Joyce's
PORTRA

Joyce's
PORTRAIT

Criticisms and Critiques

edited by
Thomas Connolly

PETER OWEN · LONDON

SBN 72060000 6

PETER OWEN LIMITED
12 Kendrick Mews Kendrick Place London SW7

First British Commonwealth edition 1964
Third edition 1967
© 1962 Meredith Publishing Company New York
Printed in the USA
Bound in Great Britain

For
MARY CONNOLLY
who came to be called Dilly

PREFACE

THE PRESENT VOLUME has been designed as a companion to the novel for all readers, both academic and nonacademic. In it, I have attempted to gather comments and studies centering on this modern classic and ranging from general evaluations of the book, to special studies, and finally to several discussions of the most controversial aspect of the novel—the theory of aesthetics that Stephen expounds to Lynch on their walk through the streets of Dublin. Although I have tried to make these selections as comprehensive as possible and representative of the best of Joycean scholarship, I must confess that many excellent studies, for a variety of reasons, have not been included. Therefore, I furnish, as an appendix, a selective bibliography of readings for those who may be interested in reading more about *A Portrait of the Artist as a Young Man.*

Acknowledgments

In addition to all who are represented in this volume and whose contributions I gratefully acknowledge with each individual essay, I am indebted to Miss Anna Russell, Mrs. Helen L. Becker, and Mrs. Marion A. Brainard of the Lockwood Memorial Library of the University of Buffalo for their help in preparing the typescript. Others of the Library staff who helped in the compilation of this book are Mrs. Nina Cohen, Mr. Gordon Kidd, and Mr. William Ernst. Rev. Richard J. Powers, S.J. was also helpful. Mr. E. J. Sully very graciously helped to prepare the final typescript. My colleagues, Dr. Ira S. Cohen and Mr. Aaron Rosen, made suggestions and comments that helped to improve the Introduction. My wife lent her sharp eyes to proofreading and helped prepare the final copy for the press. O. A. Silverman, Director of the Lockwood Memorial Library, the University of Buffalo graciously gave permission for the publication of the errata sheets in that collection, and the Yale University Library allowed them to be collated with the manuscript sheets in that collection. The Society of Authors, acting in behalf of the James Joyce Estate gave permission to include this material.

On the day that the Introduction was completed, I received news of the death, on October 14, 1961, of Harriet Shaw Weaver. Since the beginning of my interest in the writings of James Joyce, Miss Weaver has been unfailingly co-operative, kind, and helpful, and to her I owe a special debt of gratitude, one that cannot be expressed in the words of an acknowledgment.

T.E.C.

The University of Buffalo

CONTENTS

APPENDICES

Joyce's
Portrait

Introduction

A Portrait: *Provenance*

ON JANUARY 7, 1904, James Joyce took for his own use a school copybook owned by his sister Mabel and began to write in it the first draft of *A Portrait of the Artist as a Young Man*.[1] During the following month, he finished the first chapter of *Stephen Hero*, as the book was then called, and by the following summer, a good part of the manuscript. By September, 1907, he had begun to conceive of the novel in its final form and settled on its eventual five-chapter structure.

Early in 1904, however, Joyce heard that John Eglinton, whose name was W. K. Magee actually and who was on the staff of the National Library, was planning to edit a new magazine to be called *Dana*, and he decided to submit a piece of his literary work to the editors. In one day he dashed off in the appropriated copybook an autobiographical story with a romantic-philosophical cast. The usually plodding Stanislaus Joyce proposed for his brother's work the title, "A Portrait of the Artist," and the manuscript was submitted to the editor who promptly rejected it with the remark, "I can't print what I can't understand."[2] Stanislaus later made a typewritten copy of this copybook sketch of the novel[3] before the copybook itself was presented by James to Sylvia Beach, the Parisian bookseller who first published *Ulysses* as a book.

[1] This manuscript, which has been published by Richard M. Kain and Robert E. Scholes in the *Yale Review* in the spring of 1960, is now part of the Sylvia Beach Collection of James Joyce materials in the Lockwood Memorial Library of The University of Buffalo.
[2] A full account of this event is given by Professor Richard Ellmann in his *James Joyce* (New York: Oxford University Press, 1959), pp. 149-152.
[3] This typewritten copy is now in the Cornell University Library.

The holograph copybook in the Lockwood Memorial Library reveals that, even in his earliest literary work, Joyce used his draft material in the way he was to follow later in *Ulysses* and in *Finnegans Wake*. He habitually went back to a manuscript or to a notebook and crossed out passages to bring them forward to later drafts. Thus, he would shift a passage from draft to draft until it reached the final version. Such a passage as the crucial scene of the girl wading on the beach, which occupies a key position in the novel, may be found in the copybook.

Many great literary works have "ghosts"; that is, they have apocryphal or semiapocryphal stories circulating about them. *A Portrait of the Artist as a Young Man* has its ghost too. The story of the burning of the original manuscript of *Stephen Hero* was launched in 1935 by Sylvia Beach who offered in her catalogue for that year the remaining pages of the manuscript for sale.[4] Miss Beach attributed the rescue of part of the manuscript to Nora Joyce and said that she snatched as much as she could from the fire into which James had thrown *Stephen Hero* after it had been declined by publishers for about the twentieth time. Stanislaus disputed this account; he correctly identified his sister, Eileen Joyce Schaurek, as the rescuer, but he stated that the manuscript involved was that of *Dubliners*, not that of *Stephen Hero*.

The incident has been treated by Joyce's first biographer, Herbert Gorman, by Theodore Spencer in his introduction to *Stephen Hero*, and by Slocum and Cahoon in their bibliography of the writings of James Joyce. Richard Ellmann gives a brief, clear account of the incident in his definitive biography *James Joyce* (p. 325). In the early months of 1911, while in a state of depression over the trouble in publishing *Dubliners* and after an argument with Nora, Joyce threw the manuscript of the unfinished *Portrait* into the fire. It was rescued by his sister Eileen to whom he later offered, in gratitude, the appropriate gift of a pair of mittens.

After many years of revision and anxiety, serial publication

---

[4] They were eventually purchased by Harvard University and published as *Stephen Hero* (Norfolk: New Directions) in 1944 and again, with the addition of about 25 pages from the Yale University collection, in 1955.

of *A Portrait of the Artist as a Young Man* was begun in *The Egoist* in England on Joyce's birthday, February 2, 1914, and it ran in that magazine until September 1, 1915. It was Ezra Pound who interested Dora Marsden, the editor of *The Egoist* in Joyce's work. Eventually, Harriet Shaw Weaver, who was to assume such great influence in Joyce's life, also became interested in the work. Because it was difficult to find a publisher who would print the book without expurgation, *The Egoist* imported sheets from the American publisher and published the book in England on February 12, 1917. The first American edition, published by B. W. Huebsch, had appeared a bit earlier, on December 29, 1916.

Since then, more than seventy-five editions and printings of *A Portrait* have appeared in English, only a few of which are paperbound. Joyce's first novel has also been translated into at least twelve languages, among them Czech, Danish, Finnish, Japanese, Polish, and Swedish, as well the usual French, German, and Italian.

The editions of the novel referred to by the critics whose works are included in this collection are listed facing the first page of text.

A Portrait: *Theme and Structure*

Through the five chapters of *A Portrait of the Artist as a Young Man,* James Joyce traces the evolution of Stephen Dedalus from infancy to the verge of his artistic career. It has often been said that *A Portrait,* although very much concerned with the young man, is very little concerned with the artist. This remark, like many facile remarks, is true, but it leaves the wrong impression. It leaves the impression that Joyce has thereby somehow failed in his book. Joyce never intended the final version of this book to be a portrait of the mature artist as a social man, though he may have had some such intention in *Stephen Hero.* Even in *Ulysses,* a work from his full maturity as a writer, Joyce does not present Stephen Dedalus as an artist.[5]

[5] The only time Joyce attempted seriously to present the artist as artist, namely in *Exiles* (first published in 1918), he failed rather pitiably. The

Thus, the *Portrait* does not give us the full life of an artist. Rather does it depict a young man emerging from an environmental shell of faith, family, and fatherland to fix his sights on the spirit of worldly beauty. As Stephen gradually rejects the religious, household, and patriotic gods that have crowded in on him from infancy, he struggles to find a god to whose service he might dedicate himself as priest. In the end he answers the call to the priesthood of art.

The emergence of the youth is related in the first four chapters of this novel through a series of incidents that follow a fairly uniform pattern of conflict, apparent defeat, and triumphant emergence. Structurally, the book is made up, throughout the first four chapters, of a series of troughs and crests—a wave pattern—in which periods of depression and defeat yield to periods of triumph as Stephen rides the crests of the waves. After the kinetic frenzies of the preceding parts, the fifth chapter produces the static calm of relatively smooth sailing as the emergent artist rationalizes his position and plans the assumption of his new role.

Thematically, the evolution of the artistic soul is represented as a three-way struggle toward fulfillment of sexual, religious, and aesthetic desires. The sexual and religious desires initially form a nexus and later separate from each other. The aesthetic desire emerges triumphant only after the other desires have been fulfilled and found incapable of sustaining the soul. This progression may be sketched roughly as the initiation of Childe Stephen as the knight of these female figures: Eileen Vance, the Blessed Virgin Mary, Emma Clery, Mercedes, the prostitute, and the girl on the beach. The first part of this movement reaches a crest at the end of Chapter 2 in the arms of the prostitute; the second part reaches its crest at the end of Chapter 4 with the

---

probable reason for his failure in *Exiles* is that, in dealing seriously with the artist as artist, Joyce was unable to establish the proper distance between himself and his subject. He was too inextricably involved with himself as an artist to "refine himself out of existence." As a result, he clutters the stage of *Exiles* with fingernail parings of his own presence. Only when he treats an artist in satiric fashion does he succeed. The portrait of Shem the Penman, however, is the portrait of an artist drawn, as Adaline Glasheen points out, by his mortal enemy.

static joy at the sight of the girl on the beach. In effect, then, the conflict among these forces is a practical or an actual application to his own life of Stephen's borrowed theory of the good and the beautiful, of kinetic and static effects.

Bonum est in quod tendit appetitus.
(The good is that toward which an appetite tends)

Pulcra sunt quae visa placent.
(Those things are beautiful the perception of which pleases)

Ultimately Stephen sees both the sexual and the religious desires as kinetic, those things toward which appetite tends to seek fulfillment outside itself. The beautiful, toward which his aesthetic sense yearns, is that the perception of which pleases. The satisfaction of the aesthetic appetite is static; it is something that satisfies or pleases in itself; it does not move the individual to the acquisition of something or someone outside the self, be it a prostitute's body or eternal salvation.

Stephen moves to the aesthetic stage, however, only after he has passed through, sometimes alternately and sometimes simultaneously, the other two stages, and the wave structure of the book, trough and crest, defeat and triumph, gives a pattern to this struggle. The kinesis of physical and spiritual entanglement (Chapters 1 through 4) is transmuted to the stasis of the perception of the "spirit of mortal beauty." (Chapter 5)

A Portrait: *Criticisms and Critiques*

This volume has been designed as a companion to the novel for all readers, both academic and nonacademic. In it, I have attempted to gather comments and studies centering on this modern classic and ranging from general evaluations of the book, to special studies, and finally to several discussions of the most controversial aspect of the novel, the theory of aesthetics that Stephen expounds to Lynch on their walk through the streets of Dublin. Although I have tried to make these selections as comprehensive as possible and representative of the best of Joycean scholarship, I must confess that many excellent studies, for a variety of reasons, have not been included. Therefore, I furnish, as an appendix, a selective bibliography of readings for those who may be interested in reading more about *A Portrait of the Artist as a Young Man* or about James Joyce and his works.

The articles in this book range in complexity from a very simple explication of one aspect of the novel, through very complex critiques, to wide-ranging and sensitive criticisms of the book that are placed against the background of Joyce's entire literary production. The whole collection, therefore, is designed to be useful both to the beginning and to the advanced student of Joyce. Although American critics and scholars seem to have marked Joyce off as their own special province, he has, of course, received world-wide critical attention. To reflect this attention, I have included British, Australian, and Canadian criticisms of *A Portrait of the Artist as a Young Man*. The aim has been always to present a comprehensive view of this important novel.

GENERAL STUDIES

EDITOR'S NOTE

THE FOLLOWING are editions of *A Portrait* cited by critics in this volume, by list number (*P-1, P-2,* etc.), in the first footnote of the article.

P-1 New York: B. W. Huebsch, 1916 (First edition) *

P-2 New York: The Modern Library, Inc., 1928 *

P-3 *The Portable James Joyce* (New York: The Viking Press, Inc., 1949)

P-4 London: The Egoist, Ltd., 1917 (First English edition was made of sheets imported from Huebsch) *

P-5 London: Jonathan Cape, Ltd., 1924 (type reset; first truly English edition produced entirely in England)

P-6 Compass Edition (New York: The Viking Press, Inc., 1956)

* These editions, all printed from the same plates, have the same pagination.

The edition of *Stephen Hero* cited by a critic is given, by list number (*SH-1, SH-2,* etc.), at the beginning of his article.

SH-1, Norfolk, Conn.: New Directions, 1944

SH-2, Norfolk, Conn.: New Directions, 1955

SH-3, London: Jonathan Cape, Ltd., 1944

For uniformity throughout these articles, citations to *Ulysses* (*UL*) are to the Modern Library edition of 1934, and to *Finnegans Wake* (*FW*) are to Viking Press edition of 1939.

Throughout each article, page references to any edition of *A Portrait* are placed in parentheses, e.g., (264), without further notation; page references to other works by Joyce will be identified by initials, e.g., (*SH,* 264). Any number that appears as a bracketed superscript [136] indicates the end of the page in the source, periodical or book, from which that article has been taken.

HARRY LEVIN

The Artist

THE HISTORY OF THE REALISTIC NOVEL shows that fiction tends toward autobiography. The increasing demands for social and psychological detail that are made upon the novelist can only be satisfied out of his own experience. The forces which make him an outsider focus his observation upon himself. He becomes his own hero, and begins to crowd his other characters into the background. The background takes on a new importance for its influence on his own character. The theme of his novel is the formation of character; its habitual pattern is that of apprentice-ship or education; and it falls into that category which has been distinguished, by German criticism at least, as the *Bildungsroman*. The novel of development, when it confines itself to the profes-sional sphere of the novelist, becomes a novel of the artist, a *Künstlerroman*. Goethe's *Wilhelm Meister,* Stendhal's *Vie d'Henri Brulard,* and Butler's *Way of All Flesh* amply suggest the po-tentialities of the form. [41]

The *Künstlerroman* offered a tentative solution to the dilemma of Joyce's generation, by enabling writers to apply the methods of realism to the subject of art. It enabled Marcel Proust to communicate experience more fully and subtly than had been done before, because it was his own experience that he was communicating, and because he was an artist to his finger-tips. *A la recherche du temps perdu* has been described as a novel that was written to explain why it was written. But, having come to be written, it offers other novelists little stimulus toward

self-portraiture. It is singularly fitting that *Ulysses* should have
appeared in the year of Proust's death. The perverse logic of
André Gide can still present, in his *Journal des faux-monnayeurs,*
the diary of a novelist who is writing a novel about a novelist
who is keeping a diary about the novel he is writing. Of course,
the *Künstlerroman* has no logical limit; but, like the label on
the box of Quaker Oats, it has a vanishing-point. Already it is
beginning to look as old-fashioned as Murger's *Vie de Bohême.*

The *Künstlerroman,* though it reverses the more normal proce-
dure of applying the methods of art to the subject of reality,
is the only conception of the novel that is specialized enough
to include *A Portrait of the Artist as a Young Man.* In 1913, the
year before Joyce finished his book, D. H. Lawrence had published his own portrait of the artist, *Sons and Lovers.* Both books
convey the claustral sense of a young intelligence swaddled in
convention and constricted by poverty, and the intensity of its
first responses to esthetic experience and life at large. The extent
to which Lawrence warms to his theme [42] is the measure of
Joyce's reserve. Characteristically, they may be reacting from
the very different institutions behind them—evangelical English
protestantism and Irish Catholic orthodoxy—when Lawrence
dwells on the attractions of life, and Joyce on its repulsions. The
respective mothers of the two artists play a similar role, yet May
Dedalus is a wraith beside the full-bodied realization of Mrs.
Morel. The characters in *Sons and Lovers* seem to enjoy an
independent existence; in the *Portrait of the Artist* they figure
mainly in the hero's reveries and resentments. Joyce's treatment
of childhood is unrelieved in its sadness: endless generations of
choirs of children sounded, for Stephen Dedalus, the same note
of pain and weariness that Newman had heard in Vergil. "All
seemed weary of life even before entering upon it." (190)

The attitude of the novelist toward his subject is one of the
critical questions considered by Joyce's subject. Stephen expounds his own esthetic theory, which he designates as "applied
Aquinas," during a walk in the rain with his irreverent friend,
Lynch. *Solvitur ambulando.* It should be noted that the principal
action of the *Portrait of the Artist,* whether in conversation or
revery, is walking. The lingering images of *Dubliners* are those

of people—often children—in the streets. And it was reserved for
Joyce to turn the wanderings of Ulysses into a peripatetic pil-
grimage through Dublin. He was, in that respect, a good Aristotelian. But he added a personal touch to the critical theory of
Aristotle and Aquinas, when he based the distinction between
the various literary forms on the relation of the artist to his
material. In the lyric, it is immediate; in the epic, the artist
presents his material [43] "in mediate relation to himself and
others"; in drama, it is presented in immediate relation to
others. (251)

> The lyrical form is in fact the simplest verbal vesture of an in-
> stant of emotion, a rhythmical cry such as ages ago cheered on
> the man who pulled at the oar or dragged stones up a slope. He
> who utters it is more conscious of the instant of emotion than of
> himself as feeling emotion. The simplest epical form is seen
> emerging out of lyrical literature when the artist prolongs and
> broods upon himself as the centre of an epical event and this
> form progresses till the centre of emotional gravity is equidis-
> tant from the artist himself and from others. The narrative is
> no longer purely personal. The personality of the artist passes
> into the narration itself, flowing round and round the persons
> and the action like a vital sea. This progress you will see easily
> in that old English ballad *Turpin Hero,* which begins in the first
> person and ends in the third person. The dramatic form is
> reached when the vitality which has flowed and eddied round
> each person fills every person with such vital force that he or
> she assumes a proper and intangible esthetic life. The person-
> ality of the artist, at first a cry or a cadence or a mood and
> then a fluid and lambent narrative, finally refines itself out of
> existence, impersonalizes itself, so to speak. The esthetic image
> in the dramatic form is life purified in and reprojected from the
> human imagination. The mystery of esthetic like that of ma-
> terial creation is accomplished. The artist, like the God of the
> creation, remains within or behind or beyond or above his hand-
> iwork, invisible, refined out of existence, indifferent, paring his
> fingernails. (251-252)

This progress you will see easily in the succession of Joyce's
works. The cry becomes a cadence in *Chamber Music;* the mood
becomes a *nuance* in *Dubliners*. If *Exiles* is unsuccessful, it is

because the epiphany is not manifest to others; the artist has failed to objectify the relations of his characters with each other or with the [44] audience. The narrative of the *Portrait of the Artist* has scarcely emerged from the lyrical stage. Whereas *Dubliners* began in the first person and ended in the third, the *Portrait of the Artist* takes us back from an impersonal opening to the notes of the author at the end. The personality of the artist, prolonging and brooding upon itself, has not yet passed into the narration. The shift from the personal to the epic will come with *Ulysses,* and the center of emotional gravity will be equidistant from the artist himself and from others. And with *Finnegans Wake,* the artist will have retired within or behind, above or beyond his handiwork, refined out of existence.

Except for the thin incognito of its characters, the *Portrait of the Artist* is based on a literal transcript of the first twenty years of Joyce's life. If anything, it is more candid than other autobiographies. It is distinguished from them by its emphasis on the emotional and intellectual adventures of its protagonist. If we can trust the dates at the end of the book, Joyce started to write in Dublin during 1904, and continued to rewrite until 1914 in Trieste. There is reason to believe that he had accumulated almost a thousand pages—and brought Stephen to the point of departure for Paris—when the idea of *Ulysses* struck him, and he decided to reserve those further adventures for the sequel. His provisional title, *Stephen Hero,* with its echo of the ballad of Dick Turpin, marks the book as an early point in his stages of artistic impersonality. As the hero of a pedagogical novel, Stephen is significantly baptized. Saint Stephen Protomartyr was patron of the green on which University College was located, and therefore of the magazine with [45] which Joyce had had his earliest literary misadventures.

Stephen is ever susceptible to the magic of names—particularly of his own last name. Names and words, copybook phrases and schoolboy slang, echoes and jingles, speeches and sermons float through his mind and enrich the restricted realism of the context. His own name is the wedge by which symbolism enters the book. One day he penetrates its secret. Brooding on the prefect of studies, who made him repeat the unfamiliar syllables of "Dedalus," he tells himself that it is a better name than Dolan. He hears it shouted across the surf by some friends in swimming, and the strangeness of the sound is for him a prophecy:

> Now, at the name of the fabulous artificer, he seemed to hear the noise of dim waves and to see a winged form flying above the waves and slowly climbing the air. What did it mean? Was it a quaint device opening a page of some medieval book of prophecies and symbols, a hawklike man flying sunward above the sea, a prophecy of the end he had been born to serve and had been following through the mists of childhood and boyhood, a symbol of the artist forging anew in his workshop out of the sluggish matter of the earth a new soaring impalpable imperishable being? (196)

The *Portrait of the Artist,* as we have it, is the result of an extended process of revision and refinement. The original version —if an *Ur-Portrait* can be remotely discerned—must have been securely founded upon the bedrock of naturalistic narrative. It must have been a human document, virtually a diary, to which Joyce confided his notions and reactions not very long after they occurred. In turning from a reproductive to a selective method, he [46] has foreshortened his work. A fragmentary manuscript, now in the Harvard College Library, touches only the period covered by the last chapter of the printed book, and yet it is nearly as long as the book itself. What is obliquely implied in the final version is explicitly stated in this early draft. The economic situation, for example, as the Dedalus household declines from the genteel to the shabby, is attested by a series of moving vans. In the book there is just one such episode, when Stephen arrives home to hear from his brothers and sisters that the family is looking for another house. Even then the news is not put in plain English, but in evasive pig-Latin. (189) And the book leaves us with only the vaguest impression of the brothers and sisters; Stephen himself is not sure how many there are.

With revision, the other characters seem to have retreated into the background. Stephen's mother, because of the tension between her love and his disbelief, should be the most poignant figure in the book, just as her memory is the most unforgettable thing in *Ulysses*. But the actual conflict is not dramatized; it is coldly analyzed by Stephen in the course of one of his interminable walks and talks—this time with the serious-minded Cranly. In the manuscript it gives rise to a powerful scene, on the death of Stephen's sister, when his mother's orthodox piety is humbled before the mysteries of the body. The heroine of the book has been refined out of existence; she survives only in veiled allusions and the initials E—— C——. Emma Clery, in the manuscript, is an enthusiastic young lady with whom Stephen attends a Gaelic class. Their prolonged and pallid romance comes to an [47] unexpected climax when he sees her mackintosh flashing across the green, and abruptly leaves his lesson to confront her with the proposal that they spend the night together and say farewell in the morning. Her reaction explains the interview so cryptically reported in the book, when Stephen turns on the "spiritual-heroic refrigerating apparatus, invented and patented in all countries by Dante Alighieri." (298)

The esthetic theory plays a more active part in the earlier version. Instead of being dogmatically expounded to Lynch, it is sounded in the debating society, where it occasions a bitter argument. As Joyce rewrote his book he seems to have transferred the scene of action from the social to the psychological sphere. As he recollected his "conflicts with orthodoxy" in the comparative tranquility of exile, he came to the conclusion that the actual struggles had taken place within the mind of Stephen. Discussions gave way to meditations, and scenes were replaced by *tableaux*. Evasion and indirection were ingrained in Joyce's narrative technique. The final effect is that which Shakespearean actors achieve by cutting out all the scenes in *Hamlet* where the hero does not appear. The continuity of dynastic feuds and international issues is obscured by the morbid atmosphere of introspection. Drama has retired before soliloquy.

The Stephen we finally meet is more sharply differentiated from his environment than the figure Joyce set out to describe. How can he be a poet—the other boys have asked him—and not wear long hair? The richness of his inner experience is continually played off against the grim reality of his external surroundings. He is trying "to [48] build a breakwater of order and elegance against the sordid tide of life without him." (110) He is marked by the aureole of the romantic hero, like Thomas Mann's outsiders, pressing their noses against the window panes of a bourgeois society from which they feel excluded. "To merge his life in the common tide of other lives was harder for him than any fasting or prayer, and it was his constant failure to do this to his own satisfaction which caused in his soul at last a sensation of spiritual dryness together with a growth of doubts and scruples." (175) At school he takes an equivocal position, "a free boy, a leader afraid of his own authority, proud and sensitive and suspicious, battling against the squalor of his life and against the riot of his mind." (102) At home he feels "his own futile isolation." He feels that he is scarcely of the same blood as his mother and brother and sister, but stands to them "rather in the mystical kinship of fosterage, foster child and foster brother." (111)

Joyce's prose is the register of this intellectual and emotional cleavage. It preserves the contrast between his rather lush verse and his rather dry criticism, between the pathetic children and the ironic politicians of *Dubliners*. All his sensibility is reserved for himself; his attitude toward others is consistently caustic. The claims to objectivity of a subjective novel, however, must be based on its rendering of intimate experience. If Joyce's treatment of Stephen is true to himself, we have no right to interpose any other criteria. Mr. Eliot has made the plausible suggestion that Joyce's two masters in prose were Newman and Pater. Their alternating influence would account for the oscillations of style in the *Portrait* [49] *of the Artist*. The sustaining tone, which it adopts toward the outside world, is that of precise and mordant description. Interpolated, at strategic points in Stephen's development, are a number of purple passages that have faded considerably.

Joyce's own contribution to English prose is to provide a more fluid medium for refracting sensations and impressions through the author's mind—to facilitate the transition from photographic realism to esthetic impressionism. In the introductory pages of the *Portrait of the Artist*, the reader is faced with nothing less than the primary impact of life itself, a presentational continuum

of the tastes and smells and sights and sounds of earliest infancy.
Emotion is integrated, from first to last, by words. Feelings, as
they filter through Stephen's sensory apparatus, become associated with phrases. His conditioned reflexes are literary. In one
of the later dialogues of the book, he is comparing his theory
to a trimmed lamp. The dean of studies, taking up the metaphor,
mentions the lamp of Epictetus, and Stephen's reply is a further
allusion to the stoic doctrine that the soul is like a bucketful of
water. In his mind this far-fetched chain of literary associations
becomes attached to the sense impressions of the moment: "A
smell of molten tallow came up from the dean's candle butts
and fused itself in Stephen's consciousness with the jingle of the
words, bucket and lamp and lamp and bucket." (218)

This is the state of mind that confers upon language a magical
potency. It exalts the habit of verbal association into a principle
for the arrangement of experience. You gain power over a thing
by naming it; you become master [50] of a situation by putting
it into words. It is psychological need, and not hyperfastidious
taste, that goads the writer on to search for the *mot juste*, to loot
the thesaurus. Stephen, in the more explicit manuscript, finds a
treasure-house in Skeat's *Etymological Dictionary*. The crucial
moment of the book, which leads to the revelation of his name
and calling, is a moment he tries to make his own by drawing
forth a phrase of his treasure: (193)

> —A day of dappled seaborne clouds—
>   The phrase and the day and the scene harmonised in a chord.
> Words. Was it their colours? He allowed them to glow and fade,
> hue after hue: sunrise gold, the russet and green of apple or-
> chards, azure of waves, the greyfringed fleece of clouds. No, it
> was not their colours: it was the poise and balance of the pe-
> riod itself. Did he then love the rhythmic rise and fall of words
> better than their associations of legend and colour? Or was it
> that, being as weak of sight as he was shy of mind, he drew
> less pleasure from the reflection of the glowing sensible world
> through the prism of a language manycoloured and richly storied
> than from the contemplation of an inner world of individual
> emotions mirrored perfectly in a lucid supple periodic prose.

The strength and weakness of his style, by Joyce's own diagnosis, are those of his mind and body. A few pages later he offers a cogent illustration, when Stephen dips self-consciously into his word-hoard for suitable epithets to describe a girl who is wading along the beach. We are given a paragraph of word-painting which is not easy to visualize. "Her bosom was as a bird's, soft and slight, slight and soft as the breast of some dark-plumaged dove," it concludes. "But her long fair hair was [51] girlish: and girlish, and touched with the wonder of mortal beauty, her face." (199) This is incantation, and not description. Joyce is thinking in rhythms rather than metaphors. Specification of the bird appeals to the sense of touch rather than to the sense of sight. What is said about the hair and face is intended to produce an effect without presenting a picture. The most striking effects in Joyce's imagery are those of coldness, whiteness, and dampness, like the bodies of the bathers who shout Stephen's name.

The most vital element in Joyce's writing, in the *Portrait of the Artist* as in *Dubliners,* is his use of conversation. As a reporter of Irish life, for all his reservations, Joyce is a faithful and appreciative listener. It is a tribute to Stephen's ear that, in spite of the antagonism between father and son, Simon Dedalus is such a ripe and congenial character. Like Sean O'Casey's *Paycock,* with all his amiable failings, he is Ireland itself. Though he takes pride in showing Cork to Stephen, and in showing off his son to his own native city, he is really the embodiment of Dublin: "A medical student, an oarsman, a tenor, an amateur actor, a shouting politician, a small landlord, a small investor, a drinker, a good fellow, a storyteller, somebody's secretary, something in a distillery, a taxgatherer, a bankrupt and at present a praiser of his own past." (284) The improvident worldliness of John Stanislaus Joyce had made him, in the unforgiving eyes of his son, a foster-parent. So young Charles Dickens, hastening from the blacking-factory to the Marshalsea, came to look upon his father as a horrible example of goodfellowship, a Mr. Micawber. [52]

This disorder, "the misrule and confusion of his father's house," (188) comes to stand in Stephen's mind for the plight of Ireland. Like Synge's *Playboy,* he must go through the motions of par-

ricide to make good his revolt. Religion and politics, to his adult
perception, are among the intimations of early childhood: harsh
words and bitter arguments that spoil the taste of the Christmas
turkey. Again, as in "Ivy Day in the Committee Room," or in
Lennox Robinson's *Lost Leader* on the stage, it is the ghost of
Parnell that turns conversation into drama. "Dante," the devout
Mrs. Riordan, is true to the Catholic Church in denouncing the
disgraced nationalist leader. Mr. Casey, the guest of honor, is of
the anti-clerical faction. Mr. Dedalus is by no means a neutral,
and some of his mellowest profanity is enlisted in the cause of
his dead hero. Mrs. Dedalus softly rebukes him: (34)

> —Really, Simon, you should not speak that way before Stephen.
> It's not right.
> —O, he'll remember all this when he grows up, said Dante
> hotly—the language he heard against God and religion and
> priests in his own home.
> —Let him remember too, cried Mr Casey to her from across
> the table, the language with which the priests and the priests'
> pawns broke Parnell's heart and hounded him into his grave.
> Let him remember that too when he grows up.

The *Portrait of the Artist,* as Joyce's remembrance finally
shaped it, is a volume of three hundred pages, symmetrically
constructed around three undramatic climaxes, intimate crises
of Stephen's youth. The first hundred pages, in two chapters,
trace the awakening of religious [53] doubts and sexual instincts,
leading up to Stephen's carnal sin at the age of sixteen. The
central portion, in two more chapters, continues the cycle of
sin and repentance to the moment of Stephen's private apoca-
lypse. The external setting for the education of the artist is, in
the first chapter, Clongowes Wood College; in the second, third,
and fourth, Belvedere College, Dublin. The fifth and final chapter, which is twice as long as the others, develops the theories
and projects of Stephen's student days in University College,
and brings him to the verge of exile. As the book advances, it
becomes less sensitive to outside impressions, and more intent
upon speculations of its own. Friends figure mainly as inter-
locutors to draw Stephen out upon various themes. Each epiph-

any—awakening of the body, literary vocation, farewell to Ireland—leaves him lonelier than the last.

A trivial episode at Clongowes Wood seems fraught for Joyce with a profoundly personal meaning. Young Stephen has been unable to get his lessons, because his glasses were broken on the playing-field. Father Dolan, the prefect of studies, is unwilling to accept this excuse, and disciplines Stephen with the boys who have shirked their books. Smarting with pain and a sense of palpable injustice, Stephen finally carries his case to the rector, who shows a humane understanding of the situation. Many years later Father Conmee, the rector, takes a walk through a chapter of *Ulysses;* and Father Dolan—who was actually a Father Daly—pops up with his "pandybat" in Stephen's nightmare. This schoolboy incident lays down a pattern for Joyce's later behavior. When he cabled Lloyd George, who had other things on his [54] mind during the first World War, *re* a pair of trousers and *The Importance of Being Earnest,* he was behaving like an aggrieved schoolboy unjustly pandied.

The physical handicap, the public humiliation, the brooding sensibility, the sense of grievance, the contempt for convention, the desire for self-justification, and the appeal to higher authority—these are all elements of Joyce's attitude toward society and toward himself. He had begun his education by questioning the Jesuit discipline; he would finish by repudiating the Catholic faith. Having responded to the urgent prompting of his senses, he would be treated as a sinner; he would refer the ensuing conflict, over the head of religious authority, to the new light of his scientific and naturalistic studies; he would seek, in the end, to create his own authority by the light of his senses. In turning away from Ireland toward the world at large, he would appeal from the parochial Daly to the enlightened Conmee. That miserable day at Clongowes Wood, like that long evening at Combray when M. Swann's visit kept Marcel's mother downstairs, had unforeseen consequences.

Adolescence complicates the second chapter. Stephen is beginning to appreciate beauty, but as something illicit and mysterious, something apart from the common walks of life. Literature has begun to color his experience, and to stimulate his mind and his senses. His untimely enthusiasm for Lord Byron—"a heretic and immoral too" (90)—provokes a beating at the hands of his classmates. Now in jest and again in earnest, he is forced to repeat the *confiteor*. One of his essays had been rewarded with the taunt of heresy from his English master, and he takes [55] rueful consolation in the self-conscious part of the Byronic hero. He will not agree that Lord Tennyson is a poet, though he gives tacit consent to the assertion that Newman has the best prose style. But it is his other master, Pater, whose influence is felt at the climax of the chapter. Stephen's sexual initiation is presented in empurpled prose, as an esthetic ritual for which his literary heresies have been preparing him. In trying to find a cadence for his cry, he harks back to the lyricism of *Chamber Music* and the anguish of the small boy in *Dubliners:* (112)

> He stretched out his arms in the street to hold fast the frail swooning form that eluded him and incited him: and the cry that he had strangled for so long in his throat issued from his lips. It broke from him like a wail of despair from a hell of sufferers and died in a wail of furious entreaty, a cry for an iniquitous abandonment, a cry which was but the echo of an obscene scrawl which he had read on the oozing wall of a urinal.

The unromantic reader is prone to feel that a scrawl would have been more adequate to the occasion. The incidence of the word "swoon" is a humorless symptom of the Pateresque influence on Joyce's early writing. There is many "A swoon of shame" in *Chamber Music,* and "a slowly swooning soul" in the last paragraph of *Dubliners.* "His soul was swooning" at the end of the fourth chapter of the *Portrait of the Artist,* having been darkened by "the swoon of sin" at the end of the second chapter. Though the scene is clouded with decadent incense, it is clear that Stephen is still a child, and that the woman plays the part of a mother. Joyce's heroes are [56] sons and lovers at the same time; his heroines are always maternal. It is like him to lavish his romantic sensibility on an encounter with a prostitute and to reserve his acrid satire for the domain of the church. In Stephen's mind a symbolic association between art and sex is established, and that precocious revelation helps him to decide his later conflict between art and religion.

Meanwhile, the third chapter is devoted to his remorse. It embodies at formidable length a sermon on hell, suffered by Stephen and his classmates during a retreat. The eloquent Jesuit preacher takes as his object-lesson the sin of Lucifer, pride of the intellect, his great refusal and his terrible fall. Stephen's repentant imagination is harrowed by the torments of the damned. This powerful discourse provides an ethical core for the book, as Father Mapple's sermon on Jonah does for *Moby-Dick,* or Ivan's legend of the Grand Inquisitor for *The Brothers Karamazov.* Joyce is orthodox enough to go on believing in hell, and—as Professor Curtius recognized—to set up his own *Inferno* in *Ulysses.* Like another tormented apostate, Christopher Marlowe, he lives in a world where there is still suffering, but no longer the prospect of salvation. Like Blake's Milton, he is a true poet, and of the devil's party. Stephen's ultimate text is the defiance of the fallen archangel: *"Non serviam!"*

Temporarily, there is confession and absolution. When Stephen sees the eggs and sausages laid out for the communion breakfast, life seems simple and beautiful after all. For a time his restlessness seems to be tranquilized by church and satisfied by school. Seeking to order his existence, he contemplates the possibilities of the Jesuit [57] order itself: the Reverend Stephen Dedalus, S. J. After a conference with a member of that order, he is fascinated and terrified by the awful assumption of powers which ordination involves. In the fourth chapter the call comes unexpectedly—the call to another kind of priesthood. Stephen dedicates himself to art, and enters upon his peculiar novitiate. The church would have meant order, but it would also have meant a denial of the life of the senses. A walk along the strand brings him his real vocation—an outburst of profane joy at the bird-like beauty of a girl, a realization of the fabulous artificer whose name he bears, a consciousness of the power of words to confer an order and life of their own. Like the birds that circle between the sea and the sky, his soul soars in "an ecstasy of flight," in a metaphor of sexual fulfilment and artistic creation.

"To live, to err, to fall, to triumph, to recreate life out of
life!" (200)

The fifth chapter is the discursive chronicle of Stephen's rebellion. He moves among his fellow-students, an aloof and pharisaic
figure, unwilling to share their indignation at the first performance of the *Countess Cathleen,* or their confidence in a petition
to ensure world peace. His own struggle comes when his mother
requests him to make his Easter duty and his diabolic pride of
intellect asserts itself. Cranly, with the sharpest instruments of
casuistry, tries to probe his stubborn refusal. It is less a question
of faith than of observance. Stephen will not, to please his
mother, do false homage to the symbols of authority, yet he is
not quite unbeliever enough to take part in a sacrilegious communion. If he cannot accept the eucharist, he must be anathema;
he [58] respects the forms by refusing to observe them. "I will
not serve that in which I no longer believe, whether it call itself
my home, my fatherland or my church: and I will try to express
myself in some mode of life or art as freely as I can and as
wholly as I can, using for my defence the only arms I allow
myself to use, silence, exile and cunning." (291)

With this peremptory gesture, emancipating himself from his
petty-bourgeois family, and from Ireland and Catholicism at
the same time, Stephen stands ready to take his solitary way
wherever the creative life engages him. In a previous argument
with other friends, he abandoned the possibility of fighting these
issues out at home. "Ireland is the old sow that eats her farrow."
(238) Davin, the nationalist, is willing to admit that Stephen's
position is thoroughly Irish, all too typical of their gifted countrymen. "In your heart you are an Irishman but your pride is too
powerful." (237) Stephen is unwilling to compromise: "When
the soul of a man is born in this country there are nets flung at
it to hold it back from flight. You talk to me of nationality, language, religion. I shall try to fly by those nets." In exile, silence,
and cunning he trusts to find substitutes for those three forms
of subjection.

On his way to and from Belvedere College, his soul was "dis-
quieted and cast down by the dull phenomenon of Dublin." (87)

With his realization of the end he was soon to serve, a new vista
of "the slowflowing Liffey" became visible "across the timeless
air." Nomadic clouds, dappled and seaborne, voyaging westward from Europe, suggested strange tongues and marshalled
races. "He heard a confused music within him as of memories
and [59] names . . ." (194) At University College, the time-worn
texts of Ovid and Horace have filled him with awe for the past
and contempt of the present: ". . . it wounded him to think
that he would never be but a shy guest at the feast of the world's
culture and that the monkish learning, in terms of which he
was striving to forge out an esthetic philosophy, was held no
higher by the age he lived in than the subtle and curious jargons
of heraldry and falconry." (209)

English is as strange a tongue as Latin. "His language, so
familiar and so foreign, will always be for me an acquired
speech," Stephen reflects, while conversing with the dean of
studies, an English convert to Catholicism. "I have not made or
accepted its words. My voice holds them at bay. My soul frets
in the shadow of his language." (221) The last pages are fragments from Stephen's notebook, duly recording his final inter-
views with teachers and friends, with his family and "her."
Spring finds him setting down "vague words for a vague emotion," his farewell to Dublin, and to sounds of the city which
will never stop echoing in his ears: (297)

> *April* 10. Faintly, under the heavy night, through the silence of
> the city which has turned from dreams to dreamless sleep as a
> weary lover whom no caresses move, the sound of hoofs upon
> the road.

Toward the end, his purpose stiffens into a flourish of blank
verse: (299)

> *April* 26. Mother is putting my new secondhand clothes in
> order. She prays now, she says, that I may learn in my own
> life [60] and away from home and friends what the heart is and
> what it feels. Amen. So be it. Welcome, O life! I go to encoun-
> ter for the millionth time the reality of experience and to forge
> in the smithy of my soul the uncreated conscience of my race.

On the eve of departure he makes his final entry:

> April 27. Old father, old artificer, stand me now and ever in good stead.

The mythical and priestly figure of Dædalus is known for more than one work of genius—for a pair of wings, as well as a labyrinth. Stephen invokes his namesake under both aspects, the hawklike man and the fabulous artificer. Sometimes it is the cunning of the craftsman, the smithy of the artist, that is symbolized. At other times, soaring, falling, flying by the nets of Ireland, it is life itself. Yet these images of aspiration can also be associated with Icarus, the son of Dædalus. That ill-fated and rebellious spirit, who borrowed his father's wings and flew too near the sun, is an equally prophetic symbol: in a classical drama, *Icaro,* the young anti-fascist poet, Lauro de Bosis, adumbrated the heroism of his own death. The epigraph of Joyce's book is a quotation from Ovid—or rather a misquotation (the correct reference is to the *Metamorphoses,* VIII, 188). Here we are told that Dædalus abandoned his mind to obscure arts, "*et ignotas animum dimittit in artes.*" But Joyce does not tell us Ovid's reason:

$$. . . longumque \ perosus$$
$$exsilium, \ tractusque \ soli \ natalis \ amore \ . . . \ ^{[61]}$$

The artificer was weary of his long exile and lured by the love of his natal soil, the Roman poet and exile goes on to say, and the rest of his myth rehearses the filial tragedy. The father cries out for the son; Joyce's confused recollection, in *Ulysses,* makes the son cry out for the father: "*Pater, ait.*" On the brink of expatriation, poised for his trial flight, Stephen, in the *Portrait of the Artist,* is more nearly akin to the son. His natural father, Simon Dedalus, is left standing in the mystical kinship of foster-age. The Jesuit fathers, who supervised his education, no longer call him son. He has appealed from Father Dolan to Father Conmee; now he appeals from the church to another paternity. His wings take him from the fatherland. The labyrinth leads toward a father. [62]

HUGH KENNER

The Portrait *in Perspective*

From wrong to wrong the exasperated spirit
Proceeds, unless restored by that refining fire
Where you must move in measure, like a dancer.
                                        —T. S. ELIOT

Faites votre destin, âmes désordonnées,
Et fuyez l'infini que vous portez en vous!
                                        —BAUDELAIRE

And yet he felt that, however he might revile and mock her
image, his anger was also a form of homage. (259)

EVERYONE KNOWS by now that *Ulysses* must be read and reread line by line and word by word. The publication of the Hanley word index, and the erudite gymnastics that have recently been performed with its aid, indicate a dawning recognition of the kind of care with which the epic of Dublin was assembled. It is surprising, therefore, that no one has thought to apply similar attention to *A Portrait of the Artist as a Young Man*, especially since it has always been treated as a sort of vestibule to *Ulysses*, and since it is becoming more and more glaringly obvious that the planning of the one book inextricably involved the planning of the other.

Reprinted by permission of Hugh Kenner. This essay appeared originally in *James Joyce: Two Decades of Criticism*, Seon Givens, ed. (New York: Vanguard Press, 1948) to which page reference is here made, and in a revised version in Hugh Kenner, *Dublin's Joyce* (Bloomington: Indiana University Press, 1956). References to *A Portrait* are to P-1; to *Stephen Hero* are to SH-1.

For the *Portrait,* as the painstaking revision it received at [132] the *Stephen Hero* stage would suggest, must be read with un-relaxing attention. Indeed, such attention goes a long way toward revealing what *Ulysses* is all about. This may be illustrated from any random passage. Take, for example, the description of the director proposing that Stephen enter the priesthood:

> The director stood in the embrasure of the window, his back to the light, leaning an elbow on the brown crossblind, and, as he spoke and smiled, slowly dangling and looping the cord of the other blind, Stephen stood before him, following for a moment with his eyes the waning of the long summer daylight above the roofs or the slow deft movements of the priestly fingers. The priest's face was in total shadow, but the waning daylight from behind him touched the deeply grooved temples and the curves of the skull. (178)

The "waning daylight," twice emphasized, is obviously a symbol of that denial of nature which the priest's office represented for Stephen. (It must be, as we shall see, taken in its dramatic context, and not read as a sneer from James Joyce.) "His back to the light" co-operates toward a similar effect. "Crossblind" functions poetically: "blind to the cross"; "blinded by the cross." "The curves of the skull" introduces another death image: the "deathbone" associated with Shaun in *Finnegans Wake* is a freer version of an identical symbol. But the central image, the epiph-any of the interview, is contained in the movement of the priest's fingers "slowly dangling and looping the cord of the other blind"; that is to say, insolently proffering a noose. The hangman symbol in *Ulysses* is obviously adumbrated.

The reader who returns to the *Portrait* with the remainder of Joyce's output in his possession will be able to see how much symbolic material is controlled by that single image. "The lord of things as they are whom the most Roman of [133] Catholics call *dio boia,* hangman god" (*UL,* 210), the satanic prince of the natural world who in *Ulysses,* following Blake, is identified with its creator, the wielder of the thunderbolts of *Finnegans Wake,* is the obvious reading on the theological level. But the hangman image goes deeper. The hangman and the hangman god are, respectively, the civil and the supernatural defenders of the status quo. H. Rumbold, Master Barber, whose letter of application for the post of hangman is read in the citizen's tavern (*UL*, 298), is named, in sardonic insolence, after the British consul at Zurich who caused Joyce so much trouble during World War I, and there is something more metaphysical in this collocation than a personal grudge, for the civil servant defends the status quo likewise. The hangman and the things that are Caesar's are associated in the Circe episode of the epic, where a nightmarish account of an execution is followed by Stephen's remark about Edward VII: "He wants my money and my life, though want must be his master, for some brutish empire of his. Money I haven't." (*UL*, 579) And the hangman and the things that are God's are associated in the Cyclops episode, where Rumbold's letter of application is followed by a grim interjection parodying Greek and Hebrew necessitarianism: "In the dark land they bide, the vengeful knights of the razor. Their deadly coil they grasp: yea, and therein they lead to Erebus whatsoever wight hath done a deed of blood for I will on nowise suffer it even so saith the Lord." (*UL*, 299)

The *Finnegans Wake* association of Shem (Stephen) with the lifewand and Shaun (Mulligan) with the deathbone follows the same pattern; Shaun, it will be remembered, combines the priestly office with the virtues of the efficient civil servant: [134]

> —Goodbye now, Shaun replied, with a voice pure as a church-mode, in echo rightdainty, with a good catlick tug at his coco-moss candylock. . . . How them columbuses! Lard have mustard on them! Fatiguing, very fatiguing. . . . I'm off rabbited kitchens and relief porridgers. No later than a very few fort-nichts since I was meeting on the Thinker's Dam with a pair of men out of a glasshouse whom I shuffled hands with named MacBlacks—I think their names is MacBlakes—from the Head-fire Clump—and they were improving me and making me beliek no five hour factory life with insufficient emollient and indus-trial disablement for them that day o'gratises. (*FW*, 409)

This polished ennui is associated with the callous industrial reformer, the social engineer armed with statistics and minimum wage acts, and with Blake's vision of empty charity:

> They are gone to praise God & his Priest & King
> Who make up a heaven of our misery.

But it has echoes also ("Lard have mustard on them! Fatiguing, very fatiguing") of the almsgiving of the Very Reverend John Conmee, S. J.:

> The Superior, the Very Reverend John Conmee, S. J., reset his smooth watch in his interior pocket as he came down the presbytery steps. Five to three. Just nice time to walk to Artane. What was that boy's name again? Dignam, yes. *Vere dignum et justum est.* Brother Swan was the person to see. Mr. Cunningham's letter. Yes. Oblige him, if possible. Good practical Catholic: useful at mission time.
>
> A one-legged sailor, swinging himself onward by lazy jerks of his crutches, growled some notes. He [135] jerked short before the convent of the sisters of charity and held out a peaked cap for alms towards the very reverend John Conmee, S. J. Father Conmee blessed him in the sun, for his purse held, he knew, one silver crown.
>
> Father Conmee crossed to Mountjoy Square. He thought, but not for long, of soldiers and sailors, whose legs had been shot off by cannonballs, ending their days in some pauper ward, and of cardinal Wolsey's words: *If I had served my God as I had served my king He would not have abandoned me in my old days.* (*UL,* 216)

The devastating irony of this urbane prose is clearly Shaunian. The attitude to the death of Dignam ("Oblige him, if possible. Good practical Catholic: useful at mission time"), and the slick assumption that pauperdom is the wages of sin, accord thoroughly with the morality of the hangman. And all these associations—seraph, sheriff, hangman, Caesar, priest—are telescoped once more in *Finnegans Wake,* where Shem and Shaun resume their duel under the pseudonyms of Glugg and Chuff: "Hip it and trip it and chirrub and sing. Lord Chuffy's sky sheraph and Glugg's got to swing." (*FW,* 226)

If we have strayed a long way from the *Portrait,* it is only to illustrate the kind of concentration the *Portrait* can achieve in a few quiet words. For the symbol of the priest toying with the cord, however the later books may explore its significance, needs no interpretation: it is immediately evocative.

So potent a lever for interpretation should be applied from the first words on, for Joyce is always unusually careful to begin his books on a note of multiple significance. In the [136] *Portrait*, the first two pages, terminated by a row of asterisks, enact the entire action in microcosm. An Aristotelian catalogue of senses, faculties, and mental activities is counterpointed against the unfolding of the infant conscience.

> Once upon a time and a very good time it was there was a moocow coming down along the road and this moocow that was down along the road met a nicens little boy named baby tuckoo. . . .
>
> His father told him that story: his father looked at him through a glass: he had a hairy face.
>
> He was baby tuckoo. The moocow came down along the road where Betty Byrne lived: she sold lemon platt.
>
> > *O, the wild rose blossoms*
> > *On the little green place.*
> > He sang that song. That was his song.
> > *O, the green wothe botheth.*
>
> When you wet the bed, first it is warm then it gets cold. His mother put on the oilsheet. That had the queer smell.

This evocation of holes in oblivion is conducted in the mode of each of the five senses in turn: hearing (the story of the moocow), sight (his father's face), taste (lemon platt), touch (warm and cold), smell (the oilsheet). The half-blind Joyce, whose art depends so largely on his mimic's ear, puts hearing first, and connects it with a piece of imaginative literature whose bovine protagonist's encounter with baby tuckoo was to be elaborated, years later, in the fable of the Mookse and the Gripes.[1]

---

[1] Compare the opening sentence: "Eins within a space, and a wearywide space it was, ere wohned a Mookse." (*FW*, 152). Mookse is moocow plus fox plus mock turtle. The German "Eins" evokes Einstein, who presides over the interchanging of space and time.

The father with the hairy face is a traditional infantile [137]
analogue of God the Father; "through a glass" recalls I Corinthians 13:12, the mirror-symbolism of the poem *"Ecce Puer"*:

> New life is breathed
> On the glass;
> The world that was not
> Comes to pass,

and the narcissus-mirror of *Finnegans Wake* that stands between
us and the unfallen world: "Though Wonderlawn's lost us for
ever. Alis, alas, she broke the glass! Liddell lokker through the
leafery, ours is mistery of pain." (*FW*, 270)

The hairy god and his son are adumbrated again in *Finnegans
Wake*: "Derzherr, live wire, fired Benjermine Funkling outa
th'Empyre, sin right hand son." (*FW*, 289)

Derr Erzherr (arch-lord), here a Teutonic Junker, is the God
who visited His wrath on Lucifer; the "hairy" association is
given by the music-hall refrain, "There's hair, like wire, coming
out of the Empire."

The theme of Chapter IV, the predestined artist, is indicated
by the juxtaposition of dawning consciousness of his own identity
("He was baby tuckoo") and artistic performance ("He sang
that song. That was his song"). Here is a foreshadowing of the
passage in which Stephen's discovery of his vocation as artist
is associated with his discovery of the meaning of his own name:
"Now, as never before, his strange name seemed to him a prophecy . . . of the end he had been born to serve and had been
following through the mists of childhood and boyhood, a symbol
of the artist forging [138] anew in his workshop out of the sluggish matter of the earth a new soaring impalpable imperishable
being." (196)

It is noteworthy, too, that by changing the red rose to a green,
as well as by dislocating the spelling, he makes the song his
own: "But you could not have a green rose. But perhaps somewhere in the world you could." (8)

The introduction of the mother-theme follows modes to be
explored in *Finnegans Wake*:

His mother had a nicer smell than his father.[2] She played on the piano the sailor's hornpipe for him to dance. He danced:

> *Tralala lala*
> *Tralala tralaladdy,*
> *Tralala lala,*
> *Tralala lala.* (1-2)

In the nightmare drama, Shem the Penman, worsted in his quarrel with his brother, turns to his mother as to a Muse:

> To me, unseen blusher in an obscene coalhole, the cubilibum of your secret sigh, dweller in the downandoutermost where voice only of the dead may come, because ye left from me, because ye laughed on me, because, O me lonely son, ye are forgetting me!, that our turfbrown mummy is acoming, alpilla, beltilla, ciltilla, deltilla, running with her tidings, . . . babbling, bubbling, chattering to herself, deloothering the fields on their elbows leaning with the sloothering slide of her, giddygaddy, grannyma, gossipaceous Anna Livia. (*FW*, 194) [139]

And under her aegis "He lifts the lifewand and the dumb speak." Tree and stone co-operating, he composes, with her aid and to her honor, in a mighty effort of self-vindication, the *Anna Livia Plurabelle.*

Mrs. Dedalus playing the piano for her baby tuckoo to dance is a precise and evocative analogue of the relation between the Muse, *das Ewig-Weibliche,* and the artist in primal innocence. Between that innocence and its recapture through the purgation of the Wake, there is to intervene the "agenbite of inwit," the fearful hallucination of *Ulysses:*

THE MOTHER:

> (*With the subtle smile of death's madness*) I was once the beautiful May Goulding. I am dead. . . .

---

[2] Throughout Joyce's work, the sense of smell corresponds to the discrimination of empirical reality, the sense of sight to the phantasms of oppression, and the sense of hearing to the imaginative life. Touch and taste together are associated with sex.

STEPHEN:

(*Eagerly*) Tell me the word, mother, if you know now. The word known to all men. . . .

THE MOTHER:

(*With smouldering eyes*) Repent! O, the fire of hell! (*UL*, 565)

He hid under the table. His MOTHER said:
—O, Stephen will apologise.
DANTE said:
—O, if not, the eagles will come and pull out his eyes.—
  Pull out his eyes,
  Apologise,
  Apologise,
  Pull out his eyes.

  Apologise,
  Pull out his eyes, [140]
  Pull out his eyes,
  Apologise. (2)

The eagles—eagles of Rome—are a transformation of the god with the hairy face: the punisher. They are associated with Prometheus, and with gnawing, unrelenting conscience: again-bite:

  She is drowning. Agenbite. Save her. Agenbite. All against us.
  She will drown with her, eyes and hair. Lank coils of seaweed
  hair around me, my heart, my soul. Salt green death.
  We.
  Agenbite of inwit. Inwit's agenbite.
  Misery! Misery! (*UL*, 240)

The dawning of conscience in Stephen, and his hiding under the table (Cf. Shem beneath the bedclothes: "He collapsed carefully under a bedtick, . . . moaning feebly . . . that his pawdry's purgatory was more than a nigger bloke could bear." (*FW*, 176) is associated with his dawning consciousness of the existence of girls. ("When they were grown up he was going to marry Eileen.") This is the childish analogue to the experience of puberty, when to sexual experience is added a mature sense of sin. As such, it is analogous to Stephen's brothel experiences and the hellfire retreat of Chapter III, and, ultimately, to the way the sense of sin in *Ulysses* is associated with the dead mother, the humiliation of Glugg with the tempting Maggies, and the guilt-complex of H.C.E. with an unspecified episode involving two girls in the park, who appear to be themselves analogues of his own wife and daughter.[3]

This sort of exegesis gives a hint of the number of levels of analogy on which the *Portrait*, from its first few words, is simultaneously moving. Ultimately, as the insistent climax of the overture shows, its central theme is Sin: the development of Stephen Dedalus from a bundle of sensations to a matured, self-conscious, dedicated, fallen being. The development of Stephen Dedalus, however, is itself, like the whole of *Finnegans Wake*, an analogue of the childhood of the human race: the life in the Garden, the temptation, the Fall, and the duty laid on man to exact the sweat of his brow in the quest of life. It is no exaggeration to say that every theme in the entire lifework of James Joyce is stated on the first two pages of the *Portrait*. The two major works strive toward an inclusive mythopoeic vision embracing in an archetypal pattern of fall, struggle, and redemption every mode of human activity; their bulk and complexity derive from their method of counterpointing within this pattern particular chains of action at a dozen different levels: physiological, psychological, esthetic, theological, erotic—even commercial. The *Portrait*, equally inclusive in ambition, is simpler only in method. It pursues systematically one level of action: the development of a particular human consciousness and conscience. The other possible levels of analogy are indicated periodically by passages, such as those we have examined, which punctuate the melodic line with intermittent complex chords. Joyce is playing a melody with his right hand and striking periodic chords of comment with his left. It is not merely that he has yet to develop a technique for maintaining a dozen simultaneous themes; his very

[3] His uneasy defense is characteristic, and characteristically allusive: "I protest there is utterly not one teaspoonspill of evidence at bottomlie to my babad, as you shall see, as this is. . . . And I contango can take off my dudud dirtynine articles of quoting here in Pynix Park before those in heaven to provost myself, by gramercy of justness. . . ." (*FW*, 534) [141]

awareness of the archetypal implications of his narrative is still
comparatively undeveloped. Thus the *Portrait* is important not
only as an independent work of art but also as a demonstration
that the intricate analogical simultaneities of *Ulysses* and *Finnegans Wake* are not irresponsibly excogitated from esoteric
reading, but grow out of Joyce's persistent contemplation [142]
of intense psychological experience. Joyce's interest is psychological in a more than clinical sense: he is a man in quest of the
meaning of his life.

The key to all this contemplation, for Joyce as for the reader,
is the word, for reasons worth surveying briefly. A useful index
to the development of Stephen Dedalus is the growing maturity
of his attitude toward language. It is neither sufficient nor even
initially accurate to say that by naming things he acquires power
over them; on the contrary, the names of things are already given,
and it is through their names that they have power over him:

> —The language in which we are speaking is his before it is
> mine. How different are the words *home, Christ, ale, master,*
> on his lips and on mine. I cannot speak or write these words
> without unrest of spirit. His language, so familiar and so for-
> eign, will always be for me an acquired speech. I have not
> made or accepted its words. My voice holds them at bay. My
> soul frets in the shadow of his language. (221)

Here the point is not simply that the Dean is an English convert and so the bearer of a conqueror's tongue. All language is
acquired speech, imposed and to be accepted; even Erse, which
Stephen, in impatience, quickly dropped. The issue is not national but metaphysical. Words, like the physical world, are
imposed upon the artist from without. The body of language
corresponds to the creation it mirrors in intrusiveness as well
as in complexity. And by submitting himself, with an aware
sensibility, to the mysteries of language, the artist can probe
the significance of the cosmos: "Words which he did not understand he said over and over to himself till he had learnt them
by heart: and through them he had glimpses of the real world
about him." (68) [143]

Language is a Trojan horse by which the universe gets into

the mind. The business of the artist is to be constantly aware that the horse houses armed warriors, even while admitting it to his mental citadel. He has then a chance of winning them over, upon their emergence, and cross-questioning them about the collective consciousness outside, of which they are the armed representatives.

The insistent brainless rhyme of page 2:

> Pull out his eyes,
> Apologise,
> Apologise,
> Pull out his eyes,

represents this initial incursion of language, an invader armed with mysterious corrosive power which fascinates and paralyzes the will: it has power to strike terror into a child who knows nothing of eagles, or of blindness, or of Prometheus. There is grim irony in the foreshadowing of the grown-up writer, whose refusal to apologize synchronized with gathering blindness. There are many other examples in *Finnegans Wake* where the "agenbite of inwit" pounds upon the brain in the guise of a mocking rhyme.[4]

Language, then, is primarily a disturbance, an emissary of the non-ego, an alien irritant body around which the artist knowingly, as the citizen unknowingly, deposits protective coatings: pearls or padding.

To be sure of secreting pearls, the artist must subject such manifestations of a hostile universe to aware scrutiny: it is in obedience to some such subliminal awareness that six-year-old Stephen meditates on "belt." [144]

> He kept his hands in the side pockets of his belted grey suit.
> That was a belt round his pocket. And belt was also to give a
> fellow a belt. One day a fellow had said to Cantwell:
> —I'd give you such a belt in a second.
> Cantwell had answered:

[4] E.g., the chorus of mocking voices that derisively buzzes through Earwicker's mind apropos of the fall of his reputation: "Like Pate-by-the-Neva or Pete-over-Meer. This is the Hausman all paven and stoned that cribbed the Cabin that never was owned that cocked his leg and hennad his Egg." (*FW,* 205).

—Go and fight your match. Give Cecil Thunder a belt. I'd like
to see you. He'd give you a toe in the rump for yourself.
    That was not a nice expression. His mother had told him not
to speak with the rough boys in the college. Nice mother! (3)

"Belt" as an invaluable supporter or as a painful enemy epiph-
anizes through words the duplicity of things; and the further
distinction, sanctioned by his mother, between good and bad
words, introduces a disharmony, to be exhaustively explored by
the mature sensibility, between evil connected with objective
harm, and Mrs. Grundy's evil, the whole substance of which is
irrational authority. It is at this instant, incidentally, that the
mother as muse and guardian commences to put forth her malig-
nant shadow-self, the mother of restrictive duty whose shade
(her substance significantly dead) haunts Stephen throughout
Ulysses.
    A much more complex association snowballs through the first
chapter and recurs after many years of subconscious festering
to add its venom to his apostasy:

—Suck was a queer word. The fellow called Simon Moonan
that name because Simon Moonan used to tie the prefect's false
sleeves behind his back and the prefect used to let on to be
angry. But the sound was ugly. Once he had washed his hands
in the lavatory of the Wicklow hotel and his father pulled the
stopper up by the chain and the dirty water went down through
the hole in the basin. And when it had all [145] gone down slowly
the hole in the basin had made a sound like that: suck. Only
louder.
    To remember that and the white look of the lavatory made
him feel cold and then hot. There were two cocks that you
turned and water came out: cold and hot. He felt cold and then
a little hot: and he could see the names printed on the cocks.
That was a very queer thing. (6)

Here "suck" appears in two contexts: a playful sinner who toys
with his indulgent superior, and a noise following the disap-
pearance of dirty water. The connection with the forgiveness
of sins in the confessional is obvious. The habitually orthodox
penitent tangles with a God who pretends to be angry; after a
reconciliation the process is repeated. And the process is a game,

because the sleeves he tangles are false sleeves; the sins he commits are not metaphysical sins, but transgressions of authoritative fiats lacking in ontological content. And the mark of that kind of play is disgraceful servility. Each time the sin disappears, the sinner is mocked by an impersonal voice out of nature: "Suck!"

This attitude toward unreal good and evil furnishes a context for the next association-pattern: whiteness with coldness. On the next page, the link is enforced. Stephen finds himself, like Simon Moonan,[5] engaged in the rhythm of obedience to irrational authority, bending his activities to a meaningless act, the arithmetic contest. He is being, in other words, "a good little boy": obedient. And the appropriate psychological state is induced, with its color symbol: "He thought his face must be white because it felt so cool." (That he is physically sick at this point is a further analogue.)

Whiteness, the color of obedient goodness, is next associated [146] with damp repulsiveness: the limpness of a wet blanket and of a servant's apron:

> He sat looking at the two prints of butter on his plate but could not eat the damp bread. The tablecloth was damp and limp. But he drank off the hot weak tea which the clumsy scullion, girt with a white apron, poured into his cup. He wondered whether the scullion's apron was damp too or whether all white things were cold and damp. (8)

Engaged in this complex pattern, white-cold-damp-obedient, the key-words inject a portion of their moral venom into every context in which they recur. Stephen, after saying his prayers, "his shoulders shaking," "so that he might not go to hell when he died," "curled himself together under the cold white sheets, shaking and trembling. But he would not go to hell when he died, and the shaking would stop." (16) The sea, which, as in *Finnegans Wake*, is the emblem of the terrible power of God, "was cold day and night, but it was colder at night." (14) We are reminded of Anna Livia's gesture of submission: "my cold father, my cold mad father, my cold mad feary father." (*FW*,

---

5 Note the association of the name with simony. Every name in Joyce is significant.

628). Stephen is puzzled by the phrase "Tower of Ivory" in the Litany of the Blessed Virgin. "How could a woman be a tower of ivory or a house of gold?" He ponders until the revelation comes: "Eileen had long white hands. One evening when playing tig she had put her hands over his eyes: long and white and thin and cold and soft. That was ivory: a cold white thing. That was the meaning of *Tower of Ivory.*" (36)

This instant of insight depends on a sudden reshuffling of associations, a sudden conviction that the Mother of God, and symbols appropriate to her, belong in the context of cold, white, unpleasant things associated with a blindfold [147] morality of obedience. Contemplation focused on language is rewarded by moral and metaphysical insight: *"Tower of Ivory. House of Gold. By thinking of things you could understand them."* (45)

The white-damp-obedient association reappears at the moment when Stephen is about to make his confession after the celebrated retreat. Sin has been associated with fire, while the prayers of the penitents are epiphanized as "soft whispering cloudlets, soft whispering vapour, whispering and vanishing" (166). And having been absolved:

> White pudding and eggs and sausages and cups of tea. How simple and beautiful was life after all! And life lay all before him. . . .
> The boys were all there, kneeling in their places. He knelt among them, happy and shy. The altar was heaped with fragrant masses of white flowers: and in the morning light the pale flames of the candles among the white flowers were clear and silent as his own soul. (168)

This chain of associations is a vehicle for presenting from passage to passage Stephen's religious conscience, and his ultimate defection is paralleled by the ultimate association: whiteness with blankness: pallor.

These verbal leitmotivs are a technique for indicating simultaneously the alignment of ideas in the protagonist's mind and the motivation of such alignment; the emotions which Joyce's dramatic context attaches to the key-words combine, interact, and crystallize as the language indicates. The dance of feelings has its objective correlative in the dance of words. Here the language, in the mode of mimesis, is performing dramatic actions in imitation of psychological actions. Joyce as an artist is working in language, but his material is psychology. His linguistic symbols represent psychological experiences detached from their context and put [148] in motion in the new context of the printed page. There is nothing so crude here as illustrative metaphor, nor as figurative language applied from the outside to "expand the events," as the phrase goes, "to symbolic significance." The levels of significance are not applied but, through contemplation, uncovered; they are conveyed to the reader through a handling of language analogous to that of the Elizabethan drama or of the seventeenth-century lyric, as sensitive as it is profound.

The progression from the *Portrait* through *Ulysses* into *Finnegans Wake* represents the increasingly thorough transfer of dramatic action into the convolutions of the language itself. The liturgical implications are obvious; like the Mass, the linguistic actions are not merely analogous to another action: they *are* that action.

This is not to say that the *Portrait* itself is prentice-work. It corresponds to the first term in the necessary progression of the esthetic image described by Stephen to Lynch: lyric, epic, dramatic. *Ulysses,* as everyone knows, is epic, and *Finnegans Wake* is dramatic, its structural rationale being the superimposition of the *Oedipus Rex* of Sophocles upon the Mass, with the dreaming Earwicker as both chorus and congregation, acting and acted upon.

The terms in which Joyce expresses this progression must be taken philosophically, not colloquially. They are otherwise almost sure to be misread, as Aristotle's *Poetics* is commonly misread, through the supposition that "lyric" means a little poem and "drama" something enacted in a theater. Stephen's own account of the lyrical form, "the simplest verbal vesture of an instant of emotion, a rhythmical cry such as ages ago cheered on the man who pulled on the oar or dragged stones up a slope," (251) may mislead us further, until we realize that in twentieth-century civilized practice the emotion may be very complex indeed, and its "simplest verbal vesture" three hundred pages long. The

"instant of emotion" is the exalted instant, emerging at the end
of the [149] book, of freedom, of vocation, of Stephen's destiny,
winging his way above the waters at the side of the hawklike
man: the instant of promise on which the crushing ironies of
Ulysses are to fall. Since Joyce's theme is always the condition
of man, his ultimate conflict is always between metaphysics and
psychology, and its ultimate key the Fall. The task of rendering
the natural world intelligible demanded that the epiphany of
the sea of matter should be preceded by the psychological epiphany of a growing dream: a dream that would disregard the Fall
of man, a dream nourished by a sensitive youth of flying above
the sea into an uncreated heaven:

> The spell of arms and voices: the white arms of roads, their
> promise of close embraces and the black arms of tall ships that
> stand against the moon, their tale of distant nations. They are
> held out to say: We are alone—come. And the voices say with
> them: We are your kinsmen. And the air is thick with their com-
> pany as they call to me, their kinsman, making ready to go,
> shaking the wings of their exultant and terrible youth. (298)

All that is delusion, and the delusion is pricked with frequent
darts in *Ulysses:* "Fabulous artificer, the hawklike man. You flew.
Whereto? Newhaven-Dieppe, steerage passenger. Paris and back."
(*UL*, 208)

Stephen's interminable gnawing introspection of June 16, 1904,
has to do directly with the spurning of his mother's deathbed
wishes. But if we remember the mother-muse collocation, the
application of "motherland" to Ireland, and the phrase, which
Joyce also respected, Mother Church, we shall see that this
spurning involves more than a refusal to say a prayer for May
Dedalus. He does not, as is frequently supposed, become an
artist by rejecting church and country. [150] Stephen does not
become an artist at all. Country, church, and mission are an
inextricable unity, and in rejecting the two that seem to hamper
him he rejects also the one on which he has set his heart.
Ironically, he repeats exactly the pattern of the mediocre clergy
who, according to his own diagnosis, had insulted God's creation
in seeking God.

Stephen becomes, not an artist, but an esthete: he has rejected the humility before being proper to artists. "Signatures of all things I am here to read," (*UL*, 38) he says truly; but in the *Portrait* he shows no inclination even to look at them. He imagines that "the loveliness that has not yet come into the world" (297) is to be found in his own soul.

In its full context, the epigraph from Ovid, *Et ignotas animum dimittit in artes,* is a pertinent reminder of this fact. It offers on the first page an initial indication that Joyce was detached from what he was doing and understood fully that only an Icarian fall could end Stephen's flight to the Paterian never-never land. Here is a translation of the Ovid passage:

> In tedious exile now too long detain'd
> Dedalus languish'd for his native land.
> The sea foreclos'd his flight; yet thus he said,
> Though earth and water in subjection laid,
> O cruel Minos, thy dominion be,
> We'll go through air; for sure the air is free.
> *Then to new arts his cunning thought applies,*
> *And to improve the work of nature tries.*

Improving the work of nature is Stephen's obvious ambition, and it logically follows from the esthetic he expounds to Lynch. The genuine artist reads signatures; the fake artist forges them, a process adumbrated in the obsession of Shem the Penman with the most famous of literary forgeries, "Macfearsome's Ossean," studying "how cutely to copy all their various styles of signature so as one day to utter an [151] epical forged cheque on the public for his own private profit." (*FW*, 180). This accords with Stephen's interest in Blake, who, as Northrop Frye tells us, looked forward to a world "no longer continuously perceived but continually created." [6] The mature Joyce of *Finnegans Wake* confidently labels this process "forgery," and holds up its exponent, Shem, to continual ridicule. ("Shem was a sham and a low sham.") The Joyce who wrote the *Portrait* was equally enlightened (though it is a persistent and recurrent fallacy to suppose that the *Portrait* and *Ulysses* were written by a Stephen

[6] *Fearful Symmetry,* p. 44.

Dedalus), but the exigencies of his immediate task make it difficult for him to "place" Stephen as explicitly as he was later able to "place" Shem.

The peculiar difficulty of the *Portrait* may be stated in this way. The three major works of Joyce are all versions of one another: they simply repeat the same action in different modes. At the same time, they form a progression. The tension of the *Portrait* arises from vision without matter, of *Ulysses* from matter without spirit, of *Finnegans Wake* from spirit without grace. The *Portrait,* then, is complete in itself, and at the same time it leads directly into *Ulysses.* The final chapter, which in respect to the juggernaut of *Ulysses* is intended to be a vulnerable flank, in respect to the *Portrait* itself is intended to be a conclusion. Hence the moral ambiguity which makes the last forty pages of the *Portrait* such painful reading.

One may append the suspicion that Joyce himself had not yet thoroughly disentangled his emotions from Stephen's ambitions; that is why so much of the intended satire in *Ulysses* reads like self-laceration and why Joyce had to complain to Ezra Pound that none of the reviewers had called the book funny. The point is that he saw he must make this breach, and, in creating Shem the Penman, he succeeded. He had, after all, at one time been violently torn with identical ambitions [152] and disappointments, and the *Portrait,* on one level his kindly final salute to his youth, on another level does not entirely avoid being a personal catharsis.

It is high time, in short, to point out once and for all that Stephen's flight into adolescent "freedom" is not meant to be the "message" of the book. (Joyce observed to Frank Budgen that people often forgot the last four words of his title, *A Portrait of the Artist as a Young Man.*) *Ulysses* securely places Stephen as an esthete, not an artist, as Wyndham Lewis saw; his mistake was to suppose that Joyce did not see it too. The Stephen of the first chapter of *Ulysses,* who "walks wearily," constantly "leans" on everything in sight, invariably sits down before he has gone three paces, speaks "gloomily," "quietly," "with bitterness," and "coldly," and "suffers" his handkerchief to be pulled from his pocket by the exuberant Mulligan, is precisely the priggish, humorless Stephen of the last chapter of the *Portrait* who cannot remember what day of the week it is (206), sentimentalizes like Charles Lamb over the "human pages" of a second-hand Latin book (209), conducts the inhumanly pedantic dialogue with Cranly on mother-love (281-292), writes Frenchified verses in bed in an erotic swoon, and is epiphanized at full length, like Shem beneath the bedclothes, shrinking from the "common noises" of daylight: "Shrinking from that life he turned towards the wall, making a cowl [!] of the blanket and staring at the great overblown scarlet flowers of the tattered wall-paper. He tried to imagine his warm perishing joy in their scarlet glow, imaging a roseway from where he lay upwards to heaven all strewn with scarlet flowers. Weary! Weary! He too was weary of ardent ways." (260)

The irony of Stephen's inversion of the direction of the primrose path is not intended to escape the reader. But [153] the reader insensitive to irony may still convince himself that Stephen is not Joyce simply by comparing the esthetic discourses in the early *Stephen Hero* version with the final dramatic presentation in the *Portrait*. The same Joyce wrote both, but, having in the interval conceived *Ulysses*, he drastically pruned the *Stephen Hero* text of several of its key doctrines, so as to leave Stephen Dedalus unpropped against the ironic realities which were to overwhelm his soul in the epic. In the final version there is not a hint of the key doctrine of the epiphany, matter rendered intelligible; and a similar significant omission of the principle, of which Joyce was aware as early as 1902 when he framed it in his essay on *James Clarence Mangan*, that the artist's business is "to bend upon *these present things* and so to work upon them and fashion them that the quick intelligence may go beyond them to their meaning which is still unuttered" (*SH*, 78). The Stephen of the *Portrait*, ignoring "these present things," is inclined to ascribe the origin of esthetic beauty to the "soul" of the artist, and speaks of *claritas* as *quidditas*, the *whatness* of the esthetic image, without mention of any external whatnesses which the artist has first contemplated. "This supreme quality is felt by the artist when the esthetic image is first conceived in his imagination." (250)

Stephen's esthetic, in short, is inclined to be Neoplatonist

rather than Aristotelian, but Stephen's esthetic is not Joyce's.
The two are not incompatible, but Stephen's is incomplete. Joyce,
in fact, is extremely cagey. In manipulating the esthetic statement to serve a dramatic rather than a philosophical function,
he never commits Stephen to a position he himself would repudiate; he merely omits important emphases, which leaves the
distinct impression that Stephen's mind is centered on *ego* rather
than on *ens*. Of Joyce's own orientation, despite frequent charges
of subjectivism, there can be no doubt. Of the artist "bending
upon these present [154] things," there is no more triumphant
example in the whole of literature than *Ulysses*.

In a space in which it is impossible to treat it properly, I
mention the Joycean esthetic at all only to give the reader who
has been inclined to accuse Joyce of interiorism something to
chew on. The fit reader will be able to see that Stephen's introspective visions are constantly judged, and ironically, by the
terms in which they are raised, and that the vision of the final
pages, in fact, the total vision of the book, is murderously lam-
basted in *Ulysses*. The relation between Stephen and his sanctified namesake, who was stoned by the Jews after reporting a
vision (Acts VII:56), extends to parody as well as parallel.

The dashing of youthful hopes is constantly hovering, like an
ironic disembodied grin, over their genesis. Stephen's repentance
after the retreat, for example, is phrased throughout according
to standards by which it will later be judged:

> He sat by the fire in the kitchen, not daring to speak for hap-
> piness. Till that moment he had not known how beautiful and
> peaceful life could be. The green square of paper pinned round
> the lamp cast down a tender shade. On the dresser was a plate
> of sausages and white pudding and on the shelf there were
> eggs. They would be for the breakfast in the morning after the
> communion in the college chapel. White pudding and eggs and
> sausages and cups of tea. How simple and beautiful was life
> after all! And life lay all before him.[7] (168) [155]

---

[7] Cf. *Paradise Lost*, XII, 645-49:
    "Som natural tears they drop'd, but wip'd them soon;
    The World was all before them, where to choose
    Thir place of rest, and Providence thir guide:

The good life conceived in terms of white pudding and sausages needs no external satirist. Only an incurable tendency to identify himself, like a soap-opera fan, with the ups and downs of the hero could blind the reader to the mockery behind these passages. Joyce as an artist rather than a propagandist offers emotions for contemplation rather than participation. It is true that he scarcely expected to be understood in an age of soap-opera, but the difficulty of understanding his art is always a moral difficulty imposed by an immoral civilization; it has nothing to do, as the present instance shows, with deciphering the text.

A rare explicit example of an ironic effect in the early book uncompleted until the later one, is to be found early in the second chapter. Schoolboy Stephen is inhabiting his Monte-Cristo dream-world:

> He wanted to meet in the real world the unsubstantial image which his soul so constantly beheld. He did not know where to seek it or how but a premonition which led him on told him that this image would, without any overt act of his, encounter him. They would meet quietly as if they had known each other and had made their tryst, perhaps at one of the gates or in some more secret place. They would be alone, surrounded by darkness and silence: and in that moment of supreme tenderness he would be transfigured. (71)

It is true that this longing reaches temporary fulfillment in the plunge into profane love; but ultimately the "secret place" was to be Mabbot Street, outside Bella Cohen's brothel; the unsubstantial image of his guest, that of Leopold Bloom, advertisement canvasser; and the transfiguration, a transfiguration into the phantasmal dead son of a sentimental Jew: [156] *"Against the dark wall a figure appears slowly, a fairy boy of eleven, a changeling, kidnapped, dressed in an Eton suit with glass shoes and a little bronze helmet, holding a book in his hand. He reads from right to left inaudibly, smiling, kissing the page."* (*UL,* 593).

They hand in hand with wandring steps and slow,
Through *Eden* took thir solitarie way."
The allusion to the expulsion from Paradise under the auspices of a renewed compact with God is ironically appropriate.

The fact that it is meant to be completed by Ulysses explains, while it does not altogether excuse, much of the unsatisfactoriness of the latter third of the *Portrait:* the embarrassing intimacy and earnestness of its very humorless hero. This difficulty was largely inseparable from the projected carry-over of one book into the other. The attempt, which left the *Portrait* a suspended chord, unresolved as a *Ding an sich,* is justified by the triumphant success of its sequel; the tragic force of *Ulysses* depends to no inconsiderable degree upon the reader's being persuaded to bring to it sympathy for the self-regarding dream of Stephen Dedalus. Stephen must be more than a parlor esthete for whose loss no one out of Bloomsbury would shed a tear; he must be more significant than a casual butterfly caught on a Dublin wagon-wheel. And, indeed, Joyce never lets us forget that his perception is not in the least limited to the plight of an artist in Dublin. Stephen's final condition, "seabedabbled, fallen, weltering" (*UL,* 208), is the inevitable condition of created man, adrift in a sea of matter. To unite itself with the intrinsic intelligibility of matter is the compulsive appetite of the human mind; the tragedy of the human condition is that that appetite is frustrated by the Fall. The tragedy of Leopold Bloom is precisely that he can grope toward the Resurrection of the Body and achieve only a project to circumvent living burial ("An electric clock or a telephone in the coffin and some kind of a canvas airhole. Flag of distress."). While it is presented in a peculiarly modern mode, its particulars drawn from a sensate [157] culture immersed in matter as has been no preceding epoch in human history, we are never allowed to forget, in the way Bloom's musings parallel more transcendental speculations, that man's condition since the Fall has always been sufficiently materialized to lend Bloom's plight an extratemporal status.

The *Portrait* is similarly conceived in an extratemporal mode. We have seen how the thematic material on the two opening pages demands to be read at a level more comprehensive than the mere données of psychological experience. In synchronizing his thematic statement with a catalogue of the *schema potentiae hominis,* Joyce does homage to the Thomistic principle that all knowledge starts with the senses, but it is a mistake to suppose that the growth of the book out of these premises can be accounted for on a basis of Lockian associations between sense-impressions, or even between reflections. Such a concentration on the techniques of mechanical association has made nonsense of most attempts to explore *Ulysses;* it would have done the same for the *Portrait* but for the dubiously fortunate fact that no detailist has thought the *Portrait* worth exploring. One is not intended to deduce from the linked images, explored above, of coldness, whiteness, and moral virtue, that Stephen's apostasy was dictated by impersonal associative laws that took hold at the early moment when he was repelled by a white wash-basin. "The stream of consciousness" has been an unfortunate obsession with Joycean critics. The kind of exegesis running, "X makes him think of Y, which he associates with a memory of Z," is puerile precisely because it stresses the stream and omits the total object; in Joyce, the stream of consciousness is always part of an esthetic landscape, and drives a metaphysical millwheel. We are dealing with a poem within which such associations make up one kind of *consonantia;* but, like a Chinese ideogram, the whole has a total intelligibility based on the [158] interaction of the parts juxtaposed by association. Joyce's associative techniques, in short, are neither deterministic nor capricious. They are rooted in a patristic theory of language descended from the custom of viewing the universe as a book to be read, to which any written book bears an analogical relation, so that the work of art always has ontological rather than merely psychological content.

The complex psychological states evoked in the *Portrait,* then, are part of a pattern of metaphysical disharmony, generalized out of psychological particulars according to Joyce's doctrine of epiphanies, which makes the major job of the artist the raising of particulars to intelligibility.

There is an especially explicit example of this process in the paragraph which describes Stephen, in the squalor and confusion of his home, listening to his brothers singing:

> He heard the choir of voices in the kitchen echoed and multiplied through an endless reverberation of the choirs of endless generations of children; and heard in all the echoes an echo also of the recurring note of weariness and pain. All seemed weary

of life even before entering upon it. And he remembered that
Newman had heard this note also in the broken lines of Virgil,
"giving utterance, like the voice of Nature herself, to that pain
and weariness yet hope of better things which has been the experience of her children in every time." (190)

This treatment of particular manifestations as the signatures
of metaphysical reality is the common mode of Joyce's writing.
It is not to be confused with the kind of "symbolism," like Blake's
use in his drawings of an advanced left hand or foot to indicate
matter, a right hand or foot to indicate spirit, which is really no
more significant than the labeling of the figures in a political
cartoon. Joyce is not arbitrarily pinning on labels, he is scrutinizing existences for [159] their significance; the epiphany, like Hopkins' "inscape," is the reward for the artist of intense contemplation. Joyce eludes altogether the party politics of "symbolism"
and "naturalism."

In fact, a paragraph like the one above, which comes closest
to arbitrary inflation or label-pinning, is very rare; the normal
mode of the epiphany is better illustrated in such passages as
the priest dangling the cord, analyzed at the beginning of this
essay. Here the ambiguities of such key-words as "skull," "crossblind," and "temple," signal to the reader the kind of intelligibility the incident is capable of yielding; the ambiguity of the
words corresponds directly with the multiple significance of the
object.

The vitality of Joyce's prose is rooted in the way such words
supplement their grammatical function by independent life as
blocks in the mosaic. "Crossblind" as an independent entity
comments on the whole situation, and when it is perceived as
an independent entity there is also perceived the irony of the
nonchalance with which the priest leans on it, and a surrealist
dimension is added to prosaic statement. The *Portrait* is not as
far as it seems from *Finnegans Wake;* indeed, a Finneganistic
handling of language appears beneath it as a sort of subconscious.

This method, as it is employed in the *Portrait,* tends to round
off the epiphanies in tight little paragraphs. It is important therefore to realize further that Joyce's technique is not to be con-

fused with "Imagism." The quest of the isolated image, however radiant, seemed to Joyce a particularly dilettantish activity, like the "epiphanies on green oval leaves, deeply deep" which Stephen Dedalus dreamed of sending to the great libraries of the world, "including Alexandria." Ezra Pound, who has always hamstrung his use of the epiphany technique by conceiving it in terms of the limited capacity of the Chinese written character, might be content to offer as a complete, titled Imagist poem, [160]

> The apparition of these faces in the crowd;
> Petals on a wet, black bough.

Unlike Pound, however, Joyce possessed a metaphysic which made him instinctively incapable of stopping with an illuminated *morceau*. Hence his interest in Ben Jonson, whose works, read through in the hungry Paris exile of 1903, showed him how to organize clusters of naturalistic and symbolic material around controlling images: the normal method of the Elizabethan drama.

Thus, in the *Portrait*, the controlling emotion of Chapter I is fear, and its dominant image Father Dolan and his pandybat. This, associated with the hangman-god and the priestly denial of the senses, was to become one of Joyce's stock ideograms for clericalism—hence the jack-in-the-box appearance of Father Dolan in the nightmare imbroglio of Circe's brothel, his pandybat cracking twice like thunder. Stephen's comment, in the mode of Blake's repudiation of the God who slaughtered Jesus, emphasizes the cosmic dimensions of the image: "I never could read His handwriting except His criminal thumbprint on the haddock." (*UL*, 548)

Chapter II opens with a triple image of Dublin's prepossessions: music, sport, and religion. The first is associated with Uncle Charles singing sentimental ballads in the outhouse; the second with Stephen's ritual run around the park under the eye of a superannuated trainer, which his uncle enjoins on him as the whole duty of a Dubliner; the third with the clumsy piety of Uncle Charles, kneeling on a red handkerchief and reading above his breath "from a thumb-blackened prayerbook wherein catchwords were printed at the foot of every page." (67) This trinity of themes is unwound and entwined throughout the chap-

ter, like a net woven around Stephen; it underlies the central
incident, the Whitsuntide play in the Belvedere chapel (religion),
which opens with a display by the dumbbell team (sport) pre-
luded [161] by sentimental waltzes from the soldier's band (music).
(The use of the chapel for these purposes is itself an epiphany
of the squalid function of the church in Irish popular culture.)

While he is waiting to play his part, Stephen is taunted by
fellow students, who rally him on a fancied love affair and, smit-
ing his calf with a cane, bid him recite the *Confiteor*. His mind
goes back to an analogous incident, when he had been similarly
punished on his refusal to "admit that Byron was no good." The
further analogy with Father Dolan is obvious; love, art, and personal independence are thus united in an ideogram of the prepossessions Stephen is determined to cultivate despite whatever
persecution.

The tormenting schoolboys with their canes carry further the
symbolic projection of Stephen's pig-headed environment. As
Father Dolan represents the Church, so they represent Dublin,
translated into an active mode. But analogous inner torment accompanies Stephen's every contemplation of Dubliners' ways, and
the dream-world which he nourishes within himself is played off
against the manifestations of sport, music, and religion throughout the chapter. The constant ironic clash of Dublin *vs.* the
dream furnishes the dramatic life of Chapter II, as the clash of
the ego *vs.* authority furnished that of Chapter I. All these themes
come to a focus during Stephen's visit to Cork with his father.
The dream of rebellion which Stephen has silently cultivated is
externalized by the discovery of the word *Foetus* carved in a
desk by a forgotten medical student: "It shocked him to find
in the outer world a trace of what he had deemed till then a
brutish and individual malady of his own mind. His monstrous
reveries came thronging into his memory. They too had sprung
up before him, suddenly and furiously, out of mere words. . . ."
(101) [162]

The possibility of shame's gaining the upper hand is dashed,
however, by the sudden banal intrusion of his father's conversation: "When you kick out for yourself, Stephen, as I daresay you

will one of these days, remember, whatever you do, to mix with gentlemen. . . ." Against the standards of Dublin, his monstrous reveries acquire a Satanic glamour, and the trauma is slowly diverted into a resolution to rebel. After his father has expressed a resolve to "leave him to his Maker" (religion), and offered to "sing a tenor song against him" (music) or "vault a fire-barred gate against him" (sport), Stephen muses, watching his father and two cronies drinking to the memory of their past,

> An abyss of fortune or of temperament sundered him from them. His mind seemed older than theirs: it shone coldly on their strifes and happiness and regrets like a moon upon a younger earth. No life or youth stirred in him as it had stirred in them. He had known neither the pleasure of companionship with others nor the vigour of rude male health nor filial piety. Nothing stirred within his soul but a cold and cruel and loveless lust. (107)

After one final effort to compromise with Dublin on Dublin's terms has collapsed into futility ("The pot of pink enamel paint gave out and the wainscot of his bedroom remained with its unfinished and ill plastered coat") (110), he fiercely cultivates his rebellious thoughts, and moving by day and night "among distorted images of the outer world," (111) plunges at last into the arms of whores. And this final act is presented as the inversion of the image of Father Daly's and Uncle Charles's religion: his descent into nighttown is accompanied by lurid visions of a Black Mass: "The yellow gasflames arose before his troubled vision against the vapoury sky, burning as if before an altar. Before the doors and in the lighted halls [163] groups were gathered arrayed as for some rite. He was in another world: he had awakened from a slumber of centuries." (113)

This last paragraph offers significant opportunities for misreading. The reader who can see that it is not written to assist in evoking a lurid mood, rather that it is the mood that confers intelligibility on the material, is probably ready to tackle *Ulysses*.

Each chapter in the *Portrait* gathers up the thematic material of the preceding ones and entwines them with a dominant theme of its own. In Chapter III, the fear-pandybat motif is patently present in Father Arnall's crudely materialistic hell, of which even the thickness of the walls is specified, and the Dublin-*vs.*-dream motif has ironic inflections in Stephen's terror-stricken broodings, when the dream has been twisted into a dream of holiness, and even Dublin appears transfigured:

> How beautiful must be a soul in the state of grace when God looked upon it with love!
> Frowsy girls sat along the curbstones before their baskets. Their dank hair trailed over their brows. They were not beautiful to see as they crouched in the mire. But their souls were seen by God; and if their souls were in a state of grace they were radiant to see: and God loved them, seeing them. (162)

A rapprochement in these terms between the outer world and Stephen's desires is too ironic to need commentary, and it makes vivid as nothing else could the hopeless inversion of his attempted self-sufficiency. It underlines, in yet another way, his persistent sin, and the dominant theme of Chapter III is Sin. A fugue-like opening plays upon the Seven Deadly Sins in turn: gluttony is in the first paragraph ("Stuff it into you, his belly counselled him"); followed by lust; then sloth ("A cold lucid indifference reigned in his soul"); pride [164] ("His pride in his own sin, his loveless awe of God, told him that his offence was too grievous to be atoned for"); anger ("The blundering answer stirred the embers of his contempt of his fellows"). The final recapitulation fixes each term of the deadly catalogue in a phrase, enumerating how "from the evil seed of lust all the other deadly sins had sprung forth." (120)

By a peculiar irony, which accords with the priest-punisher ideogram and throws important light on the apostasy to follow, Stephen, when he is deepest in sin, is most thoroughly a theologian. A paragraph of burning experience of evil is juxtaposed, like Shem by Shaun, with a list of theological questions that puzzle Stephen's mind as he awaits the preacher:

> . . . Is baptism with mineral water valid? How comes it that while the first beatitude promises the kingdom of heaven to

the poor of heart, the second beatitude promises also to the
meek that they shall possess the land? . . . If the wine change
into vinegar and the host crumble into corruption after they
have been consecrated, is Jesus Christ still present under their
species as God and as man?

"Here he is! Here he is!"

A boy from his post at the window had seen the rector come
from the house. All the catechisms were opened and all heads
bent upon them silently. (120)

This last is a particularly telling collocation. Wine changed
into vinegar and the host crumbled into corruption fit exactly
the Irish clergy of "a church which was the scullery-maid of
Christendom." The excited "Here he is! Here he is," following
hard on the mention of Jesus Christ and signaling nothing more
portentous than the rector, makes the point as dramatically as
anything in the book. The clinching sentence, [165] with the students suddenly bending over their catechisms, places the rector
as the vehicle of pandybat morality.

The last of these theological questions is the telling question.
Joyce never doubted the existence of God nor the validity of
the priestly office—Stephen's *"Non serviam"* is not a *"Non credo"*
—but the wine and bread that were offered for his veneration
were changed into vinegar and crumbled into corruption. And
it was the knowledge of that underlying validity clashing with
Stephen's refusal to do homage to vinegar and rot that evoked
in him a split psychological state and changed the Christ of the
sacraments into "a malevolent reality behind those things I say
I fear." (287) The Hell of Father Arnall's sermon, so emotionally
overwhelming, so picayune beside the adult horrors of the Inferno of Dublin in *Ulysses,* had no more ontological content for
Stephen than had "an eternity of bliss in the company of the dean
of studies." (282)

It is to be noted that the dramatic conflict of this central chapter is again between the phantasmal and the real. What is real
—psychologically real, because realized—is Stephen's anguish and
remorse, and its context in the life of the flesh. What is phantasmal is the "Heaven" of the Church and the "good life" of the

priest. It is only fear that makes him clutch after the latter at all; his reaching out after orthodox salvation is, as we have come to expect, presented in terms that judge it:

> The wind blew over him and passed on to the myriads and myriads of other souls, on whom God's favour shone now more and now less, stars now brighter and now dimmer, sustained and failing. And the glimmering souls passed away, sustained and failing, merged in a moving breath. One soul was lost; a tiny soul: his. It flickered once and went out, forgotten, lost. The end: black cold void waste.
>
> Consciousness of place came ebbing back to him [166] slowly over a vast tract of time unlit, unfelt, unlived. The squalid scene composed itself around him; the common accents, the burning gasjets in the shops, odours of fish and spirits of wet sawdust, moving men and women. An old woman was about to cross the street, an oilcan in her hand. He bent down and asked her was there a chapel near. (162)

That wan, waste world of flickering stars is the best Stephen has been able to do toward an imaginative grasp of the communion of Saints sustained by God; "unlit, unfelt, unlived" explains succinctly why it had so little hold on him, once fear had relaxed. Equally pertinent is the vision of human temporal occupations that the sermon evokes: "What did it profit a man to gain the whole world if he lost his soul? At last he had understood: and human life lay around him, a plain of peace whereon antlike men laboured in brotherhood, their dead sleeping under quiet mounds." (144)

To maintain the life of grace in the midst of nature, sustained by so cramped a vision of the life of nature, would mean maintaining an intolerable tension. Stephen's unrelenting philosophical bias, his determination to understand what he is about, preclude his adopting the double standard of Dubliners; to live both the life of nature and the life of grace he must enjoy an imaginative grasp of their relationship which stunts neither. "No one doth well against his will," writes Saint Augustine, "even though what he doth, be well," and Stephen's will was firmly harnessed to his understanding. The tragedy of his situation is that there is no one to help him achieve understanding. It is not to be wondered at that the rank fear inspired by Father Arnall's sermon precludes any desirable outcome, for the sermon follows the modes of pandybat morality and Dublin materiality. Its only possible effect on Stephen is to lash his [167] dormant conscience into a frenzy. The description of Hell as "a strait and dark and foul smelling prison, an abode of demons and lost souls, filled with fire and smoke," with walls four thousand miles thick, its damned packed in so tightly that "they are not even able to remove from the eye a worm that gnaws it," is childishly grotesque beneath its sweeping eloquence; and the hairsplitting catalogue of pains—pain of loss, pain of conscience (divided into three heads), pain of extension, pain of intensity, pain of eternity—is cast in a brainlessly analytic mode that effectively prevents any corresponding Heaven from possessing any reality at all.

Stephen's unstable pact with the Church, and its dissolution, follows the pattern of composition and dissipation established by his other dreams: the dream, for example, of fair women, of the tryst with "Mercedes," which found ironic reality among harlots. It parallels exactly his earlier attempt to "build a breakwater of order and elegance against the sordid tide of life without him," whose failure, with the exhaustion of his money, was epiphanized in the running-dry of the pot of pink enamel paint. His regimen at that time, "He bought presents for everyone, overhauled his room, wrote out resolutions, marshalled his books up and down their shelves, pored upon all kinds of price lists. . . ." is strictly comparable with his searching after spiritual improvement:

> His daily life was laid out in devotional areas. By means of ejaculations and prayers he stored up ungrudgingly for the souls in purgatory centuries of days and quarantines and years. . . . He offered up each of his three daily chaplets that his soul might grow strong in each of the three theological virtues. . . . On each of the seven days of the week he further prayed that [168] one of the seven gifts of the Holy Ghost might descend upon his soul. (170)

The analogy between the two passages is, in fact, particularly strict; the "loan bank" he had opened for the family, out of which

he pressed loans on willing borrowers "that he might have the
pleasure of making out receipts and reckoning the interests on
sums lent" finds its significant counterpart in the benefits he
stored up for souls in purgatory that he might enjoy the spiritual
triumph of "achieving with ease so many fabulous ages of canoni-
cal penances." Both projects are parodies on the doctrine of the
economy of grace; both are attempts, corrupted by motivating
self-interest, to make peace with Dublin on Dublin's terms; both
are short-lived.

This precise analogical structure suggests that the action of
each of the five chapters is really the same action. The pattern
of dream nourished in contempt of reality, put into practice, and
dashed by reality, is worked out in the five chapters in five
main modes, and in numerous subordinate instances. The movement of the book is dialectical; each chapter closes with a synthesis of triumph which in turn feeds the sausage-machine set
up in the next chapter. The triumph of the appeal to Father
Conmee from lower authority, of the appeal to the harlots from
Dublin, of the appeal to the Church from sin, of the appeal to
art from priesthood, is always the same triumph raised to a
more comprehensive level. All the particulars are achieving the
same pattern of intelligibility, and, ironically, that pattern is
ultimately theological. Stephen's relation to God and to God's
creation is at every point the ethical center of the book. He
appeals from each inadequate vehicle of God's word to another
only less inadequate; "the exasperated spirit" proceeds, in Eliot's
phrase, "from wrong to wrong." His every dream is a blasphemy,
even when it obeys Dublin morality, and comes to grief on a
rock of metaphysical fact: that is, of Divine fact. Each successive
attempt represents on [169] the psychological level a maturer level
of comprehensive organization; an assault on life armed with successively larger and larger visions of the meaning of his own
existence. The last, the self-dramatization as the "priest of the
eternal imagination," is the most comprehensive of all, and it
permits a temporary suspension of the tensions of the book; but
it, too, is to come to grief in *Ulysses,* in a universe the rule of
whose Ruler is "all or not at all." When Stephen's comprehension finally swells past several stages of subjectivism to the

metaphysical, the root error persists, and he claims a birthright of metaphysical self-sufficiency. One does not need to go beyond the *Portrait* to understand T. S. Eliot's authoritative statement that Joyce is "the most ethically orthodox among the more eminent authors of our time."

It is worth indicating briefly, as further elucidation of this theological and moral orientation, the function in the book of physical love. The physical is an analogue of the spiritual, as St. Augustine insisted in his *Confessions* (which is as important an archetype for the *Portrait* as the *City of God* is for *Ulysses*). The poles between which this affection moves are those of St. Augustine and St. John: the Whore of Babylon and the Bride of Christ. The former is analogous to the life of the flesh, the latter to the life of the spirit. Stephen moves in a constant tension between the two. His desire to "meet in the real world the unsubstantial image which his soul so constantly beheld" (71) is figured in the visions of the shadowy Mercedes of *The Count of Monte Cristo*, encountering whom "weakness and timidity and inexperience were to fall from him." (112) That satisfaction he thinks he achieves in his first visit to a prostitute: "In her arms he felt that he had suddenly become strong and fearless and sure of himself." Yet the resolution of desire in that fashion is illusory: "fearless" is exactly what he does not become. The Dream of Fair Women transmuted into the life of the flesh brings only torture. [170]

The same dream thirsts simultaneously toward an exactly opposite, spiritual satisfaction. The wraithlike E— C—, to whom he twice writes verses, and who is barely present in the book as a physical figure,[8] preys upon his imagination with an identical torture. And E— C— is continually assimilated to the image of the Blessed Virgin and of the Church which is the Bride of Christ. The torture she costs him is the torture his apostasy costs him. His flirtation with her is flirtation with Christ. His profane villanelle (262) is composed in the mode of religious imagery

---

[8] In the *Stephen Hero* MS, Emma Clery is realistically described (66) with her loud voice and her body compact of pleasure. Joyce refined her into a wraith with a pair of initials, in proportion as his analogical purpose became clearer to him, to parallel a spiritual love and an intangible church.

(the smoking incense of praise, the eucharistic hymn, the sacrificial chalice). Her heart, following Dante's image, is a rose (255), and in her praise "the earth was like a swinging swaying censer, a ball of incense." (256)

The woman is the Church. His vision of greeting Mercedes with "a sadly proud gesture of refusal" is fulfilled when he refuses to make his Easter duty. Emma's eyes, in their one explicit encounter, speak to him from beneath a cowl. (76). "The glories of Mary held his soul captive" (118), and a temporary reconciliation of his lust and his spiritual thirst is achieved as he reads the Lesson out of the Song of Solomon. In the midst of his repentance she functions as imagined mediator: "The image of Emma appeared before him," and, repenting, "he imagined that he stood near Emma in a wide land and, humbly and in tears, bent and kissed the elbow of her sleeve." Like Dante's Beatrice, she manifests in his earthly experience the Church Triumphant of his spiritual dream. And when he rejects her because she seems to be flirting with Father Moran, his anger is couched in the anticlerical terms of his apostasy: [171] "He had done well to leave her to flirt with her priest, to toy with a church which was the scullery-maid of Christendom." (258)

That Kathleen ni Houlihan can flirt with priests is the unforgivable sin underlying Stephen's rejection of Ireland. But he makes a clear distinction between the stupid clericalism which makes intellectual and temporal life impossible, and his clearly-nourished vision of an ideal Church triumphant upon earth. He rejects the actual for daring to fall short of his vision.

The *Portrait* is throughout a tragedy of ideals without matter; the tragic conflict is always between the dream and life, "the cattle which had seemed so beautiful in the country on sunny days revolted him and he could not even look at the milk they yielded" (69). In the same way, *Ulysses* is the tragedy of matter without spirit, and *Finnegans Wake* of spirit without grace. The final reconciliation was to have been achieved in the poem which death prevented Joyce from writing, where the fundamental rhythm was to have been the sound of the sea: the sea which, in the final pages of *Finnegans Wake,* stands for God and Father and Home.

Stephen, then, is ultimately an idealistic perfectionist whose unfulfillable hunger is for God. He leaves a country which seems wholly secular, a Church which seems thoroughly enmeshed in matter, determined, if there be no true priests, to be his own priest. This constant spiritual and theological basis is perfectly consistent once we become aware of it. And while the final chapter is to image painstakingly the spiritual pride and autonomy that are to come to comprehensive grief in *Ulysses*, this same chapter, precisely because it is an attempt to finish off temporarily a book that on its own terms cannot be finished, makes heavy reading. The insufferable Stephen of the final chapter is explicable on the assumption that Joyce is preparing his bridge into *Ulysses;* but the moral difficulty of accepting the *Portrait* as satisfactorily [172] finished off in its own right imposes an intolerable strain on the reader. It is painful to be invited to close the book with an indigestibly Byronic hero stuck in our throats. We are compelled to take Stephen seriously so that *Ulysses* may have its desired tragic effect (also, one may whisper, because Joyce had known a time, to which he here does homage, when he himself had been wrapped in an identical pride), but to take him seriously is very hard indeed.

What he lacks most of all in the final chapter is humor. The dark intensity of the first four chapters is moving enough, but our impulse on being confronted with the final edition of Stephen Dedalus is to laugh; and laugh at this moment we dare not: he is, after all, a victim being prepared for a sacrifice. Humor is the last achievement of a mind striving to integrate itself on a level of supremely mature awareness, and, while Joyce incontrovertibly achieved it, it is intrinsic in the dramatic conception of Stephen that he shall not.

Ten years before he died, Joyce finally rewrote the essential action of the *Portrait* as an integral part of what was to be his last synthesis; it is the portion of *Finnegans Wake* called *The Mime of Mick Nick and the Maggies* (Bk. II, Ch. 1). Here, freed from the distraction of preparing an indefinitely postponed denouement, the comic spirit has full play. Joyce the dancer and singer is superimposed on the writhings of Stephen Dedalus with superb comic effect: "He threwed his fit up to his aers, rolled his poligone eyes, snivelled from his snose and blew the guff out of his hornypipe. The hopjoimt jerk of a ladle broom jig that he learned in locofoco when a redhot turnspite he." (*FW*, 231)

Here at last Stephen's self-dramatization as Prometheus is placed as comic absurdity; his posturings are assimilated to the antics of the damned, and "spite" establishes the torturing [173] fire as psychological: wherein he moves in measure, like a dancer. Intelligibility at every level, moral, psychological, and metaphysical, is finally achieved, and achieved with an ease and freedom that sunders our picture of Joyce, finally and forever, from the sickly, stiffnecked, introspective esthete whose development the *Portrait* so sensitively explores. Such are the necessary terms of a final judgment: the *Portrait* is a work of genius both astonishing and painful; the *Mime,* from the fullness of its realization, is supremely great literature. [174]

DOROTHY VAN GHENT

On A Portrait of the Artist
as a Young Man

. . . ONE OF THE OLDEST THEMES in the novel is that language is a creator of reality. There is this theme in *Don Quixote.* . . . Quixote is supremely a man animated by "the word"; and as the words he has read in books send him into action—creating reality

From *The English Novel: Form and Function,* by Dorothy Van Ghent. Copyright ©, 1953. Reprinted by permission of Holt, Rinehart and Winston, Inc., publishers. References to *A Portrait* are to *P*-3; to *Stephen Hero* are to *SH*-1.

for him by determining what he sees and what he feels and what he does—so Quixote in turn has a similar effect upon other people, subtly changing their outlook, creating in them new forms of thought and activity. *Don Quixote* may be looked on as an extensive investigation of the creative effects of language upon life. Joyce's *Portrait* is also an investigation of this [264] kind; appropriately so, for the "artist" whose youthful portrait the book is, is at the end to find his vocation in language; and the shape of reality that gradually defines itself for Stephen is a shape determined primarily by the associations of words. We follow in the circumstances of the boy's life the stages of breakdown and increasing confusion in his external environment, as his home goes to pieces, and the correlative stages of breakdown in his inherited values, as his church and his nation lose their authority over his emotions. Very early the child's mind begins to respond to that confusion by seeking in itself, in its own mental images, some unifying form or forms that will signify what the world *really* is, that will show him the *real* logic of things—a logic hopelessly obscure in external relations. His mental images are largely associations suggested by the words he hears, and in intense loneliness he struggles to make the associations fit into a coherent pattern.

To the very young child, adults seem to possess the secret of the whole, seem to know what everything means and how one thing is related to another. Apparently in command of that secret, they toss words together into esoteric compounds, some words whose referents the child knows and many whose referents are mysterious; and the context of the familiar words guides him in his speculation about the unfamiliar ones, the unfamiliar ones thus taking on their meaning for him in a wondrously accidental and chaotic fashion. These accidents of context, however bizarre, build up his notion of reality and determine his later responses and the bias of his soul. There is the story that Stephen's father tells him about a cow coming down along a road. There is the song about the wild rose blossoming on the green place. He, Stephen, is evidently the "nicens little boy" toward whom the cow designs its path, and he, Stephen, can make the wild rose into a green one by a transposition of ad-

jectives. The world's form, then, is apparently shaped toward
him and out from him as its center. But how to put the story
and the song intelligibly together, in a superior meaningful pattern of reality, with his father's hairy face looking at him through
a glass? or with the queer smell of the oil sheet? or with Dante's
two brushes? or with Eileen, the neighbor girl, who has a different father and mother? or with some shadowily guilty thing
he has done for which he must "apologize," else eagles will pull
out his eyes? In this extremely short sequence at the beginning
of the book, the child's sense of insecurity, in a world whose
form he cannot grasp, is established—and with insecurity, guilt
(he must apologize) and fear (the horrible eagles). With these
unpromising emotional [265] elements established in him, the ma-
turing child will try again and again to grasp his world imag-
inatively as a shape within which he has a part that is essential
to its completeness and harmoniousness and meaningfulness.

Immediately there is a transition to the children's playground
at Clongowes Wood, the child's earliest experience of a community other than that of the home. Again the auditory impression is predominant—sounds heard, words spoken—and the life-
directed attempt of the young mind is to understand their meaning in relation to each other and in relation to a governing design.
There are the "strong cries" of the boys and the "thud" of their
feet and bodies; then comes a quick succession of references to
special oddnesses in the names of things. To the child's laboring
apprehension, which assumes all names to have intimate and
honest connections with reality, the name "dog-in-the-blanket"
for the Friday pudding must represent something about the pudding which is real and which other people know but which is
obscured from him; it may have more than one meaning, like
the word "belt," which means a strap on a jacket and also "to
give a fellow a belt"; or it may have complex, mysterious, and
terribly serious associations with destiny, understood by others
but dark and anxious to himself, like his own name, Stephen
Dedalus, which Nasty Roche says is "queer" with a queerness
that puts the social status of Stephen's father in doubt. Through
words the world comes to Stephen; through the words he hears
he gropes his way into other people's images of reality. Doubts

and anxieties arise because the words and phrases are disassociated, their context frequently arbitrary, like that of the sentences in the spelling book:

> Wolsey died in Leicester Abbey
> Where the abbots buried him.
> Canker is a disease of plants,
> Cancer one of animals. (249)

The sentences in the spelling book at least make a rhythm,
and a rhythm is a kind of pattern, a "whole" of sorts; they are
therefore "nice sentences" to think about. But the threatening,
overwhelming problem is the integration of all the vast heap of
disassociated impressions that the child's mind is subjected to
and out of which his hopeful urgency toward intelligibility forces
him, entirely lonely and without help, to try to make superior
rhythms and superior unities. [266]

The technique of the "stream of consciousness," or "interior
monologue," as Joyce uses it, is a formal aspect of the book
which sensitively reflects the boy's extreme spiritual isolation.
There is a logical suitability in the fact that this type of technique should arise at a time of cultural debacle, when society
has failed to give objective validation to inherited structures of
belief, and when therefore all meanings, values, and sanctions
have to be built up from scratch in the loneliness of the individual mind. When an author assumes the right to enter his
novel in his own voice and comment on his characters—as Fielding does or George Eliot does—we are able to infer a cultural
situation in which there are objective points of reference for the
making of a judgment; the author and reader enter into overt
agreement, as it were, in criticizing and judging the character's
actions; and where there is this assumption of agreement, we
are in a relatively secure social world. The "gregarious point of
view" used by the older novelists reflects a world, comparatively
speaking, of shared standards. As the technical point of view
adopted by the novelist more and more tends to exclude the
novelist's own expression of opinion from his book, the world
which he represents tends more and more to be one whose values
are in question; and we have, for instance, in the later work

of Henry James, a work such as *The Ambassadors,* where the
subjective point of view of the main character is dominant, a
concentration on a process of mind in which values are reshifted
and rejudged from top to bottom, all in the loneliness of an
individual's personal experience. The technique of the "interior
monologue" is a modification of the subjective point of view. It
is not a departure from traditional convention, for even Fielding
used this point of view when he wanted to show "from the
inside" how a character's mind worked; but it is an employment of
the subjective point of view throughout the entire novel—instead
of sporadically, as in the older English novel—and it follows
more devious and various paths of consciousness than traditional
novelists were concerned with. Joyce's concern, in the *Portrait,*
is with the associative patterns arising in Stephen's mind from
infancy into adolescence. What we need to emphasize, however,
is that he is concerned with these only as they show the dialectical process by which a world-shape evolves in the mind. The
process is conducted in the absolute solitude of the inside of
the skull, for Stephen has no trustworthy help from the objective environment. The technique of the interior monologue is the
sensitive formal representation of that mental solitude. [267]

"By thinking of things you could understand them," Stephen
says to himself when he arrives at the conclusion that the epithet
"Tower of Ivory," in the litany of the Blessed Virgin, means
what Eileen's hand felt like in his pocket—like ivory, only soft—
and the "House of Gold" means what her hair had looked like,
streaming out behind her like gold in the sun. (286) Shortly
before, he has been puzzling over the fact that Dante does not
wish him to play with Eileen because Eileen is a Protestant, and
the Protestants "make fun of the litany of the Blessed Virgin,"
saying, "How could a woman be a tower of ivory or a house of
gold?" (278) Who was right then, the Protestants or the Catholics? Stephen's analytical quandary is resolved by the perception
of the identity between the feel of Eileen's prying hand and the
meaning of "Tower of Ivory." In the same way, by the same
dialectical process, his flooding impressions reach a stage of cohe-
sion from moment to moment, a temporary synthesis in which
he suddenly sees what they "mean." As Stephen matures, there

is mounted on the early association between the Virgin and Eileen an identification between his dream-Mercedes (ideal girl in a rose-cottage) and a whore. By extension, this association holds in it much of Stephen's struggle between other-worldliness and this-worldliness, for it has identified in his imagination flesh and spirit, while his intellect, developing under education, rebels against the identification.[1] Thus "the word"—Tower of Ivory, House of Gold—creates by accident and at random the reality of suffering and act.

Those moments in the dialectical process when a synthesis is achieved, when certain phrases or sensations or complex experiences suddenly cohere in a larger whole and a meaning shines forth from the whole, Joyce—who introduced the word into literary currency—called "epiphanies." They are "showings-forth" of the nature of reality as the boy is prepared to grasp it. Minor epiphanies mark all the stages of Stephen's understanding, as when the feel of Eileen's hand shows him what Tower of Ivory means, or as when the word "Foetus," carved on a school desk (339), suddenly focuses for him in brute clarity his "monstrous way of life." Major epiphanies, occurring at the end of each chapter, mark the chief revelations of the nature of his environment and of his destiny in it. The epiphany is an image, sensuously apprehended and emotionally vibrant, which communicates instantaneously the meaning of experience. It may contain a revelation of a person's [268] character, brief and fleeting, occurring by virtue of some physical trait in the person, as the way big Corrigan looked in the bath: "He had skin the same colour as the turfcoloured bogwater in the shallow end of the bath and when he walked along the side his feet slapped loudly on the wet tiles and at every step his thighs shook a little because he was fat." (299) In this kind of use, as revelation through one or two physical traits of the whole mass-formation of a personality, the epiphany is almost precisely duplicable in Dickens, as in the spectacle of Miss Havisham leaning on her crutch beside the rotten bridecake, or of Jaggers flourishing his white hand-

[1] Irene Hendry points this out in her admirable essay "Joyce's Epiphanies," in *James Joyce: Two Decades of Criticism*, Seon Givens, ed. (New York: Vanguard Press, 1948). See this essay reprinted in this volume on pp. 204-220.

kerchief and biting his great forefinger. The minor personalities in the *Portrait* are reduced to something very like a Dickensian "signature"—as Heron with his bird-beaked face and bird-name, Davin with his peasant turns of speech, Lynch whose "long slender flattened skull beneath the long pointed cap brought before Stephen's mind the image of a hooded reptile." (470) Or the epiphany may be a kind of "still life" with which are associated deep and complex layers of experience and emotion. In the following passage, for instance, the sordor of Stephen's home, the apprehensive and guilty image of the bath at Clongowes, and the bestiality he associates with the bogholes of Ireland, are illuminated simultaneously by a jar of drippings on the table. "He drained his third cup of watery tea to the dregs and set to chewing the crusts of fried bread that were scattered near him, staring into the dark pool of the jar. The yellow dripping had been scooped out like a boghole, and the pool under it brought back to his memory the dark turfcoloured water of the bath at Conglowes." (434)

Here the whole complex of home, school, and nation is epitomized in one object and shot through with the emotion of rejection. The epiphany is usually the result of a gradual development of the emotional content of associations, as they accrete with others. Among Stephen's childish impressions is that of "a woman standing at the halfdoor of a cottage with a child in her arms," and "it would be lovely to sleep for one night in that cottage before the fire [269] of smoking turf, in the dark lit by the fire, in the warm dark, breathing the smell of the peasants, air and rain and turf and corduroy. . . ." (258) The early impression enters into emotional context later with the story Davin tells him about stopping at night at the cottage of a peasant woman, and Stephen's image of the woman is for him an epiphany of the soul of Ireland: "a batlike soul waking to the consciousness of itself in darkness and secrecy and loneliness." (444-445; 488) The epiphany is dynamic, activated by the form-seeking urgency in experience, and itself feeding later revelations. At the point of exile, Stephen feels, "under the deepened dusk, the thoughts and desires of the race to which he belonged flitting like bats, across the dark country lanes, under trees by the edges of streams and near the pool mottled bogs." (508)

The major epiphanies in the book occur as the symbolic climaxes of the larger dialectical movements constituting each of the five chapters. As Hugh Kenner has pointed out, in his essay *"The Portrait* in Perspective," [2] each of the chapters begins with a multitude of warring impressions, and each develops toward an emotionally apprehended unity; each succeeding chapter liquidates the previous synthesis and subjects its elements to more adult scrutiny in a constantly enlarging field of perception, and develops toward its own synthesis and affirmation. In each chapter, out of the multitude of elements with which it opens, some one chief conflict slowly shapes itself. In the first, among all the bewildering impressions that the child's mind entertains, the deeper conflict is that between his implicit trust in the authority of his elders—his Jesuit teachers, the older boys in the school, his father and Mr. Casey and Dante—and his actual sense of insecurity. His elders, since they apparently know the meaning of things, must therefore incarnate perfect justice and moral and intellectual consistency. But the child's real experience is of mad quarrels at home over Parnell and the priests, and at school the frivolous cruelty of the boys, the moral chaos suggested by the smugging in the square and the talk about stealing the altar wine, and the sadism of Father Dolan with his pandybat. With Stephen's visit to the rector at the end of the chapter, the conflict is resolved. Justice is triumphant—even a small boy with weak eyes can find it; he is greeted like a hero on his emergence from the rector's office; his consolidation with his human environment is gloriously affirmed.

The second chapter moves straight from that achievement of emotional [270] unity into other baffling complexities, coincident with the family's removal to Dublin. The home life is increasingly squalid, the boy more lonely and restless. In Simon Dedalus' account of his conversation with the rector of Clongowes about the incident of the pandying, what had seemed, earlier, to be a triumph of justice and an affirmation of intelligent moral

[2] *Ibid.* See this essay reprinted in this volume on pp. 25-60.

authority by Stephen's elders is revealed as cruel, stupid indifference. In the episode in which Stephen is beaten for "heresy," the immediate community of his schoolfellows shows itself as false, shot through with stupidity and sadism. More importantly, the image of the father is corroded. On the visit to Cork, Simon appears to the boy's despairing judgement as besotted, self-deluded, irresponsible—and with the corruption of the father-image his whole picture of society suffers the same ugly damage. On the same visit, Stephen's early dim apprehension of sin and guilt is raised into horrible prominence by the word "Foetus" which he sees inscribed on the desk at Queen's College and which symbolizes for him all his adolescent monstrosity (the more monstrous in that Simon looks with obscene sentimentality on the desk carvings, thus condemning the whole world for Stephen in his own sickened sense of guilt). Meanwhile, his idealistic longings for beauty and purity and gentleness and certitude have concentrated in a vaguely erotic fantasy of the dream-girl Mercedes in her rose-cottage. Again, at the end of the chapter, Stephen's inner conflict is resolved in an emotional unity, a new vision of the relationships between the elements of experience. The synthesis is constituted here by a triumphant integration of the dream of Mercedes with the encounter with the whore. It is "sin" that triumphs, but sublimated as an ideal unity, pure and gentle and beautiful and emotionally securing.

As Hugh Kenner has observed, in the [preceding] essay, the predominant physical activity in the *Portrait* that accompanies Stephen's mental dialectics, as he moves through analysis to new provisional syntheses, is the activity of walking; his ambulatory movements take him into new localities, among new impressions, as his mind moves correspondingly into new spiritual localities that subsume the older ones and readjust them as parts of a larger whole. Living in Dublin, his walks take him toward the river and the sea—toward the fluid thing that, like the "stream" of his thoughts, seems by its searching mobility to imply a more engrossing reality. At first, in Dublin, the boy

> contented himself with circling timidly round the neighbouring square or, at most, going half way down one of the side streets; but [271] when he had made a skeleton map of the city in his

mind he followed boldly one of its central lines until he reached the Custom House. . . . The vastness and strangeness of the life suggested to him by the bales of merchandise stocked along the walls or swung aloft out of the holds of steamers wakened again in him the unrest which had sent him wandering in the evening from garden to garden in search of Mercedes. . . . A vague dissatisfaction grew up within him as he looked on the quays and on the river and on the lowering skies and yet he continued to wander up and down day after day as if he really sought someone that eluded him. (312-313)

On his visit to Cork with his father, in his wanderings in the brothel section of Dublin, on his seaward walk at the end of the fourth chapter when his chief revelation of personal destiny comes to him, on his later walks between home and the university, on his walk with Lynch during which he recapitulates his aesthetics, and with Cranly when he formulates his decision not "to serve"—on each of these peripatetic excursions, his mind moves toward more valid organizations of experience, as his feet carry him among other voices and images and into more complex fields of perception.

In the third chapter of the book, the hortations to which he is exposed during the retreat pull him down from his exaltation in sin and analyze his spiritual state into a multitude of subjective horrors that threaten to engulf him entirely and jeopardize his immortal soul. The conflict is resolved during a long walk which he takes blindly and alone, and that carries him to a strange place where he feels able to make his confession. A new synthesis is achieved through his participation in the Mass. Chapter 4 shows him absorbed in a dream of a saintly career, but his previous emotional affirmation has been frittered and wasted away in the performance of pedantically formal acts of piety, and he is afflicted with doubts, insecurities, rebellions. Release from conflict comes with a clear refusal of a vocation in the church, objectified by his decision to enter the university. And again it is on a walk that he realizes the measure of the new reality and the new destiny.

He has abandoned his father to a public house and has set off toward the river and the sea.

The university! So he had passed beyond the challenge of the sentries who had stood as guardians of his boyhood and had sought to keep him among them that he might be subject to them and serve [272] their ends. Pride after satisfaction uplifted him like long slow waves. The end he had been born to serve yet did not see had led him to escape by an unseen path; and now it beckoned to him once more and a new adventure was about to be opened to him. It seemed to him that he heard notes of fitful music leaping upwards a tone and downwards a diminishing fourth, upwards a tone and downwards a major third, like triple-branching flames leaping fitfully, flame after flame, out of a midnight wood. It was an elfin prelude, endless and formless; and, as it grew wilder and faster, the flames leaping out of time, he seemed to hear from under the boughs and grasses wild creatures racing, their feet pattering like rain upon the leaves. Their feet passed in pattering tumult over his mind, the feet of hares and rabbits, the feet of harts and hinds and antelopes, until he heard them no more and remembered only a proud cadence from Newman: "Whose feet are as the feet of harts and underneath the everlasting arms." (424-425)

The imagery is that of mobile, going things, increasingly passionate and swift—first slow waves, then fitful music leaping, then flames, then racing creatures. A phrase of his own making comes to his lips: "A day of dappled seaborne clouds." The dappled color and the sea movement of the clouds are of the same emotional birth as the images of music and flames. All are of variety and mobility of perception, as against stasis and restriction. Physically Stephen is escaping from his father—and the public house where he has left Simon is the sordid core of that Dublin environment whose false claims on his allegiance he is trying to shake off; at the same time he is realizing a "first noiseless sundering" with his mother, a break that is related to his decision against accepting a vocation in the church. Dublin, the tangible and vocal essence of his nationality, and the Roman Church, the mold of his adolescent intellect, have failed to provide him with a vision of reality corresponding with his experience, and he thinks in terms of a movement beyond these—toward another and mysterious possible synthesis. "And under-

neath the everlasting arms": the phrase from Newman implies
an ultimate unity wherein all the real is held in wholeness.
Toward this problematic divine embrace Stephen moves, but it
is only problematic and he can approach it only by his own
movement. The epiphany which confronts him in this moment
on the beach is a manifestation of his destiny in terms of a
winged movement. He hears his name, Dedalus, called out, and
the name seems to be prophetic. [273]

> . . . at the name of the fabulous artificer, he seemed to hear
> the noise of dim waves and to see a winged form flying above
> the waves and slowly climbing the air . . . a hawklike man fly-
> ing sunward above the sea, a prophecy of the end he had been
> born to serve and had been following through the mists of child-
> hood and boyhood, a symbol of the artist forging anew in his
> workshop out of the sluggish matter of the earth a new soar-
> ing impalpable imperishable being. . . . (429)

The ending of Chapter 4 presents this new consciousness in
terms of an ecstatic state of sensibility. It is marked by the
radiant image of the girl standing in a rivulet of tide, seeming
"like one whom magic had changed into the likeness of a strange
and beautiful seabird . . . touched with the wonder of mortal
beauty" (431-432), while his own life cries wildly to him, "To
live, to err, to fall, to triumph, to recreate life out of life!" (432)
The girl is a "wild angel" that has appeared to him, to "throw
open before him in an instant of ecstasy the ways of error and
glory." The batlike woman-soul of his race, flitting in darkness
and secrecy and loneliness, has given place to this angelic emissary from "the fair courts of life," of strange seabird beauty,
inviting him to exile across waters and into other languages, as
the sun-assailing and perhaps doomed Icarus. And it is in the
flights of birds that Stephen, standing on the steps of the university library, in the last chapter, reads like an ancient haruspex
the sanction of his exile.

With Chapter 5, Stephen's new consciousness of destiny is
subjected to intellectual analysis. Here, during his long walks
with Lynch and Cranly, all the major elements that have exerted

emotional claims upon him—his family, church, nation, language —are scrutinized dryly, their claims torn down and scattered in the youthfully pedantic and cruel light of the adolescent's proud commitment to art. Here also he formulates his aesthetics, the synthesis which he has contrived out of a few scraps of medieval learning. In his aesthetic formulation, the names he borrows from Aquinas for "the three things needed for beauty"—*integritas, consonantia, claritas*—are names for those aspects of reality— wholeness, harmoniousness, significant character—that he has been seeking all his life, from earliest childhood. His aesthetic formulation is thus a synthesis of the motivations of his psychological life from the beginning; and the vocation of artist which he has chosen is the vocation of one who consciously sets himself the task of apprehending and then representing in his art whatever wholeness, harmony, and meaning the world has. [274]

In an earlier version of the *Portrait,* called *Stephen Hero,* it is said that the task of the artist is to "disentangle the subtle soul of the image from its mesh of defining circumstances most exactly and 're-embody' it in artistic circumstances chosen as the most exact for it in its new office. . . ." (*SH,* 78)

The "new office" of the image is to communicate to others the significant character of a complete and harmonious body of experience. The artist is a midwife of epiphanies. Joyce's doctrine of the epiphany assumes that reality does have wholeness and harmony—even as Stephen as a child premises these, and with the same trustfulness—and that it will radiantly show forth its character and its meaning to the prepared consciousness, for it is only in the body of reality that meaning can occur and only there that the artist can find it. This is essentially a religious interpretation of the nature of reality and of the artist's function. It insists on the objectivity of the wholeness, harmony, and meaning, and on the objectivity of the revelation—the divine showing-forth.

At Clongowes Wood, there had been a picture of the earth on the first page of Stephen's geography, "a big ball in the middle of clouds," and on the flyleaf of the book Stephen had written his name and "where he was."

Stephen Dedalus

Class of Elements

Clongowes Wood College

Sallins

County Kildare

Ireland

Europe

The World

The Universe (255)

His ambulatory, dialectical journey is a quest to find the defining unity, the composing harmony, and the significant character of each of these broadening localities containing Stephen Dedalus, and the intelligible relationships making each functional in the next. It is an attempt, by progressive stages, at last to bring the term "Stephen Dedalus" into relationship with the term "The Universe." Through the book he moves from one geographical and spiritual orbit to another, "walking" in lengthening [275] radius until he is ready to take up flight. As a child at Clongowes it had pained him that he did not know what came after the universe.

> What was after the universe? Nothing. But was there anything round the universe to show where it stopped before the nothing place began? It could not be a wall but there could be a thin thin line there all round everything. It was very big to think about everything and everywhere. Only God could do that. He tried to think what a big thought that must be but he could think only of God. God was God's name just as his name was Stephen. *Dieu* was the French for God and that was God's name too; and when anyone prayed to God and said Dieu then God knew at once that was a French person that was praying. But though there were different names for God in all the different languages in the world and God understood what all the people who prayed said in their different languages still God remained always the same God and God's real name was God. (255-256)

At the end of the book Stephen is prepared at least to set forth on the "dappled, seaborne clouds" (426) that float beyond Ireland and over Europe. His search is still to find out "what came after the universe." The ultimate epiphany is withheld, the epiphany of "everything and everywhere" as one and harmonious and meaningful. But it is prophesied in "God's real name," as Stephen's personal destiny is prophesied in his own name "Dedalus." It is to be found in the labyrinth of language that contains all human revelation vouchsafed by divine economy, and to be found by the artist in naming the names. [276]

SPECIAL STUDIES

JOSEPH PRESCOTT

James Joyce's Stephen Hero

BEFORE LEAVING IRELAND IN 1904, Joyce announced that he would produce a great book within ten years. The boast was superbly fulfilled in *A Portrait of the Artist as a Young Man*. In 1944, three years after Joyce's death, Theodore Spencer edited, with an admirable introduction, a large portion of an early draft of this work, entitled *Stephen Hero* and written apparently between 1901 and 1906, during Joyce's last years at University College, Dublin, and first years on the Continent.

I

Stephen Hero is an absorbing document, straightforward, explicit, and marked by a fullness of statement which Joyce, for various reasons, denied to the *Portrait*.

Covering about two of Stephen's university years, what we have of *Stephen Hero* has a better claim to the title *A Portrait*

Reprinted by permission of the author and of *The Journal of English and Germanic Philology* where it first appeared, LIII (April, 1954), 214-223. It was reprinted as follows:
The Bell (Dublin), XIX (November, 1954), 27-35.
Letterature Moderne (Bologna), VI (November-December, 1956), 679-688.
Diliman Review (Quezon City, Phil. Is.), VII (October, 1959), 373-385.
Spanish translation in *Sur* (Buenos Aires), No. 250 (January-February, 1958), pp. 39-50.
Same translation in *Armas y Letras* (Monterrey, N. L., Mexico), Second Series, I (October-December, 1958), 64-76.
French translation in *Configuration critique de James Joyce,* ed. Joseph Prescott (Paris: M. J. Minerd, 1959-1960), I, 48-66 (also published as *La Revue des lettres modernes* [Paris], VI [Autumn, 1959], 288-306.)
In 1960, a tape recording of the essay, with voice by Prescott was added to the library of World Tapes for Education. Hebrew translation in *Moznaim* (Tel Aviv), XIV, No. 2 (January, 1962), 137-143.
References to *A Portrait* are to P-2; to *Stephen Hero* are to SH-1.

of the Artist as a Young Man than does the so-miscalled work, which treats Stephen's experience from his earliest memories to young manhood. The 383 pages of manuscript,[1] as the editor points out, coincide with the last 93 pages of the *Portrait*. In both versions Stephen is the same penurious, arrogant, and solitary young man. The hero who, invited to contribute to a college review, asks, "And tell me, will I be paid?" (*SH*, 182) is recognizable as the young man who, when invited to sign a testimonial for universal peace, asks, "—Will you pay me anything if I sign?" (229) The hero who expects "reward from the public for [his] verses because [he] believe[s his] verses are to be numbered among the spiritual assets of the State" (*SH*, 202) is recognizable as the young man who [214] goes forth "to forge in the smithy of [his] soul the uncreated conscience of [his] race." (299) And the hero who "professed scorn for the rabblement and contempt for authority," (*SH*, 122) had a "commandment of reticence," (*SH*, 124) "was very lonely," (*SH*, 161) and lived "such a strange life—without help or sympathy from anyone" that "sometimes [he was] afraid of [himself]" (*SH*, 197) is recognizable as the young man who felt keenly "that he was different from others," (71) who "was happy only when he was . . . alone or in the company of phantasmal comrades," (93) who "was destined to learn his own wisdom apart from others or to learn the wisdom of others himself wandering among the snares of the world." (188)

It is notable that the youthful preferences which Joyce records in *Stephen Hero* are perhaps more significant than those he mentions in the *Portrait*. In *Stephen Hero,* as is not the case in the *Portrait*, we have a revealing account of Stephen's devotion to two artists. Of the first, Joyce begins: "It must be said

---

[1] The 1955 edition (*SH-2*) of *Stephen Hero* incorporates the text of 25 additional manuscript pages, edited with a foreword by John J. Slocum and Herbert Cahoon. The text of 5 more pages of manuscript is made available by Slocum and Cahoon in Marvin Magalaner, ed., *A James Joyce Miscellany: Second Series* (Carbondale, Illinois, 1959). For first publication of the original version of the *Portrait,* a brief narrative essay antecedent to *Stephen Hero,* see R. M. Kain and R. E. Scholes, "The First Version of Joyce's 'Portrait,'" and James Joyce's, "A Portrait of the Artist," *Yale Review,* XLIX (1960), 355-69.

simply and at once that at this time Stephen suffered the most enduring influence of his life." (*SH*, 40) And Ibsen plays a central role in Stephen's experience, for it is in defense of him, in connection with a paper on "Art and Life" read before the University College Literary and Historical Society, that Stephen breaks a lance with the authority for which, as an artist, he professes contempt. Furthermore, in March, 1901, the nineteen-year-old Joyce wrote to Ibsen personally, praising "your highest excellence—your lofty impersonal power . . . and how in your absolute indifference to public canons of art, friends and shibboleths you walked in the light of your inward *heroism*." In October of the same year Joyce wrote, in the essay *The Day of the Rabblement:* "No man, said the Nolan, can be a lover of the true or the good unless he abhors the multitude; and the artist, though he may employ the crowd, is very careful to isolate himself"; he remarked that "every movement [of protest against the sterility and falsehood of the modern stage] that has set out *heroically* has achieved a little"; and he spoke reverently of "the old master who is dying in Christiania." I have italicized the words *heroism* and *heroically* for, written when *Stephen Hero* was presumably [215] already in process of gestation, they indicate the turn of the author's thought at the time: Ibsen is a hero, and opposition to sterility and falsehood is the act of heroes to the prototype of Stephen the hero.

Of the second artist whose work Stephen admired, Joyce begins:

> [Stephen] had found on one of the carts of books near the river an unpublished book containing two stories by W. B. Yeats. One of these stories was called *The Tables of the Law* . . . and one evening while talking with a Capuchin, he had over and over to restrain an impulse which urged him to take the priest by the arm, lead him up and down the chapel-yard and deliver himself boldly of the whole story of *The Tables of the Law*, every word of which he remembered. . . . He satisfied himself by leading Lynch round the enclosure of Stephen's Green and making that young man very awkward by reciting Mr Yeats's story with careful animation. . . . He repeated often the story of *The Tables of the Law* and the story of the *Adoration of the Magi*. (*SH*, 176-178)

Later, quotations from both stories are put into Stephen's mouth. And a further measure of Joyce's attachment to these stories is anonymously indicated in Yeats' prefatory note to the first public edition. "These two stories were privately printed some years ago. I do not think I should have reprinted them had I not met a young man in Ireland the other day, who liked them very much and nothing else that I have written." The young man, according to Yeats' biographer, Joseph Hone, was Joyce.

The leading characters of both stories stand outside established orders. Both artists whom Stephen and his creator find congenial are proud preachers of independence of social taboos. Joyce-Dedalus bears out a statement which Dedalus is later to make in *Ulysses:* "We walk through ourselves, meeting robbers, ghosts, giants, old men, young men, wives, widows, brothers-in-love. But always meeting ourselves." (*UL*, 210)

Stephen's character, as I have said, is essentially the same in both versions. What changes is the relationship between that character and the author. This is perhaps the most important qualitative difference between the two versions.

A fair illustration of the attitude of the author to his subject in *Stephen Hero* is the introductory sentence, already quoted, about Ibsen (whom, it will be remembered, Joyce admired for his impersonality): [216] "It must be said simply and at once that at this time Stephen suffered the most enduring influence of his life." (*SH*, 40) Here is the author not merely reporting a fact regarding his character but also, by his strident emphasis, announcing his own position. Other brief editorial asides ("it is as well to admit that" (*SH*, 111) "undoubtedly") (*SH*, 146) leave the reader no choice but to listen to the author's explicit point of view. The editorial phrase extends to sententious and abstract generalization:

> This quality of the mind which so reveals itself is called (when incorrigible) a decadence but if we are to take a general view of . . . the world we cannot but see a process to life through corruption. . . . When a demand for intelligent sympathy goes unanswered . . . he is a too stern disciplinarian who blames himself for having offered a dullard an opportunity to partici-

pate in the warmer movement of a more highly organized
life. . . . No young man can contemplate the fact of death
with extreme satisfaction and no young man, specialised by fate
or her stepsister chance for an organ of sensitiveness and intel-
lectiveness, can contemplate the network of falsities and trivi-
alities which make up the funeral of a dead burgher without
extreme disgust. (*SH*, 37, 83, 168)

The tendency to editorialize reaches a peak, as one might
expect, at a peak of emotion, and phrase and sentence are, in
one instance, elaborated into a long and tense essay. Joyce has
been reporting Stephen's thoughts on Catholicism.

That kind of Christianity which is called Catholicism seemed to
him to stand in his way and forthwith he removed it. He had
been brought up in the belief of the Roman supremacy and to
cease to be a Catholic for him meant to cease to be a Christian.

Then, almost imperceptibly, Joyce crosses the vague line between autobiographical creation and creator:

The idea that the power of an empire is weakest at its borders
requires some modification for everyone knows that the Pope
cannot govern Italy as he governs Ireland nor is the Tsar as
terrible an engine to the tradesmen of S. Petersburg as he is to
the little Russian of the Steppes. In fact in many cases the gov-
ernment of an empire is strongest at its borders and it is invariably strongest there in the case when its power at the centre
is on the wane. The waves of the rise and fall of empires do
not travel with the rapidity of waves of light and it will be perhaps a considerable time before Ireland will be able to understand that the Papacy is no longer going through a period of
anabolism. The bands of pilgrims who are shepherded safely
across the continent by their Irish pastors must shame the jaded
reactionaries of the eternal city by their stupefied intensity of
worship in much the same way as [217] the staring provincial
newly arrived from Spain or Africa may have piqued the loyalty of some smiling Roman for whom . . . the future of his
race was becoming uncertain as its past had already become obvious. Though it is evident on the one hand that this persistence
of Catholic power in Ireland must intensify very greatly the
loneliness of the Irish Catholic who voluntarily outlaws himself

yet on the other hand the force which he must generate to propel himself out of so strong and intricate a tyranny may often be sufficient to place him beyond the region of re-attraction.

Again almost imperceptibly, Joyce crosses back from himself to his autobiographical creation:

> It was in fact, the very fervour of Stephen's former religious life which sharpened for him now the pains of his solitary position and at the same time hardened into a less pliable, a less appeasable enmity molten rages and glowing transports on which the emotions of helplessness and loneliness and despair had first acted as chilling influences. (*SH*, 147-148)

It needed only a change of tense to transform the authorial essay into an organic part of Stephen's experience. But the young Joyce had not yet sufficiently detached himself from his own thoughts and feelings to give them to his not much younger creation. He failed, in other words, to achieve the "esthetic statis" (241) which Stephen regards as essential to the success of a work of art. "The artist, like the God of the creation," Stephen says in the *Portrait*, "remains within or behind or beyond or above his handiwork, invisible, refined out of existence, indifferent, paring his fingernails.—" (252) In *Stephen Hero* a tone of adolescently turbulent rancor, everywhere audible, inspires the reader with loathing for "Irish paralysis" (*SH*, 211)—a kinetic effect, which, according to Stephen's esthetic, makes for improper art. (240) We may, in fact, say of the author of this early version what he says in it of his titular character: "It was hard for him to compel his head to preserve the strict temperature of classicism." (*SH*, 210)

In the *Portrait*, on the other hand, from start to finish there is not a single comment or generalization; every thought, every feeling is particularly Stephen's. Now and then, to be sure, the author *reports* as author, but he never *comments*. "It was the very spirit of Ibsen himself," Joyce wrote in *Stephen Hero*, "that was discerned moving behind the impersonal manner of the artist"; (*SH*, 41) so, again to be sure, it is the very spirit of Joyce himself that is discerned moving [218] behind the impersonal manner of the artist of the *Portrait*. But such discernible-

ness is not inconsistent with the invisibility of the God of the
creation behind his handiwork.

At this point the evolution of Joyce's novel becomes interesting beyond itself, for the history of this novel repeats the history
of the genre. The change from *Stephen Hero* to the *Portrait*
mirrors the progression from the novel of the overt and partisan
manager to that of the invisible and impersonal director.

II

The reader, however, will ask not only how far *Stephen Hero*
generally resembles or differs from the *Portrait* but also what it
reveals about Joyce's work as a whole. I have already mentioned
the explicitness of the earlier version; and the economy of the
Portrait is a matter of common knowledge. As Spencer observed,
Stephen Hero clarifies obscurities in Joyce's other works and
illuminates Joyce's development as a craftsman.

To the examples of clarification cited by Spencer, I should
like to add a few which point up Joyce's sometimes excessive
economy.

Stephen Dedalus, having just refused to sign a petition for
world peace—in the *Portrait*—mocks at a friend:

> —Now that you have signed the petition for universal peace—
> said Stephen—I suppose you will burn that little copybook I
> saw in your room.—
> As Davin did not answer Stephen began to quote:
> —Long pace, fianna! Right incline, fianna! Fianna, by num-
> bers, salute, one, two!—
> —That's a different question—said Davin.—I'm an Irish na-
> tionalist, first and foremost. But that's you all out. You're a born
> sneerer, Stevie.—
> —When you make the next rebellion with hurley-sticks—said
> Stephen—and want the indispensable informer, tell me. I can
> find you a few in this college.—(236)

Twenty-five pages earlier the reader has heard of Davin's at-
tendance at a hurling match. (211-212) Sixty pages later Stephen,
having met Davin at a cigar-store, records in his diary: "He was
in a black sweater and had a hurley-stick. . . . Just then my

father came up. . . . Asked Davin if he might offer him some
refreshment. Davin could not, was going to a meeting." (296)
Of hurley-sticks in the *Portrait* there is not another word. The
reader may therefore be expected to see in [219] Stephen's
remark a bluntly contemptuous gibe inspired by the not clearly
pertinent association of Davin with hurling. But let us look at
a passage in *Stephen Hero* which is important enough to quote
at some length:

> The meetings [of the nationalists] on Friday nights were public
> and were largely patronised by priests. The organisers brought
> in reports from different districts . . . when it was time for the
> whole company to break up all would rise and sing the Rallying-
> Song. . . . His [a certain citizen's] circle was the separatist
> centre and in it reigned the irreconcilable temper. It had its
> headquarters in Cooney's tobacco-shop . . . To this circle Mad-
> den who was the captain of a club of hurley-players reported
> the muscular condition of the young irreconcilables under his
> charge . . . A glowing example was to be found [in the eyes
> of "these enthusiasts"] for Ireland in the case of Hungary, an
> example, as these patriots imagined, of a long-suffering minority,
> entitled by every right of race and justice to a separate free-
> dom, finally emancipating itself. In emulation of that achieve-
> ment bodies of young Gaels conflicted murderously in the
> Phoenix Park with whacking hurley-sticks, thrice armed in their
> just quarrel since their revolution had been blessed for them by
> the Anointed . . .
>
> Stephen said one day to Madden:
> —I suppose these hurley-matches and walking tours are prep-
> arations for the great event.
> —There is more going on in Ireland at present than you are
> aware of.
> —But what use are camàns [hurley-sticks]?
> —Well, you see, we want to raise the physique of the coun-
> try. (61-62)

With so clear and full a frame of reference—which must have
been in Joyce's mind as he wrote the *Portrait*—Stephen's dull
shaft would have been pointed and barbed.

And now for two brief specimens from Ulysses. In the library
scene, Stephen meditates: "Where is your brother? Apothecaries'

hall. My whetstone. Him, then Cranly, Mulligan: now these."
(*UL,* 208) In the brothel scene Stephen calls Lynch's cap "Whetstone!" (*UL,* 493) The reader will comb *Ulysses,* and the *Portrait*
as well, for explanation in vain, for the explanation is to be
found in *Stephen Hero,* in which "Stephen found Maurice [his
brother] very useful for raising objections." (*SH,* 36)

In the second example from Ulysses, a passage which makes
good enough sense unbuttressed by further explanation is en-
riched by *Stephen Hero* with a new and clearly pertinent association. In the brothel scene, Lynch's use of the word *pandybat*
precipitates the [220] hallucination of Father Dolan of Clongowes
Wood College, which Stephen had attended as a child: *"Twice
loudly a pandybat cracks, the coffin of the pianola flies open, the
bald little round jack-in-the-box head of Father Dolan springs
up."* (*UL,* 547) The immediate picture of the priest's head
popping out of the pianola is enough, as I have indicated, to
warrant the figure of the jack-in-the-box. But, again and again
the hallucinations in the brothel scene, as we know, are based
on reality. The vision of the priest's head is Stephen's, and
Ulysses contains no clue to its origin. The full explanation of
what must almost certainly have gone on in Joyce's mind as he
wrote this passage is to be found in *Stephen Hero:*

> [Stephen's] mother told him one day that she had spoken of
> him to her confessor and asked his spiritual advice. Stephen
> turned to her and remonstrated hotly with her for doing such
> a thing.
>
> —It is a nice thing, he said, that you go and discuss me be-
> hind my back. Have you not your own nature to guide you,
> your own sense of what is right, without going to some Father
> Jack-in-the-Box to ask him to guide you? (*SH,* 209)

To be sure, memories are carried over from the *Portrait* to
Ulysses without explanation, and their full meaning for Stephen
cannot possibly be arrived at without recourse to the earlier
work. The practice may be justified on the ground that, since
Stephen is in what, regarding his character, is a sequence of
two novels, the reader may be expected to know the first novel
before beginning the second—a justification tantamount to an
admission that, as regards Stephen, *Ulysses* does not constitute

an artistic whole, but some justification withal. What reason is
there, however, in economy beyond comprehension on the basis
of a work, which the author, regarding it as juvenile, evidently
did not intend to publish? Perhaps it may be urged that blind
spots occupy a legitimate place in one's understanding of another
mind. But since explanations for these particular spots did exist,
surely blindness here is an unnecessary affliction.

As already indicated, *Stephen Hero* not only elucidates passages in Joyce's other works; it also prefigures Joyce's later activity—in particular, his development as a craftsman. [221]

A brief description of Stephen's Uncle John may well contain
the germ of the short story in *Dubliners* called "The Boarding
House": "One of the boys' uncles was a very shock-headed asth-
matic man who had in his youth been rather indiscreet with his
landlady's daughter and the family had been scarcely appeased
by a tardy marriage." (*SH*, 166)

Stephen's remark "A man might think for seven years at intervals and all at once write a quatrain which would immortalise
him seemingly without thought or care—seemingly" (*SH*, 185)
and a passing reference to "some ardent verses which he entitled
a 'Vilanelle [*sic*] of the Temptress'" (*SH*, 211) seem to represent the germ of the marvellously vivid record in the *Portrait*
of the creation of a villanelle. (254-263)

Again, the technique of a whole episode of *Ulysses* is adumbrated in the following passage:

> [Stephen] devised the following question and answer for the
> pseudo-classical catechism:
>   *Question*—What great truth do we learn from the *Libation-
>   Pourers* of Eschylus?
>   *Answer*—We learn from the *Libation-Pourers* of Eschylus that
>   in ancient Greece brothers and sisters took the same
>   size in boots. (*SH*, 192-193)

Here, in embryo, is the technique of the penultimate episode of
Ulysses, the "impersonal" catechism which Joyce wrote with
tongue in cheek.

Similarly, *Stephen Hero* anticipates the internal monologue
of *Ulysses* more explicitly than does any part of the *Portrait.*

We hear that "Cranly grew used to having sensations and impressions recorded and analysed before him [by Stephen] at the very instant of their apparition." (*SH*, 125) The introspective habit, illustrated several times in the *Portrait*, is an appropriate base from which Joyce is later to find congenial the internal monologue in Dujardin's *Les Lauriers sont coupés* and the probing of modern psychologists.

As early as *Stephen Hero*, also, Joyce's experiments with language are foreshadowed. Stephen "put his lines [of verse] together not word by word but letter by letter. He read Blake and Rimbaud on the [222] values of letters and even permuted and combined the five vowels to construct cries for primitive emotions." (*SH*, 32) A single passage from *Ulysses*, among countless passages, will suffice to make clear the importance of such experiment for Joyce's later work: "Listen: a fourworded wavespeech: seesoo, hrss, rsseeiss ooos. Vehement breath of waters amid seasnakes, rearing horses, rocks. In cups of rocks it slops: flop, slop, slap: bounded in barrels. And, spent, its speech ceases." (*UL*, 50)

The later master of the technique of juxtaposition for the effect of simultaneity [a brief specimen from a large number of passages employing the device is Bloom's thought "Excuse, miss, there's (whh!) just a (whh!) fluff"] (*UL*, 82) is suggested in the powerful scene in which the urge to fornication with Emma Clery, and, immediately after it, the death of his sister press upon the artist the contradiction of beauty and mortality. (*SH*, 162 ff.)

III

Youthful and incomplete as it is, *Stephen Hero* should contribute substantially to Joyce's reputation. If, as I have said elsewhere, *Finnegans Wake* alienated some readers of Joyce, *Stephen Hero* may serve to remind them of two things. First, Joyce's earlier works—including the bulk of *Ulysses*, for people brought up on a literature produced largely under its influence—are eminently readable. Secondly, Joyce, who typifies the artist in exile, was paradoxically destined, as this youthful work intimates, to develop into one of the most significant spokesmen of his time.

Dealing with the turn of the century, the Irish Renaissance, the form of the novel, the establishment of modern drama, and such perennial questions as the psychology of the artist and of the work of art, and the relationship between the individual and the institutions of family, school, church, and state, *Stephen Hero* commands attention not only among admirers of Joyce but among all those interested in the history of the making of the modern mind. [223]

RICHARD ELLMANN

A Portrait of the Artist *as Friend*

REVOLUTIONARIES FATTEN ON OPPOSITION but grow thin and pale when treated with indulgence. Joyce's ostracism from Dublin lacked, as he was well aware, the moral decisiveness of Dante's exile from Florence in that Joyce kept the keys to the gate. He was neither bidden to leave nor forbidden to return, and he did in fact go back four times. But whenever his relations with his native land seemed in danger of improving, he found a new incident to solidify his intransigency and reaffirm the rightness of his voluntary exile. He even showed some grand resentment at the possibility of Irish independence on the grounds that it would change the relationship he had so carefully established between himself and his country. "Should I," he asked someone, "wish to alter the conditions that have made me what I am?"

At first he thought only his soul was in danger in Ireland. Then, when his difficulties over the publication of *Dubliners* became so great, he thought his writing career was being deliberately conspired against. Finally he came to assert that he was physically in danger. This suspicion began when his wife paid a visit to Galway in 1922. Civil war had just broken out in the west, and her train was fired on by soldiers. Joyce chose to believe that the bullets were really aimed at him, and afterwards refused to return to Ireland because he said he feared for his life. That Joyce could not have written his books in Ireland is likely enough, but he felt the need for maintaining his intimacy with his country by continually renewing the quarrel with her which prompted his first departure. [53]

In his books too his heroes are outcasts in one way or another, and much of their interest lies in why they are cast out and by whom. Are they "self-doomed," as Joyce says of himself in his broadside, "The Holy Office," or are they doomed by society? To the extent that the hero is himself responsible, he is Faust-like, struggling like Stephen Dedalus or Richard Rowan to achieve a freedom beyond human power. To the extent that society is responsible he is Christlike, a sacrificial victim whose sufferings torment his tormentors. Joyce was not so masochistic as to identify himself completely with the helpless victim; at the very moment he attacks society most bitterly as his oppressor, he will not completely deny the authorship of his own despair. Like the boy in the ballad of the Jew's daughter, he is immolated, *consenting*. Again he was not so possessed with self as to adopt utterly the part of the anarchic individual. He carefully avoids making his heroes anything but unhappy in their triumphant self-right-eousness.

Half-willing and half-forced to be a sufferer, Stephen endows the artist in *A Portrait of the Artist as a Young Man* with a rather similar mixture of qualities, the total power of a god bored by his own handiwork and the heroic impotence of a Lucifer, smarting from pain which he has chosen to bear. To be both god and devil is perhaps to be man. In *Ulysses* the paradoxes ascribed to these forces are the paradoxes of being Joyce: God begets Himself, sends Himself between Himself and others, is put upon by His own friends. Joyce and Stephen challenge in the same way the forces which they have brought into being. As Stephen says of Shakespeare, "His unremitting intellect is the hornmad Iago ceaselessly willing that the moor in him shall suffer." (*UL*, 210) If the residents of heaven were not androgynous, he says, God would be bawd and cuckold too, arranging for his own humiliation with his own creatures.

In his books Joyce represents heroes who seek freedom, which is also exile, voluntarily and by compulsion. The question [54] of ultimate responsibility is raised and then dropped without an answer. Joyce's hero is as lonely as Byron's; consequently Joyce obliterated Stephen's brother, Maurice, from the *Portrait* after using him tentatively in *Stephen Hero*, for there must be no adherent, and the home must be a rallying-point of betrayal. A cluster of themes—the sacrilege of Faust, the suffering of Christ, the exile of Dante—reach a focus in the problem of friendship. For if friendship exists, it impugns the quality of exile and of lonely heroism. If the world is not altogether hostile, we may forgive it for having mistreated us, and so be forced into the false position of warriors without adversaries. Joyce allows his hero to sample friendship before discovering its flaws, and then with the theme of broken friendship represents his hero's broken ties with Ireland and the world.

The friendship is invariably between men; here Joyce is very much the Dubliner. A curious aspect of Irish life is that relationships between men seem more vital there than relationships between men and women. It is not easy to know whether this trait is due to a misogynistic bias in Irish Catholicism, or, less impressively, to long hours of pub crawling. Whatever the cause, the trait carries over into the work of Joyce. In his writings there is a succession of important friendships between men which receive more of his attention than love affairs. He displays a man's world, in which Emma, Gretta, Bertha, Molly, Anna, and Isabel occupy, however fetchingly, only a bed or a kitchen. Frank Budgen describes a number of Joyce's diatribes against women who venture beyond their station. Once he remonstrated with Joyce a little, saying, "But as I remember you in other days, you always fell back upon the fact that woman's flesh was provoking and desirable, whatever else was objectionable about her." Joyce snorted and replied, "Perhaps I did. Now I don't care a damn about their bodies. I am only interested in their clothes." In his books the men, whether lovers or husbands, are almost always away from home, drinking in a pub, talking on the library steps, [55] walking in Phoenix Park or along the strand. Joyce remarked to his friend Ottocaro Weiss, in explanation of his principles of dramaturgy, "When things get slow, bring a woman on the stage." Women appear brilliantly in his work, but they are admitted only on condition that they remain bright accessories to the main struggles.

To isolate the male friendships in Joyce's novels does not, of course, give a complete account of the novels; but it does them surprisingly little violence. Each book has a special view of friendship, although later developments are lightly prefigured in the earliest, *Stephen Hero*. Here Joyce touches upon Stephen's amorous interest in Emma Clery, but shows his relation to her as wary and circumspect when it is not merely blunt. The main interest attaches however to his friendship with Cranly, which is much more tender and complex. Cranly's alienation from Stephen is the novel's principal dramatic action; three explanations of it are given, none of them wholly satisfactory. Stanislaus Joyce has commented that his brother was baffled by the behavior of Cranly's prototype, J. F. Byrne, and this bafflement may account for the various interpretations of it offered in *Stephen Hero*. The first reason is suggested to Stephen by his brother Maurice. "Cranly," he says, "wants to become more and more necessary to you until he can have you in his power." (*SH*, 145) Stephen repudiates this analysis, which he contends is based upon a novel conception of friendship. But it is never discredited. The second reason appears on the surface to be an aesthetic disagreement, Cranly's cool reception of Stephen's paper on "Drama and Life." The first blood between them is this partial rejection of one of Stephen's literary works. Joyce's own ruptures with good friends often came about in the same way. A chill developed between him and Wyndham Lewis after *Time and Western Man* had criticized Joyce's work, and Joyce had little more to do with Ezra Pound, in spite of all Pound had previously done for Joyce, after Pound expressed his disapproval of the early sections of *Finnegans Wake.* [56] Like many authors, Joyce always preferred to suspect that literary disagreement with him arose from personal causes, not detached intellectual judgment. When Jung wrote his critique of *Ulysses,* Joyce's comment was, "What does Jung have against me? Why does he dislike me? I haven't even met him."

Cranly's conflict with Stephen becomes more earnest when he follows his refusal of sympathy for Stephen's paper with a refusal of sympathy for Stephen's detachment towards his dying sister Isobel. Joyce too was capable of showing this utter detachment, and in later life he brought on a quarrel with Paul Léon by remarking casually of Lucia Joyce's mental collapse that it was like a story in *Dubliners.* Léon accused him of cerebralizing tragedy. It may be that Cranly's judgments of Stephen are well-founded, but we are never allowed to regard them so. They at once make Stephen suspicious of Cranly's attitude towards him. Joyce writes in a passage unconsciously full of adolescent egoism, "He fancied moreover that he detected in Cranly's attitude towards him a certain hostility, arising out of a thwarted desire to imitate. Cranly was fond of ridiculing Stephen to his bar companions and though this was supposed to be no more than banter Stephen found touches of seriousness in it." (*SH,* 209) He goes on a little pompously, "Stephen refused to close with this trivial falsehood of his friend and continued to share all the secrets of his bosom as if he had not observed any change. He no longer, however, sought his friend's opinion or allowed the sour dissatisfaction of his friend's mood to weigh with him." (*SH,* 209) Like the desire to possess, suggested by Maurice, Stephen's second diagnosis, "the thwarted desire to imitate," is self-engrossed.

The third reason is more complicated, for it involves another person. Stephen's beloved, Emma Clery, walks by the two young men, and when they bow to her she disregards Stephen to bow only to Cranly. To Cranly's question, "Why did she do that?" Stephen replies with a laugh, "An invitation perhaps." (*SH,* 215) He pretends to regard the incident lightly, but sexual rivalry and jealousy [57] seem bound to divide the two young men more decisively than the desire of Cranly to dominate or imitate Stephen. One of the main functions of female characters in Joyce is to promote division between male friends. Yet Cranly's liking for Emma is an implied compliment to Stephen's taste in women, and all three reasons, the desire to dominate and emulate and steal away his friend's girl, have in common the fact that it is Cranly who takes the first steps towards enmity, and that all explanations of his behavior are essentially proofs of his dependence upon Stephen. Cranly's feelings are reactions to Stephen's feelings.

In *A Portrait of the Artist as a Young Man* the themes introduced in *Stephen Hero* are heightened by the new unifying theme of artistic development. Friendship too is viewed with greater intensity, its collisions are more serious, and at the end of the book it begins to seem an impossibility. In later life Joyce remarked to Samuel Beckett, "I don't love anyone but my family," in a tone that implied that he did not really *like* anyone but his family either. The *Portrait* justifies the hero's renunciation of friendship more elaborately than *Stephen Hero* attempted to do. While Stephen has another important friendship, with Lynch, Cranly remains his chief confidant. He talks to Lynch about aesthetics, Lynch's coarse responses providing a ground bass for his tenor, but he talks to Cranly about his secret thoughts.

So the resolution of the book's problem, which is what Stephen should do next, comes in a climactic discussion with Cranly. What in *Stephen Hero* was only a suspicion becomes here a virtual certainty. Stephen asks Cranly to come and talk with him, but Cranly delays. During the delay Emma Clery passes by, and again bows across Stephen in response to Cranly's greeting. Stephen is affronted and pounces on this deliberate misdirection of her favor. "Was there not a slight flush on Cranly's cheek?" he asks himself. "Did that explain his friend's listless silence, his harsh comments, the sudden intrusions of rude speech with which he had shattered so often Stephen's ardent wayward [58] confessions?" (501) In the subsequent conversation, Cranly suspiciously takes the part of mothers and of women generally; he accuses Stephen of inability to love. It is this conversation which determines Stephen upon departure, for it makes him feel that he cannot hope for friendship: "Away then; it is time to go. . . . his friendship was coming to an end. Yes; he would go. He could not strive against another. He knew his part." (516)

But to give Stephen more complete mastery of the situation, Joyce adds an element not present in *Stephen Hero*. This too occurs in the final conversation. Cranly reminds Stephen that he will be alone, "And you know what that word means? Not only to be separated from all others but to have not even one friend. . . . And not to have any one person . . . who would be more than a friend, more even than the noblest and truest friend a man ever had." Stephen looks at him and wonders if he has spoken to himself. "Of whom are you speaking?" he asks at last, and receives no answer. (519) The effect of the suggestion is to bring Cranly's emotions even more completely within Stephen's circle of attraction. His attachment to Stephen and to Stephen's girl are presumably related, but Joyce does not labor the relation. In the last pages of the book Stephen writes in his journal of Cranly's growing intimacy with Emma, "Is he the shining light now? If so, I swear it was I who discovered him. . . . " (522) The artist discovers his own rival, shapes him even for the task of betraying him.

The self-centered character of the *Portrait* precludes Joyce's enlarging upon Stephen's further relations with Cranly. Stephen dispenses with both love and friendship, reluctantly but with what he considers justification. The contest of love and hate between him and Cranly is irrelevant except in so far as it compels his departure to search for freedom. The only question is how long it will take Stephen to slough off both Cranly and Emma. The *Portrait* ends in exile for one; Joyce might have ended it with exile for two, with a departure modeled upon his [59] own setting forth with Nora Barnacle in 1904; but he wished Stephen at this stage to find no one to help him. Stephen's self-isolation is heroic but presumptuous, suited as Stanislaus Joyce says to his character as Irish Faust. On the other hand, his refusal to strive against another, his endurance of gratuitous deceit, gives him also a Christlike character.

Joyce reserved for his play *Exiles* a saturnalia of the emotions of friendship. By 1914, when he began the play, he had had a series of important experiences with friends which he had not had in 1902, the last year to which his earlier books refer. The first came on his return from Paris in 1903. He had written of sexual exploits in Paris to his friend Vincent Cosgrave, the prototype of Lynch. He did so in contravention of the advice of Cranly's prototype, J. F. Byrne, who thought Cosgrave vicious, and later had his judgment confirmed. When Joyce returned to Dublin, Byrne demanded an explanation for Joyce's having flouted his advice, and when Joyce could not furnish an adequate one Byrne broke off with him. In *Ulysses* Stephen says of Cranly, "He now will leave me. As I am. All or not at all." Actually they became friends again, but Joyce has Stephen decide that Cranly's protectiveness is an attempt to keep him to himself.

A second experience that entered into *Exiles* occurred in 1909 when Joyce was making a brief visit to Dublin. He called on Cosgrave and to his consternation heard Cosgrave boast that he had seduced Nora Barnacle after her supposed allegiance to Joyce began. Joyce went in despair to Byrne, then living at 7 Eccles Street, and told him what he had just heard. He wrote home to Nora in such agony and with so much recrimination that his distressed wife showed the letters to Stanislaus Joyce. Fortunately Stanislaus was able to prove to his brother that Cosgrave was lying, because five years before Cosgrave had confidentially confessed to Stanislaus at a pub his failure with Nora. If the relationship with Byrne seemed to argue possessiveness, that with Cosgrave led Joyce to see in friendship an aspect of hatred and [60] treachery. The relationship of man and woman is bewilderingly precarious here. When Joyce's faith in Nora was shaken, he appears to have made no attempt to defend her or to heed her defense. (His attitude had not yet attained the sangfroid of Wellington in the first chapter of *Finnegans Wake*, who, in another treatment of Joyce's theme, on receiving Napoleon's message, "Fieldgaze thy tiny frow [wife]. Hugacting. Nap." replies "Figtreeyou!") (*FW*, 9) Nora had to be vindicated by someone else, and that one a man; otherwise no vindication would seem to have been possible. Joyce was unhappily quick to suspect treachery in those closest to him. At a word, his friend is a Judas, his wife a Delilah.

A third episode occurred in Trieste, when an Italian friend of Joyce, who was also an admirer of Nora, seemed to Joyce to be as much drawn to himself as to her. Little is known about this relationship, but it is probable that it reinforced his conception of the homosexual undercurrent in friendship. Finally, Joyce paid a visit to Dr. Oliver Gogarty in Dublin in 1912, and from Gogarty's account this ended in mutual hostility. From these four episodes Joyce drew the picture of friendship which appears in *Exiles,* where your friend is someone who wants to possess you mentally and your wife physically, and longs to prove himself your disciple by betraying you.

Joyce focuses attention in the play upon husband rather than upon lover. In the notes to *Exiles* he attributes to the newly published pages of *Madame Bovary* (discarded by Flaubert) the current movement in thought which takes more interest in the husband's dilemma than the lover's glamor. But principally the husband-hero was a figure through whom he could keep his own matured *persona* as the center. In his university days Joyce denounced *Othello,* and while we do not know the reasons we can guess that he already repudiated the naiveté and easy susceptibility of the hero. His own role with Cosgrave was equally undistinguished, but in the play he makes Richard a more powerful antagonist for Robert than Othello is for Iago. The two men [61] watch each other in what Joyce called three cat-and-mouse acts, with Richard's mistress-wife as the prize for the more feline.

As always, the hero's motivation cuts two ways. On the primary level Richard desires that his wife share in his own Faustian freedom; he would like, but cannot ask, that her freedom should result in fidelity. On the secondary level he longs to be wronged by her and by his best friend, so as to feel vicariously the thrill of adultery. Her infidelity and Robert's will confirm his view of the impossibility of a genuine tie between people; yet in his partial wish for this confirmation he is an accomplice in the infidelity. As for Robert, his motivation is simpler: he wishes to possess Bertha, and also to possess and dominate Richard through the body of his wife. Richard is caught in his two conceptions of himself; as Faust searching freedom he cannot try to control another, as Christ he cannot resist for himself. There is also another element, his love for his wife, to keep him from acting. For Bertha love is not what it is to Richard; rather than the bestowal of freedom, it is the insistence upon bonds. She waits for the sign which he will not give, and encourages Robert less for himself than in the hope of bestirring her husband to express his love. Richard has begotten the situation from which he proceeds to suffer.

The winner of the bout is not decided. Joyce asked Paul Suter, a friend in Zurich, whether he thought Bertha was unfaithful to Richard or not, and Suter sensed so much agitation beneath the question that he evaded answering it. Yet there can be no doubt that Robert feels he has lost, and that Richard retains his moral ascendancy. Whatever happens between the bodies of Robert and Bertha, their beings are completely dominated by Richard. "There is a faith still stranger than the faith of the disciple in his master," says Richard to Robert, "the faith of a master in the disciple who will betray him."

In *Ulysses* betrayal serves as a countertheme to the main action, which is the coming together of Bloom and Stephen. [62] When Mulligan takes Stephen's arm, Stephen says to himself, "Cranly's arm. His arm," (*UL*, 9) as if they were equally unreliable. The crime of friendship in *Ulysses*, committed by Mulligan, Lynch, and Cranly ("He now will leave me"), is the crime of leaving one's friend in the lurch. For this Stephen calls Lynch a Judas and predicts he will hang himself. Incidentally, as if to confirm Joyce's view, Cosgrave did commit suicide in the late nineteen-twenties. The sexual betrayal theme is presented ingeniously in Stephen's description of Shakespeare, with whom both he and Bloom are somewhat identified; Shakespeare, Stephen holds, was betrayed by his brother with his wife, and betrayed with the dark lady of the sonnets by his "dearmylove," that is, by Mr. W. H., for whom he had a homosexual affection.

Among all these betrayals of one man by another, the relationship of Bloom and Stephen stands forth in vivid contrast. Mulligan suspects that Bloom's interest in Stephen is homosexual, but the suspicion is only malicious. The relationship of the two is not friendly, but paternal and filial. Joyce seems to imply that only within the family, or the pseudo-family, can a solid bond be established. Even this relationship has its sexual content, for Bloom, in his desire to play the role of father with Stephen and to have him for son is motivated also by jealousy of Blazes Boylan and by a desire to free his wife from Boylan's embraces. Consequently, like Stephen's God and Stephen's Shakespeare, Bloom is bawd and cuckold, showing Stephen a picture of Molly in an alluring costume. It cannot be wholly irrelevant that Joyce himself sent a picture of Nora to Forrest Reid in 1918, shortly before he wrote this episode. Bloom continues his invitation by asking Stephen to give Molly lessons in Italian in exchange for lessons in singing. The relationship with another man is so important to him that it reduces the importance of his relationship with a woman.

The treatment of Bloom and Stephen finds no parallel in the earlier novels, but it recalls the theme of the story, "The Dead." [63] There the middle-aged husband of Gretta Conroy finds himself unexpectedly bound to his wife's young lover, whom he regards first with jealousy and then with affection. (In the story, however, the lover is dead.) Molly is offered as a pawn not in friendship but in the father-son bond. "Betray me and be my son," Bloom half-tells Stephen. Stephen, as usual, ends by committing himself to no one, but Bloom, who has also cast off friendship, is partially at least committed to him and to Molly as father and husband. Joyce perhaps found it easier to picture this triangular relationship in *Ulysses* because he put so much of himself in both his heroes that he was at once betrayer and betrayed.

Moreover the familial relationship, while not necessarily satisfactory, is at least inevitable. In *Finnegans Wake* Joyce returns to the family situation, and the book contrasts with an early work like *Dubliners*, where most of the relationships are outside the family, or with the *Portrait*, where a break with the family is essential. It is as if, having sampled all varieties of friendship, and in *Ulysees*, fosterkinship, Joyce reverts at last to the fundamental and timeless condition of the family. Betrayal continues: in a famous passage every member of the family is revealed to have illicit relations with every other member; H.C.E., for example, has an incestuous interest in his daughter as strong as Bloom's interest in his son. Stanislaus Joyce remembered his brother's saying to him, "There are only two permanent things in the world, the love of a mother for her child, and the love of a man for lies." But Stanislaus thought his brother in later life had discovered still another form of love, that of a father for his daughter. In the *Portrait* the hero moved away from his father's family to friends, but every friend betrayed him; and now the hero reverts to the family, this time a family of his own making. In the family betrayal continues, yet here all the members of the family seem principally aspects of Joyce's imaginative life, alternately embracing and rejecting each other, but bound as indissolubly as the cortexes of the brain. He is the wooer and the [64] wooed, the slayer and the slain.

The image that Joyce created of his life, and that his biographer Herbert Gorman followed him in consolidating, is heavily suffused with the character of the betrayed man, but neglects the element of desire for betrayal. No one wishes to underestimate the difficulties of writers in Ireland, which have driven so many of them to other countries. The continent of Europe is not the most miserable exchange imaginable, however. But it is characteristic of Joyce's state of mind that things never got better for him. From his talk and from Gorman's biography, one has the impression that his relations with publishers were always execrable; actually Joyce was treated extremely well by publishers from about his thirty-fourth year. In the same way, Joyce steadily represented himself as living in poverty, but as Ernest Hemingway remarked in the early nineteen-twenties, poverty found the Joyces every night at Fouquet's, where Hemingway could afford to go only once a week. Joyce forced himself into bad straits. He grew so accustomed to representing himself as a mild saint surrounded by energetic devils that Stuart Gilbert quite surprised and amused him by pointing out that he was not really in bad circumstances at all, that he was on the contrary quite lucky.

Most of the incidents in Joyce's life have to be reconsidered from this point of view. For example, in the famous quarrel in Zurich involving the English Players, Joyce represented himself as the victim of splenetic British bureaucrats. Actually, he appears to have provoked an unnecessary row quite deliberately, constructing an incident in which he would be aggrieved so he could then protest it. The humorous references to it at the end of the *Circe* episode were the artistic aftermath of his inartistic involvement. Similarly, when Mrs. McCormick abruptly withdrew her patronage from Joyce in Zurich, he fastened the blame upon a young friend of his, and Gorman says in a dark footnote which Joyce wrote for him: "Several times during Joyce's career [65] this brusque and unexplained [change of] attitude of certain admirers of his has taken place. . . . There is no single explanation so far as these different admirers are concerned that will fit all these cases, but the facts remain that all through his life he seems to have had admiration both in its spiritual and its material form spontaneously and suddenly offered him and subsequently just as suddenly transformed into passive or open hostility." Joyce's suspicions of his young friend were altogether unfounded, but they suggest how essential it was for him to believe that his friends were, at the slightest nudge, his enemies. As in his quarrel with Nora in 1909, his anger at being victimized knew no bounds, although in both cases he was his own victim. There is a certain relish for the violent breaking of friendships; a favorite word in his early work is "sunder." No doubt in some instances Joyce had cause, but even in these he helped the betrayers along. The image in one of his later poems, of plucking his own heart out and devouring it, is a recurrent pattern in his behavior as in his works.

In actual life Joyce's urge to detach himself became itself a passion, so strong that it led him into truculence or into distrust, but, in the perverse way of art, his violent renewals of exile through the persons of his friends became a virtue. As soon as he had rejected them as friends, convinced of their propensity to betray him and of his own to be betrayed, he was free to behold them in that clear light which is one of his special contributions to fiction. His characters, except for his heroes, belong to a land which he lords as an absentee. They lack the liberating recourse of art, which enables him to recover a mastery he has dissipated in quarrels; he does not treat them with coldness, but rather with the sympathy of someone who can emerge from their nerve-racked sphere, beyond love and lies to detachment and truth. As for the heroes, particularly Bloom and Stephen, while they are not as removed as their creator from attachments, they show some of the same power to withdraw themselves. A certain insouciance [66] and humor in Bloom prevent his taking his wife's adultery altogether to heart, and keep him also from entanglements with Martha Clifford and Gerty MacDowell. The more sombre Stephen too, when he propositions Emma Clery in *Stephen Hero*, stipulates that on the morning after their night of love they will say an eternal farewell; in the *Portrait*, when he finds a girl who symbolizes all that he desires, he makes no attempt to know her; and in *Ulysses* he withdraws also from the proffered friendship with Bloom. The heroes in most novels are drawn into situations; in Joyce's they extricate themselves from them.

Joyce told his friend Claud Sykes that, so long as he could write, he could live anywhere, in a tub, like Diogenes. Writing was itself a form of exile for him, a source of detachment. When a young man came up to him in Zurich and said, "May I kiss the hand that wrote *Ulysses*?" Joyce replied, somewhat like King Lear, "No, it did lots of other things too." Only in writing, which is also departing, it is possible to achieve the purification which comes from a continual re-baptism of the mind. [67]

GRANT H. REDFORD

The Role of Structure in Joyce's Portrait

A CLOSE LOOK AT *A Portrait of the Artist as a Young Man* by
James Joyce reveals a relationship between artistic proposition
and structure which has either been overlooked or too-little
emphasized. Yet unless the book is seen as both definition and
demonstration, its subject matter cannot be properly evaluated.
It will be seen merely as a thinly-veiled autobiographical record
of an arrogant, somewhat ridiculous, even "insufferable" (says
Hugh Kenner) young man with artistic pretensions who is not
understood by his family nor appreciated by his society, and
who turns his back on "all that" and decides to remake the
world nearer to his heart's desire. This partial and inexact view
supported by considerable comment over the years does dis-
service to the book. The present paper proposes to show how
the book's themes—Search and Rebellion—are made meaningful
through structure, and how the structure is the embodiment
of an artistic proposition proclaimed by the central character
himself as being basic to a work of art.

As a useful step toward this purpose, a word of reminder
needs to be said about Joyce's method of work. Frank Budgen
visited him while he was writing *Ulysses* and was told that
though he had been working hard all day he had written only
two sentences. "I have the words already," he told Budgen.
"What I am seeking is the perfect order of the words in the
sentence. There is an order in every way appropriate." This

Reprinted by permission of the author and of the Purdue Research Foundation, copyright owner. The essay originally appeared in *Modern Fiction
Studies,* Spring, 1958. References to *A Portrait* are to P-2; to *Stephen Hero*
are to *SH*-2.

search for the perfect order is revealed throughout Joyce's work, both indirectly and directly: In *Stephen Hero*, Stephen "sought in his verses to fix the most elusive of his moods and he put his lines together not word by word but letter by letter." (*SH*, 32) In *The Portrait*, he is trying to write a poem about a girl and a party; an earlier effort to write a poem about Parnell had foundered: "Now it seemed as if he would fail again, but by dint of brooding on the incident, he thought himself into confidence. During this process all those elements which he deemed common and insignificant fell out of the scene." (77-78) This process is dramatically demonstrated in the transformation of a manuscript, *Stephen Hero*, estimated by Joyce to be 150,000 words covering twenty-five chapters—[21] about half the projected work —into five chapters totalling less than 90,000 words, *The Portrait*.

A characteristic of this process is a more precise use and interweaving, as in music, of symbol and motif; e. g., the family name, Dedalus, is retained, but made the defining symbol of *The Portrait*—note the scene, pages 196-197; the motif of the bat-like soul of Ireland and thus of Stephen waking to consciousness is used at least seven times at important junctures (e. g., pp. 213, 226, 237, 238, 259, 280, 299). Everything is made to serve the "perfect order" of Joyce's vision.

The vision, the proposition which underlies the book, is stated by Stephen near the end of the book as the climax of his Search: "Truth is beheld by the intellect which is appeased by the most satisfying relations of the intelligible: beauty is beheld by the imagination which is appeased by the most satisfying relations of the sensible." (243) Such a work, he concludes, will have "wholeness, harmony, and radiance." How then does the book conform to this requirement of having the most satisfying relation of the intelligible and the sensible, of attempting to be both true and beautiful?

The first two pages introduce the major subject-matter motifs: family, friends, country, church (embodied in the aunt), and Stephen's special responsiveness to music and language. Each of the book's five chapters presents an aspect of these materials in relation to Stephen's growth, i. e. in relation to his rebellion from them—family, church, etc.—and in relation to his search for something more satisfying to the artist's necessity. The length, treatment and special emphasis given each of the chapters is a key to how Joyce wanted the reader to regard the material and to view the total work.

Considerably more than half of Chapter I is devoted to religion and politics as factors destructive of family harmony, personal dignity and justice. Sixteen pages in full scene, a method employed nowhere else in the book, reveal the harrowing experience of the bitterly ironic family Christmas dinner. Four pages concentrate the injustice of a whipping administered by a priest, Father Dolan. Stephen's attempt to obtain justice from the Rector turns out, he discovers later, to be an ironic gesture, for it merely causes laughter among the authorities. Expanded through the remaining chapters, these elements constitute part of that against which Stephen eventually rebels.

The Search is also embodied in this first chapter but indirectly as an expression of the child's, then young boy's, growing awareness of the "outside world"—a term used often and with special significance throughout the book. These beginnings of the Search are revealed through Stephen's unusual sensitivity to language. [22] Dorothy Van Ghent goes so far as to say that *The Portrait* is an investigation of the creative effects of language upon life: "and the shape of reality that gradually defines itself for Stephen is a shape determined primarily by the association of words." In addition to the verse "apologize" and its implications (2), examples of his preoccupation with language are also found in Chapter I (5, 11, 13, 22, 25, 45, 49 and others). But most directly related to the Search are pages 11-12. They present Stephen not only concerned with language but seeking to *place* himself. He writes his name and then his address progressively until he asserts himself in the universe. This is Joyce announcing in full scale the Search theme.

Chapter II extends his experience with the "outer world" and his recognition and reaction to the continuing disintegration of his family's financial and social condition. Ten pages of the fifty are devoted to a reiteration of the "apologize" theme; here it involves his judgments and the writing and speaking of them.

In class his instructor, Mr. Tate, forces submission from him regarding the phrasing of a relationship between the Creator and the soul. Mr. Tate says that the phrase "without a possibility of ever approaching nearer" was heresy. Stephen murmurs: " 'I meant without a possibility of ever reaching. . . .' Mr. Tate, appeased, folds up the essay and passes it across to him, saying, 'O . . . Ah! *ever reaching*. That's another story.' " But the boys from the class use the incident as an excuse to attempt to force an admission from him that Byron was no good. They pinioned his arms and whacked him with a cabbage stump. But at last "after a fury of plunges he wrenched himself free." (91)

His second attempt to wrench himself free—this time from the grip of the squalid family circumstances—was not successful. He had won an exhibition and essay prize of thirty and three pounds and with it had embarked on a "swift season of merrymaking" of loaning money, buying presents, groceries and delicacies, buying pink paint for his room, etc.

> How foolish his aim had been! He had tried to build a breakwater of order and elegance against the sordid tide of life without him and to dam up, by rules of conduct and active interests and new filial relations, the powerful recurrence of the tide within him. Useless. From without as from within the water had flowed over his barriers. . . .
>
> By day and by night he moved among distorted images of the outer world. (110-111)

In this chapter he writes the poem about the girl and the party and defines his method of composition: by dint of brooding on the incident, etc. In addition to this significant act we find him testing and responding to words and conducting his search: [23]

> Words which he did not understand he said over and over to himself till he had learnt them by heart: and through them he had glimpses of the real world about him. The hour when he too would take part in the life of that world seemed drawing near and in secret he began to make ready for the great part which he felt awaited him the nature of which he only dimly apprehended. (66)

> He sat listening to the words and following the ways of ad-
> venture that lay open in the coals, arches and vaults and wind-
> ing galleries and jagged caverns. (74)

Here, indirectly through the architecture of the fire's action, Joyce
introduces the major motif of the Search theme, Dedalus, the
Artificer, with whom Stephen aligns himself more and more
throughout the work and dramatically at the climax and the
book's end.

As did the first and as do all the others, this chapter ends with
a seeming of order and satisfaction: his nocturnal wanderings,
which are a manifestation of his seeking of solace from inner
and outer turmoil, land him in the arms of a prostitute who is
kind and gentle with him. "In her arms he felt that he had suddenly become strong and fearless and sure of himself." (114)

Chapter III presents a concentration of his emotional involvement with sin on the one side and the Church on the other. Over
one sixth of the book is devoted directly to this conflict. It is
an intense and harrowing experience for Stephen to find himself
involved in more, and more nerve-wracking, excursions into the
sins of the flesh while at the same time he is confronted with
the celebration of a Retreat in honor of the school's patron saint,
Xavier, wherein Stephen is subjected to a most devastating view
of hell, the horror into which he, Stephen, is to be cast as the
reward of his multiple sins. The length and intensity of this
section is proportional to its effect on Stephen. Joyce is careful
to show that others took it more casually. (143) However, in
spite of the terror of the experience, as the artist-becoming, he
does not judge. This is made clear in an earlier sequence where
he is angry for being young and being a victim of a world of
squalor and insincerity. "Yet his anger lent nothing to the vision.
He chronicled with patience what he saw, detaching himself
from it and testing its mortifying flavour in secret." (73) Later
he states directly that detachment, impersonalization of the artist,
is a necessity for art. (252)

Simply as a human being, however, the terrified young man
of sixteen seeks solace in confession in an out-of-the-way, un-
pretentious chapel. Here, though edged with irony, Joyce presents
a quiet, gentle sequence to contrast with the cacophony and

stridency of the Retreat. Stephen returns to his school a lifted soul and partakes of the sacrament. The chapter ends on a note of peace, Stephen apparently safe in the arms of the Church. [24]

But as neither the arms of a prostitute nor the bosom of the Church gave him the satisfaction that his heart desired—"the loveliness which has not yet come into the world"—the next chapter, IV, a short one of thirty pages, reveals him still searching. One of the most enticing of all the nets held out to him is offered in this chapter. The director of the school calls Stephen in and asks him if he has ever had a desire to join the order. "To receive that call, Stephen . . . is the greatest honor that the Almighty God can bestow upon a man. No king or emperor . . . no angel or archangel . . . no saint, not even the Blessed Virgin herself has the power of a priest of God. . . ." (183)

Pondering this possibility and after an encounter with his mother, which ends with him "aware dimly and without regret of a first noiseless sundering of their lives" (191), he wanders by himself to a headland overlooking the sea. "Disheartened, he raised his eyes toward the slow-drifting clouds, dappled and seaborne. They were voyaging high over Ireland, westward bound." He hears "confused music within him" that recedes, recedes. He hears the call with his whole being, paying little heed that the call also sounds from bantering school acquaintances on the beach, shouting, "Hello, Stephanos! Here comes The Dedalus!" Caught and held in the mystic moment of an overpowering vision, he sees himself the artificer winging to whatever artistic forgings his soul could achieve: "This was the call of life to his soul not the dull gross voice of the world of duties and despair, not the inhuman voice that had called him to the pale service of the altar. . . ." (197)

He lies down in a hidden sandy nook "that the peace and silence of the evening might still the riot of his blood. . . . He felt above him the vast indifferent dome and the calm processes of the heavenly bodies: and the earth beneath him, the earth that had borne him, had taken him to her breast." (200) This embrace of earth is within three paragraphs of the end of the chapter. It makes a dramatic contrast with the earlier embraces of prostitute and church, which ended chapters two and three.

Chapter IV ends, significantly enough, with Stephen awakening from the breast of earth. "He rose slowly and, recalling the rapture of his sleep, sighed at his joy." But this is no seeming. This is the awakening to true joy, the product of his Search and Rebellion.

Though this awakening is the climax of the book, and four of the book's five chapters have been used in arriving at this point, the Search, in a real sense, has just begun. Now he has simply discovered "the end he had been born to serve." How to serve that end, [25] the responsibilities and limitations of his calling are yet to be discovered.

It is something that he should know what he will *not* serve; but from here on it is absolutely necessary that he know what he *will* serve and that he discover how to serve; he must perform an extended and laborious apprenticeship before he achieves the certitude of understanding and skill which Stephen says is the gift of the artist to his generation: "He was persuaded that no one served the generation into which he had been born so well as he who offered it, whether in his art or in his life, the gift of certitude." (*SH*, 76)

In view of this necessity, it can be understood why the last chapter covers a third of the book; why its length, subject matter, and emphasis are necessary to the completion of its structure and the achieving of the wholeness, harmony, and radiance requisite to a work of beauty. Hugh Kenner finds this last third unsatisfactory: "The insufferable Stephen of the final chapter is explicable on the assumption that Joyce is preparing his bridge into *Ulysses;* but the moral difficulty of accepting the *Portrait* as satisfactorily finished off in its own right imposes an intolerable strain on the reader." As I've explained, however, the length and emphasis of this portion of the book are necessary to complete the satisfying relations of the intelligible and of the sensible. They are necessary to the completion of Stephen's proposition and Joyce's artistic problem when he assigned himself the task of transforming *Stephen Hero* into *A Portrait of the Artist as a Young Man.* Stephen, having had the vision of himself as the Artificer, the winged man climbing the air of certitude and the wide glimmering vistas of art, must make sure of his wings before flight. So it is that Joyce presents him during this last third of the book completing the severing of ties and analyzing, defining, testing the artistic and intellectual equipment which is to bear him up in his flight.

But it is not easy. The fine confidence that was born with the vision and Rebellion is often assailed. Early in this last chapter, after drinking watery tea and chewing on crusts of fried bread preparatory to his going to morning classes at the university, he leaves by the back lane and hears a mad nun crying, "Jesus! O Jesus!" beyond the wall. ". . . stumbling through the mouldering offal, his heart [was] bitten by an ache of loathing and bitterness. His father's whistle, his mother's mutterings, the screech of an unseen maniac were to him now so many voices offending and threatening to humble the pride of his youth." (204)

Later, standing on the steps of the library and seeing birds in flight, he was moved to doubt. [26] "A sense of fear of the unknown moved in the heart of his weariness, a fear of symbols and portents, of the hawklike man whose name he bore soaring out of his captivity on osier woven wings . . . was it for this folly that he was about to leave forever the house of prayer and prudence into which he had come?" (264) There are also other periods of frustration and self-doubt. But from them all he emerges stronger, surer. Buoyed up by the necessity of his developing wings, he continues to serve his apprenticeship, to forge out his own concepts.

Touched by the spirit of Ibsen "like a keen wind" or the "silver-veined prose of Newman" or a song by Ben Jonson, he wanders the dark streets of Dublin "among heaps of dead language."

> His own consciousness of language was ebbing from his brain and trickling into the very words themselves which set to band and disband themselves in wayward rhythms:

> > *The ivy whines upon the wall,*
> > *And whines and twines upon the wall,*
> > *The yellow ivy upon the wall*
> > *Ivy, ivy up the wall.*

Did any one ever hear such drivel? Lord Almighty!
Who ever heard of ivy whining on a wall? Yellow ivy: that
was all right. Yellow ivory also. And what about ivory ivy?
The word now shone in his brain, clearer and brighter than
any ivory sawn from the mottled tusks of elephants. (208)

(Here, Joyce picks up an image made use of early in the book,
p. 45. Thinking of Eileen's hands, "They were like ivory; only
soft. That was the meaning of *Tower of Ivory* but protestants
could not understand it and made fun of it.")

In this quotation—the one just quoted from page 208—is revealed the change taking place in Stephen's relationship to language. When, in the fore part of the book, he travels the coun-
tryside with his uncle he listens to the talk. "Words which he
did not understand he said over and over to himself till he had
learnt them by heart: and through them he had glimpses of the
real world about him." (68) He still responds to language; its
phrases and rhythms have been the core around which much
of his knowledge of places and events has accreted. But now,
as he says, language is beginning to form shapes of idea and
sound in his mind. He is beginning to cross over from the passive
recipient to the active maker, the artificer.

It is easy to understand, therefore, why this section presents
Stephen in the act of composing a poem. Nearly ten pages are
devoted to this emotion-charged event. (254-263) The poem,
in keeping with the rigorous self-discipline of the artist-becoming,
is one of the more demanding of verse forms, the villanelle. And
as would be expected, it makes use of a motif introduced earlier
in the [27] book, an echo of Stephen's reading of Shelley, lines
about the moon "pale for weariness? Of climbing heaven and
. . . Wandering companionless." (108) When first used, these
lines were more or less passively repeated by Stephen as an
embodiment of his mood, but now the motif is used aggressively;
now is the act of making: "Towards dawn he awoke. O what
sweet music! His soul was all dewy wet. Over his limbs in sleep
pale cool waves of light had passed. He lay still, as if his soul
lay amid cool waters, conscious of faint sweet music. His mind
was waking slowly to a tremulous morning knowledge, a morning inspiration. A spirit filled him, pure as the purest water,

sweet as dew, moving as music. . . ." As has been noted, music accompanies almost every major event of vision or "awakening" in the book.

> O! in the virgin womb of the imagination the word was made flesh. Gabriel the seraph had come to the virgin's chamber. An afterglow deepened within his spirit, whence the white flame had passed, deepening to a rose and ardent light. . . .
>
> > *Are you not weary of ardent ways,*
> > *Lure of the fallen seraphim?*
> > *Tell no more of enchanted days.*
>
> The verses passed from his mind to his lips and, murmuring them over, he felt the rhythmic movement of a villanelle pass through them. The roselike glow sent forth its rays of rhyme; ways, days, blaze, praise, raise. . . . (255)
>
> Fearing to lose all, he raised himself suddenly on his elbow to look for paper and pencil. . . . His fingers found a pencil and then a cigarette packet. He lay back and . . . began to write out the stanzas . . . in small neat letters on the rough cardboard surface.
>
> Having written them out he lay back on the lumpy pillow, murmuring them again. (256-257)

The completed poem is full of literary echoes and self-consciousness, but it achieves an objectification of the artist at his work serving his apprenticeship; it reveals discipline, knowledge of his craft, imagination and passion.

Further, it is dramatized by Joyce into a significant, semi-climactic segment of the book's structure. It follows immediately Stephen's enunciation to his friend Lynch of the principles and definitions of his esthetic philosophy. He defines pity and terror, the rhythm of beauty; he answers the question "What is art? What is the beauty it expresses?" by saying, "Art is the human disposition of sensible or intelligible matter for an esthetic end." He then defines truth and beauty and states that the form of the art is of major significance.

> The image, it is clear, must be set between the mind or senses of the artist himself and the mind or senses of others. If you bear this in memory you will see that art necessarily divides itself into three forms progressing from one to the next. These

forms are: the lyrical form, the form wherein the artist presents his image in immediate relation to himself; the epical form, the form wherein he presents his image in mediate relation to himself and to others; [28] the dramatic form, the form wherein he presents his image in immediate relation to others. . . . Even in literature, the highest and most spiritual art, the forms are often confused. The lyrical form is in fact the simplest verbal vesture of an instant of emotion, a rhythmical cry. He who utters it is more conscious of the instant of emotion than of himself as feeling emotion. (250-251)

The "instant of emotion, the rhythmical cry"—his poem—follows two and a half pages later. Here in embryo—the statement by Stephen of artistic principles followed by his objectifying them in his poem—is what characterizes the book. Joyce seems to have proceeded from definition—Stephen's—to demonstration—his own.

Before this "rhythmical cry" Stephen had made his choice between the Church and Art, but he had not overtly, publicly done so. To have declined the invitation to join the order did not mean that he was breaking with the Church. It is significant that he does not do so until he has evolved his own statement of esthetic truths. Once he has defined what the artist can and must do, once he has demonstrated to himself that his principles have validity in action—the composition of the lyric, among other things—he is ready for the more vital severing, the cutting off of himself from the Church and his family and his friend Cranly, the "unfrocked priest" who hears confessions but cannot absolve.

These three "severings" occur in the same scene near the end of the book: Stephen is talking to his friend Cranly, after conversations with others on all subjects relevant to the situation, on Universal Peace, nationalism, and a national language—with cold violence he had told his friend Davin that "Ireland is the old sow that eats her farrow" (238)—on art, truth and beauty, and personal love of women. The scene continues at some length and Stephen is forced to state precisely what his relationship to the church and his family is, whether he loves his mother, etc. This results in Stephen's saying rather sharply,

I will not serve that in which I no longer believe, whether it call itself my home, my fatherland or my church: and I will try to express myself in some mode of life or art as freely as I can and as wholly as I can. . . . I do not fear to be alone or to be spurned for another or to leave whatever I have to leave. And I am not afraid to make a mistake, even a great mistake, a life-long mistake and perhaps as long as eternity too. (291-292)

Following this scene, the book consists of six and a half pages of diary entries. These are in the main impersonal, thus conforming to Stephen's observation: "The personality of the artist, at first a cry or a cadence or a mood and then a fluid and lambent narrative, finally refines itself out of existence, impersonalizes itself, so to speak." (252) These diary entries also conform to his conclusion that art progresses from the personal to the impersonal, from first to third [29] person. The book is indeed a definition by example or a philosophy or art that its central figure espouses.

The entries cover two months and a week. The night after his talk with Cranly, Stephen writes in his diary:

Free. Soul free and fancy free. Let the dead bury the dead. Ay. And let the dead marry the dead.

April 6, he writes:

. . . I desire to press in my arms the loveliness which has not yet come into the world.

Ten days later he writes:

"Away! Away!"
The spells of arms and voices: the white arms of roads, their promise of close embraces and the black arms of tall ships that stand against the moon, their tale of distant nations. They are held out to say: We are alone—come. And the voices say with them: We are your kinsmen. And the air is thick with their company as they call to me, their kinsman, making ready to go, shaking the wings of their exultant and terrible youth. (298)

Ten days later, April 26:

Mother is putting my new secondhand clothes in order. She prays now, she says, that I may learn in my own life and away from home and friends what the heart is and what it feels. Amen. So be it. (298)

This has the bravado and terrible confidence of youth which knows all the answers. In Stephen's case, he has made an attempt at all the answers relevant to himself, the artist soul awakening to a consciousness of itself, so there is nothing left but to depart and to test in the crucible of himself the values and vision which experience and exceptionally alert and sensitive capabilities have made available to him. For him there is nothing else to say but what he says next:

> Welcome, O life! I go to encounter for the millionth time the reality of experience and to forge in the smithy of my soul the uncreated conscience of my race. *April 27.* Old father, old artificer, stand me now and ever in good stead. (299)

His Rebellion may be done, but his Search for and the achievement of form sufficient to forge the uncreated conscience of his race is just begun. The book has become the objectification of an artistic proposition and a method announced by the central character. The book has achieved its form, the most satisfying relations of the intelligible and the sensible, its wholeness, harmony, and radiance. [30]

EUGENE M. WAITH

The Calling of Stephen Dedalus

STEPHEN DEDALUS as he appears in *A Portrait of the Artist as a Young Man* is far from being a godlike hero. Groping painfully toward some understanding of himself and his place in the world,

Reprinted by permission of the author and of The National Council of Teachers of English, the copyright owner. The essay originally appeared in *College English*, February, 1957. References to *A Portrait* are to P-2.

he is sometimes laughable, sometimes pathetic, and nearly always what we should call "difficult." Yet despite his all too human failings he has the almost superhuman courage to face the world alone, and a profound conviction that the artist is quasi-divine. This conviction is brought out in one of the most closely written passages in the novel, the description of Stephen after the composition of his villanelle, standing on the steps of the library, ashplant in hand, watching the flight of some birds which he takes to be swallows. After observing the birds minutely, he begins (characteristically) to observe himself observing the birds and to think of himself as an augur in an ancient temple. As overtones of the supernatural increase in intensity, he thinks of his mythical patron, Daedalus, and then, for several moments, of a god who is closely analogous to Stephen.

> A sense of fear of the unknown moved in the heart of his weariness, a fear of symbols and portents, of the hawklike man whose name he bore soaring out of his captivity on osier woven wings, of Thoth, the god of writers, writing with a reed upon a tablet and bearing on his narrow ibis head the cusped moon.
> He smiled as he thought of the god's image, for it made him think of a bottlenosed judge in a wig, putting commas into a document which he held at arm's length. . . . (264-265) [1]

Stephen's mental image of Thoth with a headdress suggesting a judge's wig, the long beak of an ibis, and writing on a tablet held at arm's length closely resembles depictions of the god in the Book of the Dead at the ceremony of the weighing of the heart. There the deceased is assayed while Thoth, an observer slightly removed, stands ready to add this last judgment to his record of good and evil. Thoth was the scribe of the gods, but he was also much more: he was the god of wisdom, the inventor of speech and letters and, somewhat like the divine *logos*, the one at whose word everything was created. Stephen's "god of writers" is a potent symbol, emblematic in a number of ways of Stephen himself, the artist as a young man, observing, recording, creating.

[1] See W. Y. Tindall's comment on this passage in his "James Joyce and the Hermetic Tradition," *JHI*, XV (1954), 23-39; see also his *The Literary Symbol* (1955), pp. 57-58, 79-84.

The suggestion of artistic and divine creativity in this allusion is particularly important as a counterbalance to the suggestion of a satanic fall made most overtly in Stephen's "I will not serve." Two stimulating essays on the *Portrait* have emphasized recently the theme of the fall while neglecting the theme of creativity; [2] the result is a distortion, as it seems to me, of the meaning of the novel. For example, Caroline Gordon believes that one reason for the superiority of this novel to certain others which have a comparable theme "is that Joyce is convinced that his hero is damned." (393) Hugh Kenner, in the course of an excellent demonstration of the structural complexity of the *Portrait,* says, "Ultimately, as the insistent climax of the overture shows, its [the *Portrait's*] central theme is Sin: the development of Stephen Dedalus from a [256] bundle of sensations to a matured, self-conscious, dedicated, fallen being." (142) Though the theme of the fall is undoubtedly significant, it does not occur in isolation, but related and subordinated to what the title of the novel leads us to expect as its main theme, Stephen's development as an artist. The fall is assimilated into the preparations for flight—flight from Ireland and flight on the osier wings of Daedalus, the old artificer to whom Stephen prays in the last words of the novel.

If the central theme is sin, then these final preparations for flight are supremely ironic, and in this way they have been interpreted. After commenting on the "instant of promise" at the end, Kenner goes on to say that in *Ulysses* we see clearly that Stephen's dream of flight is a delusion. He concludes that we should see Stephen, even at the end of *A Portrait,* as an esthete but no artist—a would-be flyer whose fall from grace will soon be followed by another fall like that of Icarus. But there is no indication in *A Portrait* that this kind of irony exists. Ironic detachment there certainly is: no one who has studied the differences between *Stephen Hero* and the final version of the story can doubt that Joyce manipulated the materials of his own life very freely and with great artistic objectivity. He never fails,

---

[2] Caroline Gordon, "Some Readings and Misreadings"; Hugh Kenner, "The Portrait in Perspective"; see these essays reprinted in this volume on pp. 136-156 and pp. 25-60 respectively.

in painting his final portrait, to indicate what is unlikable, weak, or foolish in his adolescent protagonist. Yet to grant all this is not to say that he brands Stephen as already a failure—still less that he shows the failure to be the consequence of rejecting the church. The entire fabric of the novel seems to proclaim its concern with potentialities, with vocation, with the moments leading to the choice of a career. The depiction of this process is brilliantly successful in making the final choice seem the inevitable outgrowth of character. The time has not come for a final judgment and the book makes none, though every stroke of the depiction is informed by a keen moral awareness.

A Portrait of the Artist as a Young Man defines with elaborate care the conditions of creativity for a particular writer, Stephen Dedalus. Though the action of the novel makes these conditions reasonably clear, the subtlety of the definition lies in a delicate and complex pattern of images reflecting the hero's growing convictions. I propose to examine one part of this pattern—a number of passages related by their imagery and all bearing on the crucial question of the place of Stephen's religious experiences in his artistic development.

Two sets of images appear together in the long description of the bird-watching, part of which I have already quoted: images of flight and images of flow. Their association provides a clue which can profitably be pursued through the novel. After the circling swallows have made Stephen think of the bird-man, Daedalus, and the bird-god, Thoth, they bring to his mind some verses from Yeats's countess Cathleen:

> Bend down your faces, Oona and Aleel,
> I gaze upon them as the swallow gazes
> Upon the nest under the eave before
> He wander the loud waters.

A soft liquid joy like the noise of many waters flowed over his memory and he felt in his heart the soft peace of silent spaces of fading tenuous sky above the waters, of oceanic silence, of swallows flying through the seadusk over the flowing waters.

A soft liquid joy flowed through the words where the soft long vowels hurtled noiselessly and fell away, lapping and flowing

back and ever shaking the white bells of their waves in mute
chime and mute peal and soft low swooning cry. . . . (265)

As creative power is suggested by the flight of the swallows
through Stephen's associations with Daedalus and Thoth, so his
delight and satisfaction with words—especially the sound of
words—are conveyed in the image of the flowing water over
which the swallow flies in Yeats's lyric (Stephen's identification
of himself with the swallow is suggested by his changing the
pronoun in the fourth line [257] from Yeats's "she" to "he"). When
we look at some of the other appearances in the novel of the
images of flight and flow we find that they play a major part
in the definition of the proper conditions for creativity.

After Stephen's first successful self-assertion, his protest against
the injustice of Father Dolan, he is described "alone," "happy
and free," and as he listens to the sound of the cricket bats they
sound "like drops of water in a fountain falling softly in the
brimming bowl." (64) In the second chapter flowing water is
associated with both the disorderly life of his father's house and
the riotous imagings of his aroused sexual desire. With a little
prize money he tries to make a new life, charitable and orderly,
but the money is soon gone and the scheme collapses. The end
is thus described:

> How foolish his aim had been! He had tried to build a break-
> water of order and elegance against the sordid tide of life with-
> out him and to dam up, by rules of conduct and active interests
> and new filial relations, the powerful recurrence of the tide
> within him. Useless. From without as from within the water had
> flowed over his barriers: their tides began once more to jostle
> fiercely above the crumbled mole. (110-111)

These "sordid tides" seem very different from the dripping water
of the fountain, yet in both cases the images of overflowing
are related to a rebellion against order, that of a classroom tyrant
or of Stephen in his mood of self-reform. The pressure of "a
presence subtle and murmurous as a flood" leads finally to the
embrace of the streetwalker described at the close of the second
chapter. His experience is at least a sort of communication, "a

vague speech," and as such is briefly satisfying to the isolated adolescent.

Soon, however, sensual indulgence is presented in images which reflect a great change in attitude: "His soul was fattening and congealing into a gross grease. . . ." (127) Once more Stephen's lust is related to the life of his father's house, for he is revolted there by the thick gravies and the grease: in both his inner and his outer life there is viscosity instead of the flowing tide. Throughout the third chapter, from which these quotations are taken, Stephen conceives of his sin as revolting bestiality. In his nightmare after the famous sermons of the retreat these feelings reach a peak of horror expressed in images of excrement, which follow logically in this viscous series.

The flow of this rebellion of the senses has coarsened and thickened to the point where it has stopped itself. What was at first a release has become a horrible restraint. Yet before the process is complete there is a hint that the excursion into sensuality is not entirely worthless. As Stephen sits thinking about his sin and working at a mathematical problem, an equation in his scribbler begins to look like the unfolding tail of a peacock, and Stephen sees it as his own soul, "going forth to experience, unfolding itself sin by sin" (116), and then folding back and fading. The meaning of the passage seems to be double: the failure of Stephen's present way of life is foreshadowed, while at the same time sin is presented as an unfolding, a development. A water image suggests what value the experience may have:

> At his first violent sin he had felt a wave of vitality pass out of him and had feared to find his body or his soul maimed by the excess. Instead the vital wave had carried him on its bosom out of himself and back again when it receded: and no part of body or soul had been maimed, but a dark peace had been established between them. The chaos in which his ardour extinguished itself was a cold indifferent knowledge of himself. (116-117)

The "chaos" of Stephen's self-knowledge here anticipates his later break with "the order of life out of which he had come." (265)

The fourth chapter opens with the superbly comic description

of the religious regime Stephen imposes upon himself [258] after
he has made his confession. It is like the "new life" he began
with his prize money, but far more elaborately contrived. Once
more the temptations of the flesh return to threaten the newly
established order and once more they are portrayed in terms of
the flood. (176-177) Stephen now associates the "sluggish turfcoloured water" of the Clongowes bath with the "grave and
ordered and passionless life" of the priests at the college. (186-
187) The standing water and the "moist unsustaining air" above
it symbolize an ordered life, and they repel Stephen almost as
much as the images of grease and excrement which symbolize
complete submission to the flesh. Somewhat later in the book
(202), the grease in the kitchen at home reminds him of the
"turfcoloured bogwater," just as the life of the priests reminds
him of it here. This series of associations shows that the religious
life is ultimately as hostile to Stephen's needs as is the life of
worldly self-indulgence exemplified by his brief career in the
brothels and also by the very different but equally self-indulgent
career of his father, Simon Dedalus. The kinds of life associated
with images of viscosity and stagnation have one characteristic
in common: they seem to Stephen to threaten his freedom of
spirit.

The passage in which Stephen makes his choice of an artist's
life combines images of flight with those of flowing water. The
voices of his friends calling his strange name seem charged with
symbolic appeal: he seems "to hear the noise of dim waves and
to see a winged form flying above the waves. . . . (196) He
walks barefoot in the sea-water, "dark with endless drift," and
sees the wading girl, who seems "like one whom magic had
changed into the likeness of a strange and beautiful sea-bird."
Profoundly moved, but not sexually aroused, he looks at her for
a few moments, then turns away and strides off across the sand,
"singing wildly to the sea." (199-200) Stephen has "fallen" in
that he has taken a beautiful body as an object of contemplation instead of the religious mysteries with which he occupied
his mind after his confession and communion, yet his excite-
ment is what he is later to describe as "the esthetic emotion,"
which is static: "The mind is arrested and raised above desire

and loathing." (240) Instead of plunging Stephen again in the mire of sensuality, this "fall" advances him toward the artistic goal he envisages: "Her image had passed into his soul for ever and no word had broken the holy silence of his ecstasy. Her eyes had called him and his soul had leaped at the call. To live, to err, to fall, to triumph, to recreate life out of life!" (200)

Not only the arrangement of this series but the association of the girl with a bird and with flowing water shows that the experience, though far removed from the "grave and ordered and passionless life" of the clergy, is equally removed from the life of the senses as it is usually conceived. That the experience and the prose describing it are intensely romantic reveals to the reader that Joyce is contriving with careful particularity the career of a certain artist at a certain time.

Stephen's ecstatic contemplation of the girl on the shore is emblematic of the life which he feels himself destined to lead— in the world but not of it. Twice in Chapter Four, once plainly and once more symbolically, this destiny is described. The first passage comes shortly after his association of the priests' life with the sluggish water of the Clongowes bath: "His destiny was to be elusive of social or religious orders. The wisdom of the priest's appeal did not touch him to the quick. He was destined to learn his own wisdom apart from others or to learn the wisdom of others himself wandering among the snares of the world." (188)

"Elusive" of orders yet "wandering among the snares of the world," uncaught, moving freely. A similar distinction is [259] made at the moment when Stephen sees his true vocation: "His throat ached with a desire to cry aloud, the cry of a hawk or eagle on high, to cry piercingly of his deliverance to the winds. This was the call of life to his soul not the dull gross voice of the world of duties and despair, not the inhuman voice that had called him to the pale service of the altar. An instant of wild flight had delivered him. . . ." (197)

Stephen's artistic destiny is not to belong exclusively to either the world of the flesh or the world of the spirit. The images of flight, like those of flowing water, suggest the freedom he must have, but their emphasis is not entirely upon escape. The flight

of Daedalus is not only an escape but a widening of consciousness, an investigation of the unknown, as Joyce reminds us by
quoting on his first page Ovid's line, *"Et ignotas animum dimittit
in artes"* (*Met.*, VIII, 188). The images of flight relate freedom,
increasing perception, and creativity. In this way part of the
novel's statement is made: Stephen seeks freedom from the
world and from the church as a condition necessary for new
perception and for artistic creation. He sees sin as a stage in the
development. The image of the unfolding peacock's tail is related
to his thought of his soul, "unfolding itself sin by sin." (116)
Another bird image, that of a bat flying in darkness, also presents
his association of sin and understanding. It comes to him in
connection with the story his friend Davin tells of a country
wife who asked him in for the night. For Stephen she is the
type of her race and his, "a batlike soul waking to the consciousness of itself in darkness and secrecy and loneliness." (213)
Stephen's choice of a vocation may thus be seen as a choice of
flux rather than any already created order, of flight into the
forbidden and the unknown in order to understand and ultimately to recreate.

The fifth chapter, by far the longest in the novel, elaborates
upon the significance of the choice while presenting scenes from
Stephen's university life. In the section dealing with Davin, the
Irish nationalist, we see Stephen's rejection of the social and
political order of his country. In the conversation with Lynch
we get the description of the static nature of esthetic experience as Stephen understands it—the artist's dependence upon
the stimuli of the senses and the detachment he must yet have
from sensual indulgence. As a further example of these complex
relationships we have the transmutation of Stephen's jealousy
and his longing for "E. C." into his villanelle, "Are you not
weary of ardent ways." The composition of the poem begins
amid imaginary sensations of music and cool waters and after
a significant parody of Scripture, "In the virgin womb of the
imagination the word was made flesh." He thinks of "E. C.," like
Davin's temptress, as "a batlike soul waking to the consciousness
of itself" (259) and surmises that her soul had "begun to live
as his soul had when he had first sinned." (261) The composi-

tion of the final stanza is described as an imaginary act of sexual intercourse, in which "E. C." is metamorphosed into the words of the poem while both are symbolized by flowing water. No passage in the book links temptation more unequivocally with artistic creativity, and none makes more clear that the emphasis is not finally upon sin.

Immediately following is the scene on the library steps with which I began. With its descriptions of birds and water and music, its allusions to gods and augurs, to the "liquid joy" of words, to the play by Yeats which Dublin noisily rejected, to Daedalus and to Thoth, this passage restates the theme of Stephen's choice of a profession, reminding the reader, more by symbol than by statement, of the meaning and consequences of the choice. Daedalus, always present in the hero's name, referred to in the epigraph and in the last words, belongs to the pattern of imagery we have been tracing, and serves as a constant [260] reminder of the courage and force of artistic endeavor. The artist may be doomed to bitter disappointment as Dedalus was, but even this is not Joyce's subject in *A Portrait of the Artist as a Young Man*. He presents the potential artist, the young man not fallen but girding himself for flight—called but not yet chosen. We are not obliged to take Stephen's exaltation at face value nor, on the other hand, to see in it the corrupt will of a "fallen being." It is part of Stephen's "whatness," portrayed with neither approval nor disapproval by an "indifferent" artist, who has "refined himself out of existence." [261]

C. G. ANDERSON

The Sacrificial Butter

BETWEEN THE WRITING OF *Stephen Hero* and the conception of *A Portrait of the Artist as a Young Man* James Joyce epiphanized his esthetic. The *Stephen Hero* fragment contains most of the matter of Chapter V of the *Portrait,* and it contains most of the esthetic theory of the *Portrait* as a whole; what it lacks is the technique of arranging non-discursive symbols in such a way that they evoke directly feelings which cannot be expressed discursively. It is by means of this technique that Joyce presents the life of the young artist as a complete, harmonious, radiant image—as ". . . *that* thing which it is and no other thing." (250, *SH*, 213) [1]

As we know from *Ulysses* and *Finnegans Wake* Joyce was fond of subtly explaining his own methods to the reader. In the *Portrait* he gives the key to the technique by pointing out that Cranly is John the Baptist: "The exhausted loins are those of Elizabeth and Zachary. Then he is the precursor. Item: he eats chiefly belly bacon and dried figs. Read locusts and wild honey." (293)

But, as will be shown, it is clear from Joyce's handling of Cranly, who is not only John the Baptist but also Judas and Satan, that he did not intend to produce an allegory. In everything he wrote after *Stephen Hero* he treated his subject symbolically. The distinction is, [3] as Yeats says in *Ideas of Good*

Reprinted by permission of the author. The essay originally appeared in *Accent,* Winter, 1952. References to *A Portrait* are to P-2; to *Stephen Hero* are to SH-1.
[1] St. Thomas's *claritas,* Hopkins' inscape, and Joyce's epiphany seem to be of a piece.

and Evil, that while "a symbol is indeed the only possible expression of some invisible essence . . . allegory is one of many possible representations of an embodied thing, or familiar principle, and belongs to fancy and not to imagination: the one is a revelation, the other an amusement." Nevertheless, on the reader's part some allegorizing is necessary if he is to understand how a symbolic work achieves its effect.

Chapter V of the *Portrait* is controlled by three principal symbols: the Daedalus myth; the poet as God—creator, redeemer, and priest; and the betrayal-crucifixion. In addition to subsuming many lesser symbols, these three are themselves related. While Icarus in the Daedalus story is an analogue for the flight of the artist from home, nation, and church into exile, "old father, old artificer" Daedalus corresponds to God the Father and Creator. God the Father is united with Christ the Son, who as the Word joins in creation and as the first priest becomes a creator in Joyce's special sense. Christ, the Creator as a young man, is betrayed and crucified in a way which corresponds to the betrayal of the artist as a young man by his family, his national society, and his church. Since the Daedalus element has been, in general, clear from the beginning, this article will examine only the second and third of these principal symbols.

1

Stephen's exposition of his esthetic to Lynch in Chapter V is the intellectual climax of the novel. Stephen is here an ordained priest of art proclaiming the gospel of art. As he says of himself, he is ". . . a priest of eternal imagination, transmuting the daily bread of experience into the radiant body of everliving life." (260) But to understand his priesthood, we must understand his conversion and baptism.

When, in Chapter IV, the director of University College suggests that Stephen consider becoming a Jesuit, Stephen decides that he will ". . . never swing the thurible before the altar as priest." (188) But later, as he walks along the beach, he hears ". . . the call of life to his soul not the dull gross voice of the world of duties and despair, not the inhuman voice that had called him to the pale service of the altar." (197) He is born again, and his soul arises from the ". . . grave of boyhood, spurning her graveclothes." (197) He feels that his calling and election are sure, and he immediately accepts his vocation: "Yes! Yes! Yes! He would create proudly out of the freedom and [4] power of his soul . . . a living thing, new and soaring and beautiful, impalpable, imperishable." (197)

Stephen is baptized by wading in the sea, and he feels the regenerative power of this sacrament. He feels ". . . a new wild life . . . singing in his veins" (197) and wonders, "Where was his boyhood now? Where was the soul that had hung back from her destiny to brood alone upon the shame of her wounds . . . ?" [2] (197)

At the opening of Chapter V Stephen already has passed from baptism through ordination, and is saying mass. Contrasting with the Shelleyan swoon of the baptism and its ecstatic aftermath in the final pages of Chapter IV, the first sentence of Chapter V is a rhetorical change of pace: "He drained his third cup of watery tea to the dregs and set to chewing the crusts of fried bread that were scattered near him, staring into the dark pool of the jar." (202)

Important as this deflation is to the stylistic structure of the novel, however, the sentence is at least as important because it introduces the symbol of the eucharist—specifically, as we shall see, of the eucharist in the Maundy Thursday Mass. The tea and bread are paralleled by the cocoa which Stephen drinks with Bloom in the cabmen's shelter and at 7 Eccles Street in the Eumaeus and Ithaca episodes of *Ulysses*. After Stephen has consumed his breakfast of bread and tea (read bread and wine), he takes up ". . . idly one after another the blue and white dockets. . . ." (202) of his pawn brokers. These represent the communion wafers. After he has fingered them, he puts them

---

[2] During his baptism Stephen sees the wading figure of a girl—symbol of the fleshly beauty to which he has been converted, and symbol of Emma—on whom ". . . an emerald trail of sea-weed had fashioned itself as a sign upon the flesh." (199) Because she is baptized—chosen and marked with the sign— he sees her as a bird capable of flying with the "hawklike man," (264) although ultimately she becomes the "batlike soul" (259) who cannot soar with Icarus.

aside and gazes ". . . thoughtfully at the lid of the box [i.e., the tabernacle] speckled with louse marks." (202) Then his sister Maggie, representing the acolyte of the mass, prepares the water for the purification of his fingers, a ceremony which follows directly after, the second ablution in the mass.

As is usual with Joyce, things are not so simple as they appear at second glance. Stephen's mother washes his neck. Because the reader already knows that Stephen has abhorred water since childhood and has lice (202, 275), he realizes at once that this is a rather singular endeavor; it is not an ordinary Ordinary of the mass, but one which [5] no doubt has its Proper of the Season. What this Proper is, however, and what symbolic meaning it has, is discovered more gradually. Although Joyce knows very well what day it is, Stephen and the reader do not learn that it is Thursday until Stephen reads a news-agent's placard as he walks to school. (206) Thursday is the day which Stephen in his earlier Catholic fervor had dedicated to the Most Blessed Sacrament.[3] (170) And later, when Stephen refers to St. Thomas' *Pange lingua gloriosi,* he mentions to Lynch, who knows the fact as well as he does, that it is "a hymn for Maundy Thursday." (246) The Maundy Thursday Communion Verse, which follows the Purification in the order of the mass liturgy, says that ". . . the Lord Jesus, after He had supped with His disciples, washed their feet." Stephen ". . . allowed his mother to scrub his neck and root into the folds of his ears and into the interstices at the wings of his nose," (203) and we are reminded that Peter, in the Maundy Thursday Gospel, when he consents to Christ's washing him at all, says, "Lord, not my feet, but my hands also, and my head." [4]

After Stephen as priest has purified his fingers, his mother as server thrusts ". . . a damp overall into his hands, saying:—Dry

[3] It is also Bloomsday on June 16, 1904, and the day on which black masses are traditionally performed. There is no indication, however, that the mass in the *Portrait* is black.
[4] That Stephen's mass does not begin at the beginning does not, perhaps, require explanation, but it is interesting that in former days the Holy Thursday Mass which is now in the Missal began at the Offertory, either because two other ceremonies preceded it or because the preliminary portion was not essential to the sacrifice.

yourself and hurry out for the love of goodness." (203) The
overall, which represents the priest's napkin, is damp at the
Purification because it has already been used in the Washing-
of-the-Hands ceremony during the Offertory of the mass. The
hurry and the return of Stephen's sister ". . . making signs to
him to be quick and go out quietly by the back" (203) suggest
the hustle of the final portion of the mass. Stephen gives the
Benediction by ". . . smiling and kissing the tips of his fingers
adieu." (204) But at least two other meanings are compressed
into this single ironic action. It is the priest wiping his lips and
the priest kissing the altar before he pronounces the Benediction.[5]

As Stephen leaves the house he hears the mad nun in the
nearby asylum screech, "Jesus! Jesus! Jesus!" (204) Her exclama-
tion is in the correct mouth and in the correct ritualistic context
to signify the thanksgiving of an individual madwoman for the
mad sacrament [6] of a mad service. But it also identifies Stephen
with Christ, the first priest. That this identification is what Joyce
is actually saying is borne out later in the chapter when the
Maundy Thursday symbol is made more explicit by the consideration which Stephen and Lynch give to St. Thomas' *Pange
lingua gloriosi* and to the *Vexilla Regis* of Venantius Fortunatus.

Between the ejaculation of the nun and the discussion of the
hymns there are several symbols which carry in their complex
of meanings and tones the meaning and tone of the mass. These,
however, will be discussed in the second section of this article
because they have more direct connections with the betrayal and
crucifixion than with the Maundy Thursday ritual itself.

The two hymns are of primary importance in understanding
Joyce's method of using liturgy as symbol. The first hymn is
merely named and called the "highest glory of the hymnal."
(246) But, Stephen says, ". . . there is no hymn that can be
put beside that mournful and majestic processional song, the

[5] Skeat, whose *Etymological Dictionary* Joyce read "by the hour" (*SH*,
26), translates *adieu* as "(I commit you) to God." The priest kisses the
altar in the mass as representing Christ; but since Stephen, as we shall see,
is not only priest but also Christ, it is perhaps inevitable that he should kiss
himself.

Vexilla Regis. . . ." (246) Lynch then sings a stanza of the
second hymn from memory. In the liturgy the *Pange lingua
gloriosi* is sung after the mass on Maundy Thursday, when the
second Host, which has been consecrated to be reserved for
the Good Friday Mass in which no consecration takes place, is
carried in procession to the chapel or some other place. When
the procession arrives at this place, the chalice [*sic*] containing
the Host is incensed and placed in an urn or tabernacle. The
procession then returns, and Vespers are sung in the choir. The
Vexilla Regis is the hymn for Vespers during Passiontide.

The discussion of the hymns interrupts Stephen's expounding
of the mysteries of art to Lynch, and they are by no means
used merely to complete a parody or to give relief from what
might have become an esthetically tedious exposition of an
esthetic. The line *Pange lingua gloriosi* is translated in the
Missal as "Now, my tongue the mystery telling"; and Lynch
does not sing the first stanza of the *Vexilla Regis*, which begins
in translation with "Behold the royal ensigns fly," but the second
stanza, beginning "The mystery we now unfold." The hymns as
symbol, therefore—and this is true of all Joyce's symbols—are
not used as mere decoration, nor as extraneous allegorical signs;
the meanings they add to the narrative are intimately important
to the narrative, giving it depth of texture and expansiveness.
It is important that we know that Stephen is expounding mysteries, but it is also important that we know he is expounding
them in his symbolic office as Stephen-Christ, the first priest
of art. [7]

When Lynch has finished singing, he and Stephen turn into
Lower Mount Street. As we shall see this may be connected with
Golgotha, for when they stop the crucifixion is re-enacted: but
one of its other connections is the prophecy which Stephen made
when he accepted the call to the religion of art in Chapter IV:
". . . dawn . . . [would] show him strange fields and hills and
faces." (198) Here is the hill, and Donovan's bloated face appears.

Stephen and Lynch halt their procession; and although it is
still Thursday on the narrative level, the conversation with Dono-

van symbolically treats the Last Supper in retrospect. This is important because of the re-enactment of the crucifixion which is to take place shortly. Telling of a group of students (read disciples) who have passed their examination successfully, Donovan says, "The Irish fellows in Clark's gave them a feed last night. They all ate curry." [6] (246) These students are apostles ready to go forth to all nations: "Halpin and O'Flynn are through the home civil. Moonan got fifth place in the Indian." (246)

Food continues to be the controlling image in their conversation. Stephen asks Donovan twice to bring him "a few turnips and onions" the next time he goes on a botany field trip so that he can "make a stew" (247); Donovan mentions that his sister is to make pancakes for supper; and Lynch expresses disgust that pancakeeating Donovan can get a good job while he has to smoke cheap cigarettes. [7]

Stephen ends the delineation of his esthetic with the now famous statement, "The artist, like the God of creation, remains within or behind or beyond or above his handiwork, invisible, refined out of existence, indifferent, paring his fingernails." (252) The artist is God; God is Jesus; Stephen is Jesus. As Jesus left the companionship of his disciples on Maundy Thursday for the exile of the cross and the grave, [8] Stephen is leaving Lynch, his pope, and Emma, his Blessed Virgin, as well as his family, nation, and church for the exile of the artist and for Paris.

[6] Possibly it was curry of lamb with rice which they ate. Joyce, who knew the grail legends passed on by the medieval romancers, may have been consciously using the idea of the grail as the dish from which the disciples and Christ ate the Paschal Lamb on Maundy Thursday rather than as a chalice. Mallory uses it in this sense, and Joyce's favorite Skeat, in his *Etymological Dictionary*, traces the word to "Old French *graal, greal, grasal*, a flat dish." This definition plus the rice would connect it with ". . . the soup plate he had eaten the rice from for supper" (256), which Stephen finds on the table by his bed on the morning of what is narratively Friday. The rice, therefore, might also stand for the Host left over from Maundy Thursday, as explained above.

[7] Three comments. The cigarette-smoking business which is used all through the walk which Stephen and Lynch take together may be related to the use of incense during the mass procession on Maundy Thursday. Donovan's last field trip was on the preceding Saturday—to gather palms? Note that the basket used by Stephen to illustrate his esthetic theory to Lynch is a butcher's basket rather than a grocer's or chemist's.

2

But the symbols examined above are from only a very small portion of the chapter. What happens symbolically between the tea and fried bread of Stephen's breakfast and the curry eaten at Clark's: Thousands of things. And after the curry other thousands. Some of these are clearly symbolic, and their symbolic content can be allegorized for purposes of analysis.

In the narrative Stephen walks to school. As he walks he thinks of himself as a doubting monk (205), meets a consumptive man (206), thinks of Cranly as a guilty priest (207), reflects on his interest in words (207), recalls the temptation of Davin by a country wife (209 ff), is buttonholed by a woman selling flowers (213), thinks with something like compassion of Dublin (214), and thinks of Burnchapel Whaley, Buck Egan, and Buck Whaley. (214)

After witnessing Stephen's function as priest, it is clear to the reader why he should think of himself as a doubting monk.[8] But it may not be immediately apparent that the consumptive man is a type of Christ; and in him, as in the dwarf whom he, Cranly, and Dixon meet in the library (267), Stephen (as Christ) sees himself as he will be on Good Friday: ". . . an ugly little man who has taken into his body the sins of the world. . . . a crooked ugly body for which neither God nor man have pity." (*SH*, 116 f.) Joyce had attended the Tenebrae services of Holy Week and had taken notes on them. These notes were found with the *Stephen Hero* MS., and a photostatic copy is reproduced in *Stephen Hero*. (facing 116) He may have got the idea of the disfigured Christ from the Responsory of the second Nocturne of the Office of Holy Thursday: "Behold we have seen him disfigured and without beauty: his aspect is gone from him: he has borne our sins and suffered for us." To put it in a variety of theological language, the consumptive man and the dwarf are

---

[8] The thought recurs. (258, 260) Skeat traces "monk" to several Anglo-Saxon, Latin, and Greek words meaning "solitary" or "alone," meanings which have obvious significance in relation to Stephen.

"types" of Christ (Stephen) [9] as a scapegoat just as Noah or Jonah in the Bible are types of Christ.[9]

The time on the dairy clock is wrong because time is out of joint in the symbolic sequence of the chapter, and also because the dairy, which fuses as symbol with the temptation of Davin by the country wife, is connected with eternity before time— at least before that aspect of time called death.[10] Davin is Adam, who is tempted by this Irish Eve with a mug of milk for an apple. He is the person in the *Portrait* most closely related to "the broken lights of Irish myth" (210), and he is associated in Stephen's mind with primeval incest. (268 f.) Joyce links the country wife to the woman selling flowers (213 f.) and the temptresses in general (259), including Emma (259) and the Blessed Virgin (255), who is one of the lures of the fallen seraphim. (255) [11]

Cranly is thought of as a "guilty priest" (207) because he is, in one of his symbolic aspects, Judas. He betrays Stephen by stealing his best girl: "She passed out from the porch of the library and bowed across Stephen in reply to Cranly's greeting. He also? Was there not a slight flush on Cranly's face?" (273)

In Stephen's own interpretation of Cranly as John the Baptist

[9] The Dwarf as a type of Christ is incestuous because he has taken into his body the sins of the world. Perhaps incest may be taken as incorporating all sins since it was the sin which Joyce found most terrifying to contemplate. Cf. the father's relation to his daughter in "A Flower Given to My Daughter" and "Simples" in *Pomes Penyeach,* and Earwicker's to Isabel in *Finnegans Wake.*

Joyce gives us many clues to a character's encountering his own image. In "An Encounter," for instance, "Stephen" encounters himself in the "queer" gentleman as he ". . . chewed one of those green stems on which girls tell fortunes." In *Ulysses* (197), Stephen thinks, "His image, wandering, he met. I mine. I met a fool i' the forest." And later (*UL*, 210), he says, "We walk through ourselves, meeting robbers, ghosts, giants, old men, young men, wives, widows, brothers-in-love. But always meeting ourselves."

[10] Shortly after looking at the dairy clock Stephen hears a clock strike eleven, and it is for him (as Christ) the eleventh hour. The time and the precision of the striking make him think of MacCann, dressed in ". . . a shooting jacket and breeches" (206), the precise symbol of the Roman (or British) state—in short, the Procurator of Judea. This will be treated below.

[11] In Catholic belief, of course, Eve is the woman by whom sin enters the world, and the Blessed Virgin is the woman by whom the means of salvation from sin enters the world. Mary is sometimes referred to in Catholic writings as the "celestial temptress" since she can tempt men to Christ.

he was puzzled by St. John at the Latin Gate and sees him as the "precursor trying to pick the lock." (293) He writes in his diary, "Is he the shining [10] light now? Well, I discovered him. I protest I did." (296)

The reader is as puzzled as Stephen unless he knows or takes the trouble to find out who St. John at the Latin Gate is. The feast of St. John before the Latin Gate, celebrated in the Church on May 6, marks the anniversary of the dedication of the Basilica of St. John Lateran outside the Gate of St. John in Rome during the time of Pope Adrian. The original church was dedicated to the Savior, but later, because it was served by a Benedictine monastery dedicated to St. John the Baptist and St. John the Evangelist, the church was dedicated to the two St. Johns as well. This later dedication has now superseded the original one in popular usage; or, in the framework of Joyce's symbolism, Christ has again been betrayed. Since the station for Maundy Thursday Mass is at St. John Lateran, Joyce's irony is apparent.[12]

Stephen ponders "The soul of the gallant venal city" (214) of Dublin, which had ". . . shrunk with time to a faint mortal odour rising from the earth. . . ." (214) as Christ thinks of Jerusalem: [Jerusalem! Jerusalem! thou that killest the prophets, and stoneth them that are sent unto thee, how often would I have gathered together thy children, as the hen doth gather her chickens under her wings and thou wouldest not.] [13]

Several Irish prophets who have been killed by Irish men are mentioned in Chapter V, and all of these are connected with Stephen's own crucifixion. Yeats at the opening of the National Theatre is one of these: ". . . the catcalls and hisses and mocking cries ran in rude gusts around the hall." (266) And Stephen says to

[12] In "Tilly," the "extra measure" of *Pomes Penyeach,* Cranly is represented as "my torn bough." The poem is the "extra measure" as Judas became the "extra" disciple, and he is torn from Stephen (read Christ) as one of the branches of the true vine. He is also Satan (another betrayer) tempting Jesus to be a material Messias—Cranly was sidestepping the priesthood of art to open a porkstore in Wicklow; hence he drives cows in the poem. But since Stephen said, "Satan, really, is the romantic youth of Jesus reappearing for a moment" (*SH,* 222), perhaps we can come full circle to John the Baptist as the romantic youth of Jesus.

[13] Matthew 33:37. Cf. the Tenebrae service for Maundy Thursday evening, the office of Good Friday.

Davin: "No honorable and sincere man . . . has given up his life
and youth and his affection from the days of Tone to those of
Parnell but you have sold him to the enemy or failed him in need
or reviled him and left him for another." (237)

The Bucks Egan and Whaley and Burnchapel Whaley were
infamous for many reasons. They performed, according to rumor,
black [11] masses while living in what was to become the University College building. Burnchapel also burns chapels, but it is
Buck, his son, who is important for his connection with Cranly.
Buck's second alias was "Jerusalem" Whaley because he won
a bet, estimated to be between 10,000 and 15,000 pounds, for
walking to Jerusalem and playing ball against the walls. This is
the key to the mysterious grey handball which Cranly carries.
(229, *etc.*) He and Davin play handball with it, "Cranly insisting
his ball should be used," and in answer to its thud, he exclaims,
"Your soul!" (238) In Stephen's ironic theology this supports the
demonic character of Cranly as the betrayer, and it is made
doubly ironic by Cranly's being the most "Roman" of Stephen's
Catholic male friends.

The thoughts of the Bucks bring the narrative to Stephen's
arrival at University College, where he enters the physics classroom to find the dean of studies lighting a fire in the fireplace.
Stephen sees his actions as religious ritual: "Kneeling thus on
the flagstone to kindle the fire . . . he seemed more than ever
a humble server making ready the place of sacrifice in an empty
temple, a levite of the Lord." (215)

But the position of this scene in relation to Buck Whaley, and
the thoughts which Stephen has concerning the priest indicate
that it is the ritual of the Catholic priest which is defective rather
than the ritual of the priest of art. The dean's ". . . very soul
had waxed old in that service without growing towards light
and beauty" (216), ". . . in his eyes burned no spark of Ignatius'
enthusiasm" (217), and ". . . it seemed as if he loved not at all
the master." (217)

During the physics class Stephen considers offering himself as
a "subject for electrocution." (255) And afterwards, as Stephen
goes into the crowd of students in the entrance hall, "Cranly's
dark eyes were watching him." (227) The crowd has gathered

to watch his trial. He is tried by MacCann as Pilate for not sub-mitting to Caesar in the form of the Tsar. MacCann, who is "ready to shed the last drop" (228) for the "universal peace" of the Tsar (or Augustus) even pronounces Pilate's *Ecce homo!* while clearing his throat, "Hom!" (229)

Stephen and Cranly cross the "weedy garden" (234) of Geth-semane together and find Lynch, the disciple to whom Stephen will confide the innermost mysteries of the religion of art, asleep; and the parallel with Matthew 26:40 and the Responsory to the eighth Lesson of the third [12] Nocturne of the Holy Thursday is complete: "Could ye not watch one hour with me?"

Stephen and Lynch then set out on their peripatetic discussion of Stephen's esthetic, and Stephen symbolically reassures Lynch that he is not only God but "also an animal!" This may encourage the reader to recall Stephen's doubly ironic question of a few pages earlier, "Do you fancy I am going to pay in my own life and person for debts they made?" (237) And later, in the pas-sage dealing with Stephen's lineage, the question "Did an angel speak?" (271) carries not only narrative and obscene levels but also refers directly to the means of conception between the Holy Ghost and the Blessed Virgin.

Although the crucifixion of Stephen is represented fully only by the book as a whole, it is symbolically re-enacted on the steps of the National Library at the end of Stephen's and Lynch's walk. As they approach the library, the sky is appropriately "veiled" and it begins to rain. Emma stands silently among her companions (the "other Marys" of the gospels) and Stephen watches her with "conscious bitterness" (253), thinking of her as a lure for him and Father Moran. She is specifically identified with the Virgin by the medical students' otherwise pointless talk of obstetrics, which the dying Stephen hears ". . . as if from a distance in interrupted pulsations." (254) As she prepares to go away with her companions, Stephen considers forgiving her.

The church year is continued in the burlesque Easter Mass which Stephen celebrates in the Circe episode of *Ulysses*, but the resurrection is foreshadowed in the *Portrait* by the sleep and waking which immediately follow Stephen's symbolic cruci-fixion: "A spirit filled him, pure as the purest water. . . . But how faintly it was inbreathed. . . . as if the seraphim themselves were breathing upon him!" (254) ". . . The night had been enchanted. In a dream or vision he had known the ecstasy of seraphic life." (255)

This explication does not exhaust the meanings of even these few strands of symbols in a single chapter of the *Portrait*, a book which is a rich, closely woven fabric of symbol and narrative. But since all of the elements treated as symbols in the *Portrait* were either omitted or treated on a simple narrative level in *Stephen Hero,* the tracing of the few strands through a small part of the whole cloth may add to our understanding of the growth of Joyce as an artist. [13]

CAROLINE GORDON

Some Readings and Misreadings

TWO PASSAGES IN JACQUES MARITAIN's *Art and Scholasticism* illuminate the work of certain great nineteenth-century novelists, as well as the work of some of the novelists of our own day. In a discussion of Christian art he says:

> By Christian art I do not mean *ecclesiastical* art, an art specified by an object, an end and definite rules. By Christian art I mean art bearing on the face of it the character of Christianity. Christian art in this sense is not a particular genus of the species art; we do not talk of Christian art as we do of pictorial art or poetic, Gothic or Byzantine art. A young man does not say to

Reprinted by permission of the author. This essay originally appeared in *The Sewanee Review,* Summer, 1953. Copyright ©, 1953, by The University of the South. References to *A Portrait* are to P-1.

himself: "I am going in for Christian art" as he might say "I am
going in for agriculture." There is no school for teaching Christian art. The definition of Christian art is to be found in its
subject and its spirit; we talk of Christian art or the art of a
Christian as we talk of the art of the bee or the art of man. It
is Christianity redeemed.

   . . . wherever art, Egyptian, Greek or Chinese, has attained
a certain degree of grandeur and purity, it is already Christian.
. . . Christian in hope, because every spiritual splendour is a
promise and a symbol of the divine harmonies of the Gospel.

The novel as we know it today did not exist until the early
part of the nineteenth century, when men were given over to
industrialism in the social order, materialism in philosophy, and
skepticism in religion. Our own century bears the stamp of the
century that preceded it; comparatively few men today live consciously by the Christian virtues, to say nothing of Christian
philosophy [384] or Christian social order. But the creative imagination—I am speaking particularly of the fiction writer's imagination—does not reckon time in the way in which it is ordinarily
reckoned. A novelist's conscious mind may be influenced by what
is going on around him, he may announce himself a pragmatist,
a skeptic, an atheist while his creative faculties seem to move
in and subscribe to a totally different order. Maritain says that
after the Renascence "art was so disheartened that it took to
living its own life." From this point of view, I have examined
some of the great nineteenth century novels. On the surface the
action seems to run in one direction while the current, in its
depths, runs in quite another. I believe that it could be shown
that in the nineteenth century and in our own century as well
the fiction writer's imagination often operates within the pattern
of Christian symbolism rather than in the patterns of contemporary thought. The peculiarly Christian element of the great
nineteenth century novels is their architecture. Many of them
are based on the primal plot: the Christian Scheme of Redemption. *Madame Bovary,* for instance, is strung as tightly as a bow-
string on two arcs, which coincide two visions of Emma. Emma,
as she appears on the occasion when Charles is first alone in
a room with her, standing tiptoe, her neck on the strain, pouting

because she cannot, with her tongue, lick all the sweets from
the bottom of her wine-glass, and Emma, who, in the same
attitude, except that now she lies prone, takes the chalice of
salvation and, dying, presses upon the figure on the crucifix "the
fullest kiss of love she has ever given." (The description of the
administering of Extreme Unction to Emma is simply a page
out of the Paris liturgy put into French, Flaubert wrote Madame
Maurice Schlésinger, "but the good folk who watch over the
preservation of the liturgy are rather weak in their catechism.")

The Christian Scheme of Redemption is a strange and original [385] plot. Two modern psychologists have commented on its
strangeness and originality. In *The Integration of The Personality*
Carl Jung conceives of the drama of the human psyche as "a
work of redemption." He says: "The life and death of the God-
man . . . a unique sacrifice, bring about the reconciliation of
man, who craves redemption, and is lost in materiality, with God
. . . man is potentially redeemed at the moment when the eternal
Son of God returns to the Father after suffering crucifixion. . . ."

In *Totem and Taboo* Sigmund Freud says: "We are much
disturbed by the spectacle of a youthful god sacrificing himself,"
then adds, "but let us pass that over." In the mystery religions
of the East, which were so popular in the early days of Christianity and which, in diluted and refined form, are so popular
today, the worshipper sacrificed to the god in order to constrain
him, to get some of his power, or the god was torn to pieces,
as was Dionysos Zagreus, in order that the multitude might feed
on him. (In *Totem and Taboo* Freud's imagination is so possessed by this symbolism that parts of the book, if written out
of professed faith, might read as an interpretation of the Eucharist.) But pagan gods do not sacrifice themselves. Freud has put
his finger on the primary difference between Christianity and
other religions.

The primal plot is so deeply rooted in us all that, like Freud,
we may apprehend it without realizing what we are doing. This,
I think, is the case with Henry James. His father, Henry James,
Sr., a follower of Emmanuel Swedenborg, had an antipathy to
any kind of orthodoxy. In *Notes of a Son and Brother*, the
novelist records himself as "never having been allowed to divine

an item of devotional practise," and Graham Greene, in an essay which he has written on "The Altar of the Dead," has commented on James's ignorance of Catholic rites. It would [386] seem that James was ignorant of dogma as well as rites, both Catholic and Protestant. And yet all his novels have one theme: *caritas*, Christian charity.

William Troy, in a provocative essay entitled "The Altar of Henry James," concludes that in all his work James *is* erecting an altar.[1] "And in that case, his altar—what would it be but the sometimes splendid and exultant, sometimes mangled and ignoble body of humanity stretched out in imagination in time and space?" This smacks more of the elder James than the younger. James himself considered "The Ambassadors" the best rounded of all his books. In the crucial interview between Lambert Strether and Madame de Vionnet it is clear that the altar has been erected for a particular sacrifice: the sacrifice of Eros, or pagan love, in order that Agapé, Christian love, may be born.

James spares no pains to set his stage for a sacrifice. Madame de Vionnet's drawing-room, ordinarily lamp-lit, is lit tonight by "a pair of clusters of candles that glimmered over the chimney-piece like the tall tapers of an altar. The windows were all open, their redundant hangings swaying a little, and he heard once more, from the empty court, the small plash of the fountain. From beyond this, and as from a great distance—beyond the court, beyond the *corps de logis* forming the front—came, as if excited and exciting, the vague voice of Paris."

James tells us that Strether feels that the voice of Paris had come in thus on "the great recorded dates, the days and nights of revolution. They were the smell of revolution, the smell of the public temper—or perhaps simply the smell of blood."

Madame de Vionnet is dressed in "simplest, coolest white, of [387] a character so old-fashioned . . . that Madame Roland, on the scaffold, must have worn something like it." She still seems to Lambert Strether "the finest and subtlest creature, the happiest apparition it had been given him in all his years to meet," but tonight she seems also "less visibly exempt from the

[1] The essays by Mr. Troy and Mr. Greene are to be found in the volume *Contemporary Essays*, edited by Sylvia Norman.

touch of time." She seems to him, indeed, as "vulgarly troubled
. . . as a maid-servant crying for her young man."

> What was at bottom the matter with her, embroider as she
> might, and disclaim as she might—what was at bottom the mat-
> ter with her was simply Chad himself. It was of Chad that she
> was, after all, renewedly afraid; the very strength of her passion
> was the very strength of her fear. . . . With this sharpest per-
> ception yet, it was like a chill in the air that a creature so fine
> could be, by mysterious forces, a thing so exploited. For, at the
> end of all things, they *were* mysterious: she had but made Chad
> what he was—so why could she think she had made him in-
> finite?

James never presents a crucial scene without painstaking prepara-
tion. Strether has before this reflected that the trouble with
Chad is that he is *"pagan."* Madame de Vionnet, the high-born
lady, is, at bottom, like Emma Bovary, the bourgeois wife: they
are both romantics, demanding the infinite of the finite. It is
largely through her realization of Chad's limitations—a realization to which she has to be helped by Strether—that Madame
de Vionnet arrives at her profession of faith, Christian charity,
which she makes that night to him: "The thing is to give, never
to take."

It is also possible that the primal plot may operate in a work
of art not only without the artist's conscious knowledge but almost against his will. Such a work is James Joyce's *A Portrait
of the Artist as a Young Man.* I suspect that this book has been
misread by a whole generation. It is not primarily a picture of
the artist rebelling against constituted authority. It is, [388] rather,
the picture of a soul that is being damned for time and eternity
caught in the act of foreseeing and foreknowing its damnation.
Joyce's story is based on a Greek myth, the story of Dedalus,
who created the labyrinth in which King Minos of Crete confined
the Minotaur. Stephen Dedalus, Joyce's hero, has for surname
the name of the pagan artificer. But his first or Christian name
is that of the first martyr, Saint Stephen. The Jesuits who have
trained him think that he may take orders. The director calls
him in one day to question him as to whether he has a vocation.

Stephen listens to the director in "reverent silence . . . through the words he heard even more distinctly a voice bidding him approach, offering him secret knowledge and secret power. . . ." (184-185)

But Stephen knows that he will never become a priest:

> The voice of the director urging upon him the proud claims of the church and the mystery and power of the priestly office repeated itself idly in his memory. . . . His soul was not there to hear and greet it . . . a definite and irrevocable act of his threatened to end forever in time and eternity, his freedom. . . . The snares of the world were its ways of sin. He would fall. He had not yet fallen but he would fall silently, in an instant. Not to fall was too hard, too hard. . . . (188)

When he resists the call to a vocation he knows that it is forever, and as he walks back to his father's house after the conversation with the director he turns his eyes "coldly for an instant towards the faded blue shrine of the Blessed Virgin which stood fowl-wise upon a pole in the ham-shaped encampment of poor cottages. . . . The faint sour stink of rotted cabbages came to him from the gardens on the rising ground above the river. He smiled to think that it was this disorder, the misrule and confusion [389] of his father's house and the stagnation of vegetable life which was to win the day in his soul. . . ." (188)

He enters his father's house by the back door. In the kitchen he finds his younger brothers and sisters still sitting about the table. They have just finished tea and over the small glass jars and jam-pots which do service for tea-cups, among discarded crusts and lumps of sugared bread, turned brown by the tea which has been poured over them, are singing "Oft in the Stilly Night."

Stephen "waited for some moments, listening, before he too took up the air with them. He was listening with pain of spirit to the overtone of weariness behind their frail fresh innocent voices. Even before they set out on life's journey they seemed weary already of the way. . . ." (190) And he is setting out on the same journey, with wings of wax. Stephen, though a believer—he never loses his faith, he denies it—is an anti-Christ and has his precursor, his John the Baptist, to make his way straight for him. He does not love any of his classmates and Cranly is the only one in whom he has confided. He has told Cranly all his sins and his soul-searchings. He asks himself:

> Why was it when he thought of Cranly he could never raise before his mind the entire image of his body but only the image of his head and face? Even now against the grey curtain of the morning he saw it before him like the phantom of a dream, the face of a severed head or death mask, crowned on the brows by its stiff black upright hair as by an iron crown? (207)

At last he has a conversation with Cranly in which the way he is to go is revealed to him:

> —It is a curious thing, do you know—Cranly said dispassionately—how your mind is supersaturated with the religion in which you say you disbelieve. Did you believe in it when you were in school? I bet you did.— [390]
> —I did—Stephen answered.
> —And were you happier then?—Cranly asked softly—happier than you are now, for instance?
> —Often happy—Stephen said—and often unhappy. I was some one else then.—
> —How some one else? What do you mean by that statement?
> —I mean—said Stephen—that I was not myself as I am now, as I had to become.—
> —Not as you are now, not as you had to become—Cranly repeated—Let me ask you a question. Do you love your mother?
>   Stephen shook his head slowly.
> —I don't know what your words mean—he said simply.
> —Have you never loved any one?—Cranly asked.
> —Do you mean women?—
> —I am not speaking of that—Cranly said in a colder tone.—I ask you if you ever felt love towards anyone or anything.—
>   Stephen walked on beside his friend, staring gloomily at the footpath.
> —I tried to love God—he said at length.—It seems now that I failed. It is very difficult. I tried to unite my will with the will of God instant by instant. In that I did not always fail. I could perhaps do that still. . . . (283-284)

In her *Seraphic Dialogues* St. Catherine of Siena tells us that it is impossible to love God directly; we must love Him through his creatures, our fellow-men. Stephen has tried to achieve the impossible. His "disordinate" love will, in the end, bring him to ruin. His sin is the same as Lucifer's; he has said what Lucifer said: "I will not serve."

Stephen's sin, intellectual pride, like all sin, begets in him a terrible restlessness. He is impelled to leave his home and college and seek a new life. His mother, as she puts his *secondhand* clothes in order, prays that in his own life, away from home and friends, he may learn what the heart is and what it [391] feels, but Joyce has given us to understand that this will never happen. Stephen has told Cranly that he is not afraid to make a mistake, "even a great mistake, a lifelong mistake and perhaps for eternity, too." (292)

These two passages throw considerable light on Joyce's intentions. He was a good classicist and had been steeped in Greek mythology. He was also one of the most conscientious literary craftsmen that ever lived. He was not likely to base his action on a Greek myth without realizing its full implications, nor could he have been guilty of the kind of cheap "modernistic" invention that characterizes Jean-Paul Sartre's play, *Les Mouches*. In that play the Eumenides descend to the hero's level and after an unconvincing struggle, follow him off the stage like whipped curs. In Joyce Furies remain Furies. The story follows the myth to its unhappy end. Stephen's father, Dedalus, the artificer, is a man of the nineteenth century. His skepticism and materialism have helped to construct the labyrinth from which both he and his son are trying to escape. Mr. Dedalus escapes through his love of his fellow men. When Stephen goes with his father to his father's college he is amazed at his father's love for his old cronies—there was not one of his set, Simon Dedalus tells his son, who did not have some talent, some merit that lifted him above the ordinary. Stephen, listening, feels that his own heart is as cold as the craters of the moon; the only one of his classmates with whom he is intimate is Cranly and they are intimate only because Cranly feels an almost scientific curiosity about the workings of Stephen's mind. Mr. Dedalus escapes from the trap which his own hands have built, as Dedalus escaped of old. But Dedalus' son, Icarus, flies too near the sun. The wings which his father have made for him are only of wax. They melt under the sun's fierce heat and he falls into the sea and is drowned.

I suspect that Joyce's novel is sounder theologically than a [392] novel by a contemporary novelist which deals with the same situation: a soul choosing damnation. I think that one reason why *A Portrait of the Artist as a Young Man* is superior is that Joyce is convinced that his hero is damned. The other writer, Graham Greene, seems to me to be in some doubt himself as to the outcome of his action, and his book ends in an anticlimax.

Henry Scobie, the hero of Greene's *The Heart of the Matter,* is a major in the British police force of a colonial port—a place where a noise on the tin roof means that a vulture has settled down for the night. Scobie is a long-suffering, much-harassed man who longs only for peace. He sometimes dreams of it. Greene says that "Once in sleep it had appeared to him as the great glowing shoulder of the moon heaving across his window like an iceberg arctic and destructive in the moment before the world was struck."

We are given to understand that Scobie might have been a different man if his little daughter had lived. But she is dead when the action begins. The only person for whom he now feels any affection is his native servant, Ali, who has been with him for fifteen years, longer than he has been married. He does not love his wife. The only time he is able to endure her is when he feels pity for her. Pity—aside from his attachment to Ali and to his dead daughter—is the only emotion he feels towards any human being, although he is scrupulously considerate and just in his dealings with his colleagues and with the natives over whom he has supervision. His wife, who has an annoying habit of hitting the nail on the head, sometimes refers to the fact that he does not love her and says that she would like to go away so he can have the peace of which he is always dreaming. Scobie feels so sorry for her that he goes against his principles and puts himself in the power of a native gangster, Yusef, [393] by borrowing from him the money for her passage to South Africa. She no sooner gets there than she realizes that she should not have left her husband and takes the next boat back.

It is too late. The events which will lead to Scobie's ruin have already been set in train. Yusef has begun to blackmail him and he has become involved in an adulterous love affair. A ship is wrecked off the coast. A young Englishwoman is one of the few persons who survive forty days in open boats. Her name is Helen Rolt and she is brought on the scene half-dead, or, at least, unconscious, one hand clasping a stamp album. At first glance she seems just the girl for Scobie. Her interest in stamp collecting—the album is the only possession she has saved—might make us think that the blood ran calmly in her veins, but as soon as she gets her strength back she is just like every other woman who fails to find love where it has been promised, suspicious, jealous and, finally, given to the same kind of tantrums that Scobie's wife has. Between the two women Scobie's sufferings are so acute that he no longer dreams of peace but actively desires damnation. He has a vision of ultimate happiness: being "alone, with the rain falling, without love or pity."

His wife has come back anxious to devote herself to him and wants to seal what she thinks of as their reconciliation by their taking Communion at the same time. He has sworn to his mistress that he will never desert her and he puts off the ordeal as long as he can, until, driven by what Greene calls "that terrible, promiscuous passion which so few experience," pity, he goes with his wife to Mass and, kneeling at the rail, makes one last attempt at prayer, offering up his own damnation for the two women for whom he has never been able to feel any emotion livelier than lust or pity.

I take it that Mr. Greene means us to accept Scobie as a hero, a man who would not only give his life but would risk damnation for his fellow creatures. There have been saints who have [394] told God that they were willing to be damned if their damnation would save their fellow creatures, but they made this prayer out of love, not out of pity. Scobie is a Manichaean hero, engaged from the first in the kind of denial of the natural order that can end only in despair. He admits to himself that he has never loved his wife but he has "taken a terrible private vow to make her happy." He denies the natural order by attempting the impossible; we can only assure people that we love them, we cannot assure their happiness. Greene has a curious paragraph in which he celebrates despair:

> He would still have made the promise even if he could have foreseen all that would come of it. He had always been prepared to accept the responsibility for his actions, and he had always been half aware how far *this* action might carry him. Despair is the price one pays for setting oneself an impossible task. It is, one is told, the unforgivable sin, but it is a sin the corrupt or evil man never practises. He always has hope. He never reaches the freezing point of knowing absolute failure. Only the man of good will carries always in his heart this capacity for damnation. . . .

Joyce's novel ends dramatically on the note of eternal damnation. Joyce does not need to tell us the kind of life Stephen will lead; it is explicit in the action. Greene's action goes on for several chapters after Scobie has committed suicide. The last chapter is an argument between his wife and the priest, Father Rank, as to whether or not he is damned. When Louise Scobie says, "It's no good even praying," Father Rank says: "For goodness' sake, Mrs. Scobie, don't imagine that you—or I—know a thing about God's mercy." When she begins, "The Church says . . ." he replies, "The Church knows all the rules. But it doesn't know what goes on in a human heart. . . . It may seem an odd thing to say when a man's as wrong as he was—but I think, from what I saw of him, that he really loved God." To [395] which the wife replies: "He certainly loved no one else." "And you may be in the right of it there, too," Father Rank says.

The ending is so inconclusive that there has been argument about whether Scobie was bound for Hell or Purgatory—an argument which Evelyn Waugh once tried to settle by taking his cigar out of his mouth long enough to say: "Where is Scobie? In Hell, of course." My own feeling is that in *The Heart of the Matter* Mr. Greene's craftsmanship would have been better if reenforced by sounder theology; one should not have to ask oneself exactly how a book ends. The ending should seem the only one possible. Greene's book ends with an anticlimax because

Scobie tries to "eat his cake and have it, too" maintaining what we are told is theologically impossible, that he loves God even if he cannot love his fellow men.

In the light of what Maritain has said, I should like to glance at the work of three other novelists. They are: George Bernanos, François Mauriac, and Evelyn Waugh.

Bernanos fills me with more awe than almost any of my contemporaries. No other novelist, except Dostoevsky, has been so bold in exploring the frontiers of the human spirit. The divinity in man seems to be his chief preoccupation, even, when, as in *Sous Le Soleil de Satan,* he is writing about the Devil. He tells us the kind of things the saints tell us and in the same authentic accents. As a result, he has a tremendous power, a whole register, so to speak, that is out of the reach of most of his fellow novelists. A writer like Ernest Hemingway seems flat and one-dimensional beside him. Even William Faulkner, in his flights, often sounds a note that is strained beside Bernanos' organ tones. And yet I think that Faulkner is, on the whole, a more Christian writer.

Maritain says the novel differs from other forms of literature "in having for object not the manufacture of something with its own special beauty in the world of *artefacta* . . . but the [396] conduct of human life itself. . . . It may therefore be understood how honest, universal and authentic the novelist's realism ought to be: only a Christian, nay a mystic, because he has some idea of *what there is in man* can be a complete novelist."

Maritain makes some further remarks about art in general which, I think, apply to the novel as well as any other form of art. Art, he says, must be "gratuitous" and "disinterested" and goes on to explain what he means by these terms:

> In the actual production of the work the virtue of art has only one object, the good of work to be done; to make matter resplendent with beauty, to create a thing in accordance with the laws of its being. . . . At the same time its desire is that there shall be nothing in the work eluding its control, that it alone shall regulate the work directly, handle it and shape it.
>
> There are many ways of failing to obtain this "gratuitousness." A man may think, for example, that excellent moral in-

tentions may make up for the deficiencies in the craft or the
inspiration, and are sufficient for the construction of the work.
Or a man might go so far as to alter the work itself as the rules
and the determined way of art require it to be, by the forcible
application of alien elements.

Faulkner's *As I Lay Dying* seems to me an example of the kind
of work of art Maritain is talking about, a work which is "gratuitous" and "disinterested" and a work which is important in the
history of the novel as an art form. With it he takes his place
among the writers whom Ezra Pound has called "the innovators,"
men who have presented "the conduct of human life" in a way
in which it has not been presented before, men who, as it were,
have originated a new vehicle for its presentation. In *As I Lay
Dying*, Faulkner shows a dramatic grasp as firm and almost as
comprehensive as James's and a faithfulness [397] in rendition
moment by moment that has been surpassed only by Joyce. Two
main currents of fiction meet in this admirable work, which—
to change the figure—resembles in its action a football game in
which passing, signals and foot-work are all faultless, each character taking the ball from the character who precedes him and
running his required number of yards. The result is action that
is as brilliant, as dense and seemingly as credible as life itself,
a work that is not only "gratuitous" and "disinterested" but
created "in accordance with the laws of its own being."

Bernanos dazzles us by showing us cloud-wrapped heights,
but he never, for me, at least, achieves the "honest, universal
and authentic realism" in which Faulkner excels.

His novel, *La Joie*, for instance, is the kind of conception that
comes only to a first-rate imagination—the life and death of a
saint. On the surface, the life of Chantal de Clergerie is like
that of any well-brought-up, dutiful young—French!—girl. But
the Russian chauffeur, sent to summon her to lunch one day
when she has not heard the bell, finds her praying, her eyes
wide open, a strange expression on her face, and realizes that
they have a saint in their midst. He threatens to reveal her
secret and when she will not be blackmailed, murders her. That
is what we are all tempted to do to saints, I suppose, and that
is the bold, simple outline of Bernanos' story. A writer less gifted

might have had difficulty in persuading us that this young girl
was a saint or that a man hated her enough to murder her because she was a saint. But Bernanos makes us believe that
Chantal's life and death were as he says they were. What gives
us pause is the Abbé Cénabre. The Abbé Cénabre, who appears
in another novel of Bernanos', is a priest who has lost his faith
without leaving the Church or relinquishing his priesthood. He
has confided his terrible secret to only one person, the Abbé
Chévance, Chantal's confessor, and he suspects that when
the [398] Abbé Chévance was dying he confided it to Chantal.
The spectacle of Chantal's life and martyr's death unhinges his
reason and he falls in a fit on the floor beside the body, crying
"Pater Noster" in "a superhuman voice," to die later in an asylum
for the insane. The action would be more aesthetically satisfying
if Bernanos had more regard for his craft, whose first requirement is the contrivance of the illusion of life. It took Lambert
Strether several months to find out what kind of woman Madame
de Vionnet was. Yet her whole character is revealed—if he had
had the wit to read it—when she first comes on the scene:

> . . . dressed in black, but in black that struck him as light and
> transparent; she was exceedingly fair, and, though she was as
> markedly slim, her face had a roundness, with eyes far apart and
> a little strange. Her smile was natural and dim; her hat not
> extravagant; he had only perhaps a sense of the clink, beneath
> her fine black sleeves, of more gold bracelets and bangles than
> he had ever seen a lady wear.

The roundness of her face, her "strange" eyes, the bracelets and
bangles that she wears under her "fine, black sleeves," all tell
us—after the event, the way life usually tells us—that though
conventional by up-bringing and inclination, she is, nevertheless,
a woman who is capable of having an illicit love affair. But the
part the Abbé Cénabre plays in *La Joie* is not prepared for in
such painstaking and realistic fashion; his name is not even mentioned until the last part of the book.

If fiction has for its primary concern "the conduct of human
life itself" no pains are too great to achieve the desired effect,
no pains too small, which is, perhaps, one of the reasons why

Maritain says that only a Christian can be "a complete novelist"
—even if he be Christian only "in hope." A pagan, attempting
to write fiction, is handicapped by the lack of example. Minerva
sprang full-grown from the head of Jove, and was not Bacchus
taken out of the side of his father's leg? But Christ [399] spent
nine months in the Virgin's womb and thirty years in solitude
and obscurity. It is the fiction writer's arduous task to imitate,
on however lowly a scale, the patience that stooped low enough
to lift up a fallen universe. For that patience no detail is too
insignificant and no effect will have its full dramatic value unless
prepared for. (If Our Lord had begun His ministry with His
Transfiguration His Incarnation would doubtless not have been
complete. Ford Madox Ford used to say that the worst horror
story he knew was the one about the man who was visiting in
a country house strange to him and, being wakeful and wanting
to smoke in bed, was appalled at having an unseen hand offer
him a match. I do not think that there is as wide a discrepancy
between these two examples as may at first appear. At any rate,
I believe that each of them has significance for the writer of
fiction.)

François Mauriac has lately been awarded the Nobel prize
for imaginative literature. This strikes me as astonishing. Mauriac's novels aroused my admiration long before he was awarded
this prize, but the admiration is always mixed with exasperation.
Mauriac and Bernanos have opened up to the contemporary
novelist who takes his art seriously whole vistas that, in our time,
at least, remain almost unexplored. Secrets of the human heart
seem to have been revealed to each of them that do not seem
to have been revealed to writers as great as Balzac or George
Eliot. The future of the novel as an art form will be glorious,
indeed, if any young writer has the strength and daring to follow in their footsteps. But why are they not better artists? Why
is Mauriac's art not more like that of the bee—to use Maritain's
figure? Everything the bee makes is perfection for the purpose
to which it will be put. Art is made by human beings but it
should always be approaching perfection. Mauriac's novels are
crudely put together; he has little regard for his craft. [400]

In *Le Noeud de Vipères,* he tells his story in the first person.

Henry James called this "one of the most barbarous of devices," yet scored one of his greatest triumphs with it in "The Turn of the Screw." The inventions, the devices which serve a novelist best grow, usually, out of his necessity. A writer wants to get something over that he feels nobody else has ever got over, but the conventions of the craft, the very medium itself all seem against him. He stands with his back to the wall, straining at his bonds and, suddenly bursting them asunder, evolves a new device which will serve fiction writers to come for many a year. But he has to feel his bonds constricting him before he can burst them. The great revolutionaries in the arts have been those who take the limitations of their medium seriously. Flaubert was such a writer, James was such a writer. So is William Faulkner. But Mauriac, as far as I can judge, has given little thought to the fundamentals of his craft, the basic problem of viewpoint, for instance. He adopts a viewpoint, uses it as long as it suits his convenience, then flings it down to adopt another, seemingly without taking into account the effect such shifts may have on the structure of his novel.

The story of *A Knot of Vipers* is told in the journal in which the old miser, Louis, records his hate of the members of his family. He feels that his revenge will come when they read the journal after his death. But his wife dies first! In the fireplace in her bedroom he finds great masses of charred paper and deciphers enough of what has been written on the paper to discover that she, too, kept a journal. He discovers, too, that his miserliness and his infidelities have caused her all her married life to "be racked by passions that only God can master"—in short that she has longed for his love.

At sixty-eight he feels the "wild delight" that a man might feel at setting out on what promises to be a splendid life. In thinking of his family as *A Knot of Vipers* he has chilled his [401] own life-blood so that, until now, he has hardly lived at all. But his wife is dead. His children and servants—he has no friends— are accustomed to thinking of him as "a monster of solitude and indifference." How can he swim against the stream, impose on them the vision of the person he is and always has been? He feels that for this "some especial strength" is needed: "Yes, but what strength? The aid of some *person*, of some one in whom we might all have been reunited, of some one who would, in the eyes of my family, have guaranteed the victory which I had won over myself, of some one who would stand my witness, who might relieve me of my hideous burden, and bear it on his own shoulders. . . ."

Mauriac's theme is on the grand scale—a dramatization of the redemption of a human soul—but many of his crucial scenes are marred by careless execution. He literally will not give the reader time to take in what is happening. And the whole action is made to turn on coincidence. The husband and wife each reveals his soul through the medium of a journal. It is hardly likely that two people would keep such journals simultaneously. Mauriac fails to convince me that they did.

There is in every artist a still, small and at times intensely disagreeable voice. This monitor has perhaps advised Mauriac that his action is not convincing. He has written an irritable preface to *Le Noeud de Vipères* in which, it seems to me, he shifts the blame to his readers:

> The man here depicted was the enemy of his own flesh and blood. His heart was eaten up by hatred and by avarice. Yet, I would have you, in spite of his baseness, feel pity and be moved by his predicament. All through his dreary life squalid passions stood between him and that radiance which was so close that an occasional ray could still break through to touch and burn him; not only his own passions, but, primarily, those of the luke-warm Christians [402] who spied upon his actions, and whom he himself tormented. . . .
>
> It was not money that this miser really treasured, nor, in his blind fury, was it vengeance that he sought. What it was that he truly loved you may discover who have the strength of mind, and the courage, to follow his story to the end, to that ultimate moment of confession which death cuts short.

Oscar Wilde, who, like King Charles II, uttered words wiser than his acts, says, "He who speaks a word loses faith." He is referring to the risk the imaginative writer runs if he talks about his conception while it is in the process of execution, but the contriver of illusion who yields to the temptation to thrust his

head out from behind the curtain and explain to the audience
what is going on runs a risk that is almost as great. If he speaks
a word he is likely to shatter the audience's faith in his illusion.
It takes a great deal more strength and courage to write a novel
than to read one. Yet there have been great novelists—Henry
James, for example—who could justly complain of never having
been properly read. But Mauriac, in explaining in his preface
what his story is about, is confessing his own weakness, his own
lack of courage, not the reader's. He ought not to have to tell
us what his story is about. That ought to be implicit in the action.

Mauriac's work might, I think, be compared with that of another Nobel prize-winner, William Butler Yeats. Yeats was not
an avowed Christian. He even dabbled in magic for many years,
but his artistic triumphs are all solidly based on the natural
order. "In Memory of Major Robert Gregory" shows the poet just
moved into the old tower which is to be his new home and
thinking of the friends whom he would like to have sup with him.
The poem, after he has called them all to mind, turns into an
elegy on the friend whom of all men he has ever [403] known he
found most naturally good. He defines Robert Gregory's character in terms of *objects* he loved:

> For all things the delighted eye now sees
> Were loved by him; the old storm-broken trees
> That cast their shadows upon road and bridge;
> The ford where drinking cattle make a stir
> Nightly, and started by that sound
> The water-hen must change her ground;
> He might have been your heartiest welcomer.

That kind of patient, passionate portrayal of natural objects
is a recognition of the natural order which I can only call Christian, "Christian in hope." Mauriac's loftiest edifices, lacking such
a solid foundation, seem always on the verge of toppling. The
lurid flames that light up his scenes make them appear less
rather than more substantial. He has said that he regrets that
he does not find human nature more admirable but that he must
portray it as he sees it. One wonders if he would not be a better
novelist if he found it more *natural?*

The novelist's foremost concern, certainly, is human nature or, as Maritain puts it, "the conduct of human nature." But Nature in itself is not Art! In this connection I think that the French philosopher has said something else that is of practical value to the novelist:

> In our time the *natural* gift is lightly taken for art itself, especially if it be disguised in clever faking and a voluptuous medley of colours. Now a natural gift is merely a prerequisite condition of art, or again a rough sketch (inchoatio naturalis) of the artistic habit. Such an innate disposition is clearly indispensable; but without a culture and a discipline which the Ancients considered should be long, patient and honest, it will never turn into art.

It seems to me that in America the natural gift, the innate [404] predisposition to the writing of fiction has been too much emphasized, and has received too much encouragement. "Flaubert me no Flauberts," Thomas Wolfe, who lived and died an amateur writer, wrote Scott Fitzgerald when Fitzgerald, overwhelmed with admiration for Wolfe's talent and appalled to reflect how much he had to learn, wrote, offering him advice. There is a feeling in the air that a novelist who admits that he has anything to learn about his craft is that much less of a novelist. As John O'Hara, who considers Ernest Hemingway a better writer than Shakespeare, puts it: "No can do, can teach." (Yeats, attempting to appraise himself as a writer, prophesied that he "would dine at journey's end with Landor and with Donne." Hemingway, attempting the same feat, repudiates the company of fellow writers and defines his own eminence in a figure from the prize-ring. He is not a master, learning what the masters who have gone before him have to teach, but a champion, taking them on, one by one, and defeating all of them except Tolstoi, with whom he has never been matched since they fight in different classes.) The brilliant but unschooled young fiction writer, James Jones, has already received so much praise, so much money for his amateurish efforts that it would seem almost impossible for him to turn into a real novelist. Writers like Somerset Maugham and Louis Bromfield have been so richly rewarded for peddling their natural gifts, "enhanced by clever faking and a voluptuous medley of colours," that neither of them has made a serious effort in years. I think that what I say of America holds true of England, too. Men like Joyce Carey and V. S. Pritchett are bad craftsmen. If there is any British novelist who has mastered any of the great lessons in technique that are to be learned from Henry James I do not know his name or his work.

A trend towards orthodoxy in religion has made itself felt, not only in the world at large but among fiction writers. Among [405] Catholic novelists, Evelyn Waugh is conspicuous for his "honest" and "authentic" realism, but it is hard to consider him "a complete novelist." His early novels are brilliant but fragmentary. His characters are not presented in the round but in cinematic flashes. Miss Runcible, sitting up in a hospital bed, smiling deliriously, bowing her bandaged head to imaginary visitors:

> Darling . . . how *too* divine . . . *how* are you? . . . and how are *you?* . . . how angelic of you all to come . . . only you must be careful not to fall out at the corners . . . ooh, just missed it. There goes that nasty Italian car. . . . I wish I knew which thing was which in this car . . . darling, do try and drive more straight, my sweet, you were nearly into me then. . . . Faster. . . .

Miss Runcible, her head cracked in a head-on collision between two automobiles, not knowing "which thing is which," is a brilliant symbol of our times, but she is not a character in fiction in the sense that Emma Bovary or Isabel Archer or Julien Sorel are characters. Mr. Waugh does not explore the consciousness of any one of his characters in these early books. He simply presents them acting in or being acted upon by events which arouse his righteous indignation. You might say that moral indignation is the hero and heroine of all his early novels. It is the only emotion which he seems to feel is worth dealing with. As a result, his early novels are like splinters shattered from some marmoreal block whose outlines are so vast that he has not yet taken their measure.

Edmund Wilson, in a review of *Brideshead Revisited,* has complained that Waugh is not as brilliant, not as much fun to read since he "got religion." I think that Mr. Wilson may be right. Waugh is not as sure of himself as he was. He is out after bigger game and goes more cautiously than he used to. The wit which crackled in the early books is gone. Waugh has [406] a new subject, which arouses not moral indignation but awe, a rendering of the mystery of human existence. Lord Marchmain, Lady Marchmain, Sebastian, Julia, Cordelia, Captain Ryder are all more mysterious and hence truer to life than his Ninas or Brendas or Adam Fenwick-Symeses. His realism has always been "honest" and "authentic," even when fragmentary. In *Brideshead Revisited* I think it approaches the universal. In this novel the whole action is permeated by a recognition, a love of the natural order which I do not find in Mauriac, Bernanos or Greene. I think that he was "Christian in hope" long before he entered the Roman Catholic Church. [407]

JANE H. JACK

Art and A Portrait of the Artist

D. H. LAWRENCE once recorded that he found Joyce boring, "too terribly would-be and done-on-purpose, utterly without spontaneity or real life." But Lawrence was not primarily an artist: he was a twentieth-century Sage or Prophet of great sincerity and remarkable literary ability. The successful creation of a work of art requires a considerable degree of deliberateness not only in the design and presentation but in the conception of the subject, in what might be called the exercise of a disciplined vision, a vision modified by considerations of the potentialities

Reprinted by permission of the author and of *Essays in Criticism* where it first appeared in October, 1955. References to *A Portrait* are to *P*-4; to *Stephen Hero* are to *SH*-2.

and limitations of the medium in which the artist has chosen to work.

Had Joyce died after writing *A Portrait of the Artist as a Young Man* his reputation as a novelist of stature could have rested on that one work alone. Its flaws—too much Ruskinesque prose and the discharge of some muddled emotional experience of whose objective value in the pattern of the work as a whole we are not sufficiently assured—are faults which a long work in prose may override as a poem may not; and the *Portrait* does, triumphantly. Yet it has rarely received its due. Interest in it as a novel has been dissipated by its obvious autobiographical content. And the attitude underlying Lawrence's aversion is not as uncommon as one might hope. Of all Joyce's works the *Portrait* has suffered most from this distrust of the constructive intellect in art. The existence of an earlier version, *Stephen Hero*, undisciplined and extravagant of detail, has induced a general easy acquiescence in the view that the *Portrait* is by comparison, deliberate, artificial and cold-blooded. It does not in fact lack feeling. Its inspiration is to be traced to far more profound and integrated experiences than anything behind the adolescent *Stephen Hero*, however warm and appealing some scenes in the latter may be. And the organization, the deliberate economy, the firm employment of a definite technique, [354] mark the birth of an artist. *Stephen Hero* is a series of exclamations, shrill and often touching, at the shocks of birth itself.

The earlier novel is a straightforward naturalistic narrative, comprehensive, frank, humorous and partisan. All that is important to Stephen's life and development receives generous and detailed description and while there is some attempt at objectivity the writer's criterion of importance is obviously closely personal. *Stephen Hero* does present a picture of the hero and his notions on art, but it is set against a very rich background of family, friends, city and religion—a family consisting of father, mother, a brother who is a close friend, a sister and minor relatives, friends who have distinct personalities and whose opinions are not only independent of Stephen but important to him; Dublin, which is both a city and a language; and Catholicism as religion and the channel of education. Stephen, as hero, reads essays to his mother as she does the ironing and lends her Ibsen, talks long and earnestly with his brother Maurice—"the elder smoked cigarettes and the younger ate lemon drops" (*SH*, 36)— is present to comfort his sister on her deathbed and reads an elaborately prepared paper on Art and Life, in whose reception he is nervously much bound up, to the college debating society. This may be sufficient to illustrate that the earlier draft is a study of a son and a brother, of a very human though consciously clever and eccentric student, at once painfully and happily growing into a writer. The *Portrait,* on the other hand, is the work of an accomplished artist creating directly out of the experiences and responsibilities of his calling.

It has not always been sufficiently emphasized that, in the *Portrait,* Joyce makes considerable use of the techniques of symbolism. Harry Levin's comment, "*A Portrait of the Artist as a Young Man* stands squarely in the naturalistic tradition," has left the emphasis too heavily on the difference between the modes of imaginative expression in this early work and those employed in *Ulysses.* Particularly towards the end of the *Portrait* Joyce created a fairly elaborate metaphorical design for the expression of the complexity and totality of the modern artist's reaction to his environment and to the characteristics [355] of his own personality. Failure to grasp the metaphorical values and relations which Joyce establishes has often led to the distortion and oversimplification of his meaning in the last part of the work. Levin describes the closing chapter of the book as "a discursive account of Stephen's rebellion." The novel is not *about* the youth Stephen Dedalus, alias James Joyce: it has a theme which may only be defined in abstract terms.

The *Portrait* is built on the proposition that art is a main artery in the body of life. All that nourishes art is living: all that stifles art is dead. Joyce works outwards from the conviction that the artist, as artist, must have no loyalties, must make no judgments except in distinguishing between what is relevant or irrelevant to his art. It is with art, not with himself or his environment, that Joyce is preoccupied in the *Portrait,* and such criticisms of the circumstances of his youth as are implicit in the novel are by-products of his concentration on the phenomenon in himself

of artistic vitality: men, women and institutions become images
and stresses in an imaginative awareness of the tension between
the life of art and the death of the spirit.

The basic symbolism of the last third of the *Portrait* springs
from an apprehension of the birth of art as a struggle with death.
Like many post-Renaissance writers, Joyce found it necessary to
express his awareness of this truth in a work which is at once
definition, dedication and positive achievement. Like Keats in
Hyperion he utilizes a fragment of classical mythology; but like
Wordsworth in *The Prelude* he leans most heavily on a selected
chain of autobiographical incidents for the plot of the work,
filling his canvas with material drawn from his own early life,
from Ireland and the Church, from his family relations, his love
affair, the University College and his friends. No one would deny
the realism of the finished work, the crude vivacity of the student
scenes, the almost material presentation of the dirt, fog, occasional beauty and noise of Dublin. But beneath the realism of
the physical description there is a network of relations which
are symbolical. The sum total of the experience expressed in
the novel is to be grasped by attention not only to statement—
"Stephen thought," "Stephen saw," "Stephen felt"—but to varying
degrees of obliquity, to the nexus of connections between different aspects [356] of Stephen's life, to the different stresses laid
from time to time on the same phenomena, to the telling juxtaposition of incidents in a deliberate symbolical pattern.

In establishing the considered seriousness with which Joyce
employed various techniques in the *Portrait* the early draft, *Stephen Hero*, can be of considerable assistance. Joyce's reworking
of the material in the early book was far more than an economical
pruning designed to make the long-winded *Stephen Hero* acceptable to a publisher. *Stephen Hero* may be ransacked legiti-
mately by the biographer of Joyce: the *Portrait* can only suffer
from a reading which keeps Joyce in the forefront of attention.
But both works employ the same raw material and to consider
the changes which Joyce makes, the different functions which
the same characters, incidents and places are induced to fulfil
in the later book, is to gain some insight into the manner in
which the modern artist achieves unity and universality by a

dependence on technique. Since only a fragment of *Stephen Hero* has survived—about two hundred printed pages, covering much the same ground as the last ninety pages of the *Portrait*—I shall restrict this note to that part of the novel for which we have the early draft.

Theodore Spencer pointed out in his introduction to *Stephen Hero* that there are in that work "five main themes, . . . Stephen's family; his friends, male and female; the life of Dublin; Catholicism; Art." (*SH*, 13) In the *Portrait* the last-mentioned is the only theme, and it is illumined by images of varying richness which may be grouped under the other four heads. In the early work Spencer's first four topics are discussed in detail. Dublin and the Irish peasantry revolt Stephen. He castigates the hypocrisy and illogicality of the political life of Dublin and the power, corruption and decadence of the Church. He produces long arguments in conversation directed against contradictions in the moral and economic order of Irish life after the manner of Ibsen's *Pillars of Society.* "One of your professors in the Medical School who teaches you Sanitary Science . . . is at the same time the landlord of a whole streetful of brothels not a mile away from where we are standing . . ." (*SH*, 65) In the *Portrait* he discards the cloak of the amateur critic of society. He is no longer anxious to express his contempt for Irish life and home-grown panaceas. [357] He is not creating out of a desire to see Ireland as it is (that was to come later), but to express the one body of truth his youth had discovered—that a corrupt consciousness is the death of art, that art is the visible life-force of every generation, that the modern age is inimical to art. The Church as a church does not have its turn in the forefront of attention; it becomes an image for one of the forces which impede the attainment of objectivity or threaten the integrity of the artist.

In the last part of Chapter IV, for which there is no corresponding part of the manuscript, Stephen is portrayed accepting his vocation in a series of passages of highly imaginative prose: these supply us with a key to the value of the imagery in the later part of the book. The Church is given the meaning it is

to maintain to the end of *Stephen Hero*. When Stephen asserts
that the duty of the artist is to create from a direct impression
of life hampered neither by human ties nor by the inhuman
"pale service of the altar," (197) he makes a clear distinction
between these two impediments to artistic freedom. The Church
is unequivocally death. But although love and friendship are
dangerous they are also Stephen's subject matter. This is the
ambivalence which gives Dublin and things Irish generally their
symbolical ambiguity and richness in succeeding parts of the
work. In so far as it is Stephen's native soil, an inheritance of
political and spiritual passions, Ireland is a danger: as a microcosm of the human world it must be embraced and known as
a subject. And simply as land, with grass and trees, washed by
the sea, it is a symbol of elemental life. So in the most profound
moment of his youth he portrays himself near "the wild heart
of life." (199) The erotic imagery is identical in significance
with "the seaharvest of shells," the arid grasses and the earth.
The word mortal is used twice of the girl he finds wading. The
word grapples sex to life and therefore to his art; it is set off
against the death-image of the Church. The girl is an angel
"of mortal youth and beauty, an envoy from the fair courts of
life." (200)

The first comparable passages in *Stephen Hero* and the *Portrait* are those dealing with Father Butt, the lighting of the fire,
and the "aesthetic question." In *Stephen Hero* the incident is
prefaced by a series of remarks about Stephen's explorations of
the language which he studies by listening in the streets and [358]
reading Skeat's etymological dictionary. There is an account of
the style of his weekly English composition, his reputation in the
English class, and of Father Butt's encouraging remarks about
the possibility of future publication. It is then reported that Stephen launched into an account of his theories—of which only
the point about the debased value in common usage of the word
"detain" is given. The following morning Stephen finds Father
Butt lighting a fire and the only remark made is in the way of
repartee, "We have the useful arts and the liberal arts." (215)
This is followed by a description of Stephen's love of walking in

the streets, listening and watching, and of his invariable dis-
pleasure on entering the Green and seeing on the far side the
gloomy building of the college.

Father Butt as he appears here and elsewhere in *Stephen Hero*
is portrayed as an enemy. Stephen's respect for him is over-
balanced by the hatred he feels for an obscurantist. It is doubtful
how much more real he is as a person in *Stephen Hero:* in the
Portrait he has certainly more imaginative force. The simple
description in the *Portrait of an Artist* of the humble old man,
an Englishman exiled in Ireland, is much more telling than the
dramatic scenes in *Stephen Hero* in which the priest is portrayed
as a severe and destructive critic.

The two morning conversations with Father Butt find their
way into the *Portrait,* but not in their own right: they focus
attention on the powers of the priesthood and its hostility to
originality. Fused into one encounter and prefaced by Stephen's
silent soliloquy as he walks through the Dublin streets on the
way to the college, they become part of a complex expression
of the artist's reaction to certain aspects of experience. As he
walks through the city Stephen recalls the story of the girl at
the cottage door asking Davin to be her lover. He meets an
Irish flower-seller with "young-blue eyes" (213): he finds Stephen's Green "fragrant of rain giving forth its mortal odour."
(214) The reflective interspersions which surround Stephen's
conversation with Father Butt evoke a contrasting atmosphere.
The metaphorical significance of the Jesuit college is placed in
the epithets chilly, grey, dusty, lean, pale, loveless and mortified.
Dublin is here an image of life and Catholicism of the living
death which is an insensitive and corrupted consciousness.
"Or [359] was the Jesuit house extra-territorial and was he walking among aliens?" (215)

It would be quite mistaken to imagine that the difference
between these incidents in the two versions is due to the exercise
of a rigorous economy in the second. In *Stephen Hero* the al-
tercation with Father Butt, though divided between two successive mornings, amounts to only one page of the text. In the
Portrait, excluding the closely related episodes which precede it,
the incident occupies seven pages. Here Joyce has actually ex-

panded his material with the obvious intention of creating a balanced set of metaphors. The conversation about the "tundish" (funnel) is completely new and gives fresh emphasis to the native/foreign imagery. Father Butt is not only a priest but "a poor Englishman in Ireland." (220) In the extracts from his diary which bring the book to a close Stephen notes that this word "tundish," which is unknown to Father Butt, is good old blunt English. Stephen turns away from the Irish flower-seller before she offers her wares "to a tourist from England or a student of Trinity." (214)

While Catholicism has a constant symbolical value, Ireland and Dublin shift and fluctuate in significance. When not being contrasted with the Church, Ireland is "the old sow that eats her farrow," (238) an importunate allegiance which the artist cannot entertain. Sex and friends have a similarly fluctuating significance. Like Ireland, sex may be thought of as a force of life or as a form of slavery. It is with the latter significance that Emma Clery is most often introduced in the last book of the *Portrait*. It is an aspect of the unity and impersonality of the later work that even she is viewed strictly in relation to Stephen as artist. So regarded she has strong associations with the other powerful symbols of artistic death and encumbrance, the Church and Irish Nationalism. She flirts with a priest and learns Irish. In his meditations on the girl Stephen contrasts himself with the Church and regards it as his successful rival. "To him [the priest] she would unveil her soul's shy nakedness, to one who was but schooled in the discharging of a formal rite rather than to him, a priest of the eternal imagination, transmuting the daily bread of experience into the radiant body of everliving life." (259-260)

A glance at *Stephen Hero* will again supply us with our proof [360] of the singleness of purpose and objectivity of the later work. In the earlier book Stephen is in love, after an adolescent fashion, with Emma Clery, and his preoccupation with art is a minor attribute of his whole personality; it is simply as a proud and volatile youth that he woos Emma and ponders her reaction to himself. "Emma allowed him to see her home several times but she did not seem to have reserved herself for

him. The youth was piqued at this for above all things he hated
to be compared with others." (*SH*, 66) And as for his artistic
interests—"She treated femininely everything that young men
are supposed to regard as serious but she made polite exception
for Stephen himself and for the Gaelic revival." (*SH*, 67) In
Stephen Hero Emma is a person: she is described in action and
appears in different situations in widely separated parts of the
story. Her flirtation with a priest, for example, is described just
as it happened one evening at the Daniels'. In the *Portrait* E. C.
is a symbol of ambivalent significance; she is merged with other
images of the "batlike soul" of Ireland, "waking to consciousness
of itself in darkness and secrecy," (259) for Stephen appreciates
the possibility of piercing through her to the consciousness of
his race, while aware of those limitations in her which Ireland
has imposed and from which he himself must escape. In his
recollections of this girl Stephen sees her beauty at the same
moment as he remembers her "with dove's eyes" (258) flattered
by the attentions of a priest. The Emma of the *Portrait* is subordinated to the claims of a larger subject. He leaves her along
with other encumbrances to his art and carefully retains or
invents links between her and these encumbrances.

In *Stephen Hero* the artist's family is treated in considerable
detail, as are his friends at University College. They have each
an independent life of their own, and are dramatically presented
as they cross Stephen's self-blazed path. In the *Portrait* they are
symbols: the demands of the symbolical pattern break down
their independence of each other and show them linked together
by religious, ideological or personal ties. Stephen's antipathy is
no longer personal: it is now an expression of the dilemma of
the post-Renaissance artist in terms of the life and death symbolism through which Joyce has chosen to project his vision.
Stephen's mother is a woman to whom he is expected [361] to
bow his mind. She intercedes with him on behalf of the Church,
and his friend Cranly constitutes himself her advocate. And
Cranly is coupled with Emma: they are cut off together. In
Stephen Hero Cranly does not intercede with Stephen on behalf
of his mother, nor is he Stephen's successor in Emma's interest.
It is clearly a neat tying together of loose metaphorical threads.

Harry Levin has complained that Stephen's mother is lost in the *Portrait* and the drama of her personal claims on her son sacrificed. While the Easter-duty scene in *Stephen Hero* is highly dramatic and humorous—"The next time he [your confessor] asks you 'What is that mistaken young man, that unfortunate boy doing?,' you can answer, 'I don't know, father. I asked him and he said I was to tell the priest he was making a torpedo'" (*SH*, 210)—it must be admitted that it is a very high degree of art that has subordinated so personal a struggle to the demands of unity and proportion. The loss of varied personality in the later work is the opposite of increasing self-centredness in Joyce. As Stephen records his likes and his dislikes and stresses the inferiority of all the other inhabitants of his world, we see clearly that the theme of the book was himself. "The young men in the class laughed and Stephen as he looked contemptuously at the laughing faces thought of a self-submersive reptile. No one would listen to his theories; no one was interested in art." (*SH*, 33-34) This self-regarding tone almost disappears in the later work.

Cranly, who wavers in Stephen's affection and finally loses it, is depicted as contrasting rudely as an Irishman with what Stephen admires in Ireland: he is also associated with those characteristics of women which have been condemned as a bar to artistic activity. His speech, contrasted with the romantic tones and occasional beauties of Davin's, is suggestive of "a bleak decaying seaport" or "a Wicklow pulpit." (228) During his last friendly conversation with him Stephen reflects that Cranly "felt then the sufferings of women, the weaknesses of their bodies and souls: and would shield them with a strong and resolute arm and bow his mind to them. Away then it is time to go." (289) The end of this friendship in *Stephen Hero* is quite different. The aspects of the friendship which relate to Stephen's art play a small part in it. Its end is forecast by Maurice in conversation with Stephen. "He will grow to dislike you when [362] you begin to play the god to someone else. He will give you nothing in exchange for what you give him whether he has it or not because his character is naturally overbearing." (*SH*, 145) And when the break does indeed come its cause is personal jealousy. "He fancied, moreover, that he detected in Cranly's attitude towards him a certain hostility, arising out of a thwarted desire to imitate." (*SH*, 209)

But the value assigned to sexual love in the *Portrait* is not impaired by the condemnation of Cranly for his attitude to women and his relations with Emma. In the extracts from Stephen's diary which bring the book to a close, Stephen remembers Cranly's parentage. "Told me once in a moment of thoughtlessness, his father was sixty-one when he was born . . . But his mother? Very young or very old? Hardly the first. If so, Cranly would not have spoken as he did. Old then. Probably, and neglected. Hence Cranly's despair of soul: the child of exhausted loins." (293) And later this is more firmly built into the metaphorical pattern of life and death. "Ay. And let the dead marry the dead." (293) Emma's metaphorical association with Cranly is also fixed in Stephen's last remarks on her. He records that his last conversation with her takes place in Grafton Street and is terminated by one of his dramatic gestures, "I must have looked like a fellow throwing a handful of peas into the air . . . She shook hands a moment after." (298) *Stephen Hero* throws some light on this. In the early work Stephen unfolds to a sceptically bored and cryptic Cranly his belief that there should be an art of gesture.

> Of course I don't mean art of gesture in the sense that the elocution professor understands the word. For him a gesture is an emphasis. I mean a rhythm. You know the song "Come unto these yellow sands"?
> —No—
> This is it, said the youth making a graceful anapaestic gesture with each arm. That's the rhythm, do you see?
> —Yes—
> I would like to go out into the middle of Grafton St. some day and make gestures in the middle of the street.
> —I'd like to see that— [363]
> —There is no reason why life should lose all grace and nobility. . . . (*SH*, 184)

The metamorphosis perhaps most indicative of Joyce's increasing humanity and objectivity is that undergone by Madden. In

Stephen Hero Madden is the young Fenian dedicated to the freedom of Ireland. Stephen despises him. He is depicted as a personally ambitious, sliding and stupid young man. It is Madden who shows Stephen two English poems by Hughes which are so inept that they occasion "a long staining blush of anger." (*SH*, 83) The Madden of *Stephen Hero* becomes the Davin of the *Portrait*, descended from Mat Davin the athlete, with an imagination nourished by the broken lights of Irish myth. His speech is beautiful. He is a sort of personification, a doubtful admission of the possibility of innocence and simple idealism. The fear and hatred of ignorance and stupidity remain, these qualities being personified by the Irish peasant, with "his red-rimmed, horny eyes." (298) But it is Davin who tells Stephen the story of the peasant woman asking him to her bed and it is Davin whose hands appear to him as he broods on his father's story of the incestuous love of Forster's ancestors. "Why were they not Cranly's hands? Had Davin's simplicity and innocence stung him more secretly?" (269) And it is Davin whom Stephen tells that "the shortest way to Tara is via Holyhead." (296) [364]

BARBARA SEWARD

The Artist and the Rose

TO EVEN THE CASUAL READER of James Joyce it must soon become apparent that the rose is a recurrent symbol in both *A Portrait of the Artist as a Young Man* and *Ulysses*. Its central importance

Reprinted by permission of the University of Toronto Press and of Mr. John P. Seward on behalf of his daughter, the late Barbara Seward (Mrs. Walter Price). The essay originally appeared in the *University of Toronto Quarterly* in January, 1957. References to *A Portrait* are to P-2.

in *Ulysses* as a symbol of Molly Bloom has been adequately demonstrated,[1] and the interrelationship between the *Portrait* and *Ulysses* is universally acknowledged. It is therefore surprising that no one has yet seen fit to examine the flower's complex function in the earlier novel. Taking a place beside water and birds as one of the *Portrait*'s leading symbols, the rose plays a far from negligible role in the development of both structure and theme. Roses blossom at crucial stages of Stephen Dedalus's experience in association with three of his principal concerns: women, religion, and art. Since his conceptions of all three are ambivalent and inseparable, the use of a symbol capable of suggesting various levels of conscious and unconscious meaning is essential to the full expression of his emotional state. Beyond this, his emotional state itself is dynamic and fluctuating, so that the rose takes on additional significance in conveying vital changes in attitudes and reactions determining Stephen's course on the road to maturity.

Joyce, as we know, saw analogies everywhere. In choosing the rose as a dominant symbol for Stephen's intricate emotions, he was choosing a symbol admirably suited to suggesting a complex of these analogies. For centuries the rose has served as emblem of many of man's fundamental concerns, among them those concerns most significant to Stephen. As the flower of beautiful women, it has long been allied with both sensual and spiritual love; and association with the beauty of women is but a short step from association of the rose with the beauty of art. Further, Joyce, who was impressed by such symbolic achievements as the four-fold allegory of Dante's *Comedy* or the indefinite suggestiveness of the early Yeats, could find in these precursors conspicuous roses used as symbols of women, religion, and art. With traditional analogies [180] supporting and enhancing private preoccupations, he was able to enrich Stephen's rose by introducing evocations of objective beliefs into the interplay of subtle subjective impressions.

The symbol's association with Stephen is made on the very first page of the *Portrait*. This in itself is surely an indication of

---

[1] William York Tindall, "Dante and Mrs. Bloom," *Accent*, XI (Spring, 1951), 85-92.

its intended importance; for Joyce, who was notably exacting about every word and the position of every word in his books, was anything but negligent of his opening pages. Here Stephen learns a song about a rose:

> *Oh, the wild rose blossoms*
> *On the little green place.*
> He sang that song. That was his song.
> *Oh, the green wothe botheth.* (1)

The little green place clearly suggests Ireland, while the wild rose hardly less clearly suggests Stephen, who is at this time in the blossoming stage, who specifically claims the song as "his," and who is to be essentially rebellious, alone, and in his own terms "wild" throughout his Irish youth. With the green rose in the child's own version of the song, hints of Stephen's artistic inclinations are introduced. By altering the wording he is exercising incipient creativity, and by positing a green rose he is creating in imagination that which does not exist elsewhere. As a flower whose colour is that of Ireland and whose creation is dependent upon Stephen's imagination, the green rose of the child's initial artistic effort acts as a symbolic foreshadowing of the young man's final determination "to forge in the smithy of my soul the uncreated conscience of my race." (299)

The green rose also appears to be related to Stephen's emotional condition. Green is suggestive of fertility and therefore of potentiality, but at the same time implies present unripeness or immaturity. In this respect the flower is associated not only with Stephen's youth but also with his persistent desire to discover an impossible, subjective ideal in the actual world. The association is made specific when, during Stephen's first school experience, the War of the Roses in his mathematics class calls his song to mind again (8): "But you could not have a green rose. But perhaps somewhere in the world you could." And his thought here is simply an early expression of the longing that later dominates his adolescence, "to meet in the real world the unsubstantial image which his soul so constantly beheld." (71)

This interpretation is supported by the fact that Stephen's fantasies of Mercedes, the "unsubstantial image" in question,

always have a rose [181] garden for their setting. The ideal of
Mercedes was derived from Stephen's reading *The Count of
Monte Cristo* and identifying himself with the novel's hero in
his love for the girl of that name. In fact, Stephen's fantasy
owes to Dumas almost every romantic detail: a lady who embodies all goodness and virtue, a love that will weather untold
hardships, and, when his dream shall have been betrayed, a
triumph no less glorious than the passion that provokes it. But
Stephen's ideal is framed with roses which do not appear in
Dumas: "Outside Blackrock, on the road that led to the mountains, stood a small whitewashed house in the garden of which
grew many rosebushes: and in this house, he told himself, another
Mercedes lived." (68) Since no rose garden is to be found in
Dumas (although almost all else down to the whitewash is Dumas), Joyce undoubtedly adds it with symbolic intent. Through
associating Mercedes with roses he is able to make more evident
her relation to other women in the *Portrait* who are also associated with roses. Further, his use of symbolism in the treatment
of Mercedes enables him to express more than a single meaning
and thus to suggest the complexity of young Stephen's attitude
towards women.

The ideal lady in her rose garden is on one level reminiscent
of Beatrice, who leads Dante to the rose of heaven and is herself
enthroned on one of its petals. Other features of Stephen's fantasy support this association. The Count of Monte Cristo, with
whom Stephen identifies himself, is named Edmond Dantes. In
addition to the likeness of names, both Dante and Dantes were
proud and angry exiles, intense moral idealists, and devoted
lovers. In each, love for the lady remained chaste and unconsum-
mated; in each it served as moral guide throughout an otherwise
troubled life.[2] Then, reinforcing the clear Dantesque parallels
to *The Count of Monte Cristo* (which Joyce, if not Dumas, was
surely aware of), are two further parallels to Dante, pointed

---

[2] Dantes, throughout his long career of vengeance, regarded himself as a
veritable agent of Providence sent to punish his betrayers. Mercedes, the
chief motive behind his fierce justice, was alone able to temper his vengeful
excesses when they threatened the life of her innocent son.

up by Joycean modifications of Dumas. While Dantes is in his teens at the time of falling in love with Mercedes, Stephen, like Dante, is still a child. More important, while Dantes' Mercedes lives on a promontory, Stephen's lives on a road leading to mountains. The substitution of mountains for promontory seems deliberate: Dante's attempt to climb the holy hill when he lost his way in the dark wood of sense and his success in climbing Purgatory by grace imparted through Beatrice both find their echo in Stephen's later youth when he, lost in his own dark wood, experiences relief in remembering his early vision of purity: (111-112) [182] "In the pauses of his desire, when the luxury that was wasting him gave room to a softer languor, the image of Mercedes traversed the background of his memory. He saw again the small white house and the garden of rosebushes on the road that led to the mountains."

The association of Mercedes with roses that have perceptible Dantesque hues links her to other rose-women in the *Portrait* who are also in some sense Beatrice-like. Whether secular or spiritual, the later roses have roots in Mercedes' garden, for Stephen's childhood fantasy-woman embodies within herself the seeds of those to follow. First among her descendants is the Virgin herself. As a chaste, ennobling influence Mercedes plays a role in Stephen's consciousness (as does Beatrice in Dante's) which is similar in some ways to that of Mary. During his struggles with lust and guilt, when memories of Mercedes brought transitory balm, the idea of the Virgin was a still more potent source of inspiration and relief. Since the rose is traditionally symbolic of the Virgin as well as of womankind, Stephen's experience of penance as expressed in prayers to Mary is appropriately conveyed by the same flower that has been associated with his earlier female idol: "his prayers ascended to heaven from his purified heart like perfume streaming upwards from a heart of white rose." (168) The use of rose symbolism for both Mary and Mercedes to evoke analogous moods of elevated serenity makes apparent a parallel between Stephen's divine and earthly ideals.

But the correspondence between ideals and roses is devious.

While Stephen's conscious worship of chastity at this time is strongly influenced by his unquestioning Catholicism,[3] his unconscious reactions to womankind are not entirely in accord with Catholic ideals. In a novel told entirely from Stephen's conscious point of view, such unconscious reactions must be conveyed primarily by symbolic indirection. The roses of Mercedes and the Virgin indicate Stephen's suppressed sensual desires as well as his acknowledged admiration for holiness. Mercedes' dwelling in a garden of rosebushes, through suggesting the idealized sexuality of the *Roman de la Rose,* clarifies the nature of the "strange unrest" Stephen felt when he "brooded upon her image." (70) And the "heart of white rose" he offers to the Virgin at the end of the religious retreat ironically recalls his sensations at its outset: "Stephen's heart had withered up like a flower of the desert that feels the simoom coming from afar." (123)

Such intimations of unconscious sexual stirrings are reinforced by [183] association with other symbols. Stephen's painful, ascetic attempts to transform the "withered" flower of his sensual nature into the purified "white rose" of the Virgin evoke the novel's recurrent associations of white, the colour of Catholic purity, with cold, dank, unpleasant things.[4] More specifically, the Virgin's flower recalls the only other white rose in the *Portrait,* that worn by Stephen during the early War of the Roses in his mathematics class. On this occasion Stephen's white rose is defeated by the opposing red rose, just as later his religious ideal of chastity, associated with the Virgin's white rose, was to be defeated by a victorious sensual ideal, associated with the more commonly secular red rose.

Red and white roses, then, symbolize Stephen's conflict between the flesh and the spirit. It is notable that Joyce assigned no colour to the roses surrounding Mercedes, and this is possibly because she is Stephen's "unsubstantial image," the green rose of the child's still undefined longing. Certainly the fantasy of Mercedes contains in embryo both religious and profane poles

[3] An unresolved Oedipus complex also seems to be influential. In Freudian theory guilt over unconscious incestuous desires often results in a dichotomizing of women into pure women, placed in the mother category, and women who are sexually attractive but therefore evil.

[4] See Hugh Kenner, "The Portrait in Perspective," pp. 25-60.

of Stephen's conflict, while his subsequent worship of the Virgin represents his first conscious choice between opposites. Since the choice is contrary to his nature, his repudiation of the Virgin in favour of a secular ideal is almost inevitable. Significantly, his reversal, the climax of the book, again reminds us of Mercedes and this time culminates in a gigantic red rose.

Through his encounter with the girl on the beach Stephen is converted from the worship of things divine to the worship of things earthly. The significance of this inverted conversion is to a great extent communicated by symbolism which expresses opposition to Catholicism through association with a markedly secular rose. Throughout the experience, Stephen's most frequent adjective is "wild," indicating both rebellion and release, and echoing the "wild rose" with which he identified himself in infancy. The girl, recalling Mercedes, is suggestive of Beatrice: like Beatrice, she has come as a messenger of ultimate truth, and, like Beatrice, she will guide Stephen by her eyes to his vision of ineffable glory. But going beyond Mercedes, the girl on the beach is a now avowedly sensual Beatrice, and the vision to which her inspiration leads will be an avowedly secular vision: "Her eyes had called him and his soul had leaped at the call. . . . A wild angel had appeared to him, the angel of mortal youth and beauty, an envoy from the fair courts of life to throw open before him in an instant of ecstasy the gates of all the ways of error and glory." (200)

Stephen's "instant of ecstasy" follows almost immediately his experience of the girl. He is no longer near her (as Dante was no longer [184] beside Beatrice in his final ecstasy), but "her image had passed into his soul for ever." (200) Lying down upon the beach to calm his agitation, he is granted a vision of a rose of heavenly light which is a temporal image of Dante's rose of God (200-201):

> His eyelids trembled . . . as if they felt the strange light of some new world . . . fantastic, dim, uncertain as under sea, traversed by cloudy shapes and beings. A world, a glimmer, or a flower? Glimmering and trembling, trembling and unfolding, a breaking light, an opening flower, it spread in endless succession to itself, breaking in full crimson and unfolding and fading

to palest rose, leaf by leaf and wave of light by wave of light, flooding all the heavens with its soft flushes.

Stephen's ecstasy is brief and Dante's is protracted, so that a thorough comparison between the two would necessitate a reading of the *Paradiso's* last four cantos. Nevertheless, it is possible to gain some conception of the close parallel (in light, water imagery, shapes and beings, vast opening flower) from Dante's description of the rose's initial manifestation to him (XXX, 106-117):

> *Fassi di raggio tutta sua parvenza*
> *riflesso al sommo del Mobile Primo, . . .*
> *E come clivo in acqua di suo imo*
> *si specchia. . . .*
> *sì soprastando al lume intorno intorno*
> *vidi specchiarsi in più di mille soglie,*
> *quanto di noi lassù fatto ha ritorno.*
> *E se l' infimo grado in sè raccoglie*
> *sì grande lume, quant' è la larghezza*
> *di questa rosa nell' estreme foglie?*

Joyce's presentation of Stephen's climactic vision through symbolism strongly reminiscent of the *Paradiso* emphasizes the simultaneous opposition and kinship between Stephen's experience and Dante's. Stephen being inspired by primarily sensual feelings, the crimson rose represents his supreme affirmation of the "wonder of mortal beauty," in direct contrast to Dante's white rose of spiritual beauty. At the same time the analogy with Dante's rose enhances the tremendous significance of Stephen's. It is notable that Stephen, like Molly Bloom and Anna Livia, is granted his moment of supreme affirmation in the borderland between sleep and waking when the relaxation of the critical intellect presumably facilitates cosmic insights.[5] His twilight vision of a Dantesque rose of mortal glory, symbolizing his new comprehension of life's meaning, clearly implies that Stephen's

[5] Cf. Yeats's "moment when we are both asleep and awake . . . in which the mind liberated from the pressure of the will is unfolded in symbols"— *Essays* (New York, 1924), 193; and T. S. Eliot's visionary lady "who moves in the time between sleeping and waking" (*Ash Wednesday*).

ecstasy has for him something of the transcendent import that Dante's had for Dante.

Beneath the experience, however, lurks an ironic undertone that [185] becomes magnified in retrospect. The immediate effect of Stephen's conversion to the worship of mortal beauty is his realization of his true vocation. Dedication to art fills the place left vacant by his repudiation of the priesthood, and after developing an aesthetic theory applying Thomistic concepts to art for art's sake doctrine, Stephen is ready to write a poem putting theory into practice. The symbolic atmosphere surrounding the creation of this poem parallels that of his experience on the beach in almost every detail. Again inspired by a girl who is for the moment the centre of Stephen's emotional universe, the poem is composed in a like state of visionary ecstasy expressed by clouds, water, light, and most notably another Dantesque rose. Since this experience is more extensive and complex than its earlier counterpart, a close analysis of the symbolism through which it is conveyed illuminates the real conflict underlying Stephen's attitude and the irony of his ecstatic conviction.

Stephen's second vision simultaneously encompasses the three main levels of meaning associated with the rose: religion, woman, and art. Like its predecessor, it takes place in the borderland between dream and waking and unfolds in cloudlike rays of rosy light (254-255):

> Over his limbs in sleep pale cool waves of light had passed. He lay still, as if his soul lay amid cool waters. . . . His mind was waking slowly to a tremulous morning knowledge, a morning inspiration. . . . In a dream or vision he had known the ecstasy of seraphic life. . . . The instant flashed forth like a point of light and now from cloud on cloud of vague circumstance confused form was veiling softly its afterglow . . . deepening to a rose and ardent light.

Here the *Paradiso* is recalled by the imagery of watery light at the outset of Stephen's vision as well as by the emerging rose. Just as Dante's mystic rose of heaven first appeared to him as a river of light (*E. vidi lume in forma di riviera: Par.* XXX, 61), so Stephen's second Dantesque rose now evolves from a dream-like impression of light and waters.[6] The inescapable analogy with Dante is again made partly to mark the comparison between Stephen's experience of mortal beauty and Dante's of heavenly beauty. But as a symbol of specifically creative ecstasy, the rose of the *Paradiso* is still more suggestive. Not only is it the culmination of one of the world's greatest literary creations, but it also symbolizes therein the divine fulfilment of God's eternal creation. Stephen's exalted conception of the artist could scarcely have found more appropriate expression.

As the vision unfolds, further implications for art develop. Stephen's rose, like Dante's, becomes the Virgin's flower. And, in accord with [186] Stephen's customary conversion of spiritual entities to secular uses, the Virgin herself becomes associated with his markedly secular theory of art. The art for art's sake doctrine, already presented explicitly in Stephen's talk with Lynch (241-250), is here presented by symbolic indirection. The Annunciation is made to symbolize artistic inspiration (255): "O! in the virgin womb of the imagination the word was made flesh. Gabriel the seraph had come to the virgin's chamber." And the Annunciation as symbol of poetic inspiration is presently complemented by the Eucharist, symbol of poetic composition (260): ". . . transmuting the daily bread of experience into the radiant body of everliving life." Following Stephen's aesthetic theory, artistic creation is presented as a dual process in which inspiration first makes the word flesh (i.e., gives rise to an "epiphany" or illuminating insight), and artistic discipline then makes the flesh word (i.e., gives the insight "wholeness, harmony, and radiance," thereby moulding it into an aesthetic form).

It is notable that these concepts, here associated with Dante's flower of heaven and Mary, are again associated with a rose by Stephen's remarks in *Ulysses* (385): "Desire's wind blasts the thorntree but after it becomes from a bramblebush to be a rose upon the rood of time. . . . In woman's womb word is made

[6] Water here also suggests rebirth, as has Stephen's wading in the first vision. His poem's completion employs similar imagery to indicate his rebirth as artist through acceptance of sex (262): "Her nakedness . . . enfolded him like water with a liquid life . . . the liquid letters of speech . . . flowed forth over his brain."

flesh but in the spirit of the maker all flesh that passes becomes the word that shall not pass away." Stephen, still identifying the artist with the divine Creator, still associates the rose with the process of artistic creation. Although he has now substituted Yeats's "rose upon the rood of time" for Dante's rose of heaven, there is small difference in effect. For Yeats's rose of Eternal Beauty, like Dante's rose of Eternity, symbolizes the beginning and end of art and life; and Yeats, like Dante, believed (or tried to believe) that art was a bodying forth of spiritual mysteries. Joyce, seeking symbolic expression for Stephen's secular aesthetics, continues to choose the most transcendental of literary roses to emphasize the supreme importance to Stephen of his doctrine of earthly beauty in art.

Beauty has become Stephen's highest value in life as well. Since beauty throughout the *Portrait* has been associated with women at least as much as with art, and since the sensual charm of a woman has been directly responsible for Stephen's conversion to mortal beauty, it is not surprising to find yet another woman involved in his creation of a poem. Again the rose as the Virgin's flower is important, and here the opposition to Dante is most strongly marked. Stephen's girl, who has inspired his creative ecstasy, is a virgin and a Catholic, "her life . . . a simple rosary of hours." (254) But in his fantasy she becomes a [187] temptress awakening man's lust, a universal embodiment of all that is opposed to Mary (255):

> That rose and ardent light was her strange wilful heart, strange that no man had known or would know, wilful from before the beginning of the world: and lured by that ardent roselike glow the choirs of the seraphim were falling from heaven. . . . Its rays burned up the world, consumed the hearts of men and angels: the rays from the rose that was her wilful heart.

In the sacrilegious spirit of the *fin de siècle*, this passage recalls the "mystical rose of the mire" of Swinburne's "Dolores" or the "rose that is rooted in hell" of Arthur Symons's "Rosa Flammae." Stephen, still preoccupied with the religion he is repudiating, has used Dantesque imagery to translate his sexual desire into anti-Catholic terms and to create of its object an inverted Virgin who is as potent a force for damnation as Mary is for salvation.

His conceptions of art and woman are, then, at this time inseparable. Both are aesthetic, sensual, and anti-Catholic, and both rest on the same infirm emotional foundation. Two further analogies complement the analogy with Dante in revealing the attitudes underlyng Stephen's ecstasy. His idealized rose-woman, existing "from before the beginning of the world" and sending forth rays of beauty that "consumed the hearts of men and angels," echoes Yeats's "Rose of the World," who existed before there were angels "or any hearts to beat" and for whose beauty "Troy passed away in one high funeral gleam." Stephen's rose, like Yeats's, is at once the inspiration of his art, the particular woman to whom he is attracted, and the embodiment of his ideal of beauty; and Stephen, like Yeats, is limited at this stage by highly subjective, romantic, and immature attitudes which he too is later to repudiate. A passage from Joyce's own early essay on James Clarence Mangan completes the picture. Writing of the moving spirit in Mangan's poetry, Joyce describes it as a feminine symbol of ideal beauty, a "flower of flowers" remarkably similar to Yeats's or Stephen's:

> the presence of an imaginative personality reflecting the light of imaginative beauty is . . . vividly felt. . . . Music and odours and lights are spread about her. . . . Vittoria Colonna and Laura and Beatrice . . . embody one chivalrous idea . . . and she whose white and holy hands have the virtue of enchanted hands, his virgin flower, the flower of flowers, is no less than these an embodiment of that idea.[7]

It is significant that this essay was published in *St. Stephen's* for May 1902, a few months before Joyce's winter flight from Dublin and therefore at approximately the time when the autobiographical Stephen was composing his poem. [188]

Despite his elaborate conversion to mortal beauty, Stephen is still in much the same frame of mind as the child who dreamed of a green rose that couldn't exist. He had set out to discover

[7] Quoted in Herbert Gorman, *James Joyce* (New York, 1948), 76-77. Joyce borrows "flower of flowers" from Mangan's "Dark Rosaleen," a version of the traditional Irish song, allusions to which are also present in Yeats's rose poems.

his "unsubstantial" ideal "in the real world," but sought it in
Virgin and anti-Virgin, heaven and hell, ironically ignoring the
solid earth in between. His adherence to the lush, world-weary
romanticism of the 1890's reflects the introverted adolescence
of his present emotional orientation, while his use of Dante in
expressing rebellion against the Church reveals his continuing
preoccupation with the religion he has rejected. Turning from
the spirit to the flesh, Stephen has simply substituted one side
of his conflict for the other without working out a satisfactory
resolution. His reaction to woman is now a purely sensual thing
and his artistic ideal does not go beyond the aesthete's hollow
shell of formal beauty. He himself is dimly conscious of dissatisfaction when, at the very pinnacle of creative ecstasy, inspiration suddenly fails him (260):

> The full morning light had come . . . he knew that all around
> him life was about to awaken in common noises, hoarse voices,
> sleepy prayers. Shrinking from that life he turned towards the
> wall . . . staring at the great overblown scarlet flowers of the
> tattered wallpaper. . . . Weary! Weary! He too was weary of
> ardent ways.

But he remains unconscious of the nature of his trouble, also
hinted at in this passage. The awakening of daily life causes
Stephen's roses to appear "overblown" because he cannot yet
come to terms with that life. He is suffering primarily from an
egocentricity that excludes charity, and he will achieve neither
a true resolution of conflicts nor an adequate conception of art
until his discovery of humanity, the subject of *Ulysses*.

A little epiphany towards the close of the *Portrait* illuminates
Stephen's condition and serves almost as a forecast of his course
in *Ulysses*. The epiphany is associated with a woman who is
again a rose. Stephen and Cranly overhear a servant singing
"Rosie O'Grady," and in Stephen's mind she is alternately related
to each of his unreconciled conceptions of woman, the spiritual
and the secular. He first envisions "the figure of woman as she
appears in the liturgy of the church" (288), thereby evoking
the Beatrice-Virgin-Catholic aura of his earlier rose-women. The
image passes and he later thinks of his girl, the rosy temptress

of his recent villanelle, whom he now realizes he is losing to Cranly (289): "Yes; he would go. He could not strive against another. He knew his part." But the singer herself is actually a typical Irish servant, a representative of the ordinary humanity from which egocentric Stephen holds himself aloof. [189]

Cranly, well ahead of Stephen in tolerance and sympathy, unites all these women through the phrase, *"Mulier cantat"*; for in their fundamental kinship, which Stephen fails to comprehend, lies a potential resolution of his difficulties. Commenting on the lyrics of "Rosie O'Grady," Cranly attempts to point out to Stephen the charity that is lacking in his cold art and selfish life (289):

> —There's real poetry for you—he said.—There's real love.—
> He glanced sideways at Stephen with a strange smile and said:
> —Do you consider that poetry? Or do you know what the words mean?—
> —I want to see Rosie first—said Stephen.
> —She's easy to find—Cranly said.

But Stephen is not yet ready to understand, can understand only his own isolation. Not until his comprehension of Molly Bloom, the ultimate rose of human life, will he learn what the words love and poetry mean and find his fulfilment "in the real world." [190]

THE AESTHETIC THEORY

A. D. HOPE

The Esthetic Theory of James Joyce

JAMES JOYCE IS BETTER KNOWN FOR HIS NOVELS than for his theory of art. Yet this theory of art is embodied in his novels and it is important that critics of the novels should understand it because of the light that it throws on the structure and themes of the works themselves. Of course the theory is presented dramatically. It is put into the mouth of Stephen Dedalus, a character in *Ulysses* and in *A Portrait of the Artist as a Young Man,* so that it cannot be strictly attributed to Joyce. But there is plenty to show that Joyce did hold these views at the age at which Stephen is represented to be, and there is no reason to think that he ever changed them.

Joyce goes to Aristotle and to St. Thomas Aquinas for the basis of his theory, though he does not claim to derive it in any systematic way from the work of either. They simply provide him, says Stephen, in *A Portrait of the Artist,* with one or two ideas in the light of which he elaborates his own theory: "If the lamp smokes or smells I shall try to trim it. If it does not give light enough I shall sell it and buy another." (212-213) It is important to remember this in discussing the implications and consequences of Joyce's theory, but it is also true, I think, that the ideas Joyce borrows involve him in accepting certain other features of scholastic philosophy from which these ideas are systematically derived.

Reprinted by permission of the author and the Editor of *Australasian Journal of Psychology and Philosophy,* XXI (December, 1943), where the essay originally appeared. Readers interested in further discussion of Joyce and Thomism should consult William Noon, S. J., *Joyce and Aquinas* (New Haven: Yale University Press, 1957). References to *A Portrait* are to P-5.

The problems with which Stephen Dedalus deals in the last few sections of *A Portrait of the Artist* appear in fairly logical order and form a connected discussion, a fact which is not quite clear owing to the dramatic form in which they are presented. The topics are: [93]

(*a*) the nature of beauty,

(*b*) the nature of a work of art, as distinguished from other beautiful things and from other human products,

(*c*) the general characters of a work of art,

(*d*) the types of works of art and the distinction of literary modes (tragedy and comedy),

(*e*) the conditions of producing a work of art and the nature of the artistic process.

Each of these questions is made to depend on the answer to those preceding[1] it so that the theory, although by no means complete, can be regarded as an attempt at a coherent system.

The crux of this system is the problem of the nature of beauty. The definition given both by Joyce in his notebooks[2] and by Stephen in *A Portrait of the Artist* (211, 236) is that of Aquinas: *Pulcra sunt quae visa placent*,[3] "That is beautiful the apprehension of which pleases," and he links this with Aquinas's definition of the good: *Bonum est in quod tendit appetitus*,[4] "The good is that towards the possession of which an appetite tends." These are Joyce's translations. Beauty in fact is regarded as a particular class of "good." Now the good in Thomistic philosophy forms one of the five "transcendental" properties which all beings possess. The most important of these transcendental properties are unity, truth and goodness. These are not properties in the sense that colour, for instance, is a property of some beings but characters which all things possess in virtue of their relations with other things. To say that a thing is one is, in a way, no more than to say that it is a complete being in itself distinguish-

---

[1] In the order in which I have placed them; the order in which they occur in the book is slightly different.

[2] H. Gorman, *James Joyce: A Definitive Biography*, p. 133.

[3] *Summa Theologica*, I, Q.V, art. 4.

[4] *Ibid.*

able from all the other beings in the universe. To say that it is
true is to say that it is intelligible, and to say that it is good is
to say that it is desired. But if we ask why one being desires
another we find [94] that it does so by the law of its own nature
which disposes it to desire this thing and not another: "that to
which an agent tends definitely must needs be befitting to that
agent, since the latter would not tend to it save on account of
some fittingness thereto. But that which is befitting to a thing
is good for it. Therefore every agent acts for a good." 5 Thus
goodness is not merely a relation in which beings stand to one
another. The agent and its object form a "set" analogous to
that of a wireless receiver and transmitter. It is necessary to
know the nature of both agent and object in order to be able
to say in what respect the object is good, but that is not to say
that by "good" we simply mean a relation in which one stands
to the other. The good *is* the end which the agent seeks in order
to perfect a lack in its own nature. A substance is only to be
called food in view of the fact that it nourishes a specific animal.
And it is in virtue of the fact that the animal seeks to eat this
substance that we call it food. But the character of the substance
does not depend on the animal but on its own nature. When an
archer lets fly at a target, both the archer and the arrow act each
for its appropriate good and that good is the actual target.6 The
properties of the target do not vary and they are determined
by the kind of thing it is in itself. Otherwise we should have to
say that the arrow and the archer aimed at different things.

The beautiful is distinguishable from other kinds of the good
in several ways. The most important of these are: (*a*) the specifically intellectual nature of the beautiful, whereas St. Thomas
uses "the good" to describe the end of *any* activity; 7 (*b*) the
fact that the beautiful has the character rather of a formal than
of a final cause. The good is defined simply as that by which
an appetite is appeased. And everything that acts does so because
it has an appetite. But it pertains to the nature of the beautiful

5 *Summa Contra Gentiles*, Bk. III, Ch. III; English translation by Dominican Fathers; Burns, Oates and Washbourne, 1928. (References are to the
same text throughout this article.)
6 *Summa Contra Gentiles*, Bk. III, Ch. II, p. 4.
7 *Ibid.*

that the appetite in question is appeased by the mere sight or contemplation of its [95] object. This distinction of intellectual from other acts is a fundamental one in the system of Aquinas and it comes up again in connection with Joyce's discussion of the characters of a work of art. For the moment it is enough to say that the intellect is not swayed by the desire and loathing which are characteristic of animal natures but is that part of man in which he transcends his animal nature. The importance of the distinction, as we shall see, is that it allows us to distinguish esthetic and intellectual activities and enjoyments from practical. Aquinas for instance makes a sharp distinction between the senses of taste and smell, appetites which are appeased by sensual gratification, by actual possession of their objects, and those of sight and hearing which are appeased by contemplation of them.[8] So that when Stephen Dedalus says that Aquinas uses the word "visa" to cover esthetic apprehension of all kinds, whether through sight or hearing or through any other avenue of apprehension (236), he is only correctly understood if we remember that Aquinas does not regard all the senses as sharing equally in the intellectual nature. Not that the intellect is without its specific and proper appetite. The beautiful like the true can only be classed as types of the good in so far as they are the objects of some appetite,[9] and as knowledge is an activity it argues an appetite in the agent.

Aquinas connects beauty and goodness in another way. As a thing is said to have an appetite for the good in so far as it is perfected by the attainment of its natural desires, so it is said to have an appetite for the beautiful inasmuch as it is modified, or attains the specific characters of the sort of thing it is, by the exercise of its natural appetite.[10] Aquinas regards all finite beings as in a process of becoming, of self-realisation. Only in complete realisation, when the potential characters of a being in act are perfected by the attainment of the end of its natural activity, does a thing exhibit the wholeness and due [96] proportion of

[8] *Summa Theologiae*, I, Q.XXVII, art. 2; also 1, II, Q.XXXI, art. 6, in which Aquinas deals with the sense of touch.
[9] "Commentary on the Sentences," Bk. I, Dist. XXXI, Q.II, 4.
[10] *De Veritate*, Q.XXII, art. I, 12.

its parts in virtue of which it is called beautiful. Thus the activity of the intellectual nature, which is to know, induces finally the completeness, harmony and due proportion that is beauty in the agent. This is an aspect of Aquinas's doctrine of the unity of the knower and the known in the act of comprehension.

Joyce, however, does not adopt this side of Aquinas's theory, though he seems to touch on it in his treatment of the quality of "Claritas" or radiance which he says a work of art should possess. As far as concerns what he calls the phenomena of artistic conception, artistic gestation and artistic reproduction, he finds Aquinas inadequate. (238)

The second main distinction of the beautiful from the good in Aquinas lies in the fact that an agent is said to be able to seek its ends in virtue of the fact that it is proportioned to those ends. The senses, for instance, are duly proportioned to their objects and are gratified by virtue of a similarity in themselves to those objects.

> The sensitive object affects the sense by its quality so as to impress itself upon it like the form of the seal impressed on wax. If we were to suppose the wax conscious, then in consciously taking on the form of the seal it would know the shape of the seal by becoming it in terms of itself. This image, though employed by St. Thomas, is inadequate, as the process is on a higher level than that of material analogy, but it serves to bring out the two sides in sensation, the part played by the external object and the immanent activity implied in sensation. . . .[11]

In man sensation is accompanied and completed by intellectual act which it furnishes with the means by which, by abstraction, the formal structure of things is made clear. For a being to become intelligible, however, it must exhibit four types of cause, material, efficient, final and formal. The object of sense is called good because it is the object of the sensory appetite without which sensation would not be possible. The good has the character of a final cause. But we call it beautiful inasmuch as the senses are gratified by the [97] correspondence of a certain form in the object with the induced form in the subject. Without

[11] M. C. D'Arcy, "Thomas Aquinas"; O.U.P., 1937, p. 203.

this correspondence of forms sensation would not be possible. So that the beautiful has the character of a formal cause.[12]

This view of the nature of beauty has two important consequences for esthetic theory, though Aquinas nowhere develops a systematic esthetic theory himself.

In the first place it involves a clear contradiction of the popular view that some things are intrinsically ugly, and of the view that, if art is concerned with the beautiful, some subjects are improper for the artist. On the contrary, whatever is intelligible is beautiful since a thing is beautiful in so far as it is capable of being the object of intellectual contemplation. Ugliness, like all forms of evil, must consist in defect. It must consist in things of incomplete or discordant, irrational or contradictory nature of which complete intellectual comprehension is impossible. In nature it will rarely, if ever, arise, but in works of art, owing to the defects of man's intellectual nature and the confusing irrelevancy introduced by his animal passions,[13] it will frequently arise.

Joyce's notebooks written at Pola in 1904 [14] show that he realised and extended this implication of Thomism. Like Aquinas he divides the act of apprehension into two parts: simple perception and recognition. The first, in Aquinas, is the activity of the *sensus communis* which differentiates and compares the impressions of the various senses. This is the *species impressa* which is largely passive perception. Partly the work of memory and partly the work of the *intellectus agens,* however, is a second activity by which the universal and formal characters of experience are presented to the mind as a *species intelligibilis.* Joyce is not necessarily committed to this machinery but it certainly seems to underlie his division of the act of apprehension. The importance of his view is that all objects, in so far as they satisfy the separate [98] activities of the act of apprehension, must be said to be beautiful. "Consequently even the most hideous object may be said to be beautiful for this reason (viz. that it is rec-

[12] *Summa Theologica,* I, Q.V, art. 4, 1.
[13] *Summa Theologica,* 2, II, Q.CLXXX, art. 2.
[14] Gorman, *op. cit.,* pp. 133-135.

ognised) as it is *a priori* said to be beautiful in so far as it encounters the activity of simple perception.[15]

It is hardly necessary to point out the importance of this view
in connection with the criticism so often levelled at *Ulysses* that
it deals with subjects improper to a work of art. Joyce's view
is precisely that nothing is improper to art in so far as its treatment exhibits certain general characters. In themselves all natural objects are potentially beautiful. On the other hand, unless
we understand Joyce to accept Aquinas's theory of knowledge,
he would appear to be putting forward a relational theory of
the beautiful. "Beauty is that quality of a sensible object in virtue of which its apprehension pleases or satisfies the esthetic
appetite which desires to apprehend the most satisfying relations of the sensible." [16]

For it is only the assumption that there is either a hierarchy
of appetites or a clear distinction between lower and higher
appetites that gives us a criterion of "the most satisfying relations of the sensible." If all appetites are on an equal footing
any of the qualities which satisfy them in the highest degree
would, by definition, be those which the esthetic appetite desires
to apprehend. And, if not, then the statement means no more
than: Beauty is that quality of a sensible object which satisfies
the appetite for Beauty. But in fact Joyce does seem to make
a distinction between intellectual and other appetites similar
to that made by Aquinas:

> The true and the beautiful are spiritually possessed; the true
> by intellection, the beautiful by apprehension, and the appetites
> which desire to possess them, the intellectual and esthetic ap-
> petites, are [99] therefore spiritual appetites.[17]

Elsewhere of course Joyce defines beauty not in terms of esthetic
appetite, but in terms of the qualities themselves which a beauti-

[15] *Ibid.*, p. 134.
[16] *Ibid.*, p. 133.
[17] *Ibid.* See also *A Portrait of the Artist:* "The desire and loathing excited
by improper esthetic means are really not esthetic emotions not only because
they are kinetic in character, but also because they are not more than physical. Our flesh shrinks from what it dreads and responds to the stimulus of
what it desires by a purely reflex action of the nervous system." (234)

ful object must possess, the qualities of wholeness, proportion
and radiance, and it is on his definition of these that the real
test of whether his view of esthetics is a relational one, must
finally depend.

The second important consequence of Aquinas's theory of
beauty lies in this clear distinction between the animal appetites
and the intellectual or contemplative appetites. Aquinas regards
man as a link in the hierarchy of beings between the purely
intellectual and spiritual beings and the material things. He
partakes of both natures. Inanimate objects are moved by external forces; living creatures of a lower sort move themselves
but their activity is tied to specific ends outside the creature
and they are not able to modify their activity because it is not
conscious of its ends. Higher animals, bound by instinctive behavior as they are, are, however, conscious and able to modify
their behaviour in a limited way. But as they are unable to
reflect on their behaviour and unable to form universal concepts, their consciousness is bound to the objects of the animal
appetites. In man and higher creatures, however, we see a new
type of free behaviour. Man is a creature capable not only of
animal consciousness, but of an activity which is tied to no
specific objects. Intellection has as its object anything in the
whole universe and therefore is the first example of *free* activity.
But as the essence of a substance determines its type of activity
this argues the existence of a specific intellectual substance, the
soul. The appetites of this substance and its pleasures are not
like those of lower substances bound to specific objects. Its
"good" consists not in possession but in contemplation of its
objects. This is, of course, a very inadequate account of Aquinas's
theory of the soul. But it is enough to give some notion of the
background against which Joyce's theory is developed.

Joyce, too, puts forward a theory of the soul as something
which grows or emerges within man's animal nature. For him,[100]
too, the soul's activity is a free intellectual activity and is contrasted with that other part of man's behaviour which is concerned with and bound by movements of desire and loathing,
the instincts and appetites of his animal and social nature. The
problem touches his esthetic theory when he asks whether beauty

is a stasis or a kinesis. How is it that different races of men, for
instance, admire seemingly incompatible types of female beauty?
One answer is that what we call an esthetic appetite is simply
a disguised form of animal desire connected with the instinct
of propagation. (237) Stephen Dedalus admits that this is possible but prefers the alternative that there are certain characters
in all things called beautiful which satisfy a specific intellectual
appetite and which arouse a specific esthetic pleasure.[18] He does
not say why he prefers this view but it seems clear from the
whole discussion that he bases it on some division of appetites
similar to that put forward by Aquinas. He speaks of the birth
of the soul in terms which suggest the same thing (231) and
among his early notes [19] occur the following sentences from
Aristotle:

> The soul is the first entelechy of a naturally organic body.
>
> Only when it is separate from all things is the intellect really
> itself, and this intellect separate from all things is immortal and
> divine.
>
> The intellectual soul is the form of forms.

and so on. . . . He obviously does not use the word soul in any
merely literary sense.

What Joyce's precise theory of the soul may have been and
how far it was the same as that of Aquinas is not at all certain.
The important point is that his esthetic theory seems to involve
him at the outset in two assumptions that may present considerable difficulties. One is the assumption that there are specific
intellectual motives of a disinterested kind as opposed to those
which are connected with the preservation of the species or of
the individual, those which are tied to [101] practical ends. The
other is the assumption there are two ways of knowing or types
of apprehension. In Aquinas the first assumption depends on
the second and both rest on the vulnerable logical doctrine of
essences. Whether Joyce could have found other grounds for
defending either view is uncertain. But in the discussion on

[18] "Certain relations which satisfy and coincide with the stages in themselves of all esthetic apprehensions." (238)
[19] Gorman, *op. cit.*, pp. 95-96.

Hamlet in *Ulysses* there is a hint that he regarded free intellectual activity, specifically, that of the artist, as made possible not by a superior intellectual faculty but by achieving a balance or harmony of the conflicting motives such that none could be too dominant, the achievement of a kind of democracy of motives within the individual made possible in turn by "exile," by cutting oneself off from the forces in one's society which tend to dominate opinion and behavior.

However that may be, one consequence of Joyce's solution of the problem of the unity of the characters of the beautiful in the various and sometimes apparently incompatible examples of what different races think beautiful in a woman, is this: it tends to free art from the tyranny of techniques and recipes. The whole tendency of modern European art has been to stress the esthetic importance of styles, of tricks of the trade. On Joyce's view there seems no reason to think that schools of painting, for instance, which are often claimed to be putting forward incompatible views of art, are doing more than advocating different styles adapted to different types of beauty. It may be that they are actually painting different things. If impressionists set out to paint light and atmosphere while the pre-Raphaelites set out to paint shapes and contours, the details of objects, it is inevitable that they will require different styles, but there is not necessarily any conflict of esthetic theory involved. This indicates that the whole question of schools of art should be examined anew. The primary distinction between good and bad art would be that between disinterested and propaganda art. "The feelings excited by improper art are kinetic, desire or loathing. Desire urges us to possess, to go to something; loathing urges us to abandon, to go from something. The arts which excite them, pornographical [102] or didactic, are therefore improper arts. The esthetic emotion . . . is . . . static. The mind is arrested and raised above desire and loathing.[20] (233)

This view, of course, is important in any consideration of the common assertions that *Ulysses* is a pornographic or obscene work. It is interesting to see that Aquinas like Joyce discusses the problem in terms of our ideas of personal beauty. Beauty he

[20] *Ibid.*, p. 96.

says is like health in this respect; the physical balance of humours which would make for health in a boy would not do so in an old man, yet health in all cases consists in a certain kind of balance or proportion of humours adapted differently to the needs of each nature. It may even be that health for a lion is death for a man. Similarly, examples of bodily beauty can vary tremendously while beauty in all cases consists of the balance or proportion of the limbs and colouring suited to that type. If the Bible says that Christ was beautiful we are not entitled to understand that he had yellow hair.[21]

When we come to the question of what constitutes a work of art as distinguished from other beautiful things and from other human works Joyce's definition is: "Art is the human disposition of sensible or intelligible matter for an esthetic end." [22] (235)

The distinction between sensible and intelligible matter here is that of Aquinas between the objects of sensory and intellectual apprehension. The intellect deals with the formal and universal. One might ask whether Joyce means that a purely intellectual or abstract art is possible as opposed to those which deal with sensibles and particulars. The answer is: no! Art is an activity which consists in the contemplation of the intelligible through the sensible aspects, of the universal through the particular. This is to be inferred from Aquinas's theory of knowledge: "Movement and action do not follow from a universal concept save through the medium of a particular apprehension: because [103] movement and action are about particular things." [23]

One consequence of this, though it is a view that Joyce only indirectly indicates, is that it defines the relationship of art and science. Art deals with the particular but reveals its structures, the universal characters which it exemplifies. Science deals with abstract and general relationships as such. "Truth is beheld by the intellect which is appeased by the most satisfying relations of the intelligible; beauty is beheld by the imagination which is appeased by the most satisfying relations of the sensible." (236)

[21] "Commentary on the Psalms" (Psalm 44, verse 2).
[22] Gorman, op. cit., p. 98.
[23] Summa Contra Gentiles, Bk. II, Ch. XLVIII, p. 115. See also Summa Theologica, I, Q.LXXXIV, art. 5, 6 and 7.

Again the language, the distinction of intellect and imagination is thoroughly Thomistic.[24]

Another interesting implication of this definition of art in the light of the scholastic theory from which it proceeds is that it would imply that literature, as the art in which intellectual analysis is most possible would have to be considered the highest of the arts (244) in much the same way that sight is regarded by Aquinas as the highest of the senses. Moreover it is the only art which uses words with their superior power of presenting conceptual knowledge, and the final and highest intellectual act in Aquinas's description of the operation of the intellect is called *"dictio"* or *"productio verbi mentalis."* [25]

As far as I know Aquinas does not discuss the fine arts at all, though his theory of beauty and his distinction of the terms *"utile"* and *"honestum"* [26] lead us to suppose that had he done so he would have placed them on a different footing from that on which he places the practical arts [27] and that like Joyce he would have arranged the arts in an intellectual hierarchy.

Joyce gives some examples of human products which are not works of art, excrement, lice, children, photographs, an [104] image of a cow made fortuitously by a man hacking in fury at a block of wood.[28] (243-244) Once again the scholastic background of his argument is important. A photograph is not a work of art because it is not a *human* disposition of sensible matter for an esthetic end. This looks like saying that my hat is not a hat unless it was made by a hatter. It seems to make the criterion of art a purely formal one. Joyce, however, is not thinking of a formal requirement. A photograph may be beautiful but if what it represents is not the result of the human selection, arrangement and elimination by which the mind presents its material as a work of "imagination," that is, so disposed as to bring out more than the immediate impression of sensible particulars, to

[24] See, for instance, the discussion of the distinction between the imagination and the possible intellect in *Summa Contra Gentiles,* Bk. II, Ch. LXVII.
[25] D'Arcy, "Thomas Aquinas," pp. 216-217.
[26] *Summa Theologica,* I, Q.V, art. 6.
[27] *Summa Contra Gentiles,* Bk. III, Ch. XXXVI.
[28] Gorman, *op. cit.,* pp. 98-99.

bring out the "*quidditas*" or essence of the thing, then it will be lacking in the "*claritas*" which is essential to a work of art.

The art of the crude realist, of the writer who offers you a "chunk of life," of the merely representational or "photographic" artist are all equally incompatible with Joyce's view.

In the same way the cow cannot be a work of art because it is not produced for an esthetic end. This seems to suggest that the intention of the artist is itself the criterion of art rather than the character of the work. What Joyce appears to be saying, however, is that, since every act is proportionate to its end, then, as rage comes under the head of the appetites of fear and loathing, it will tend to produce something with the characters that satisfy this appetite and this will not be a work of art, because that can only be produced by the specific esthetic appetite. The argument is not: that to decide whether a work is art or not we must know the intention of the maker. It is more the type of argument that might underlie the statement that a hen cannot lay a duck egg. There is the further possibility that the man might be an artist and that while he hacked in fury at the wood he was also actuated by his habitual artistic impulses. For instance there is the type of argument which says that there is no reason why a work of [105] art should not be both pornographic and artistic, or both didactic and artistic. But both Aquinas and Joyce would have to reject this. An essential of beauty for both is a balance or due proportion of the parts, and a completeness, a freedom from merely accessory or irrelevant features. Where two so different appetites as the esthetic and irascible are aiming at the same end, the hacking away of the block of wood, it is impossible that the result of the conflicting appetites should have the coherence and proportion necessary for beauty. Moreover, Aquinas argues that intellectual beauty is actually incompatible with the operation of certain appetites: "especially is it in temperance, which restrains the concupiscences which especially darken the light of reason." [29]

Aquinas here is speaking of intellectual beauty of the higher sort. In another place he does, it is true, make a sharp division

[29] *Summa Theologica,* 2, II, Q.CLXXX, art. 6.

between corporal and spiritual beauty in men. Physical beauty
is not incompatible with lustful appetite. Spiritual beauty is.[30]
This however only indirectly affects the argument since men are
not works of art.

Joyce, in keeping with his theory that the characters of beauty
are general characters which any object may possess, does not
deny that things which serve practical ends may be works of
art.[31] A chair in so far as it is a chair is made for a practical end.
Its *"bonum"* consists in *"utile"* according to Aquinas's classifica-
tion. But if the maker constructs it to an esthetic end, that is
to say if he finds that its nature as a chair is compatible with
its possessing the requisite characters of wholeness, proportion
and radiance, and if he constructs it to that end, then a chair
can be a work of art. Architecture then can be classed with the
fine arts, though like sculpture it would probably be classified
by Joyce as an inferior art. (244)

The nature of the whole theory, of course, depends on the
three essential characters of a work of art. Joyce describes these
essential characters in the terms of Aquinas: [106] *"Ad pulcri-
tudineum tria requiruntur integritas, consonantia, claritas. I translate it so: Three things are needed for beauty, wholeness, harmony and radiance."* (241)

These three characters correspond to the phases of apprehension. *Integritas* is the esthetic image "apprehended as self-
bounded and selfcontained upon the immeasurable background
of space and time. . . . You apprehended it as *one* thing. You
see it as one whole. You apprehend its wholeness." (241)

Consonantia is the esthetic image apprehended in its coherent
complexity. "You apprehend it as balanced part against part
within its limits; you feel the rhythm of its structure. In other
words, the synthesis of immediate perception is followed by the
analysis of apprehension. Having first felt that it is *one* thing
you feel now that it is a *thing* . . . made up of its parts, the
result of its parts and their sum, harmonious." (241-242)

Claritas is the esthetic image apprehended in its essence.
"When you have apprehended that basket as one thing and have

[30] *Summa Theologica*, 2, II, Q.CXLV, art. 2.
[31] Gorman, *op. cit.*, p. 99.

then analysed it according to its form and apprehended it as a thing you make the only synthesis which is logically and esthetically permissible. You see that it is that thing which it is and no other thing. The radiance of which he speaks in the scholastic *quidditas,* the *whatness* of a thing. This supreme quality is felt by the artist when the esthetic image is first conceived in his imagination. . . . The instant wherein that supreme quality of beauty . . . is apprehended luminously by the mind . . . is the luminous silent stasis of esthetic pleasure. . . ." (242)

It is obvious that these three characters are simply Aquinas's three transcendental characters of all being, *unum, verum,* and *bonum,* as they appear specifically in the esthetic image and that the three phases of artistic apprehension correspond to his three main levels of apprehension, that in which the mind receives the image passively, that in which the *intellectus agens,* the active intellect views the object of contemplation by means of the phantasma or image, lights up [107] the image as it were by the process of abstraction of its formal structure, and finally that by which the intellect in its highest act totally comprehends its object and is united with it. In this final act the appetite is appeased and this is the stasis, the state of intellectual delight which arises from the perfection of the act.

The passage to which Joyce refers seems to be the following from the *Summa Theologica.* Aquinas is discussing beauty as an attribute of a member of the Trinity: *"Nam ad pulchritudinem tria requiruntur. Primo quidem, integritas sive perfectio. Quae enim diminuta sunt, hoc ipso turpia sunt. Et debita proportio sive consonantia. Et iterum claritas unde quae habent colorem nitidum, pulchra esse dicuntur."* [32]

In other passages Aquinas mentions only one [33] or two [34] of these characters essential to beauty, omitting the first; but there seems to be nothing inconsistent in this for when one examines these passages it is clear that he mentions just those characters

---

[32] *Summa Theologica,* I, Q.XXXIX, art. 8.
[33] *Summa Theologica,* I, Q.V, art. 6; "Commentary on the Sentences," Bk. I, Dist. XXXI, Q.II, 4; "Commentary on the Psalms," Ps. XLIV, verse 2.
[34] *Summa Theologica,* 2, II, Q.CXLV, art. 2; 2, II, Q.CLXXX, art. 2; "Commentary on the Sentences," Bk. I, Dist. III, Q.I, 1; Commentary, *In Dionysium de divinis Nominibus,* Ch. IV, Lect. 5.

which are relevant to the particular point under discussion. We must remember that Joyce's hero is speaking of the "esthetic image," that is to say, not the butcher's boy's basket at which he and Lynch are looking, but the artist's image of it which, when reproduced in the medium of words or paint, will be the work of art. This explains the fact that he describes the characters of beauty in psychological terms, as though they were ways of seeing the object rather than characters of the object itself. The basket as a work of art may be contrasted with the basket as it appears to the bucher's boy in that the work of art presents the spectator with the artist's analysis as well as with the basket —this is the meaning of the esthetic image. It is not that the characters of beauty are added by the mind. The mind elicits them and makes them explicit in the image. There is a close correspondence between this theory and Aquinas's theory of [108] "imagination." The esthetic image as it first appears in the mind corresponds to the *phantasma* of Aquinas, and the process described by Joyce corresponds fairly closely to the process of the *intellectus agens* on the phantasm. Joyce's account also preserves the Thomistic type of realism. It is the actual basket at which the two students are looking, the "esthetic image" is not the object but the means by which the lower faculties enable the *intellectus agens* to apprehend the basket itself, somewhat as, using what is of course an inadequate analogy, a map may help the traveller to apprehend the landscape spread out before him on the hill top. It is likely, therefore, that when Joyce speaks of the apprehension of the beautiful by the imagination and the true by the intellect (236) he is strictly following Aquinas. For the *intellectus agens* acts in a mediate capacity providing the concepts by means of which the final intellectual act is accomplished. Not that, in man, it is possible to have knowledge which is entirely without intellectual form. Knowledge, though a complex, is a single process and the whole intellect through its complex machinery of sensation, imagination, conception has as its actual object the real world. This is because it is a self-conscious process. It is immediately aware of its own activity.

This mediate position of the imagination throws light on the technical structure of Joyce's two later books *Ulysses* and *Fin-*

negans Wake. It is the function of higher powers than the imagination to complete the work of abstraction which is seen in scientific thought. On the esthetic plane of apprehension the abstract and general aspects of the being apprehended remain, as it were, emergent but "embedded" in their particulars. *Ulysses* deals with the theme of the conditions of freedom, but it would be improper to the method of art for the author to treat the theme "scientifically," to elucidate his theme in abstract terms, to comment or explain. Instead he uses the method proper to the art of literature. Taking Vico's theory of the law of history by which the history of races and civilisations is conceived to repeat itself in much [109] the same general way as the life history of human beings repeats itself in each individual, Joyce shadows his esthetic image with another, the image of the *Odyssey*. Neither *integritas* nor *consonantia* is broken, for in a sense the two stories are the same, Bloom *is* the Ulysses of Irish Dublin. It is not an allegory. For the book *is* about Bloom, he is not a mere cover for a concealed meaning, not a symbol. The method of the book is that of a complex metaphor worked out in minute detail. It is by presenting the esthetic image in two forms that the mind is led to that in their structure which is common, to apprehend the abstract elements of the form in their particularity. Tolstoi, facing a similar problem in *War and Peace*, finds himself constrained to pass every now and then from art to science, from the presentation of his esthetic image to abstract historical analysis and comment. Thus the method of *Ulysses* is no mere *jeu d'esprit*. From Vico Joyce derives the theory that art is a form of myth-making. But from Aquinas he draws the philosophical justification of the myth as a proper esthetic method in literature. At the same time he recognises a progression from the simplest to the most complex arts. The simplest objects are more simply apprehended in their unity and coherence because they *are* simpler and more immediately familiar. The mere presentation and apprehension of the rhythm of their structures makes them esthetically intelligible. (234-235)

The most difficult of Joyce's three esthetic characters to conceive as an actual character of the work of art itself is that of *claritas* or radiance. He admits some doubt as to Aquinas's mean-

ing here and rejects as "literary talk" the view that Aquinas
had in mind "symbolism or idealism, the supreme quality of
beauty being a light from some other world, the idea of which
the matter is but the shadow, the reality of which it is but the
symbol," the idea that "*claritas* is the artistic discovery and representation of the divine purpose in anything or a force of gen-
eralisation, which would make the esthetic [110] image a universal
one, make it outshine its proper conditions." (242) The Commentary on the Divine Names does suggest such a view [35] and
in other passages the sense of *claritas* is perhaps ambiguous—
e.g. that *claritas* in bodies may be a physical property.[36] But
Joyce's explanation of the term, within "the proper conditions"
of the imagination, seems to be the correct one. As the passage
stands, however, *claritas* hardly seems to be a *quality* of the
esthetic image at all. It would seem to be more accurately described as a response of the mind to the image or an emotion
accompanying and produced by the mind's operation. Joyce also
calls it "supreme" among the qualities of beauty though the
sense of the epithet is not clear, and he calls its apprehension
a *synthesis,* though it seems to make no composition or combination that has not been already comprehended under the account
of *integritas* and *consonantia.*

Once again we must return to Aquinas's theory of knowledge.
If we take the metaphor of the traveller pausing on the hill top
and surveying the landscape before him with the help of a map
it may be possible to give some idea of the nature of the conception that underlies Joyce's description of *claritas.* If we imagine
the map as in the traveller's mind and as the work of his mind,
such that instead of the formal signs of roads, houses, fields and
hills the mind has constructed a map-picture, we shall have
something like the phantasma, or in the case under discussion,
the esthetic image. We can further imagine the map-picture to
be a transparent one such that when it is held between the
intellectual eye and the landscape the traveller not only perceives the landscape endowed with its formal meaning, he is
also able to observe the exact correspondence of the details of

[35] Ch. IV, Lect. 4 and Lect. 5.
[36] *Summa Theologica,* I, Q.XXXIX, art. 8.

the map with the details of the landscape before him. He becomes aware of the truth of his mental work. His impression becomes a formal judgement. This *is*, in fact, the act of judgement that now takes place, the assertion or judging of the nature of what he sees in [111] terms of the map. It is necessary to stress that this is no more than a metaphor, that it oversimplifies and in some respects distorts Aquinas and that it omits several very important aspects. But it will serve to illustrate the nature of Joyce's theory. This final judgement is the synthesis to which Joyce refers and, as he is speaking of the esthetic image, it can be truly described as a character or quality of the image in which it exists "potentially" or formally according to the Thomistic distinction of act and potency. Secondly, as the apprehension of *integritas* and *consonantia* were mediate operations by which the image was constructed, it is clear in what sense it may be described as the supreme quality among the qualities of beauty. Thirdly, as the act by which the intellectual and the esthetic appetite is appeased and consummated it will be a joy unmixed with desire, and as a moment of complete consciousness both of the essence of the object and of the activity of the mind itself it can be described as an illumination—or as Joyce describes it: "the luminous silent stasis of esthetic pleasure, a spiritual state very like to that cardiac condition which the Italian physiologist Luigi Galvani . . . called the enchantment of the heart." (242-243)

The fact that the apprehension of *claritas* is a state for which Aquinas uses the technical term "*gaudium*," joy, is the initial step in Joyce's discussion of the literary modes of tragedy and comedy. Tragedy he defines as the form of art which "aims at exciting in us feelings of pity and terror. Now terror is the feeling which arrests us before whatever is grave in human fortunes and unites us with its secret cause and pity is the feeling that arrests us before whatever is grave in human fortunes and unites us with the human sufferer." [37]

Aquinas's doctrine that a thing is only intelligible when its causes and its proper act are apprehended here excludes from true tragedy those literary works which simply present us with

[37] Gorman, *op. cit.*, p. 96.

disastrous events without laying bare their "secret causes." The death of a young girl killed in a street accident [112] is not tragic. (232-233) Comedy is the art which while not urging us to seek something beyond itself (desire) excites in us a feeling of joy and it is to be judged as more or less excellent according as this feeling of joy is excited by whatever is substantial or accidental in human fortunes: "And even tragic art may be said to participate in the nature of comic art so far as the possession of a work of tragic art (a tragedy) excites in us the feeling of joy. From this it may be seen that tragedy is the imperfect manner and comedy the perfect manner in art." [38]

This illuminates Joyce's realism, particularly that aspect of it which has been so much attacked; his faithful presentation of aspects of life that are usually considered unpleasant or obscene. Critics are often heard to praise what is called "stark realism" in literature, the unflinching presentation of the unpleasant as unpleasant or loathsome. Joyce has sometimes been treated as a writer of this sort of "realism." This is entirely to misunderstand his view of art. On the other hand what has bewildered or misled some of his critics is that he presents his subject in all its aspects as an image imbued with a kind of serene joy. It is perhaps the aspect of his work that most clearly distinguishes it from that of the majority of writers of the so-called Realist school. It is the aspect of his art in which it can most significantly be described as classic. Even Dante whose greatest work is based on and inspired by the philosophy of Aquinas, though in the very agony of Hell he twice refers to his poem as a comedy, yet treats comedy as the lower and tragedy as the higher art.[39]

Finally Joyce has something to say about literary forms. He distinguishes three forms progressing from one to the next: "These forms are the lyrical form, the form wherein the artist presents his image in immediate relation to himself; the epical form, the form wherein he presents his image in mediate relation to himself and to others; the dramatic form, the form in which he presents his image in immediate relation to others." (243) [113]

---

[38] *Ibid.*, 97.
[39] Letter to Can Grande della Scala, § 10.

His treatment of these forms is clear enough not to need comment, but it is perhaps not entirely fanciful to see in the three forms a suggestion of Aquinas's theory of the mind's three stages of consciousness of its object.

It is clear then that Joyce's esthetic theory is indebted in a more systematic way to scholastic philosophy than his own statement might suggest and that in particular it is rooted in a theory of knowledge that is open to the sort of criticism that can be levelled at a system based on the Aristotelian notion of causation and on the doctrine of essences. Such criticism need not however affect the three most important aspects of Joyce's theory, namely the notion that beauty is a positive character of works of art, the notion that this character is one of unity and coherence of theme and the notion that art is intrinsically a contemplative and analytic rather than a persuasive and superficially representational activity. For these notions can be supported in other ways.

There is another side of Joyce's theory which concerns the conditions under which the artist is produced and functions. As this, however, is not, strictly speaking, a theory of esthetics, as it derives more from Joyce's study of Vico than from his study of Aquinas, and as it forms part of the theme of another work, *Ulysses*, it would be more properly treated in another place. [114]

IRENE HENDRY CHAYES

Joyce's Epiphanies

By an epiphany he meant a sudden spiritual manifestation,
whether in the vulgarity of speech or of gesture or in a memorable phase of the mind itself. He believed that it was for the
man of letters to record these epiphanies with extreme care,
seeing that they themselves are the most delicate and evanescent
of moments.—*Stephen Hero.*

I

STEPHEN DEDALUS' esthetic in *A Portrait of the Artist as a Young
Man* has the same specious quality as his Hamlet thesis in
Ulysses and is a product of the same talent for parody; as Stephen's friend Lynch remarks, it has "the true scholastic stink."
Both theories are, of course, more than parody: the speculations
on Hamlet serve to crystallize Stephen's broodings on his spiritual
parentage, and the esthetic is actually Joyce's, which he followed
faithfully in his own literary method. Just how closely method
and principle were related in Joyce's work is shown by his little-
noticed theory of epiphanies, which is mentioned fleetingly in
Ulysses, but is given explicit statement only in *Stephen Hero,*
the fragmentary first draft of the *Portrait* recently published in
book form for the first time.[1]

Reprinted by permission of the author. Copyright ©, 1946, by The University of the South. The essay appeared originally in *The Sewanee Review* in
July, 1946. References to *A Portrait* are to P-2; to *Stephen Hero* are to SH-1.

[1] *Stephen Hero: A Part of the First Draft of A Portrait of the Artist as a
Young Man.* By James Joyce. Edited from the manuscript in the Harvard
College Library by Theodore Spencer. (Norfolk, Conn.: New Directions,
1944).

The theory of epiphanies, presented as Stephen's, is bound up with the three cardinal esthetic principles, or conditions of beauty, that he expounds to Lynch in one of their dialogues in the *Portrait*. (In *Stephen Hero*, the passive listener is Cranly, a character apparently based on Joyce's own college friend Byrne.) These principles have a respectable philosophic origin in the *integritas, consonantia* and *claritas* of Aquinas. *Integritas* Stephen explains in pseudo-scholastic language as "wholeness"— the perception of an esthetic image as *one* thing, "self-bounded and self-contained upon the immeasurable background of space or time [1] which is not it." (249) *Consonantia*, similarly, is symmetry and rhythm of structure, the esthetic image conceived as "complex, multiple, divisible, separable, made up of its parts and their sum, harmonious"; "the synthesis of immediate perception is followed by the analysis of apprehension." (249) The third principle, *claritas*, is given the approximate meaning of "radiance" and equated with another Thomistic term, *quidditas*, or the "whatness" of a thing. *Quidditas* is the link with the theory of epiphanies; in this case, the definition in *Stephen Hero* is the more revealing:

> *Claritas* is *quidditas*. After the analysis which discovers the second quality the mind makes the only logically possible synthesis and discovers the third quality. This is the moment which I call epiphany. First we recognise that the object is *one* integral thing, then we recognise that it is an organized composite structure, a *thing* in fact: finally, when the relation of the parts is exquisite, when the parts are adjusted to the special point, we recognise that it is *that* thing which it is. Its soul, its whatness, leaps to us from the vestment of its appearance. The soul of the commonest object, the structure of which is so adjusted, seems to us radiant. The object achieves its epiphany. (*SH*, 213)

Joyce's epiphanies are mentioned by Harry Levin, who had access to the manuscript of *Stephen Hero* in preparing his New Directions study, and by Theodore Spencer, who edited and wrote the preface to the published version of the fragment. Both Levin and Spencer, however, emphasize only the obvious aspect of the epiphany: its effect on the observer and his relation to the object "epiphanized." Spencer calls the theory one which "implies a lyrical rather than a dramatic view of life," (*SH*, 17) thinking apparently of Stephen's definition of the "lyrical" form of art as "the form wherein the artist presents his image in immediate relation to himself." Levin takes the stories in *Dubliners* as pure examples of epiphany and the collection of which Stephen resolves (in *Ulysses*) to leave copies to all the libraries of the world; Joyce's [2] later works, he says, are "artificial reconstructions of a transcendental view of experience," and his "dizzying shifts" of technique, "attempts to create a literary substitute for the revelations of religion."

But these descriptions do justice to neither the concept nor Joyce's use of it. In the first place, of course, the epiphany is not peculiar to Joyce alone. Virtually every writer experiences a sense of revelation when he beholds a fragment of his ordinary world across what Bullough has called "psychic distance"—dissociated from his subjective and practical concerns, fraught with meaning beyond itself, with every detail of its physical appearance relevant. It is a revelation quite as valid as the religious; in fact, from our present secular viewpoint, it perhaps would be more accurate to say that the revelation of the religious mystic is actually an esthetic revelation into which the mystic projects himself—as a participant, not merely as an observer and recorder —and to which he assigns a source, an agent and an end, called God. What Joyce did was give systematic formulation to a common esthetic experience, so common that few others—writers, if not estheticians—have thought it worth considering for its own sake.

Again, many writers use "revelation" as a technical device in achieving their effects; Joyce, however, used it more consciously and with greater variation than anyone with whom he can be compared. More than "a transcendental view of experience" is involved in Joyce's application of his theory of epiphanies, just as there is more than mysticism in religion, particularly the Roman Catholicism that shaped his whole outlook as a young man. The theory furnished Joyce with a technique of characterization which evolved generally in the "lyrical-epical-dramatic" progression that Stephen describes: from the first person to the third, from the personal to the impersonal, from the kinetic to the static. It is a technique in which *integritas* and *consonantia* are always necessary to *claritas*, and *claritas* itself comes more and [3] more to reside in *quidditas,* the soul, the essential identifying quality of the thing, than in a mystic, emotional exhilaration on the part of someone who looks on. *Claritas is quidditas* is the key the theory itself gives us.

In *Dubliners, claritas* is achieved most often, although not always, through an apparently trivial incident, action or single detail which differs from the others making up the story only in that it illuminates them, integrates them and gives them meaning. It is like the final piece which is added to the child's pile of lettered blocks and completes the spelling of a word or gives form to the "house" or "tower" he is building. Farrington's treatment of his son attaches to himself the petty tyranny we recognize first in his employer. Little Chandler's brief rebellion against domesticity frightens his child, and his dreams of being a poet are swept away by his remorse. After a drinking bout, Mr. Kernan is persuaded by his friends to take part in a retreat, at which Father Purdon's metaphor of the "spiritual accountant" crystallizes a businessman's religion that is only a reflection of their daily lives. And in *The Dead*, the artistic highpoint of the collection, the conviviality of the banquet, Gabriel Conroy's confident rejection of the dead past, his scorn for Irish nationalism and his desire of his wife are ironically drawn together and then dispersed by the story of Michael Furey.

Joyce used the *Dubliners* "block" technique again, with some modification, in the Nausicaa episode in *Ulysses*, where, after having sexually aroused Leopold Bloom and indulged in erotic day dreams of her own, Gerty MacDowell walks away with a limp. It is a technique that is obvious to us because it is familiar; although their origin is probably Katherine Mansfield or Chekhov rather than Joyce, similar "revelations" of character are vouchsafed regularly by the *New Yorker* and its imitators. Such stories are usually considered to be "objective" because the author offers no overt interpretation of his material but merely arranges it so that its meaning is "revealed" directly to the reader. [4] The *Dubliners* stories seem to conform to Stephen's definition of "dramatic" art as the form in which the artist "pre-

sents his image in immediate relation to others" (251); "life
purified in and reprojected from the human imagination." (252)
Joyce was not satisfied with such an easy attainment of the
esthetic stasis, however, and this may have been because the
"block" technique did not fulfill equally all three of his basic
principles of art. *Claritas* is achieved, but the *quidditas* that
constitutes it is dilute; *consonantia,* the parts and their sum, is
in evidence, but *integritas* is not, at least to the same degree.

II

The example of epiphany which Joyce employs in *Stephen
Hero* (*SH,* 211)—a fragment of conversation between a girl and
a young man, overheard on Mr. Bloom's own Eccles Street—is
actually the final "block" of the *Dubliners* method without the
foundation; one may guess that the foundation in each story
was laid down later, in an effort to insure the impersonality of
the epiphany Joyce originally experienced in a very personal
fashion. It may be, too, that the collection of epiphanies Stephen
wishes to leave to posterity is not *Dubliners* at all but a collection
of just such fragments as the one he acknowledges.

A number of these "most delicate and evanescent of moments"
occur throughout both *Stephen Hero* and the *Portrait,* taking
up residence in Stephen's consciousness with neither elucidation
nor relation to anything beyond themselves: factory girls and
boys coming out to lunch; the witless laughter of an old woman;
the screeching of a mad nun; a servant singing; the salutation of
a flower girl. In *Ulysses,* too, the peregrinations of Bloom and
Stephen about Dublin are rich in epiphanies of this sort; the
shout Stephen hears in the street and calls a "manifestation of
God" is only the most obvious.

Occasionally we are given a suggestion of what is "revealed"
in Joyce's epiphanies. The black straw hat and the greeting of [5]
the prostitute in *Stephen Hero* have an inordinate fascination
for Dedalus; "mustn't the devil be annoyed to hear her described
as an evil creature?" (*SH,* 190) he asks. In order to fill in the
background of an epiphany, he sometimes makes a reconstruction of an event in the past: a forgotten medical student cutting

the word *Foetus* in the wooden surface of his desk, or an imagined incestuous meeting in the rain, suggested by the dwarfish reader in the library and the rumors about his birth. And in at least three instances an epiphany helps Stephen to decide on the future course of his life: the snatch of song from the street, contrasting suddenly with the unsmiling face of the Jesuit who has been urging him to enter a novitiate; the vision of the girl wading at the shore; and the flight of birds about the college library, symbolizing the "fabulous artificer" after whom he is named.

The moment of revelation without its narrative base is the most conventional of Joyce's epiphanies; we find it elsewhere even in fiction which does not make use of revelation as a specific technique in the *Dubliners*-Chekhov-Mansfield-*New Yorker* manner. This is particularly true among writers who, like Virginia Woolf and John Dos Passos, have modified Joyce's stream-of-consciousness method. And in poetry the isolated moment of revelation dates at least from Wordsworth's experiences in the presence of mountains, leech-gatherers and the lights about Westminster Bridge. The epiphanies in Joyce's own poetry, in such pieces as "The twilight turns from amethyst," "My love is in a light attire," "A Flower Given to My Daughter," "On the Beach at Fontana," fit so well into the familiar lyric pattern that the poetry is usually dismissed as something outside the main stream of his work.

Joyce's second epiphany technique does quite clearly conform to Stephen's definition of lyrical art. Although *claritas* is ultimately generated by *quidditas*, we are first aware of an effect on the beholder—Stephen, or ourselves through Stephen—not of an objectively apprehensible quality in the thing revealed; if we [6] are to penetrate through to the *quidditas*, we must try to identify ourselves with Stephen or wrest a meaning of our own from the revelation. From the standpoint of eliminating the artist's personality from his work, this particular technique was a retrogression from the method of *Dubliners*, but it did have the advantage—in Joyce's esthetic theory, an extremely important one—of realizing the three principles, *integritas*, *consonantia* and *claritas*, in a single image. The next step toward impersonal creation was to modify the image so that its *quidditas* would be unmistakable, with its radiance attached to itself rather than to a perceiving consciousness: Joyce's third epiphany technique, which explains the differences between *Stephen Hero* and *A Portrait of the Artist.*

In the *Portrait,* which covers in 93 pages events that require 234 pages in the *Hero* fragment, the original elements of Joyce's first novel, particularly the characters, are subjected to a process of compression and distillation that rejects all irrelevancies, all particularities and ambiguities, and leaves only their pure essence. In *Stephen Hero,* the common people at the Good Friday service are diverse in their submissive ignorance and their unquestioning respect for the clergy; the old women scrape their hands over the dry bottom of the holy-water font and speak in broad, realistic dialect. But in the *Portrait* the simple faithful are represented by pious sighs and a peasant smell "of air and rain and turf and corduroy," (14, 15) or by kneeling forms and whispering voices in the confessional box—"soft whispering cloudlets, soft whispering vapour, whispering and vanishing." (164) In the first draft of the novel, Maurice and Isabel Dedalus appear specifically as characters; in the *Portrait,* Stephen's brothers and sisters are merely voices at the tea-table, replying to his questions in pig-latin or singing with an "overtone of weariness behind their frail fresh innocent voices." (190) "He heard the choir of voices in the kitchen echoed and multiplied through an endless reverberation of the choirs of endless generations of children: [7] and heard in all the echoes an echo also of the recurring note of weariness and pain. All seemed weary of life even before entering upon it." (190)

The character of Stephen itself undergoes a transformation. The *Hero* draft is often marred by adolescent particularities: Stephen baiting his cruder classmates, sneering at his mother's pious superstitions, or trying to convert his parents to Ibsen. In the *Portrait,* however, the Ibsen episode is omitted entirely, the intellectual distance between Stephen and his contemporaries is given less emphasis, and the quarrel with his mother over his failure to do his Easter duty is mentioned only indirectly. The details of Stephen's debauches similarly remain obscure; what we are shown, in the boy's dreams of temptation, the sermons he listens to during the retreat, and his hallucinations of damnation and punishment, is actually an apotheosis—or epiphany—of sin and repentance, far removed from the adventures of the Eugene Gants who for a generation have been storming the brothels of the world in imitation of Stephen.

But the most striking attenuation occurs in the character of Emma Clery. In the *Hero* fragment, she is a healthy, middle-class girl who studies Gaelic with enthusiasm, flirts with priests, and is only confused and offended by Stephen's unconventional offer of himself. In the *Portrait*, however, we are told nothing of her appearance and are never allowed a clear conception of her as an individual. The Gaelic lessons shrink to an Irish phrase-book, the flirtation becomes a bitter recollection in Stephen's mind, associated with the scorn he feels for the Church, and there is only the barest hint of the circumstances of the rejection. The girl herself is never more than a shadowy presence—a provocative glance or speech, a shawled head, "fresh warm breath," laughter and tapping footsteps, a sash or a nodding hair ornament. Her etherealization extends even to her name, which in the *Portrait* becomes "E————— C—————."

In Stephen's discussion of *quidditas*, the necessary condition to [8] radiance is a perfection of formal organization, or *consonantia* itself; "when the relation of the parts is exquisite, when the parts are adjusted to the special point, we recognize that it is *that* thing which it is." (*SH*, 213) The formal adjustment in the examples of *quidditas* I have been citing is simpler and more tangible than the metaphors "distillation," "essence" and "etherealization" might suggest; it consists in nothing more mysterious than the division of a whole character into its separate parts, analogous to the "analysis of apprehension" Stephen matches up with *consonantia*. Although she represents an almost opposite conception of woman, Emma is an essence by virtue of the same process of formal disintegration as Molly Bloom, whom we know through most of *Ulysses* as drowsy breathing, untidily scattered garments, the rattling of the brass quoits on her bed, an odor, or a chance remark, when we know her directly, and as a collection of separate physical charms when we know her through Bloom. Stephen, only somewhat less than Bloom in his celebrated stream of consciousness, is the sum of fleeting memories, sense impressions, shifting thoughts and associations, each "a memorable phase of the mind itself." The *integritas* of the character is sacrificed to the *integritas* of the esthetic image, and we are presented with generalities resynthesized from individuals: not the pious poor, but Faith; not Stephen's brothers and sisters, but Childhood; not Emma Clery, but Virginity. In *A Portrait of the Artist,* Stephen Dedalus and Emma already foreshadow the great male and female abstractions of Joyce's later work, which express on successively higher levels of sublimation the *quidditas* of each sex.

Emma's etherealization is, incidentally, suggested in other figures of women in Joyce's early work: Gretta Conroy in *The Dead;* the "memories of the girls and women in the plays of Gerhart Hauptmann" and "their pale sorrows," which the wet branches of trees call forth in Stephen's mind; the boyish figure of the Virgin in the liturgy, which Stephen visualizes as he listens to a servant singing *Rosie O'Grady.* Joyce's feminine characters [9] in general tend to become essences before his men. In fact, he conceived of only three types of woman, the Virgin, the Temptress and the Mother—all curiously Catholic, all complementing the naïve misogyny of *Stephen Hero,* where Stephen sneers at the notion of "votes for the bitches" (228) and refers to women inaccurately but with effective insult as "marsupials." (*SH,* 176) Anna Livia Plurabelle ranges through all three essences; Molly Bloom combines the qualities of temptress and mother, and Emma is transformed into a temptress in Stephen's dreams, so that the boy's abortive passion becomes a conflict between carnal and spiritual love, centered in one object. This is the conflict that is made part of a "problem" formula in Joyce's play *Exiles,* with Bertha Rowan set off against the consumptive music teacher, who is significantly named Beatrice. (In at least one scene of the *Portrait,* incidentally, there is also a suggestion of *La Vita Nuova,* with ironic overtones: Emma standing silently in the school porch surrounded by her girl companions, while Stephen regards her from a distance, remembering her flirtatiousness in the presence of Father Moran.)

And when a character is broken down into its parts and re-synthesized, what is the new integrating agent which assists the "synthesis of immediate perception" (249) and serves both *consonantia* and *claritas?* Appropriately enough in Joyce's case, it is language itself. We are most familiar with the plays on etymology and multiple accretions of meaning in his later work, but at first he achieved his effects through all the poet's or orator's traditional devices of cadence and balanced period, metaphor and apostrophe, verbal connotation and subtle variation of sound. This is apparent in the examples of *quidditas* that have been cited ("soft whispering cloudlets," (164) "frail fresh innocent voices" (190)), where we are given auditory impressions rather than adequate visual description. Epiphany is, in fact, one purpose of Joyce's amazing virtuosity of language, which grows as much between *Stephen Hero* and the *Portrait* as between the *Portrait* and *Ulysses* or [10] *Ulysses* and *Finnegans Wake*. It is not an attempt to "create a literary substitute for the revelations of religion"; it is the vehicle of the radiant esthetic experience itself, and at the same time it is intimately related to the plan of Joyce's work as a whole.

It has not been sufficiently emphasized, I think, that the three major books, as well as the play and the poetry, together repeat on the scale of the author's entire career the childhood-adolescence-maturity pattern of the *Dubliners* stories. Youth—hope and rebellion; maturity—disillusion and repentance; middle age —conformity and loneliness; age—resignation and death; in spite of palimpsests of Vico and Homer, psychoanalysis and Irish history, there is a clear and continuous line of development in Joyce's literal subject-matter from his first writings to his last. His theme is, quite simply, the life of man, and his own life was devoted to writing piece by piece a vast Human Tragedy, an epiphany of all mankind, in which a profound anthropological sense of the mystery and power of death takes the place of the Christian's traditional faith in union with God and the life everlasting. It was mainly in the service of his theme, I believe, that Joyce incorporated smaller "growth" patterns (often regarded as mere pedantic conceits) in his separate works: the passage of the day from morning to night, a river flowing to the sea, a child growing to manhood. One of the most prominent of these is the Oxen of the Sun episode in *Ulysses,* where the successive stages of the child's development in the womb are paralleled by successive stages of the development of the English language; but there are other examples of the adaptation of linguistic techniques to his theme as well as to the epiphany principle. Even in the early works there is a lyrical or rhetorical passage wherever there is a climactic epiphany of particular emotional significance, or where a generalized rather than an individual *quidditas* is revealed. In *Dubliners* we find the disillusion of *Araby* and the elegiac closing pages of *The Dead. Stephen* [11] *Hero* has Stephen's rhetorical outbursts against the Church and the "nocturne" scene just preceding Isabel's death, which in mood and setting is very like Joyce's lyric "The twilight turns from amethyst," while passage after passage in *A Portrait of the Artist,* some frankly dyed with purple, make Joyce's first novel as much a vocal book as *Ulysses* or *Finnegans Wake.*

The final epiphany in the *Portrait* is Stephen's famous journal entry marking the point at which the young man becomes an artist: "Welcome, O life! I go to encounter for the millionth time the reality of experience and to forge in the smithy of my soul the uncreated conscience of my race." (299) Although we are supposed to think of it as written, this is pure oratory (Joyce refused to set off the written word from the spoken and exploited the possibilities of both to the utmost) and an exact formal counterpart of both Molly Bloom's remembered affirmation as she sinks into sleep and Anna Livia Plurabelle's valediction at dawn. Moreover, it is balanced by the fragmentary, unpersonalized impressions of the infant Stephen at the beginning of the book precisely as the soliloquies of Molly and Anna Livia are balanced by the impersonal narrative beginnings of *Ulysses* and *Finnegans Wake.* In a reversal of the progression in Stephen's theory (which actually describes the relation of the artist to his work rather than artistic form), Joyce moves from the third person to the first, and achieves in each case a simultaneous progression on another level. In the *Portrait,* the biological development from child to man becomes also a psychological and moral development, from passive receptivity to the self-conscious will. In *Ulysses* with the progress of the day we are taken from the matter-of-fact blasphemies of Buck Mulligan to the nostalgia of middle age, a development away from the delusive optimism of the will. (For the eagerness of youth which Molly Bloom celebrates belongs as much to the past as the dead son Bloom himself has been seeking during the day, and Molly's memories—Anna Livia has them also—serve to bring into focus, or "reveal," what [12] has gone before in much the same way as Gretta Conroy's story in *The Dead.*) And in *Finnegans Wake* the concluding first-person passage is the final epiphany of the generalized human *quidditas*, the thinking and feeling soul (Joyce shows sensibility surviving will), before it enters a new cycle of existence and is dissolved in the inorganic beginnings we encountered on the first page of the book: "riverrun, past Eve and Adam's, from swerve of shore to bend of bay," the river flowing through the city. Here at last is a perfect unity of technique, theme and esthetic principle, and a distillation of essence so complete that Being becomes quite literally the Word.

III

Joyce's work is a tissue of epiphanies, great and small, from fleeting images to whole books, from the briefest revelation in his lyrics to the epiphany that occupies one gigantic, enduring "moment" in *Finnegans Wake*, running through 628 pages of text and then returning upon itself. His major technique and the best illustration of his theory is the one just discussed, revelation through distillation of the pure, generalized *quidditas* from an impure whole, by which *consonantia* (here analysis of the whole into its parts) and *integritas* (resynthesis of the parts into a larger whole through the agency of language itself) interact to produce *claritas* directly. It is also his best-known technique (anyone who has grown up since the publication of *Ulysses* knows in advance, for instance, that Molly Bloom is female essence—Magna Mater and all that!) and in its high points it is his most spectacularly successful. It has, however, the defects of virtuosity. Usually the scale is too large to comprehend with ease, and the means to unity and diffusion, even in the intricate Joycean patterns of language, tend to become too mechanically ingenious, like Tchelichew's devices for hiding children's figures among the images of trees. In spite of the author's intention, his method often separates from his meaning and actually becomes [13] an obstacle to it, turning a serious work of art (which one cannot doubt *Finnegans Wake* is) into a parlor game.

Although it is less conspicuous and plays a fixed and minor role in the larger scheme of his work, Joyce makes use of one more epiphany technique which is worth considering because it is his closest approach to that austere impersonality of creation Stephen describes to Lynch: when "the artist, like the God of the creation, remains within or behind or above his handiwork, invisible, refined out of existence, indifferent, paring his fingernails." (252) Under this, the intervention of a consciousness, even indirectly through the medium of language, is ruled out. A character is broken down into its separate parts, as it is under the "distillation" technique, but only one or two of the detached "parts"—"the vulgarity of speech or of gesture," (*SH*-211) a detail of figure or expression, an item of clothing—are recombined. Although it is free of irrelevancies, the *quidditas* represented by the recombination is not the *quidditas* of a generality but an individual; its function is to identify rather than to abstract.

In *Stephen Hero* to some degree, and especially in *A Portrait of the Artist,* we can watch this technique take form. A priest is invariably marked by the fluttering of his soutane. Father Dolan steadies Stephen's hand before administering the pandying, and the cruelty of his gesture extends to his "firm soft fingers," "his grey-white face and the no-coloured eyes behind the steel-rimmed glasses" (56); when the priest reappears in *Ulysses,* he is signified only by the pandybat. In the same way, Mr. Casey's three cramped fingers symbolize his activities as an Irish patriot and hence his loyalty to Parnell, which for the boy Stephen is the peculiar essence of his father's friend. Again, the humility and joylessness of the church office are represented in the movements of the Jesuit dean of studies as he lights the fire, in his old, lean body—literally *similiter atque senis baculus*— (217)

and his face, compared by Stephen to "an unlit lamp or a reflection hung in a false focus." (219) [141]

Gesture and clothing, in particular, are as important in creating an individual *quidditas* as voice and breathing in creating a generalized *quidditas*. "There should be an art of gesture," (*SH*, 184) Stephen tells Cranly in *Stephen Hero*. In the *Portrait*, he finds his "image of the soul in prayer" in "the raised and parted hands, the parted lips and eyes of one about to swoon" (174) of religious art, and during his period of repentance visualizes himself "accomplishing the vague acts of the priesthood which pleased him by reason of their semblance of reality and of their distance from it." (183-184) Clothes, in their turn, are true repositories of the soul, as they are for Lévy-Bruhl's primitives. When he comes upon his schoolmates swimming, Stephen thinks pityingly of their nakedness: "How characterless they looked! Shuley without his deep unbuttoned collar, Ennis without his scarlet belt with the snaky clasp, and Connolly without his Norfolk coat with the flapless sidepockets!" (195) In *Stephen Hero*, he is first impressed by the prostitute's black straw hat, the outward and visible sign of her essence, and the clothes of the characters in Joyce's play *Exiles* are so important that they are not only described in the stage directions but are mentioned by the characters themselves, with a green velvet jacket playing a significant part in the action. Finally, in the nighttown episode of *Ulysses*, changes of costume are as frequent as in the charades in which Stephen takes part at Mr. Daniel's house (*Stephen Hero*), and the hallucinatory images of Bloom at successive stages of his past are all carefully dressed for their rôles.

Gesture and clothing, details of physical appearance, peculiarities of speech and intimate material appurtenances all serve to identify Stephen's friends in the *Portrait*, in dialogue passages which might be scenes from a play. Amid the profane, witty or banal conversations of the students, the author intervenes only as a sort of property man, to mark each one with his objectified *quidditas*, which adheres to him from scene to scene virtually without change and in some instances even carries over into [15] *Ulysses:* Cranly's "iron crown" of hair and priestly pallor, his profanity and Latin affectation of speech; Lynch's whinnying laugh, his habit of swearing "in yellow," and his gesture of putting out his chest; the shooting-suit and fair goatee of McCann, the reformer; Davin's brogue and Dixon's signet ring; Heron's cane and smile; the pedant Glynn's umbrella. In these scenes Stephen himself, the individual Stephen, is often a participant; he has his ashplant, his "familiar," which he carries also in *Ulysses,* and his soul moves rapidly and elusively through a series of metamorphoses which never quite leave the realm of the literal: the lamp mentioned in his conversation with the dean of studies; Epictetus' bucketful of water; Cranly's handball; the louse he picks from his neck; the fig Cranly tosses into the gutter.

This technique represents the ultimate in "objective" characterization, "revealing" an individual essence by means of a detail or an object to which it has only a fortuitous relation; the pandy-bat expresses Father Dolan's soul not because it resembles him in any way but because it is associated with him in an act that marks him forever in Stephen's eyes. Through Joyce's fourth epiphany technique (in which *claritas* is a tiny, perfunctory flash, all but absorbed by *quidditas*) we can trace out a virtual iconography of the characters, like the systematic recurrence of emblems and attitudes among the figures in sacred art. This was probably intentional on the part of Joyce, who was curiously "influenced" by medieval concepts and methods, probably more so than any other writer of our time, and whose preoccupation with symmetry and correspondence and the-microcosm-within-the-macrocosm would have been worthy of Dante. (There are indications in the *Portrait* of his attraction to religious iconography, which itself had a literary origin in the Middle Ages. During his period of sin, the adolescent Stephen still delights in the traditional symbols of Mary, and saints and their emblems —St. Ignatius Loyola with his book, St. Francis Xavier indicating his chest, Lorenzo Ricci and his berretta—are noted with particular [16] interest by Stephen the boy in the paintings at Clongowes.) In *Ulysses,* where the individual Mr. Bloom is signified variously by his hat, his newspaper and cigar, the lemon soap, the yellow flower, and the pork kidney, much of the medieval flavor of the Witches' Sabbath passages is due to the highly formalized iconography of the apparitions: King Edward with his bucket ("for identification bucket in my hand," the king explains himself), the dead Rudy with his Eton suit and his lambkin (a genuine epiphany to Bloom as he appears over the prostrate body of Stephen), Gerty MacDowell with her bloody clout, Lord Tennyson and his Union Jack blazer, the corpse of Stephen's mother with her faded orange blossoms and torn bridal veil, her breath of "wetted ashes" and *Liliata rutilantium.*

The emblematic *quidditas* is used with greatest virtuosity in *Ulysses*, but it is a technique of characterization that runs through all of Joyce's work. There are remnants of it in *Finnegans Wake,* in the signatures (tree and stone, river and hill, HCE and ALP) of Anna Livia and Earwicker, and it appears even in *Dubliners.* Father Flynn's chalice and old Maria's saucer of clay are clear examples; in *Two Gallants,* the coin takes part in the conventional narrative "revelation" and at the same time serves as the *quidditas* of the gallants; in *The Dead,* the absent Michael Furey is represented obliquely and ironically by the snow, *The Lass of Aughrim,* the overshoes, and the sore throat of Bartell D'Arcy, the vain concert tenor. In Joyce's poems we have the flower in "A Flower Given to My Daughter" and the snood "that is the sign of maidenhood" in "Bid adieu, adieu, adieu." *Exiles* has already been mentioned: its detailed descriptions of the dress and attitudes of the characters are not so much evidence of meticulous naturalistic accuracy as an effort to transmit to the actors the special objectified *quidditas* of each character as the author conceived it; the play is a failure largely because the stage directions cannot take the place of Joyce's own handling of the scenes. And finally, I think the same iconographic technique was ultimately [17] responsible for the Joycean compound epithet that has now seeped down into Mr. Luce's editorial offices. In "shameclosing eyes," "dewsilky cattle," "saltwhite corpse," "snotgreen sea," modelled on the "winedark sea" and "rosy-fingered dawn" that have been deified by scholars, a unique quality is wedded to its counterpart to produce a compact representation of *quidditas* in its smallest unit.

And so the individual *quidditas* is concentrated in a physical image, often, though not always, visual, as the generalized *quid-*

ditas is diffused in a stream of sound. The soul of the thing, its whatness, truly "leaps to us from the vestment of its appearance." Basically, perhaps, there is no difference between Joyce's final epiphany technique and the symbolism of other writers—such as the *leitmotiv* of Thomas Mann—but in its development and its use there are very real differences. Following Freud, we have come to think of a symbol chiefly in terms of its representational qualities (Pribislav Hippe's pencil in *The Magic Mountain*); through a combination of experimental science and philosophical idealism, we tend also to find a value of their own in "things," which we conceive more or less as absolutes. Joyce's conception of the symbol is much closer to the conception of the medieval Church: a symbol has a specific function to perform in a given situation, and when that function has been performed, nothing prevents the use of the symbol again in a totally different context. This flexibility results eventually in the intimate interpenetration of the parts and the whole that is one of the chief manifestations of Joyce's principle of *consonantia,* reaching a high degree of complexity in his later work. In *Finnegans Wake,* where, as the writers of exegeses remind us, every part presupposes every other part and their sum as well, it is difficult to separate out the individual threads of the pattern. But we can see its outlines already in the "Christmas" symbolism of the *Portrait,* where the significance of the velvet-backed brushes (maroon for the *quidditas* of Michael Davitt, green for the *quidditas* of Parnell) [18] is expanded in Stephen's "red and green" impressions as he anticipates the school holiday, and the Irish church and Irish politics are ironically united at the dinner party on Christmas day in the violent quarrel between Aunt Dante and Mr. Casey; we see it also in the "bowl" symbolism in the early pages of *Ulysses,* where the bowl of shaving-lather, introduced as the *quidditas* of Buck Mulligan, becomes successively the bay, the bowl of incense Stephen carried at Clongowes, and the bowl of green bile at his mother's deathbed. Although these are only minor examples of Joyce's method, few could illustrate it more effectively. [19]

GEDDES MacGREGOR
Artistic Theory in James Joyce

In *A Portrait of the Artist as a Young Man,* one of Joyce's easiest novels, there is some reference to an artistic theory. But in a fragmentary early version of that work, the manuscript of which is now in the Harvard College Library, and which was published three years ago as *Stephen Hero,* one may find peculiarly interesting and explicit passages omitted from the work in its final form. Here is presented very ingenuously a theory which may throw considerable light on the later Joycian technique. In *Ulysses* and other later works there are but passing allusions to such a theory. Even in the finished *Portrait* Joyce has begun to pontificate, and in *Ulysses* he speaks with all the *hauteur* of the artistic temperament letting art speak for itself. It is from the immature Joyce that we may hope to understand some of the principles that lie behind his later telegraphic utterances.

Much of what Joyce's *alter ego* says in his paper on æsthetics in the early draft of the *Portrait* is in fact extremely superficial, much more superficial than it evidently professed to be. It was certainly also not original by the time the manuscript was written. The influence of Croce's *Estetica* at the turn of the century was rapid, and much of it but expressed in an exceptionally lucid manner an attitude towards which European reflection on art had been moving for a very long time. An Irishman aspiring to be a Good European, and characteristically contributing an essay on Ibsen to the *Fortnightly Review* while still an undergraduate at the college where Gerard Manley Hopkins, the Jesuit

Reprinted by permission of the author. This essay appeared originally in *Life and Letters,* LIV (July, 1947). References to *Stephen Hero* are to SH-1.

poet, had once taught Greek, James Joyce was set to absorb
this continental influence as a sponge to drink in water. The
future expatriate who, leading a particularly conventional life
with his wife and children, was to toil in Trieste as a Berlitz
language-teacher, spend the [18] war years in Exile at Zürich—
with an interlude as a bank clerk in Rome—and end up in Paris,
all while writing a literature that was to scandalize both hemi-
spheres, had swallowed his artistic theory neat as an undergraduate, and once for all. It needed but patience to work it
out, and Joyce had this virtue abundantly.

But in spite of all this, there was much in the theory that is
profoundly true. The artist is a kind of priest standing between
the world of his experience and the world of his dreams; or,
if we may reinterpret this, between the world of his experience
as artist and that of his experience as common man. He has
twin faculties—a selective and a reproductive one—and to equate
these faculties is his *métier*. The domain of art is to be conceived
as cone-shaped; poetry is the perfect coincidence of the two
faculties, while "literature" is, according to Joyce, no more than
a vast, dull space that lies between the apex and the base of the
cone, that is, between poetry and the chaos of unremembered
writing. But his kingdom of art is no anarchy, for Joyce insists
on classicism as integral to all true art. A classical style is described, indeed, as the "syllogism of art." It is this love for the
classical, hand in hand with his cosmopolitan tastes and his incurable but repressed nostalgia for Ireland, which gives his
work much of its extraordinarily distinctive flavour. A born
linguist, he knew the limitations of language, and though he
tried as perhaps no one else has ever tried to overcome them,
he never forgot them. What he valued in the classical temper
was its spatial catholicity; it is a constant state of the artistic
mind. The romantic temper, by impatiently throwing the inevitable limitations of sense to the winds, loses its moorings and
dissipates itself. Joyce always remained far too much an Irishman to forget the fatally easy fluency of his race. He perceived,
however unconsciously, that the vigorous eloquence which was
his Irish heritage needed something hard to chew if it were to
survive, and his life was in great part a quest for this.

It is in his earlier work that we find Joyce willing to take the trouble of repudiating the puritanical conception of didactic art. Genuine art should no more be didactic than it should be [19] pornographic; it should be content to be art. To prohibit the artist's course as an artist is as absurd as it would be for a police-magistrate to prohibit a triangle from having three sides. Nothing on this subject, however, is particularly well said in the *Ur-Portrait,* and had been said far better by æstheticians years previously. But one would hopelessly misunderstand Joyce if one were to think of him as an apostle of libertinism, as was D. H. Lawrence, for instance, in the sense that the latter deliberately fought against the contemporary ethical code, which he regarded as an insult to life. Joyce is no more anti-puritan than he is puritan, no more unconventional than conventional. As Sisley Huddleston depicts them, Joyce's birthday parties in his flat on the *rive gauche* show how much he was the artist and how little the literary snob; and only the most intolerable literary snob could have failed to enjoy these evenings to which the guests were invited simply because they were family friends. Far from being acts of literary homage or a Joycian cult, they were rather more like a Yorkshire family party. The guests went not to encircle James Joyce, but to meet Mr. and Mrs. Joyce at a long table on which were piles of cakes and sandwiches, jugs of champagne and Irish whisky. And as befitted such parties, one was pressed to eat more than one wanted, but never asked whether one had even read Joyce at all. They must have been almost the last places in the world at which the race of pretentious, Joyce-worshipping literary faddists would have expected to find him. One of Joyce's greatest secrets was that he never ceased to be wildly shocked by the immoral without being in the least shocked at writing about it with not the slightest vestige of reproof. His artistic theory never lost his most faithful allegiance; but he carried into his art, unwittingly perhaps, something of the conventional standards of morality that had captured his vivid imagination.

But there was an even stronger influence at work: his spiritual Mother, the Roman Church. For while he seemed to delight in ribald blasphemy against her theology, he always reverted to

her structure. No apostate was ever more irrevocably captivated
by the Church from which the apostasy [20] took place. This was
partly due to his exaltation of the classical temper, but more to
the simpler fact that his Catholicism was so embedded in his
mind that he could never wholly escape the pattern. I think one
of the best introductory remarks one could make to a prospective
student of James Joyce is that of Valéry Larbaud, who observes
that he is closer to the Jesuit casuists than to the French nat-
uralists. Even so, it is certainly bizarre that Joyce should turn
to Saint Thomas for an æsthetic, as he does in *Stephen Hero*,
while flouting the theological authority of the great Doctor of
the Church. It would be hard to find even the most enthusiastic
neo-Thomist so content with the widely discredited, naïve æsthetic of Thomism. Stephen, however, recalling the three things
which Thomas said were necessary for beauty (integrity, symmetry, and radiance), boldly rushes into an exposition. When
one is confronted by an æsthetic object, one divides the universe
into two parts, the object and the void which is not the object;
so one recognizes its integrity, which is declared in a sudden
synthesis in the faculty which apprehends. Then follows analysis;
the mind traverses every cranny of its structure, thus receiving
the impression of the symmetry of the object. But it is about the
third quality, radiance (*claritas*), that Stephen has most exercised his mind. *Claritas*, Stephen roundly asserts, is *quidditas*.
This is Thomist terminology, but little more. It is, however,
from the rock of this æsthetic theory that *Ulysses* itself is pre-
sumed to have been hewn.

After the synthesis that is followed by analysis, there comes
synthesis again. This is the moment which Joyce calls "epiphany," turning again inevitably to Mother Church. Joyce had
no Greek, and it is probable that Oliver Gogarty is right when
he suggests that Father Darlington had taught Joyce incidentally, in the Latin class, that "epiphania" (for instance, "epiphania Domini") meant "a showing forth." At any rate, Joyce defines "epiphany" as a *manifestation*, which is the usual alternative
term in English to describe the liturgical event. We ought to
beware of looking for subtle explanations of Joyce's theory and
technique, as critics too often have done, lest the simpler and

probably true explanation elude us. What is a Joycian "epiphany," after all, but the equivalent of a [21] Crocean "moment of expression"? You see a clock daily; but at last you "intuit" it. So Joyce: "Yes," said Stephen. "I will pass it time after time, allude to it, refer to it, catch a glimpse of it. It is only an item in the catalogue of Dublin's street furniture. Then all at once I see it and I know at once what it is: epiphany." (*SH*, 211)

He goes on to compare the process with that of focussing physical vision: the moment the object comes into focus it is "epiphanized." It is a question of attaining purity in artistic experience. One recalls Edward Bullough's theory of "psychical distance." Joyce was fascinated by his idea of "epiphanies," which keeps cropping up in various guises throughout his work, so that we even find that when the remarkable company of saints and martyrs, acolytes and mitred abbots, proceeds down Little Britain Street to a firm of "wholesale grocers, wine and brandy shippers," the mullioned windows of which are censed by priests standing beneath a canopy of gold, it is the introit "in *Epiphania Domini* which beginneth *Surge, illuminare*" that they sing. (*UL*, 333-334) Not a few *raconteurs* have become literary cameramen under the influence of Joyce's technique; a literature of the most subtle sophistication and eccentric preciosity has developed round short-story writing; but it is plain that, however masterly and original was this technique, his artistic theory remained always almost incredibly simple.

Nor had Joyce, in spite of the contrast between his conventional manner of life and the audacious unconventionality of his writing, the slightest capacity for the kind of artistic detachment which enables an artist to submerge his own personality in his work. Harry Levin's insight is never more penetrating than when he observes that Joyce lacks the precision in parody which made it possible for Max Beerbohm to draw caricatures which were acutely critical masterpieces quite independent of the cartoonist's personality. We can admire his style, as versatile as it is recognizable, almost without wondering who the superb craftsman was. Consider only Beerbohm's work in 1913: the immaculate and debonair Lord Alexander Thynne, all smooth and black, "enchanting the Labour Party"; or Masefield con-

templating in poetic [22] ecstasy on the roof of a "rustic slum"
the artistic significance of a "swear-word" in the alley below;
or the "mild surprise of someone who, revisiting England after
long absence," finds Shaw still standing on his head; or the dons
of Magdalen scrupulously avoiding a forlorn new undergraduate,
the Prince of Wales, so as "to incur no imputation of flunkeyism."
They are all of a piece, yet tell us little of the craftsman who
has produced them, as it were behind an iron curtain. Joyce,
on the other hand, spills himself all over his *pastiches*. When
he parodies, he parodies himself; not Dickens or Carlyle or
Wardour Street, but Joyce the Dickensian, Joyce playing at
Carlylese, Joyce in Wardour Street. His work is always as Mil-
tonic as it is Rabelaisian, and it is very much both; but it is
always above all Joycian. There is hardly a phrase in *Ulysses*
that does not scream Joyce at you; yet it is Joyce the artist,
hardly ever Joyce the man. This is one reason why, of all the
errors of judgment ever committed by the censor, surely that
which caused the ferocious persecution of Joyce and resulted
in the ridiculous litigation that ended with his triumph in the
United States Court of Appeals, must be the worst; worse even
than the prosecutions of Flaubert's *Madame Bovary* and Baudelaire's *Fleurs du Mal*. A pornographer who wrote anything
so sexually disgusting as *Ulysses* would die of starvation if he
were not locked up as mad. A blasphemer who did so would
be no less pathetically inefficient; there was perhaps more
wisdom than may appear in the Papal Index of 1929 that kept
all Zola and even some of Kant and Locke on the forbidden
list while Joyce had not found his way into it.

By the time he wrote *Ulysses* Joyce had steeped his art in
two fast dyes, sex and religion. This is not, of course, a unique
arrangement. Sex is at the root of human life, and religion
professes to be its fullest flower; it is natural that the artist
should find extremes peculiarly interesting. But the manner of
Joyce's handling of the antinomy is certainly unique, and it is
somehow increased by, if not entirely dependent on, the fact
that the Catholic tradition which held him spellbound is one
which knows pre-eminently how to express itself. Joyce does

not try to shock either the conventional or the pious; [23] he is too shocked himself by the polarity of sex and religion. He could hardly have failed to have been much influenced not least during his Zürich period, by the psychoanalysis movement, and there is little doubt that his artistic theory was to some extent, to say the least, affected by the psychoanalytic idea of free association. He is "yung and easily freudened." Confessing a debt to Dujardin, he writes a *monologue intérieur,* but one which has been deliberately brought out into the light of consciousness, and seen in the perspective of the conscious. It was a reaction from Ibsen's naturalistic drama. Impressionism had looked at life passively; expressionism, as Hermann Bahr said in 1916, looks at it actively through the mind's eye; and Joyce never forgets to bring his internal monologue on the glaring stage of conscious mind however fleeting each glimpse may be. But when all this is said, it remains true that Joyce never radically modified his own far more unsophisticated artistic theory. One will learn no more psychology from *Ulysses* than from many inferior "psychological" novels, perhaps not even as much. But the key-note of the Joycian theory, the idea of artistic arrest, is invariably manifest in his technique. One by one, with astonishing patience and skill, ideas are arrested in the black darkness of the unconscious, and, held firmly in the craftsman's grasp, brought forth boldly into the light of day, so that we have the feeling that Joyce is almost as much surprised at his catch as we are.

Theoretically, all art is a basis for further mental activity, for instance intellectual or moral reflection, because the artistic experience is that upon which all other experience rests. But Joyce's art does not ordinarily fill this role, for its strength and weakness lie in the fact that it appears but momentarily on the stage of consciousness. Artists are all accustomed to wrest artistic truth from the artificiality of ordinary experience, but Joyce does this facing, as it were, in the opposite direction. He has to create a barrier against the torrential stream of unconscious mind, to impose stasis on kinetic energy, and the result is sometimes jerky, even irritating, because he is trying to produce a still film out of a motion picture, to make the picture dominate the motion. This is, of course, what music [24] does, and to do the same in letters demands consummate craftsmanship.

There seems to be nothing in Joyce's very primitive artistic theory to suggest anything so technically clever as *Ulysses*. That Joyce was able to accomplish it was due rather to his uncannily acute sense of hearing. His eyesight was, it is well known, extremely defective, and he evidently made good the deficiency by a sense of hearing so vigorous and delicate that he was capable not only of distinguishing but of creating *nuances* that would escape most people. It is surely due to this gift, rather than to any theory, that word-play is so much part of his technique. The pun is proper to only a certain level of mental activity. Rustics are generally insensitive to it, and intellectual people usually find it tiresome; but it is at home in the strongholds of city life; the Parisian finds it amusing (French is a paradise for punsters), and the Cockney enjoys it, as he enjoys rhyming slang, its near cousin. Joyce loves nothing better than linguistic medley, and his pun has often a cosmopolitan character. He spins gaily from one tongue to another as he skims across the waters of human experience, love and obscenity, blessings and blasphemies, what you will. The Church itself, he announces, was founded on a pun, "thuartpeatrick." Chamberlain's foreign policy is "umbroglio." Joyce can go on like this for hours. His malapropisms expand till his entire work becomes one vast malapropism symbolic of the *malaise* between art and life. Sometimes it is impossible to escape the conclusion that he is too inhumanly clever with words to lay hold on human life; yet is not such failure the failure of our century to relate art to the chaos of the city?

No student of Joyce can have failed to notice how much easier he is when read aloud; indeed, to read him silently is almost like reading a musical score. In the opening paragraph of *Dubliners* he confesses how the sound of certain words has always fascinated him; "gnomon," "simony," and above all, "paralysis." He was constantly analysing the bare sounds words made, so that by the time he wrote *Ulysses* he was able to make almost the whole work onomatopœic. Some of the difficulty of his synthetic language (*Ulysses* contains 260,430 words, with a vocabulary of 29,899) disappears as we recognize [25] his extreme preoccupation with sounds and accustom ourselves to a constant tendency to onomatopœia. "Enjoy a bath now: clean trough of water, cool enamel, the gentle tepid stream." (*UL,* 85) "Jingling hoofthuds." (*UL,* 166) "He came a step a sinkapace forward on neatsleather creaking and a step backward a sinkapace on the solemn floor." (*UL,* 182) "Heartbeats her breath, breath that is life. And all the tiny tiny fernfoils trembled of maidenhair." (*UL,* 281) But to solve all the "messes of mottage" we must be on the *qui vive* for a quite incalculably complex combination of devices, especially alliterations, assonances, spoonerisms, rhymes, puns, and other such auditory frolics, but also all linguistic puzzles, anagrams, acrostics, and so forth, and these often with a *double-* or even *triple-entendre* in a Babel of foreign tongues. So we have "viceking's graab," since Ireland is at once the loot of Albion's viceroy and the grave of old Norsemen; and "pratschkats at their platschpails," because in Russian *prachka* and *plach* mean "laundress" and "weeping" respectively is a phrase to denote old women by the Liffey, whose "rivering," "chittering," "hitherandthithering" waters are presented to us in many guises. (*FW,* 215-216) There is, plainly, no end to the possibilities of linguistic fun of this kind, and Joyce certainly never goes out of his way to help the reader. By the time he was at *Finnegans Wake* he had become, it would seem, obsessed with a mania for the cryptic, almost as if it were an end in itself. All this has little to do with his naïve artistic theory, and much to do with his innate and freakish genius as a linguistic conjuror.

The extraordinary richness and versatility of Joyce, which has led Pierre Courthion, in his fairly recent book, *Le Visage de Matisse,* to compare him to Picasso, is likewise to be considered to a great extent quite apart from his artistic theory. His plethora of material has more connection with the mischievousness of his temperament, goading him on to outdo the surrealists at their own game, than with his proper art to which it is more often than not quite incidental. He could be pellucid when he pleased, even in *Pomes Penyeach:*

The moon's greygolden meshes make
All night a veil,
The shorelamps in the sleeping lake
Laburnum tendrils trail. [26]

His obscurities may have been sometimes intentional—he was certainly brimming over with fun, which saved him constantly from the spiritual jaundice to which his fastidious disgust at the tragedy of life's antitheses otherwise pointed—but oftener they arise from the fact that he has to take for his material that which is timeless, so that his range must be catholic. Giambattista Vico predicted a new, timeless history, and more recently Croce's historiology has prepared us for literary phenomena of this kind. This timelessness is among the essential features of Joycian theory and technique; he refuses to recognize any fundamental difference between myth and "historical fact"; he hammers all together just as he welds "thurifer" to "crucifix" to give us "thurifex." But we must distinguish Joyce, the literary alchemist who never forgot the Rabelaisian dictum, *"mieulx est de ris que de larmes escrire,"* from Joyce the artist, who like most artists was no æsthetician, but unlike most artists clung with astonishing tenacity to the shallow though not unwholesome artistic theory he had framed while no more than a big schoolboy rebelling against his Jesuit preceptors.

HASKELL M. BLOCK

The Critical Theory of James Joyce

WHILE IT IS GENERALLY RECOGNIZED that Joyce's outstanding artistic achievements developed from less important early writings, the role of critical theory in his works has too often been neglected. Joyce's first three publications were critical essays; his first work of major proportions, *Portrait of the Artist as a Young Man*, is devoted in large measure to the resolution of the young artist's aesthetic, and all during his formative years Joyce was occupied with the study of aesthetic theory and with the elaboration of what was to have been a highly-wrought philosophical system. And although Joyce's concern with critical theory seems to be limited to his youth, it will be readily apparent that his aesthetic exerted a pervasive influence on his writings during the whole of his literary career.

I

Born in Dublin in 1882, Joyce received a rigorously scholastic education at the hands of the Jesuits. Instructed in a strong religious and classical atmosphere, he acquired an excellent knowledge of Latin, and an extant translation of a Horatian ode made at fourteen bears witness to his early linguistic aptitudes.[1] He took his baccalaureate degree at University College, Dublin, in Romance languages, studying Italian constantly, and obtaining an excellent command of French as well. His early works with

Reprinted by permission of the author and the *Journal of Aesthetics and Art Criticism*. The essay appeared originally in that journal in March, 1950. References to *A Portrait* are to P-2; to *Stephen Hero* are to SH-1.

[1] H. Gorman, *James Joyce: A Definitive Biography*, pp. 45-46.

their copious allusions indicate clearly the wide range of his
reading in the literature of his day. He translated Maeterlinck,
Verlaine, Hauptmann and Ibsen, and during his last years at
University College, from 1900 to 1902, he composed a large
amount of verse, much of which was written in fixed French
forms in the manner of Andrew Lang, Edmund Gosse or Arthur
Symons. We may conclude merely from this cursory treatment
of the young writer's intellectual interests that the most important sources of his inspiration were three-fold: the aesthetic
movement in England, continental drama and the scholastic
tradition inculcated by his Jesuit mentors.

The most powerful single influence on the young Joyce was
Henrik Ibsen,[2] and it was with an article entitled "Ibsen's New
Drama" that he officially began his literary career.[3] The occasion
was the appearance of a new Ibsen play, *When We Dead
Awaken,* and Joyce's essay is little more than an extended review
of this work. When it is recalled that Joyce was but eighteen
years of age when his article was published, it must be recognized that his literary knowledge and critical ability indicate a
remarkable precocity.

It would nonetheless be generous to consider the essay a systematic critical appraisal. Joyce is more largely concerned with
the presentation of the heroic image of the dramatist whom he
clearly regards as a creative giant, towering over [172] all his
critics and contemporaries. After presenting this image, Joyce
goes on to render an excellent critical account of the new drama,
reviewing carefully the conduct of the action, clarifying his statements with frequent citation, and allowing Ibsen to speak for
himself whenever possible.

While it is unnecessary to consider Ibsen's work in the same
detailed manner pursued by Joyce in his essay, it is important
to indicate what elements in Ibsen's drama made the strongest
impression on the young writer. It is significant, first of all, that
he prefers the late drama to the better known "problem-play,"
and in concluding his éloge, he suggests that *When We Dead*

---

[2] Cf. V. K. Macleod, "The Influence of Ibsen on Joyce," *PMLA,* LX (1945),
879-898 and LXII (1947), 573-580.
[3] *The Fortnightly Review,* LXXIII (1900), 575-590.

Awaken may well be considered Ibsen's greatest work. In this drama, written at the end of his career, Ibsen is more concerned with psychological conditions symbolically interpreted than with social problems, and as Joyce clearly indicates, his psychological strength is most apparent in his "analytic method" by which characters are moved through "soul-crises" of mounting intensity, compressing whole lifetimes into a few moments. Even more important for Joyce is Ibsen's crucial concern with the relation of art and life. This central theme of *When We Dead Awaken* is built around the relations of a sculptor, Rubek, and his former model, Irene. The lives of both are spiritually dead; Rubek's, because increasing age has not been accompanied by a happy married life, and Irene's, because Rubek had enclosed her soul in a work of art, leaving her inwardly barren. The play is climaxed by their mutual perception of their present lives as a living death, and they find relief and communion in a love suicide, a triumph and a vindication of the beauty of aesthetic perfection, and a resolution through love of the basic dramatic conflict between isolation and union, between art and life.

Joyce stresses with admiration Ibsen's objectivity and detach‚ ment in the treatment of his subject: "Ibsen . . . treats all things with large insight, artistic restraint, and sympathy. He sees it steadily and whole, as from a great height, with perfect vision and an angelic dispassionateness, with the sight of one who may look on the sun with open eyes." [4]

There are more than echoes of Matthew Arnold here; there is the whole aesthetic tradition of the late nineteenth century, colored by the youthful reviewer's hero-worship. It is no surprise to find Joyce concluding his essay as he began it, with a succession of rhapsodic apostrophes on Ibsen's stature as a man. While it is true that Joyce's review contains many perceptive insights into Ibsen's writing, it would be most inaccurate to describe this essay as a systematic critique. There is no evidence of a carefully defined aesthetic which offers an objective basis of critical judgment.

Joyce seems to be fully aware of the unphilosophical aspect of his essay, but considers this of little importance. Since Ibsen is

[4] *Ibid.*, p. 588.

a great writer, his dramas are their own justification: "Appreciation, hearkening is the only true criticism. Further, that species
of criticism which calls itself dramatic criticism is a needless
adjunct to his plays. [173] When the art of a dramatist is perfect
the critic is superfluous. Life is not to be criticized, but to be
faced and lived." [5]

Clearly, this anti-intellectualism would render all criticism impossible in the absence of definite criteria of artistic excellence.
The rigorous opposition between "criticism" and "life" can perhaps be accounted for by Joyce's hero-worship, and by a possible
reaction to the excessive intellectualization of scholastic logic
which occupied Joyce's studies at this time. Yet the dominant
motif accords well with the thought of Joyce's English predecessors; there is a whole critical tradition at work in the attitude that
a perfect work of art constitutes its own *raison d'être*.

We have already alluded at length to Joyce's intense and
almost religious veneration of the Norwegian. At the same time,
the essay presents a tone of violent resistance to canting and
self-righteous opponents of the new drama, and at times the
work reads more like a manifesto than a review; the young critic
has identified himself with the dramatist, and Ibsen has become
a weapon against Philistine aesthetic indifference.

This polemic quality of Joyce's review suggests that his audience was not at all the customary audience of *The Fortnightly
Review*. For well-informed readers, Ibsen had been a common
topic of discussion for over fifteen years, and while a bitter
controversy had raged in England over his work between 1889
and 1896, from that time onward the dramatist's reputation was
secure and his work was generally accepted. [6] Writing in 1900,
Joyce was summarizing a struggle that had long since taken
place, and it is likely that his pugnacity was directly aimed at
his local Irish environment; in England it was hardly necessary. [7]

The same tone and tenor of thought pervades Joyce's next

[5] *Ibid.*, p. 589.
[6] Cf. C. R. Decker, "Ibsen's Literary Reputation and Victorian Taste," *SP*,
XXXII (1935), 632-645, and U. Ellis-Fermor, *The Irish Dramatic Movement*, p. 213.
[7] It should be remarked that the impression of Joyce's article on his fellow-
students in Dublin was overwhelming. Cf. Gorman, *op. cit.*, p. 65.

publication, which appeared in October, 1901. This was a brief essay in the form of a two-penny pamphlet entitled *The Day of the Rabblement,* and embodied one of the most serious and violent attacks on the policies of the newly-formed Irish Literary Theater. We have indicated the extent to which Joyce was immersed in modern European drama, and his antagonism evident throughout the essay toward the isolation of his countrymen from European artistic traditions is a product of his wide reading and growing cosmopolitan attitude. Vividly and forcefully, he contrasts the productions of Ibsen and Hauptmann with drama presented in Ireland, and proceeds to denounce the Irish Literary Theater vigorously for succumbing to popular taste in the choice of its productions. Throughout, the young writer is declamatory and contemptuous, yet the brief article embodies a closely reasoned argument, and the style itself indicates considerable literary merit.

The Irish Literary Theater had been founded in January, 1899, by W. B. Yeats, Lady Gregory and Edward Martyn, and George Moore was rapidly drawn into the organization.[8] At the time of Joyce's attack, the group was commencing its third year of performances, and it must be admitted that apart from Yeats' [174] *Countess Cathleen,* little drama of artistic merit was produced. The bulk of the financial backing was supplied by Edward Martyn, a devout Catholic anxious to remain on good terms with the clergy, and constantly difficult to manage when the question of new productions came up. Between the additional problems of keeping the actors contented and not offending the audience, it is remarkable that the Irish Literary Theater succeeded as well as it did. It should be added, however, that by October, 1901, the organization was becoming more closely associated with the Gaelic League, and it is quite clear from his brief essay that even at this early stage of his career, Joyce thoroughly condemned the subservience of art to nationalism.

The opening sentence of Joyce's attack on the Irish Literary Theater enunciates his cardinal aesthetic principle, the artistic necessity of self-imposed isolation: "No man, said the Nolan, can be a lover of the true or the good unless he abhors the multitude;

[8] U. Ellis-Fermor, *op. cit.,* p. 33. Also cf. J. Hone, *W. B. Yeats,* pp. 165-171.

and the artist, though he may employ the crowd, is very careful
to isolate himself."

It is interesting to remark that in expounding this "radical
principle of artistic economy," Joyce cites the authority of Giordano Bruno, alluding to his town of origin. He could have readily
found contemporary sources in support of this same position, and
it would not be difficult to point out the remarkable extent to
which this doctrine was accepted by many of Joyce's immediate
predecessors. At the same time, Joyce is intent on more than
a merely theoretical statement of his position. The principle of
isolation is based on a total philosophical attitude, and implies
a sharp dichotomy between the artist and his society. This separation is all-pervasive in Joyce's condemnation of the Irish pop-
ulace: "Now your popular devil is more dangerous than your
vulgar devil. Bulk and lungs count for something, and he can
gild his speech aptly. He has prevailed once more, and the Irish
Literary Theater must now be considered the property of the
most belated race in Europe."

Joyce insists firmly on the primary importance of a literary
tradition, and Irish drama is deficient because it is divorced from
the more genuine art produced on the continent. Furthermore,
the presentation of plays by the Irish Literary Theater is gov-
erned by canons of moral propriety with which the artist has
absolutely nothing to do. By retaining his personal integrity the
artist becomes heroic in his isolation, and by separating himself
from the mass of mankind, he becomes the preserver of art and
the heir of his artistic precedessors, unimpeded by any servility
to popular taste.

Joyce goes on to condemn the efforts of Martyn and Moore
unreservedly, and concludes the essay with a plea for the extension of the dramatic tradition of Ibsen and Hauptmann. The
closing lines are of particular interest for their suggestion of
Joyce's self-identification with his continental idols: "Elsewhere
there are men who are worthy to carry on the tradition of the
old master who is dying in Christiania. He has already found
his successor in the writer of *Michael Kramer,* and the third
minister will not be wanting when his hour comes. Even now
that hour may be standing by the door." [175]

We have already observed the extent of Joyce's admiration and his enthusiasm for his psychological drama as opposed to more purely social plays. A similar interest may be recognized in his praise of Hauptmann, whose works Joyce was arduously translating at this time.

Michael Kramer (1900) resembles Ibsen's *When We Dead Awaken* in its central theme, the search of the artist for security, for a unifying force that can give meaning to life. It is significant that Joyce voiced his preference for this particular play of Hauptmann, for in it the author is moving away from the tendentious presentation of sordidness and misery to a more direct concern with philosophical attitudes and psychological reactions. It is also important to recognize the dominant antagonism in the play between the Philistine bourgeois and the creative artist, and the insistence of the central figure on self-imposed isolation as the condition of artistic achievement: "*Das wächst nur aus Einsiedeleien auf! Das Eigne, das Echte, Tiefe und Kräftige, das wird nur in Einsiedeleien geboren. Der Künstler ist immer der wahre Einsiedler.*" [9]

It must be emphasized that by the turn of the century, Joyce's "principle of artistic economy" was not the exclusive property of any particular movement as had earlier been the case. One must also remember that the scholastic tradition was presumably operative continually during Joyce's early period, and it is not remarkable that he should attempt to reconcile his educational background with what he considered the most significant contemporary literature, particularly in the formation of his aesthetic. Joyce was moving in well-defined traditions, but at the beginning of his career, his eclecticism should not appear unnatural. And at bottom, it cannot be too strongly insisted, theory for him was but a stepping-stone, a necessary condition of further artistic achievement rather than an end in itself.

As might well be expected, the reaction of Joyce's fellow students at University College to *The Day of the Rabblement* was most unfavorable. After paraphrasing Joyce's argument all too briefly, the college magazine, *St. Stephen's*, remonstrated with severe indignation against the lone apostle of art:

[9] Hauptmann, *Das gesammelte Werk*, Bd. III, p. 394.

Now, as we understand the Literary Theater, its object was to *educate* a vulgarised public, in a word, to rescue the Irish rabblement from the influences which, from the point of view of the artist, were working havoc. But this rabblement clung to a standard of morality—the tradition of the Catholic Church, the ethical teaching of Christendom. For a spiritual life based thereon it had sacrificed material prosperity and well-being, and it now showed itself willing, in the same interest, to forego all that art might add to the surroundings of life. So it happened that when this rabblement protested against "Countless Cathleen," our fellow-students approved and supported the protest. Mr. Joyce alone, to our knowledge, stood aloof. If Mr. Joyce thinks that the artist must stand apart from the multitude, and means that he must also sever himself from the moral and religious teachings which have, under Divine guidance, moulded its spiritual character, we join issue [176] with him, and we prophesy but ill-success for any school which offers an Irish public art based upon such a principle.[10]

One can only surmise what Joyce's reaction to this pronouncement may have been. It must be admitted that such sweeping criticism was far from common. For while Joyce is sometimes ridiculed by his colleagues, he is often admired and there seems to have been little doubt of his genuine literary ability. At the same time, it is questionable whether Joyce's isolation was simply intellectual. The criticism and satire directed at the young artist in *St. Stephen's* would suggest that his spiritual dislocation was accompanied by a physical isolation from all but a few close intimates alluded to in later works.

Joyce's next critical statement was an essay on the Irish poet, James Clarence Mangan, and appeared in *St. Stephen's* in May, 1902.[11] Here, as in the earlier essays, there is no systematically

[10] *St. Stephen's: A Record of University Life,* December, 1901, p. 43. I am indebted to the Librarian of the British Museum for the use of Joyce's college magazine as well as of the original editions of his early critical essays. It should be remarked that the reprint of "The Day of the Rabblement" in Gorman's *James Joyce,* pp. 71-73, abounds in textual errors that cause serious distortion of Joyce's argument.

[11] This essay is evidently a reprint of a paper read by Joyce before the "Literary and Historical Society" of University College, February 1, 1902. An interesting review appears in the March issue of *St. Stephen's.* The only complete reprint of this essay appeared in an unauthorized limited edition, published by the Ulysses Press, London, in 1930.

formulated critical theory. The work is largely an appreciation of an unrecognized Irish poet whom Joyce admired, and despite the interesting light it sheds on Joyce's reading, it must not be regarded as a rigorous pronouncement of critical dicta.

On the other hand, it is possible to distinguish the presence of immediate literary influences, as well as some attempt on Joyce's part toward theoretical formulation. The analysis of the classical and romantic schools with which the essay begins is quite suggestive of Walter Pater's "Postscript" in *Appreciations,* while the philosophical principles by which Joyce judges Mangan are more closely allied to Shelley's *Defence of Poetry.* Thus, he asserts that "poetry in any art transcends the mode of its expression," and introduces the distinction between "poetry" and "literature" to separate the incommunicable regions of art from the profanities of common life.

It is important to consider Joyce's representation of Mangan as an adumbration of the concept of the artist elaborated in his later work. Mangan is described as the artist spiritually exiled in his native land, "a rare and unsympathetic figure in the streets, where he is seen going forward alone like one who does penance for some ancient sin." It is more with the man than with the poetry that Joyce is concerned, insisting that the poet must be in revolt against actuality, fleeing from common reality to dreams which serve as the primary source of poetic inspiration and which are expressed in the intensity of the poet's life.

In full accord with the logical conclusions of his arguments in *The Day of the Rabblement,* Joyce left Ireland for Paris in November, 1902. His return to Dublin in April, 1903, was forced by the death of his mother, and he remained there until [177] October, 1904, when he left Ireland to take up definite residence on the continent, and to begin his difficult career, wandering in voluntary exile over the face of Europe.

During his first sojourn in Paris he occupied himself with researches in scholastic philosophy and with careful notations toward a critical theory.[12] As we shall see from our consideration of Joyce's later work, the scholastic tradition was deeply imbedded in his intellectual attitude, and his severe attempts to

12 Cf. Gorman, *op. cit.,* pp. 96-99.

elaborate an aesthetic, attempts which were pursued at Pola and Trieste the following year, indicate the measure of Joyce's effort to accommodate his earlier training to critical canons implicit in contemporary literature. This fundamental concern with critical theory represents a conscious attempt at self-integration in an artistic tradition that would at once permit him complete freedom and guide him toward the creation of enduring works of art.

II

The theoretical formulation of Joyce's aesthetic rigidly followed Thomistic principles. In view of the young Joyce's education and environment, this fact in itself is not astonishing, but it is remarkable to observe with what degree of likeness and persistency Joyce conformed to his model. At the same time that the young writer occupied himself with poetic composition, his mind searched "for the essence of beauty amid the spectral words of Aristotle or Aquinas" and he had frequent recourse to Aristotle's *Poetics* and to a *Synopsis Philosophiae Scholasticae ad mentem divi Thomae.* (205) It should be remembered that Saint Thomas treated art only as ancillary to metaphysics, and Joyce was forced to construct his system from scattered and disjunct fragments, welded together in such a way as to provide the young artist with sanctified authority that would justify his seemingly revolutionary ideas in a hostile milieu.

The elements of Joyce's aesthetic were tied closely together by a rigid subordination of parts. Art he defined as "the human disposition of sensible or intelligible matter for an aesthetic end" (242), and he further subdivided it into three categories, based on the manner of representation. These three kinds of art are the lyrical, the epical and the dramatic. (251-252, *SH*, 77) In lyrical art the aesthetic image is presented by the artist in immediate relation to himself, and may be rendered by a fleeting emotion or moment of pure feeling. In epical art, the image is presented in mediate relation to the artist and his audience, the "centre of emotional gravity" is equidistant between the two.

In dramatic art, the image is presented in immediate relation to others; the artistic personality "refines itself out of existence, impersonalizes itself." It is this latter condition which represents the highest stage of artistic creation.

Closely related to this set of distinctions is Joyce's separation of poetry from all other writing, expounded earlier in his essay on Mangan,[13] and his conception [178] of the end of art as the attainment of formal purity and aesthetic perfection. We have already observed Joyce's attitude toward the use of art for nationalistic purposes in *The Day of the Rabblement*. Similarly, with the conventional moralistic and didactic notions of the end of art, he had nothing whatsoever to do. In his paper entitled "Drama and Life" the first Stephen Dedalus wrote: "I am unable to find even a trace of this Puritanic conception of the aesthetic purpose in the definition which Aquinas has given of beauty . . . or in anything which he has written concerning the beautiful." (*SH*, 79)

Clearly the classical two-fold end of art, to instruct and to delight, has no place in Joyce's critical theory. Practical morality goes the same way as political propaganda, and art is justified completely on the basis of sheer aesthetic pleasure *per se*.[14]

It should be evident to even the casual reader that Joyce's doctrines bear a marked resemblance to theories of *l'art pour l'art* maintained by his older contemporaries. Notwithstanding the brilliant inferences made by the young Joyce toward the construction of an aesthetic on Thomistic principles, it must be emphasized that Saint Thomas considered art as subordinate to prudence in the effecting of human ends, and all temporal activity as subject to divine sanction.[15] On Thomistic principles, Joyce would have arrived at ultimate spiritual objectives, although aesthetics would necessarily be subordinated to metaphysics. As has been well remarked, Joyce accepted the sanction of Saint Thomas for his art and denied it in his belief.[16] His

[13] *Stephen Hero* (79) presents an example of direct transference, almost word by word, of statements in Joyce's early critical essays to his later work.
[14] This attitude is reaffirmed in *Stephen Hero*, p. 170.
[15] Cf. J. Maritain, *Art et scolastique*, pp. 138-143.
[16] H. Levin, *James Joyce*, p. 25.

aesthetic was wholly functional, developed with the only precise instruments at hand when a critical theory was considered necessary.

It is significant that in both versions of *Portrait of the Artist* Joyce depicts himself as a fiery revolutionist in an unfriendly environment. On several occasions he expounds parts of his aesthetic theory, and his conflict with orthodox opinion is marked throughout. The president of his college objects strongly that Joyce's theory, "if pushed to its logical conclusion—would emancipate the poet from all moral laws." He queries Joyce directly, "I suppose you mean Art for Art's sake," to which Joyce offers no definite reply other than the simple statement that he has only pushed Aquinas' definitions to their proper conclusion. (*SH*, 95) Here too the young aesthetician encounters opposition, for at a later point one of his priests objects pointedly that he has completely neglected St. Thomas' metaphysics, and Joyce's interpretations are seriously questioned. (*SH*, 104) It should not be inferred that he wilfully distorted Thomistic doctrine in order to shape a personal aesthetic, yet it seems quite certain that Joyce's critical theory represents a rationalization of contemporary literary tenets on scholastic principles.

The extent to which Joyce's aesthetic approaches the theory of *l'art pour l'art* can be more markedly observed in his conception of the artist. The artistic temper, he felt, must be exercised in an atmosphere of complete freedom, and the [179] artist as a creative agent is subject only to the laws of his art. As he had declared in *The Day of the Rabblement,* Joyce asserted, "Isolation is the first principle of artistic economy." (*SH*, 33) In self-imposed separation from the world of practical affairs, Joyce felt that the artist was employing the only means which would enable him to realize his destiny. Isolation is his only form of protest against aesthetic indifference, against a world in which "No one would listen to his theories; no one was interested in art." (*SH*, 34) He recognized that the artist had a secret destiny to fulfill, and the "hawklike man" after whom Stephen Dedalus took his name represents for him "a symbol of the artist forging anew in his workshop out of the sluggish matter of the earth a new soaring impalpable imperishable being." (196) Heroic in his isolation, Joyce's revolt against a hostile society is a logical consequence of his recognition of his superhuman destiny.

Accordingly, the artist violently rejects the conventional seats of authority, and for Joyce, the problem of spiritual survival in Ireland is made even more acute by the environment. The only remedy, he declares, consists in flight and voluntary exile: "When the soul of a man is born in this country there are nets flung at it to hold it back from flight. You talk to me of nationality, language, religion. I shall try to fly by those nets." (238)

All of the ties that bind the individual to his society are thus sundered by the demands of the artistic temper. He not only feels consciously different from his fellow men, he comes to ignore them completely and to create his own world. From the moment when Joyce began to regard himself seriously as a literary artist, he tells us, "he professed scorn of the rabblement and contempt for authority." (*SH*, 122-123) We have already observed expressions of Joyce's utter indifference to the world of practical affairs, a total preoccupation with aesthetic matters that verges on the border of artistic anarchism. One of his socially-minded colleagues remonstrates that he has "yet to learn the dignity of altruism and the responsibility of the human individual." (232; *SH*, 52) But with social progress or individual responsibility the artist has nothing whatsoever to do. His whole task is to poetically interpret the world of his experience and his dreams, using the twin faculties of selection and reproduction to produce a new world of richness and of personal meaning. Art thus becomes a means of self-knowledge and self-liberation, and by dint of the sheer necessity to create, the artist rejects the world of his environment with a violent *"Non Serviam"*: "I will tell you what I will do and what I will not do. I will not serve that in which I no longer believe, whether it call itself my home, my fatherland or my church: and I will try to express myself in some mode of life or art as freely as I can and as wholly as I can, using for my defence the only arms I allow myself to use, silence, exile and cunning. (291) [180]

Thus Stephen's exile is a necessary consequence of his artistic vocation, and is insisted on throughout as a vital prerequisite of creative activity.

It should be emphasized, however, that if art gives sanction to all other pursuits, it is itself contingent on a steadfast devotion of the artist to his task. Artistic creation for Joyce was no matter of spontaneous inspiration; it demanded the full employment of all of the artist's faculties. "He persuaded himself that it is necessary for an artist to labour incessantly at his art if he wishes to express completely even the simplest conception and he believed that every moment of inspiration must be paid for in advance." (*SH*, 32-33)

Thus the artist, heroic in his isolation, consecrates himself with full devotion to that duty which takes precedence over all other forms of action, immolating himself before the altar of beauty, striving perpetually to create richer and fuller aesthetic forms which in themselves justify his existence.

III

We have already observed in his account of the conception of the artist how Joyce transformed Thomistic principles to accord with contemporary theory and practice. In his consideration of the artistic process he followed Aquinas even more closely, yet did not hesitate to blend scholastic doctrine with critical tenets that bore the stamp of his predecessors of the *fin de siècle*.

Thus a primary principle of Joyce's critical theory is that of impersonality. The most purely personal form of art, we have already seen, consists in the lyrical form which represents direct emotional expression. In the fullest aesthetic creation, however, there is no expression of personality whatsoever. "The artist, like the God of the creation, remains within or behind or beyond or above his handiwork, invisible, refined out of existence, indifferent, paring his fingernails." (252) [17]

It should be remarked that Joyce does not preclude the indirect expression of personality, such as the representation of the author as a character in the work: to some degree all of Joyce's work is autobiographical. Yet it is clear that he does not consider the artist's personal opinions and prejudices fit aesthetic

[17] Cf. Flaubert, *Correspondance*, Ed. Conard, IV, 164.

material; the direct expression of the artist's personality leads only to bad art.

Joyce declared that the artist's primary objective is the creation of beauty. He carefully examined and redefined the notions of beauty stated by St. Thomas, and considered this portion of his aesthetic simply "applied Aquinas." He is careful, however, to point out the restricted sphere in which Thomistic principles are applicable and the need for a personally constructed critical theory: "When we come to the phenomena of artistic conception, artistic gestation and artistic reproduction, I require a new terminology and a new personal experience." (245-246)

Aquinas held that beauty consists in that which having been seen, pleases: *"Pulchra enim dicuntur, quae visa placent."* [18] Joyce interprets this to mean that [181] the beautiful is confined to that which satisfies the aesthetic appetite, pleasing by its mere apprehension. (216; *SH*, 95) This inference is supported by a further statement which Joyce found in Aquinas: *"Pulchrum dicatur id cuius apprehensio placet,"* [19] hence the analysis of beauty must be based on an inquiry into the nature of apprehension.

In November, 1904, we find Joyce at Pola continuing the aesthetic speculations he had made the preceding year in Paris.[20] He concluded that the act of apprehension is a three-fold activity, consisting of cognition or simple perception; recognition or the satisfaction consequent on simple perception; and satisfaction or the evaluation of objects as beautiful or ugly. It should be observed that the analysis of the process of apprehension is extremely important in Thomistic aesthetics, for it is by this process that Aquinas distinguishes the beautiful from the good or the true. Only the beautiful is concerned primarily with cognitive powers and arouses delight by the mere fact of its contemplation.[21]

Following this account of the nature of apprehension, Joyce

18 *Summa Theologiae*, I, q. 5, art. iv, ad. 1m.
19 *Summa Theologiae*, I, q.5, art. i, ad. 3m.
20 Excerpts from Joyce's notebook are reprinted in Gorman, *op. cit.*, pp. 133-135.
21 Cf. Maritain, *op. cit.*, p. 41.

expounded his theory of "stasis" as the emotional condition proper to dramatic art. Since beauty is the contemplation of that which pleases, the emotions proper to the highest art seek to arrest the mind and raise it above feelings which are properly "kinetic": "The feelings excited by improper art are kinetic, desire or loathing. Desire urges us to possess, to go to something; loathing urges us to abandon, to go from something. The arts which excite them, pornographical or didactic, are therefore improper arts." (240)

Joyce returned to this notion of beauty as "stasis" in his drama, *Exiles*, wherein the central character, Richard Rowan, declares, "Even if we are often led to desire through the sense of beauty can you say that the beautiful is what we desire?" [22] Clearly, the beautiful can have no functional use or conduce to any further end; it exists as its own excuse for being.

Joyce's theory of epiphanies, perhaps his most original contribution to critical theory, is closely related to his discussion of the beautiful. Stephen declares to his friend Lynch that the phases of artistic apprehension correspond to the qualities of universal beauty. "Aquinas says: *Ad pulcritudinem* [*sic*] *tria requiruntur integritas, consonantia, claritas.* I translate it so: Three things are needed for beauty, wholeness, harmony and radiance." (248; *SH*, 212-213) An epiphany is defined as the means by which the third supreme quality of beauty is apprehended. Joyce equates *"claritas"* with *"quidditas,"* the whatness of an object, which in its fullest radiance makes possible its epiphany. (*SH*, 213) Thus the process is largely one of [182] recognition arising out of a thorough penetration, an intimate knowledge of an aesthetic object, and it is the fullness of this knowledge that the artist must capture and embody in his work: "By an epiphany he meant a sudden spiritual manifestation, whether in the vulgarity of speech or of gesture or in a memorable phase of the mind itself. He believed that it was for the man of letters to record these epiphanies with extreme care seeing that they themselves are the most delicate and evanescent of moments." (*SH*, 211)

It should be emphasized that the process by which such mo-

22 *Exiles,* Act I, p. 43.

ments of intrinsic recognition take place is by no means discursive or analytic. Rather it is synthetic and immediate, indeed, intuitive in its operation. This seizing of the crucial revelation rests at the center of the artist's interaction with his subject-matter, and has marked application in Joyce's technique. Based on his essentially static conception of beauty, it offers one of the foremost examples in Joyce's writing where theory and practice cohere to a common end.

A further example of the coherence of Joyce's aesthetic is presented in his theory of comedy. Like tragedy, Joyce contends that comedy aims at inducing a condition of "stasis" in the beholder, and does so through arousing joy. Desire is the product of bad comedy and of improper art. Joy is defined as the feeling excited by the possession of some good, and desire, as we have already seen, can have reference only to some further, external object. Joyce declares that insofar as a work of tragic art may arouse the feeling of joy it is able to participate in the nature of comic art, but it cannot do so in the same degree, and hence he concludes that "tragedy is the imperfect manner and comedy the perfect manner in art."

It must be admitted that Joyce's conclusion assumes a hierarchy of feelings wherein joy is placed considerably above pity and terror, and is founded on the reaction aroused in the percipient rather than on the formal relation of parts within the work. Whether the subordination of tragedy to comedy can be made contingent on audience reaction is itself a debatable issue.

In any case it is clear that Joyce's treatment of the passions is closely allied to his doctrine of "stasis" and to his insistence that a work of art must not conduce to any external end. This central tenet of the theory of *l'art pour l'art* is joined by his repeated declaration that the question of the morality of art is irrelevant and inapplicable, either for the artist or for the critic. Rejecting the conventional attitude of his immediate society which held that art was worthless, dangerous and "probably immoral," (*SH*, 34) Joyce stressed the complete freedom of the artist in his choice of subject-matter, as well as his right to shun religious, social or patriotic propaganda in the rendering of his art. Here, as in all phases of his aesthetic, Joyce protested vigorously against any binding dogma that would impede the full exercise of the artist's freedom and impair the autonomy of the artistic conscience. [183]

IV

In the light of his total development it would be difficult to underestimate the importance of Joyce's critical theory. Keenly aware of the antagonisms of a hostile milieu, it would seem that he felt a well-organized and systematic aesthetic necessary before he could proceed to create new modes of artistic endeavor. In the realm of critical theory his basic importance consists not in the ideas he himself elaborated, but in the way in which he extended critical notions that had been earlier set forth by Joyce's English predecessors, and before them, by such writers as Gautier and Flaubert. It is true that the complexities of Joyce's intellectual development demand the consideration of scholastic philosophy as a major formative influence. Yet it must be emphasized that an aesthetic theory formulated on Thomistic principles will clearly result in a theory identical in all important respects with the idea of *l'art pour l'art* if aesthetics is divorced from metaphysics. Joyce could not accept Aquinas' total philosophy of experience and selected only those aspects conducive to his personal use, welding them into an aesthetic of direct contemporary applicability, in harmony with the conditions of his temperament and environment.

It would be insufficient to consider Joyce's aesthetic as merely of historical importance. Like Flaubert before him, Joyce gave full expression to the fundamental antagonisms confronting the modern artist, to which he replied by enforced isolation and voluntary exile. Ultimately, Joyce's critical theory must be considered a necessary prelude to his practice, and his development in his later works cannot be separated from the aesthetic attitude embodied in earlier writings. Despite its inadequacies, Joyce's critical theory embodies a major aspect of his early literary development, and it is of some importance that his aesthetic was elaborated to the full extent that we have observed. There can be no doubt that Joyce was consciously aiming at a complete and coherent critical system and in so doing, he has afforded us a direct perception of his attitude toward artistic experience. Yet Joyce's critical system is essentially the work of a youth, seeking a liberation that would enable him to create, and if this aesthetic remains incomplete, it is only because Joyce himself considered his theory as a device, a means, toward the creative realization of aesthetic perfection. [184]

H. M. McLUHAN

Joyce, Aquinas, and the Poetic Process

ANYONE FAMILIAR with the persistent use which Joyce makes of the labyrinth figures as the archetype of human cognition, will have noticed the same figure as it appears in the dramatic action of a thomistic "article." There is first the descent into the particular matter of the "objections." These are juxtaposed abruptly, constituting a discontinuous or cubist perspective. By abrupt juxtaposition of diverse views of the same problem, that which is in question is seen from several sides. A total intellectual history is provided in a single view. And in the very instant of being presented with a false lead or path the mind is alerted to seek another course through the maze. Baffled by variety of choice, it is suddenly arrested by the *"sed contra"* and given its true bearings in the conclusion. Then follows the retracing of the labyrinth in the *"respondeo dicendum."* Emerging into intellectual clarity at the end of this process, it looks back on

Published by permission of the author and of *Renascence: A Critical Journal of Letters,* the copyright owner. The essay appeared in its original form in *Renascence* in Autumn, 1951. References to *A Portrait* are to *P*-2; to *Stephen Hero* are to *SH*-1.

the blind alleys proffered by each of the original objections. Whereas the total shape of each article, with its trinal divisions into objections, is an "S" labyrinth, this figure is really traced and retraced by the mind many times in the course of a single article. Perhaps this fact helps to explain the power of Thomas to communicate a great deal even before he is much understood. It certainly suggests why he can provide rich esthetic satisfactions by the very dance of his mind—a dance in which we participate as we follow him.

His "articles" can be regarded as vivisections of the mind in act. The skill and wit with which he selects his objections constitute a cubist landscape, an ideal landscape of great intellectual extent seen from an airplane. The ideas or objects in this landscape are by their very contiguity set in a state of dramatic tension; and this dramatic tension is provided with a dramatic peripeteia in the respondel, and with a resolution in the answers to the objections.

This, and much more, was grasped by the young Joyce, who seems to have been the first to make explicit the relation in Aquinas between the stages of apprehension and the creative process. In Aristotle the same view is also implicit, as Joyce was aware. In the *Poetics* (Chap. 4) Aristotle mentions imitation as connate to man, being the process by which men learn. But this fact is not linked with the power of abstraction which in the *De Anima* he attributes to the *nous poietikos,* or the agent intellect. That there is, however, a degree of poetic imitation in abstraction, itself, is plain from the fact that even in sensation "things [3] exist in the soul without their proper matter, but with the singularity and individuating conditions which are the result of matter." (St. Thos., *De Anima,* article 13) That this is so is the effect of the *nous poietikos,* which has the power of individuating anew in a bodily organ that which it has abstracted from existence. "For in things made by art the action of an instrument is terminated in the form intended by the artisan." (St. Thos., *De Anima,* article 12) Again, "For every object produced by art is the effect of the action of an artificer, the agent intellect being related to the phantasms illuminated by it as an artificer is to the things made by his art." (article 5) And in the same place the creative efficacy of the *nous poietikos* as "illuminative" is referred to the text in the Psalms (4:7) "The light of thy countenance is signed upon us, O Lord."

For Joyce and Eliot all art is a shadow of the Incarnation, and every artist is dedicated to revealing, or epiphanizing the signatures of things, so that what the *nous poietikos* is to perception and abstraction the artist is to existence at large: "The artist who could disentangle the subtle soul of the image from its mesh of defining circumstances most exactly and re-embody it in artistic circumstances chosen as the most exact for its new office, he was the supreme artist." (*SH*, 78)

Ordinary experience is a riot of imprecision, of impressions enmeshed in preconceptions, cliches, profanities and impercipience. But for the true artist every experience is capable of an epiphany:

> By an epiphany he meant a sudden spiritual manifestation, whether in the vulgarity of speech or gesture or in a memorable phase of the mind itself. . . . Imagine my glimpses of that clock as the gropings of a spiritual eye which seeks to adjust its vision to an exact focus. The moment the focus is reached the object is epiphanized. It is just in this epiphany that I find the third, the supreme quality of beauty. (*SH*, 211)

Joyce identified the three notes of beauty of St. Thomas with the three operations of the intellect:

> Now for the third quality. For a long time I couldn't make out what Aquinas meant. He uses a figurative word (a very unusual thing for him) but I have solved it. *Claritas* is *quidditas.* After the analysis which discovers the second quality the mind makes the only logically possible synthesis and discovers the third quality. This is the moment which I call epiphany. First we recognize that the object is *one* integral thing, then we recognize that it is an organized composite structure, a thing in fact: Finally, when the relation of the parts is exquisite, when the parts are adjusted to the special point, we recognize that it is *that* thing which it is. Its soul, its whatness leaps to us from the vestment of its appearance. The soul of the commonest object, the structure of which is so adjusted, seems to us radiant. The object achieves its epiphany. (*SH*, 213) [4]

Obviously the business of the artist in this context is that of an impersonal agent, humble before the laws of things, as well as before his own artistic activity as revealer. He must strip himself of all but his mere agency:

> "I have only pushed to its logical conclusion the definition Aquinas has given of the beautiful."
>
> "Aquinas?"
>
> "*Pulcra sunt quae visa placent.* He seems to regard the beautiful as that which satisfies the esthetic appetite and nothing more —that the mere apprehension of which pleases . . ." (*SH*, 95)

The passage in St. Thomas formally distinguishing beauty and goodness has wide but precise bearings for everything Joyce did as an artist:

> But they differ logically, for goodness properly relates to appetite (goodness being what all things desire), and therefore it has the aspect of an end (the appetite being a kind of movement towards a thing). On the other hand beauty relates to a cognitive power, for those things are said to be beautiful which please when seen. Hence beauty consists in due proportion, for the senses delight in things duly proportioned, as in what is like them—because the sense too is a sort of reason, as is every cognitive power. Now, since knowledge is by assimilation, and likeness relates to form, beauty properly belongs to the nature of a formal cause.
>
> (St.T. Q 5, a4 ad i)

That the senses themselves are *properly* analogous, as are the other cognitive powers, was not a fact lost on Joyce, who knew that the creative process itself was a retracing of the stages of apprehension. In this passage from St. Thomas can also be seen the reasons for Joyce's preferring comic to tragic art. Any movement of appetite within the labyrinth of cognition is a "minotaur" which must be slain by the hero artist. Anything which interferes with cognition, whether concupiscence, pride, imprecision or vagueness, is a minotaur ready to devour beauty. So that Joyce not only was the first to reveal the link between the stages of apprehension and the creative process, he was the first to understand how the drama of cognition itself was the

key archetype of all human ritual, myth and legend. And thus
he was able to incorporate at every point in his work the body
of the past in immediate relation to the slightest current of
perception. He could well afford to look patronizingly on the
psychological gropings of Freud and Jung and on the inferior
poetic consciousness of a Yeats or Proust, saying in "The Holy
Office,"

> So distantly I turn to view
> The shamblings of that motley crew,
> Those souls that hate the strength that mine has
> Steeled in the school of old Aquinas.

There was no shambling and no guess-work in anything Joyce
did as an artist. An absolute clairvoyance and precision attended
his work from the first page of [5] *The Portrait* to the end of
Finnegans Wake. And the reason for this, as he insisted, was
his grasp of the full creative implications of the Thomistic analysis of cognition: "But, during the formulation of his artistic
creed, had he not found item after item upheld for him in
advance by the greatest and most orthodox doctor of the Church
. . . while the entire theory in accordance with which his entire
artistic life was shaped, arose most conveniently for his purpose
out of the mass of Catholic theology?" (*SH*, 205)

It is the Thomistic view that beauty relates to a cognitive
rather than a volitional power that led Joyce to prefer comedy
to tragedy. The long passage from his notebooks given by Herbert Gorman (*James Joyce,* pp. 96-97) will become a *locus clas-
sicus:*

> An improper art aims at exciting in the way of comedy the feel-
> ing of desire but the feeling which is proper to comic art is the
> feeling of joy. . . . The feeling which the possession of some
> good excites in us. . . . For desire urges us from rest that we
> may possess something but joy holds us in rest as long as we
> possess something. . . . All art which excites in us the feeling
> of joy is so far comic and according as this feeling of joy is ex-
> cited by whatever is substantial or accidental in human for-
> tunes the art is to be judged more or less excellent. . . . From
> this it may be seen that tragedy is the imperfect manner and

comedy the perfect manner in art. All art, again, is static for the feelings which arrest us. It will be seen afterwards how this rest is necessary for the apprehension of the beautiful. . . . For beauty is a quality of something seen but terror and pity and joy are states of mind.

It is hard to know where to begin to discuss any phase of Joyce because he is so much of a piece. Anything of his includes all the rest. Thus, for example, his statement of the problem of *genres* seems simple and natural:

> . . . There are three conditions of art: the lyrical, the epical, and the dramatic. That art is lyrical whereby the artist sets forth the image in immediate relation to himself; that art is epical whereby the artist sets forth the image in mediate relation to himself and to others; that art is dramatic whereby the artist sets forth the image in immediate relation to others. (*Ibid.*, pp. 97-98)

But the complex genetic idea operative here is a shadow at once of the three operations of the intellect and of the procession of Persons in the Trinity. There is also a note of Joyce's dated at Paris (March 27, 1903) which concerns Aristotle and imitation: "*e tekhne mimeitai ten physin*—this phrase is falsely rendered as "Art is an imitation of Nature." Aristotle does not here define art; he says only, "Art imitates Nature" and means that the artistic process is like the natural process . . ." (*Ibid.*, 98) [6]

It is in *Stephen Hero* that there are the texts which explain what Joyce understood by "natural process": "For Stephen art was neither a copy nor an imitation of nature: the artistic process was a natural proces. . . . a veritably sublime process of one's own nature which had a right to examination and open discussion." (*SH*, 171)

That this process is that of ordinary apprehension is made plain:

> What we symbolize in black the Chinaman may symbolize in yellow; each has his own tradition. Greek beauty laughs at Coptic beauty and the American Indian derides them both. It is

almost impossible to reconcile all tradition whereas it is by no means impossible to find the justification of every form of beauty that has ever been adored on earth by an examination of the mechanism of esthetic apprehension whether it be dressed in red, white, yellow or black. We have no reason for thinking that the Chinaman has a different system of digestion from that which we have though our diets are quite dissimilar. The apprehensive faculty must be scrutinized in action. (*SH*, 212)

It is impossible to exaggerate the importance of this last phrase for an understanding of Joyce's art, because he never ceased to evolve techniques for scrutinizing sensations and impressions "at the very instant of their apparition." And this meant for Joyce neither impressionism nor expressionism but the revelation of the profoundly analogical drama of existence as it is mirrored in the cognitive powers in act: "They sat sometimes in the pit of a music-hall and one unfolded to the other the tapestry of his poetical aims while the band bawled to the comedian and the comedian bawled to the band. Cranly grew used to having sensations and impressions recorded and analysed before him at the very instant of their apparition." (*SH*, 125)

Dubliners, for example, is a tapestry of such arrested apparitions woven with the cognitive design of childhood, youth, maturity, and age. *The Portrait* is likewise static as the title insists, an inclusive moment focussing the stages of artistic apprehension in a *vivisection* of the young artist. It is noteworthy that Joyce excludes from the esthetic discussion in *The Portrait* just those features of the Thomistic analysis of cognition which were most important to him as a mature artist—namely the fact of the creative process as the natural process of apprehension arrested and retraced. The Stephen of *The Portrait*, (probably named after the Dedalian Stephane Mallarmé) understands Aquinas via Mallarmé whereas Joyce the artist while led to Aquinas by Mallarmé and the symbolists, finally was able to complete the work of the symbolists because he discovered how to perfect their insights by means of Aquinas. Yet it needs also to be said that the feebleness of grasp among Joyce critics is not so much [7] their ignorance of St. Thomas as their half-awareness of what Joyce saw in Flaubert, Rimbaud, and Mallarmé. Because Joyce and Eliot have surpassed these writers, only, however, with their assistance, it is enforced on the English critic to perfect his knowledge of them if only that the French in turn may come to enjoy the achievement of Joyce and Eliot.

There is a passage in *Stephen Hero* which well serves to suggest the kind of debt Joyce owed to Flaubert and his successors:

> The modern spirit in vivisective. Vivisection is the most modern process one can conceive. The ancient spirit accepted phenomena with a bad grace. The ancient method investigated law with the lantern of justice, morality with the lantern of revelation, art with the lantern of tradition. But all these lanterns have magical properties: they transform and disfigure. The modern method examines its territory by the light of day. . . . It examines the entire community in action and reconstructs the spectacle of redemption. If you were an esthetic philosopher you would take note of all my vagaries because here you have the spectacle of the esthetic instinct in action. The philosophic college should spare a detective for me. (*SH*, 186)

The use of the words "vagaries" and "detective" is here precise and significant. For, on one hand, the figure of the labyrinth is used everywhere by Joyce as the archetype of cognition and esthetic apprehension, and the modern detective since Poe employs the technique of retracing in order to reconstruct an action exactly as it occurred. Edgar Poe is rightly regarded in France as the father of symbolism because he was the first to formulate the poetic process as one of discovery by retracing. The precise poetic formula for any emotion, he pointed out, was to be found by working backwards from effect to the arrangement of words which would produce that effect. So that it is also his esthete Dupin who first displays the same method in the service of crime detection. The modern psychologist, historiographer and archaeologist use this method in common with the physicist, the chemist, and the "private eye." Professor Gilson's *Unity of Philosophical Experience* has the distinction of being the first work of philosophy in which this method of reconstruction is fully employed.

But a great deal of poetic experiment and development pre-

ceded the discovery of the technique of reconstruction as discovery. And most of all is owing to the practitioners of the pic-
turesque school of landscape that began with James Thomson in
1724. By the time of Scott, Byron, and Chateaubriand, the possibilities of discontinuous landscape as a means of including and
controlling a vast range of otherwise chaotic material was available to the novelist as a means of examining "the entire community in action." First, Stendhal and then Flaubert and Dickens
went ahead on these lines. But Flaubert was the first to see in
his *Sentimental Education* that it meant the abandonment of the
continuity of unilateral narrative in favor of the more profound
effects to be [8] achieved by analogical juxtaposition of characters, scenes, and situations without copula. So that the Cartesian
cries against cubist discontinuity have always been raised by
those ignorant of analogy and equivocity.

But Joyce, while alert to all that Flaubert had achieved for
him, was not content with controlling just the larger areas of
his discontinuous landscapes. He wanted and got a simultaneous
control of widest perspectives and the most intimate and evanescent moments of apprehension. And this he was able to achieve
by analysis of the labyrinth of cognition which Aristotle and
Aquinas had revealed to him. It is thus, for example, that he is
able to include in the first two pages of *The Portrait* the entire
experience of the race, the ground plan of all his unwritten
work, and the most individual features of Stephen's expanding
awareness. The opening words place the hero in the traditional
labyrinth and confront him with a minotaur adopted to his infant
years; "Once upon a time and a very good time it was there was
a moocow coming down along the road and this moocow that
was down along the road met a nicens little boy named baby
tuckoo. . . ." (1)

Stephen Hero is so named because the artist in that work
confronts and slays scores of minotaurs. The book swarms with
labyrinths of many kinds and levels: "At the door he had to
resign her to others and see her depart with insignificant cour-
tesies and as he came home alone he led his mood through
mazes of doubts and misgivings." (*SH*, 159)

Following this passage there is another labyrinth which is both exterior and interior. It presents one of the family migrations inside Dublin.

> . . . on the night before the day fixed for his legal eviction he moved his camp by night. The little furniture which remained to them was carried on a float and Stephen and his brother and his mother and his father carried the ancestral portraits themselves as the draymen had drunk a good deal more than was good for them. It was a clear night of late summer freshened with cold as they walked in a body beside the sea-wall. . . . The tide was lapping softly by the wall, being at the full, and through the clear air Stephen heard his father's voice like a muffled flute singing a love-song. He made his mother stop to listen and they both leaned on the heavy picture-frames and listened:
>
> Shall carry my heart to thee . . . (*SH*, 159-160)

Traditionally there are two kinds of labyrinth, stone and sea, eye and ear. Joyce uses both constantly. Here both are fused in the "sea-wall," the family treading the maze between two powers (earth and sea) and carrying the household gods, is arrested by the song. The moment of arrest is an epiphany, a moment not in time's covenant, and it is by the bringring of complex perceptions to a focus in such moments that the minotaurs of the labyrinths are always overcome.

But the means of capturing these moments is by landscape as [9] Wordsworth and others were aware. The Pre-Raphaelites and then Swinburne, Pater, and early Yeats had sought for the means to prolong these moments. But the symbolists discovered that the moment was not an end but a beginning. It was a point from which to begin a retracing of the labyrinth of apprehension in order to find the inevitable art form for that moment: "In the centre of her attitude towards him he thought he discerned a point of defiant ill will and he thought he understood the cause of it. He had swept the moment into his memory, the figure and the landscape into his treasure-room, and conjuring with all three had brought forth some pages of sorry verse." (*SH*, 67)

Since the relation of labyrinth and landscape calls for separate treatment it will serve for now to have pointed out that the conjunction of landscape and labyrinth provided Joyce with that vivisection of the stages of esthetic apprehension of which he was the only begetter. As much, therefore, as the ancient Daedalus who made the labyrinth in Crete, Joyce had the right to name his hero "Stephen Dedalus" (the French form of the word). But it is not only the labyrinth of cognition in which Joyce made himself at home, tracing and retracing with delicate precision. The labyrinthine structure of the eye it is that gives such salience in his work to the figure of the cyclops. Most of all he was at home in the labyrinth of the inner ear where he met Persse O'Reilly, who is *per se*, son of the Real. On the labyrinth of the ear, organ of the Incarnation, Joyce built those metaphysical analogies which enabled him to restore the orchestra of the seven liberal arts to its plenary functions. He is never less than the artist of the word. *Ulysses* is reared on the labyrinth landscape of the human body as the body politic; and *Finnegans Wake* whispers throughout with the voice of the river of human blood and immemorial racial consciousness. Joyce was at home in all labyrinths because of his original conquest of the stages of apprehension, of the mind in act.

Having suggested that Joyce took up the analysis of this matter at the very promising stage at which Mallarmé had left it at his death in 1898, I should like to point to what is, so far as I know, the first stage of philosophic awareness concerning the retracing apprehension as the poetic process. It occurs in Thomas Brown's posthumously published lectures on *The Philosophy of the Human Mind*, 1820. And it is in lecture 37 where he is considering the "secondary laws of suggestion" as they affect genius that he states the difference between the imagination of genius and the fancy of ordinary minds. The mind of genius, he suggests, works in some sort of reverse direction to ordinary minds: [10]

> In a poetic mind of a higher order, the conception of this very subject cannot exist for a moment, without awakening, by the different tendency of the suggesting principle, groups of images which had never before existed in similar combination . . . new forms, of external beauty or of internal passion, would crowd upon his mind, by their analogy to ideas and feelings

previously existing; and this single change of the direction of
the suggesting principle would be sufficient to produce all those
wonders, which the poet of imagination ascribes to the influence of inspiring genii. . . . The inventions of poetic genius,
then, are the suggestions of analogy: the prevailing suggestions
of common minds, are those of mere contiguity.

In these lectures, Brown is a severe critic of Locke and Hartley
and the associationists, and seems to use "analogy" in a traditional sense. To what extent he was aware of the speculations
of Coleridge, I cannot say. But Coleridge seems not to have had
any inkling of the retracing process as the poetic process. It is
noteworthy however that his celebrated definition of the primary
imagination coincides with the notion of Aristotle and Aquinas
concerning the *nous poietikos* or the agent intellect: "The primary
imagination I hold to be the living power and prime agent of
all human perception, and as a repetition in the finite mind of
the eternal act of creation in the infinite I AM."

That this has not been noticed as the *nous poietikos* is only
less curious than the fact that Coleridge never seems to have
commented on it again. His definition of the poetic or secondary
imagination has aroused great interest and enthusiasm but is
far from the precision of his definition of the primary imagination: "The secondary Imagination I consider as an echo of the
former, co-existing with the conscious will, yet still as identical
with the primary in the *kind* of its agency, and differing" only
in degree, and in the mode of its operation. It dissolves, "diffuses,
dissipates, in order to recreate: or where this process is rendered
impossible, yet still at all events it struggles to idealize and
unify."

Nothing could well be vaguer than this. It does not look very
impressive beside Brown's statement. And Brown's view is in
the line that leads through Burke to Poe, Baudelaire, Rimbaud,
Mallarmé, and Joyce. [11]

[*The remaining pages of this essay have been added by the
author to the original essay and appear in this volume for the
first time.* Ed. note]

The student of the Joyce-Aquinas axis will find a great deal of aid in *Reality and Judgment according to St. Thomas* by Peter Hoenen, S.J. (Henry Regnery and Co.; Chicago, 1952). In Chapter Ten he discusses the concept of St. Thomas of *"facientes cognoscunt."* ("By constructing they come to know."):

> St. Thomas uses the expression, "By constructing they come to know." *(facientes cognoscunt)* at the end of the passage where he discovers and explains the origin of the intellectual intuition of a geometric truth in a structure of a geometric figure which had been actuated by the seeker. . . . But St. Thomas has a detailed theory which has this truth as its foundation. He deduces this theory from the activity of the artisan and he applies it frequently. It is his theory of the "knowledge which is the cause of things . . ." *(scientia quae est causa rerum)* as opposed to the "knowledge received from things" *(scientia accepta a rebus).* . . . St. Thomas uses this theory, for example, to determine and classify the objects of God's knowledge.

In 1893 the German sculptor Adolf Hildebrand published *The Problem of Form.* Like "Le Demon de l'Analogie," by Mallarmé, this book revealed the proportion that is between knowing and making. But Hildebrand's small book had a great and immediate effect on the artists and critics of his time. In 1907 it was translated into English by Max Meyer and Robert Morris Ogden.

One reason why Hildebrand had such an immediate effect on the artists of his time is that he was able to explain why synesthesia is not only normal human experience, but he showed why the isolation of the retinal or the haptic or any other impression was, artistically, a disaster. Humanly speaking, the separation of the senses is the formula for insanity. *King Lear* is a study, as is *Othello,* of the effects of the isolation of the senses. Hildebrand saw with absolute clarity that photography and photo-engraving were effecting an isolation of retinal impression from the other senses. After his book appeared, the critics like Bernard Berenson and later Roger Fry and Clive Bell began to stress the urgency of haptic, tactile quality in retinal impression. Professor Sheila Watson, in an unpublished doctoral dissertation on Wyndham Lewis has gone into the matter. The role of Hildebrand in shaping the *vortex* idea of Lewis, Pound, and T. S. Eliot is as decisive as his effect on Heinrich Wölfflin and the Bauhaus.

A few brief samples of his discussion will indicate his importance for the Joyce student.

> Since Art does not depend on a mere knowing, but on a doing which puts this knowledge into practice, a treatise on artistic problems can be fruitful only when it follows the artistic process in its practical, as well as in its theoretical aspects. We must strive to understand clearly the connection between the artist's inner mental process and the realization of his ideas in his work. Unless we can show this mental process, demonstrate it, so to speak, ad oculos, then all insight into Art remains obscure and it is left to each individual to interpret the process this way or that according to the refinement of his senses. Finding that most theories of Art exhibit a useless quantity of reasoning and a dearth of practical experience, I have attempted to avoid this in my work by giving prominence, not to theoretical considerations, but to the actual process of creating a work of art. Accordingly, my book culminates fittingly in the chapter on stone carving; for work of this nature is, as a matter of fact, only the realization of all those artistic ideas which we shall treat in the chapters leading up to the last. The idea which informs the artist's creation is one thing, the process of the creation is another. The true connection between these two could scarce be understood except when placed at the end of the treatise. An insight into this connection seems all the more imperative since the technical progress and factory work of our day have led us to lose our appreciation of the manner in which a thing is made, and have caused us to value a product more for itself than as a result of some mental activity.

Hildebrand everywhere testifies to the crux of formal causality as necessary in artistic understanding, but he never separates formal from material, efficient or final causes:

> Nature, as she moves, produces alterations in her appearance, upon the most comprehensible of which we seize as characteristics and indices of her process. The perception of these indices suggests to us the idea of the whole process, and in imagination we perform the process and thus comprehend this inner action as the cause of the external appearance.
>   The mimetic play of laughter and of weeping in others is comprehended by the child only through imitating it and then

comparing it with his own muscular acts which accompany his pleasures and pains. Indeed, it is in this way that we all come to understand the mimetic activity of others and to translate their movements as we perceive them into the comprehensible expression of certain mental processes. We even go so far as to interpret a novel bodily expression by imitating it and thus comparing it with certain more or less similar expressions with which we are familiar, and which signify to us certain definite feelings. In this way a fund of indices to processes is accumulated, the value of each index being proportional to its clearness.

If we expand this conception to cover all bodily form, we find it applicable everywhere in Nature. Our ideas of *function* are everywhere vitalizing agents, and thus, for both spectator and artist determine the form of the representation. What we call, off-hand, the life of Nature is, in reality, the animation of Nature through our ideas. The expression of function is to be taken here in its widest sense; not merely for a direct momentary process or act but also for the state of repose. Such states of repose may require of the spectator more in the way of subjective interpretation than do states of motion.

Always with Hildebrand, then, is the prime stress on the interplay of knowing and making. The intelligible is Being, says Aquinas; and it is the splitting up of knowing and making which impoverishes art, experience, and Being alike says Hildebrand in a passage relevant to "dissociation of sensibility":

In view of the foregoing, a comparison of the Art of earlier times with that of to-day must reveal the undoubted fact that the logic of visual representation was far more highly developed then than it is now; and upon this fact is founded the superiority of earlier Art over ours. In times when Art is enjoying freedom of growth, the natural drift of ideas will follow the regular course of mental organization. Of this dependency on the laws of mental organization the artist is conscious only in so far as he may desire to be logical, and to give true expression to his natural impulses. No influence sways him in his work save that of the natural laws of Art embodied in the artistic Problem of Form. There is as yet no discord between his mental representation and his actual observation. The natural unity of idea and perception still reigns.

Other periods may be termed inartistic for the reason that this *naiveté* no longer exists, and that in its stead false interests and abnormal points of view confuse the natural artistic tendency and deflect it from its course. If we but consider that the artistic idea is in essence nothing more than a further evolution in the natural process of learning to see—a process which each one of us begins to perform in childhood; and if we remember that in childhood visual imagery is most vivid; then we may gain some idea of the sudden end to all this play of fancy which must follow the child's entrance into school. For school turns the much prized hours of youth to activities and disciplines inimical to Art. Deflected thus from his natural course, the child develops his artificial rather than his natural resources, and it is only when he reaches full maturity that the artist learns to think again in terms of the natural forces and ideas which in his childhood were his happiest possession. How many of us have preserved our inborn desire for expression? In most cases only physical ability has survived, and we are ignorant even as to the means and ends of using it. Into what devious by-ways does will lead when only instinct should direct!

As Aquinas indicates everywhere, there is a proportion between the modes of Being and the modes of our human knowing. Hildebrand points the corollary for Art: "If one would speak, then, of a mission of Art, it can be no other than this: In spite of all temporal eccentricities, to re-establish and make felt the sound and natural relations between our thought and sense activities." This is surely close to Baudelaire's notion that the role of Art is to diminish the traces of original sin.

Among the numerous ideas of Hildebrand which figure prominently in the esthetics of the next generation we find the idea of "significant form" so much used by Fry and Bell, but without Hildebrand's lucid meaning:

. . . Art consists in giving shape to these ideas of spatial values, thus taking what may have been in Nature insignificant and fortuitous, and rendering it expressive and inevitable. However, in order to be effective in a work of art, these elements must be so combined that each may have its full significance. Since in Nature it is entirely a matter of chance whether or not this condition is met in the appearance, an artistic representation cannot be a mere mechanical counterfeit of Nature, but must comply with those conditions which render visual values effective. Thus an artist's single representation is, in fact, an expression for the whole world of form as he has worked it out in his mind into effective spatial values.

He then rejects the "innocent eye" notion of art as postulating a separation rather than an interplay of the senses: "The height of positivism would be attained if we could perceive things with the inexperience of a new-born child. This theory would lead us to regard the sculptor's art as appealing exclusively to the tactual-kinesthetic sense of the esthetic percipient; the painter's art, on the other hand, as appealing entirely to the visual sense quite apart from all experience of form. . . . In true Art the actual form has its reality only as an effect. By conceiving Nature as a relation of kinesthetic ideas to visual impressions, all combined and inter-related in a totality Art frees her of change and chance."

Both for the student of Joyce and of Eliot, Hildebrand's luminous presentation of the idea of Art as impersonal will be extremely relevant:

> The historic point of view from which Art is generally considered, has not produced this consciousness of the universal laws of Art. Instead, it has tended to emphasize the differences manifest in artistic production. Consequently Art is treated either as an emanation of personal qualities in various individuals, or as a product of temporal conditions and national traits. This gives rise directly to a false conception of Art as primarily a manifestation of personality, of Art as a product of what in truth is the absolutely non-artistic side of man. The result is simple: no universal measure of artistic value is left. The greatest emphasis is laid on accessory relations, while the real artistic content obeying its internal laws unaffected by the alterations of time, is ignored. It is as though a gardener were to let his plants grow under glass vases of different shapes and then ask our attention wholly to the strange forms thus produced, expecting us to forget entirely that the really important thing is the plant itself and its inner mode of life, concerning which these artificial effects of shape and size can give us no true information whatsoever.

THOMAS E. CONNOLLY
Joyce's Aesthetic Theory

THE AESTHETIC THEORY advanced by Stephen Dedalus in *A Portrait of the Artist as a Young Man* has been critically discussed and interpreted more frequently than any other element in the book. It is therefore obviously absurd to attempt anything more than a superficial treatment of such a problem in a paper as brief as this. The theory as presented in the *Portrait,* however, is unfortunately incomplete: it makes no direct mention of the subject matter of art, and it is sketchy with respect to the "epiphany," the one element of the aesthetic theory which has most stimulated critical attention. For a synthesis of Joyce's theory it is necessary to examine and compare three texts: *A Portrait of the Artist, Stephen Hero* (the incomplete first draft of the *Portrait*), and Gorman's biography of Joyce. The theory, it will be found, divides itself into four general parts: the good and the beautiful, the subject matter of art, the static principle of art, and the method of apprehending the beautiful.

Stephen first begins to discuss the good and the beautiful in the scene in *A Portrait of the Artist* in which he talks with the dean of studies while he is lighting the fire. It is interesting to notice that in the corresponding scenes with Father Butt in *Stephen Hero* no mention of the good and the beautiful is made at all; they speak briefly of the two levels of meaning for words, and only one sentence is devoted to the distinction between the useful arts and the liberal arts. In *A Portrait* (216) Stephen sets forth the two principles from Aquinas upon which his theory

Reprinted by permission of the author and *The University of Kansas City Review.* The essay originally appeared in that journal in October, 1956. References to *A Portrait* are to *P-2*; to *Stephen Hero* are to *SH-1*.

is based: *Pulcra sunt quae visa placent:* those things are beautiful the perception of which pleases. (Stephen, of course, properly interprets *visa* not in the restricted sense of "sight," but in the wider sense of "esthetic intellection," or apprehension.) *Bonum est in quod tendit appetitus:* the good is that toward which the appetite tends. After merely stating these principles with no attempt to apply them to anything beyond the fire before them, Stephen receives the approval of the dean for his understanding of St. Thomas, and the conversation gets off on a discussion of the levels of usage of words. It is upon these two principles, however, that Stephen's entire theory rests. All that follows evolves from his conviction that the creative artist is concerned only with the creation of the beautiful, whereas the productive artist (or the artisan) is concerned with the production of the good.

For the next aspect of Stephen's theory it is necessary to depend entirely upon *Stephen Hero,* for it will be found in no other place. In the argument with the president of the university Stephen says: "Even admitting the corruption you speak of I see nothing unlawful in an examination of corruption." (*SH*, 92) The president uses stronger language than [47] Stephen in describing the subject matter of the writers whom Stephen praises in his lecture; he calls it "the garbage of modern society." (*SH*, 91) During his debate Stephen is simply defending the subject matter which the naturalistic school has chosen as appropriate for art. He rejects the attempt to limit the subject matter of art to the sublime:

> —I have only pushed to its logical conclusion the definition Aquinas has given of the beautiful.
> —Aquinas?
> —*Pulcra sunt quae visa placent.* He seems to regard the beautiful as that which satisfies the esthetic appetite and nothing more—that the mere apprehension of which pleases . . .
> —But he means the sublime—that which leads man upwards.
> —His remark would apply to a Dutch painter's representation of a plate of onions. (*SH*, 95)

The subject matter of art, then, for Stephen is anything that pleases the aesthetic sensitivity.

This question of subject matter, however, is not the rock upon which the president and Stephen split. Their basic difference is on the interpretation of the purpose of art. This difference leads us naturally to the consideration of the next aspect of Stephen's theory, the principle of stasis in art. In *Stephen Hero* this part of the theory, stasis in art, is never as clearly stated as in the *Portrait*. In the earlier version the principle is implied on two occasions. While his mother irons, Stephen reads his essay to her. She misunderstands his theory of art, and Stephen instantly corrects her: "You evidently weren't listening to what I said or else you didn't understand what I said. Art is not an escape from life. It's just the very opposite. Art, on the contrary is just the very central expression of life. An artist is not a fellow who dangles a mechanical heaven before the public. The priest does that. The artist affirms out of the fulness of his own life, he creates . . . Do you understand?" (*SH*, 86)

Later, in his argument with the president of the university, Stephen is more emphatic in his insistence that the artist seek nothing outside of the effect of the work of art which he produces.

> —The lack of a specific code of moral conventions does not degrade the poet, in my opinion.
> —Ah, if he were to examine even the basest things, said the President with a suggestion of tolerance in store, it would be different if he were to examine and then show men the way to purify themselves.
> —That is for the Salvationists, said Stephen.
> —Do you mean . . .
> —I mean that Ibsen's account of modern society is as genuinely ironical as Newman's account of English Protestant morality and belief.
> —That may be, said the President appeased by the conjunction.
> —And as free from missionary intention. The President was silent. (*SH*, 92)

In the *Portrait*, the discussion of the aesthetic theory with Lynch divides itself into two parts. The problem of the proper subject matter of art is not, as I have said, discussed. It is assumed. Stephen begins by talking of the static effect of art upon the beholder, and then introduces his theory of the beautiful, and finally his theory of the way the beautiful is apprehended by the mind. Three of the four aspects of his aesthetic theory are contained in this one dialogue.

The first half of the conversation [48] is merely the dramatic presentation of a rather lengthy notebook entry, dated 13 February 1903, which is reproduced by Gorman. (239-244) Stephen explains to Lynch that art must produce a stasis in the observer. This is merely an application of Stephen's first principle: the creative artist is concerned with the beautiful, not with the good. Good art, therefore, cannot produce a desire or a loathing in the beholder, cannot be kinetic. Rather, it must produce an emotion which in itself satisfies the aesthetic sense alone. Beyond this art cannot go; if it attempts to excite either desire or loathing (for either the good or the bad), it ceases to be creative art, since it then assumes the aim of a useful art, such as rhetoric. It is in this sense that Stephen speaks of kinetic art as "improper" art.

At this point in the *Portrait* Stephen has established two aspects of his aesthetic theory and has taken for granted the third. In the scene with the dean of studies he sets forth the basic principle, the distinction between the good and the beautiful. The proper subject of art (which he does not bother to elaborate upon in the conversation with Lynch) was argued with the president of the university in *Stephen Hero*. In the first half of the conversation with Lynch, the principle that art must produce a stasis, must seek no end other than the satisfaction of the aesthetic sense, is established. In the second half of the conversation with Lynch (after the interruption by Donovan) Stephen goes on to present the fourth aspect of his theory, the method by which the intellect apprehends the beautiful.

Ad pulcritudinem tria requiruntur, Stephen quotes Aquinas, *integritas, consonantia, claritas.* Three things are required for the perception of beauty: wholeness or integrity, harmony or proportion, and clarity or radiance. (248)

Before any object can be apprehended as beautiful it must be seen to be *one* thing; that is, it must be seen as a unified whole, distinguished, for example, from a totality. By using the notebook entries reproduced by Gorman (134-35) we are able to expand the theory at this point. Since the act of simple perception gives pleasure (his basic assumption from Aquinas and Aristotle), it is possible at this level—recognition of the *integritas* of a thing—to say that all objects, even hideous objects, which can be simply perceived are, to the extent of the pleasure derived from the act of perception, beautiful. But in a larger sense a thing cannot be said to be beautiful simply because we have apprehended it as *one* thing, as a whole composed of parts. (249)

The next step in the apprehension of the beauty of an object is the apprehension of the proportion or balance of its parts, both with respect to each other and with respect to the whole which they compose. This is to apprehend the *consonantia.* "You feel," as Stephen explains it, "the rhythm of its structure." (249) Again at this level, beauty, to a degree, may be predicated of the object, because, once again, a pleasure has been derived from the simple perception of the proportion and order of the parts. Still, the beauty of the object, in the final sense, cannot yet be said to be apprehended, for the third step in the process has not yet been [49] taken.

Finally, to *integritas* and *consonantia* must be added *claritas* to make possible the full apprehension of the beauty of any object. What Aquinas meant by *claritas* puzzled Stephen at first, but as he eventually explains it to Lynch it is the realization or the understanding of the *quidditas* of the object, the *whatness* of it. Stephen explains it very clearly: "The instant wherein that supreme quality of beauty, the clear radiance of the esthetic image, is apprehended luminously by the mind which has been arrested by its wholeness and fascinated by its harmony is the luminous silent stasis of esthetic pleasure, a spiritual state very like . . . the enchantment of the heart." (250)

Here is the essence of the epiphany which Spencer laments as having been "left out of the *Portrait* entirely." It is true that in *Stephen Hero,* in his conversation with Cranly, which is a rough parallel of the second half of the conversation with Lynch in the *Portrait,* Stephen definitely identifies the moment of the apprehension of the *claritas* of a thing as the epiphany: "This is the moment which I call epiphany." (*SH*, 213) When these three acts of perception have been accomplished by the mind, when the object has been finally epiphanized, its full beauty is apprehended.

With this aspect of his theory, Stephen has completed the formal construction of it. He then quickly applies it to literature in general, and he is able to make a triple division of the various forms of literature. This division is based upon the relationship existing between the artist and the image represented. In the lyrical form the "center of emotional gravity" (252) is in immediate relationship to the artist. The epic form is no longer purely personal. The "center of emotional gravity is equidistant from the artist and from others." (252) In the dramatic form the artist is "refined out of existence." (252) Like the creator of the universe, the dramatic artist stands apart from his work and the dramatic form exists in and for itself in a static condition. The synthesis of Stephen's aesthetic theory is complete with this pronouncement. The rain conveniently begins to fall, and Stephen, who has no more theory to advance, seeks shelter with Lynch on the library porch.

The aesthetic theory as it is presented in the *Portrait* is an admirable approach to the climax of the book, the scene in which he announces to Cranly that he has left the Church and is about to leave Ireland. When the ties with family, church, and country are cut, Stephen has as his sole possession his completely developed aesthetic theory, the theory which forced him to cut the ties. And it is the height of the novel's irony that the theory of aesthetics which drove him from the Church is derived from Aquinas. [50]

MAURICE BEEBE

Joyce and Aquinas:
The Theory of Aesthetics

WHILE MOST CRITICS of James Joyce agree that the theory of art presented by Stephen Dedalus in *A Portrait of the Artist as a Young Man* is both a key to the novel in which it appears and a programme for Joyce's later writings, they disagree on the extent of Joyce's alleged indebtedness to Saint Thomas Aquinas. When Stephen has finished expounding his theory, his friend Lynch comments, "That has the true scholastic stink." (245) Some critics agree. According to Padraic Column, for example, Stephen "is unable to analyze his ideas or shape his life except in terms of the philosophy that the Catholic Church has evolved or adopted." [1] S. Foster Damon asserts that Stephen "has mastered Aquinas and Aristotle so well that he saw the whole world through their eyes." [2] Haskell M. Block, in what is perhaps the most complete and illuminating discussion of the theory, writes: "The theoretical formulation of Joyce's aesthetic rigidly followed Thomistic principles." [3] And according to Harry Levin, Joyce "required the sanction of Saint Thomas Aquinas for his art, though not for his belief." [4]

If Joyce's art were Thomist, it would be necessary to qualify

Reprinted by permission of the author and *Philological Quarterly*, the copyright owner. The essay originally appeared in *Philological Quarterly* in January, 1957. References to *A Portrait* are to *P-1*; to *Stephen Hero* are to *SH-1*.
[1] *The Road Round Ireland* (New York, 1926), p. 321.
[2] "The Odyssey in Dublin," in *James Joyce: Two Decades of Criticism,* ed. Seon Givens (New York, 1948), p. 222.
[3] "The Critical Theory of James Joyce," *Journal of Aesthetics and Art History,* VIII (1950), 178. See pp. 231-249.
[4] *James Joyce* (Norfolk, Conn., 1941), p. 25.

the usual interpretation of Joyce-Stephen as an exile. Presumably he turned from the religion of his fathers to a religion of art. If his aesthetic remained orthodox, his self-proclaimed revolt from God, Home, and Country would appear to have been only a matter of convenience—and since he insisted that only art justifies alienation, unnecessary. It would follow that Joyce's art is sanctioned and that Joyce the artist, if not Joyce the man, may be claimed for the Church. However, the point is in dispute, and there are critics who argue that Joyce's aesthetic does not follow the Thomist [20] line. William York Tindall, for example, asserts that Joyce diverged considerably from Aquinas, "who, liberally interpreted and applied, is made to serve other ends than his own." [5] According to Francis Fergusson, "the divergence from Aquinas and Aristotle is completely self-conscious and consistent. Joyce must diverge . . . making his Thomism godless, interpreting Aristotle in a neoclassic sense, if the freedom of exile is to have its demonic completeness." [6]

Neither of these conflicting opinions has thus far been carefully defended or documented by means of a close scrutiny of the exact extent to which Joyce does follow Aquinas. Such an examination, a point-by-point comparison of Joyce's theory with the Thomist sources from which it derives, will reveal that Joyce follows the form of certain scholastic principles, but by denying the premises upon which they are based, distorts the meaning. Aquinas alludes to questions of art and beauty only in passing; his statements must be culled from their context, yet seen in their context. By taking Aquinas's definitions of beauty out of their context and by insisting upon his right to interpret them literally, Joyce draws some conclusions which would be—and have been—the despair of neo-Thomists, who see the theory of art in relation to Thomism in general. For this reason, it seems necessary to compare Stephen's theory not only with the actual text of Aquinas, but also with the explanations of Aquinas provided by such interpreters as Jacques Maritain (from whose *Art*

---

[5] *James Joyce: His Way of Interpreting the Modern World* (New York, 1950), p. 20.
[6] "A Reading of *Exiles,*" in Joyce's *Exiles* (New York: New Directions, n.d.), p. xvii.

and Scholasticism, first published in 1920, Thomist aesthetics properly dates), Thomas Gilby, and Herbert Ellsworth Cory.

The theory advanced in the *Portrait* appears fragmentarily in two earlier forms: in Joyce's notes, first published in Herbert Gorman's 1940 biography, and in the rejected version of the *Portrait,* published in 1944 as *Stephen Hero.* Since there is only one important difference among these separate versions—one which will be discussed in detail—and since the earlier versions often clarify points passed over quickly or inadequately in the *Portrait,* they may safely be considered as a single unit.

Joyce draws three main principles from two statements by Aquinas; thus, there is some overlapping. An outline of the entire [21] theory may therefore serve as a useful point of reference for discussion of the parts:

I. Art is a *stasis* brought about by the formal rhythm of beauty.
  A. The tragic emotions, pity and terror, arouse and arrest the mind in a condition of *stasis* rather than *kinesis.*
  B. Comedy is proper and perfect when it arouses the static emotion of joy rather than the kinetic emotion of desire or loathing.
  C. The aesthetic *stasis,* an ideal pity, terror, or joy, is awakened or induced by the formal rhythm of beauty.
II. Art or beauty, divorced from good and evil, is akin to truth; therefore, if truth can best be approached through intellection, beauty or art is best approached through the three stages of apprehension.
  A. Beauty is separated from good and evil because good and evil excite the kinetic emotions of desire or loathing.
  B. Beauty is related to truth because both are static.
  C. Just as the first step in the direction of truth is to comprehend the act of intellection, the first step in the direction of beauty is to understand the process of aesthetic comprehension; the stages of apprehension and the qualities of beauty are akin.
III. The three qualities of beauty which correspond to the three stages of apprehension are, in the terms of Aquinas, *integritas, consonantia,* and *claritas.*
  A. *Integritas* is wholeness—*one* thing.
  B. *Consonantia* is harmony—a *thing.*

    C. *Claritas* is radiance—*that* thing.
       1. *Claritas* is not to be considered a manifestation of the
          sublime or divine; it is simply the whatness of a
          thing.
       2. (In *Stephen Hero* only). *Claritas* is revealed through
          the experience of epiphanies.

A fourth main division of the theory is Stephen's explanation of the three forms of art: the lyrical, the epical, and the dramatic. But this part is concerned more with the problem of creating art, the artist's relationship to his materials, than with the problem of the nature of art and beauty. Stephen claims the authority of Aquinas only for his discussion of the latter: "So far as this side of esthetic philosophy extends Aquinas will carry me all along the line. When we come to the phenomena of artistic conception, artistic gestation and artistic reproduction, I require a new terminology and a new personal experience." (245-246) [7]

But to what extent does Saint Thomas carry Stephen "all along the line"?

I. ART AS STASIS

Stephen bases two main principles of his theory—art as *stasis* and the separation of beauty from good and evil—upon one sentence [22] by Aquinas: *Pulchra sunt quoe visa placent,* which he translates "that is beautiful the apprehension of which pleases." (243) Slight variations in the Latin text appear in Joyce's several versions. *Pulcra,* the form in both *Stephen Hero* and the *Portrait,* is *pulcera* in the original notes, and *quoe* is *quae* in the notes and *Stephen Hero.* (*SH,* 95) [8] Although these changes may be typographical errors, it can be demonstrated that whenever Joyce cited Aquinas he was anything but meticulous in adhering to the original Latin. If he deliberately misquoted, we have the first sign of his irreverent attitude towards the Angelic Doctor. At

[7] Although Joyce's theories of the three forms of art and of the creative process are beyond the province of this study, it may be noted in passing that the parts for which Stephen does not claim Thomist authority appear to be more Thomistic than the parts for which he does claim such authority. See H. M. McLuhan, "Joyce, Aquinas, and the Poetic Process," *Renascence,* IV (Autumn 1951), 3-11. See pp. 249-265.
[8] Herbert Gorman, *James Joyce* (New York, 1948), p. 133.

any rate, the text of the *Summa Theologica* has *pulchra enim dicunter quae visa placent*. A translation by the Dominican Fathers makes it apparent that Joyce had read the paragraph in which the sentence appears:

> Beauty and goodness are identical fundamentally; for they are based upon the same thing, namely, the form. Consequently goodness may be rightly praised as beauty. But they differ logically, for goodness properly relates to the appetitive faculty (goodness being what all men desire); and therefore it has the formal aspect of an end (the appetitive faculty being a kind of movement towards a thing). Beauty relates to the cognoscitive faculty; for *beautiful things are those which please when seen*. Hence beauty consists in due proportions; for the senses are satisfied in things duly proportioned, as in what is after their own kind—because sense is a sort of reason; and so is every cognoscitive faculty.[9]

The complete passage at least partly clears up the mystification of Stephen's explanation of the one sentence drawn from it: "He uses the word *visa* . . . to cover esthetic apprehensions of all kinds, whether through sight or hearing or through any other avenue of apprehension. This word, though it is vague, is clear enough to keep away good and evil, which excite desire and loathing. It means certainly a stasis and not a kinesis." (243)

On this foundation, the first part of the theory is developed. Stephen begins by discussing the true nature of tragedy:

> Pity is the feeling which arrests the mind in the presence of whatsoever is grave and constant in human sufferings and unites it with the human sufferer. Terror is the feeling which arrests the mind in the presence of whatsoever is grave and constant in human sufferings and unites it with the secret cause. . . . You see I use the word *arrest*. I mean that the tragic emotion is static. Or rather the dramatic emotion is. The feelings excited by improper art are kinetic, desire or [25] loathing. Desire urges us to possess, to go to something; loathing urges us to abandon,

---

[9] *Summa Theologica*, Part I, question 5, article 4. Translations of the *Summa* throughout this essay are taken from The *"Summa Theologica" of St. Thomas Aquinas, Literally Translated by Fathers of the English Dominican Province* (New York, 1911-1912; London, 1913-1922), 22 vols.

to go from something. The arts which excite them, pornographical or didactic, are therefore improper arts. (239-240)

Stephen's ultimate purpose is to establish beauty in the objec-
tivity of the art-work rather than in the subjectivity of the artist.
The missing link between *stasis* and formal rhythm is found in
Joyce's original notes, in the discussion of comedy:

> An improper art aims at exciting in the way of comedy the feel-
> ing of desire but the feeling which is proper to comic art is the
> feeling of joy. . . . For desire urges us from rest that we may
> possess something but joy holds us in rest so long as we possess
> something. . . . this rest is necessary for the apprehension of
> the beautiful—the end of all art, tragic or comic,—for this rest is
> the only condition under which the images, which are to excite
> in us terror or pity or joy, can be properly presented to us and
> properly seen by us. For beauty is a quality of something seen
> but terror and pity and joy are states of mind.[10]

If beauty is a quality of something seen, then it is to be found in
the rhythm or proportion of the art-object: "Beauty expressed by
the artist . . . awakens, or ought to awaken, or induces, or ought
to induce, an esthetic stasis, an ideal pity or an ideal terror, a
stasis called forth, prolonged and at last dissolved by what I call
the rhythm of beauty. . . . Rhythm . . . is the first formal esthetic relation of part to part in any esthetic whole or of an
esthetic whole to its part or parts or of any part to the esthetic
whole of which it is a part." (241)

Although Saint Thomas has nothing to say about tragedy and
comedy, it would seem that, read literally, he supplies sanction
for the main features of this part of Stephen's theory. The separation of beauty, the product of cognition, from goodness, the
goal of appetition, and the dependence of beauty on form are
found in the paragraph from the *Summa Theologica* cited above.
Naturally, neo-Thomists support these aspects of Aquinas's
theory. For example, Father Thomas Gilby says that the experience of beauty "comes as a rest in human activity, as something desirable for its own sake" and that "it is of the es-

[10] Gorman, *op. cit.*, p. 97.

sence of Beauty that with the knowledge of it desire is at rest." [11]
Jacques Maritain, commenting on Aquinas's definition of the
beautiful, says: "The beautiful is that which gives joy, not all joy,
but joy in knowledge; not the joy peculiar to the act of knowing,
but a joy superabounding and overflowing from such an act because of the object known. If a [24] thing exalts and delights the
soul by the very fact of its being given to the intuition of the
soul, it is good to apprehend, it is beautiful." [12]

It is only when one considers the context that Joyce's divergence from Aquinas becomes apparent. Aquinas's definition of
beauty appears as a passing reference in a section on "God, the
Divine Unity." Implied in the above sentences by neo-Thomists
is the scholastic understanding of the unity of Being and the
presence of God in all beauty. For example, both Joyce and
Father Gilby use the word *rest*. What is the orthodox interpretation of *rest?* According to Herbert Ellsworth Cory, Aquinas "tells
us that 'it is of the nature of the beautiful that the appetite is
allayed by the sight of it.' I am sure that he would like us to
recall, in this connection, our refrain from St. Augustine: 'Thou
hast made us for Thyself; and our hearts are restless until they
find rest in Thee.' The aesthetic experience is seldom mystical;
but if ever it is *fully* conscious, if its recipient is thoroughly self-
disciplined in holiness, and if he is given extraordinary graces
by God, it will be mystical." [13]

Joyce stops short before *what*, according to the Thomists, the
aesthetic *stasis* reveals. If the context is denied, the rhythm of
art reveals only the mechanical harmony of parts to parts and
parts with whole: "the first formal esthetic relation of part to
part in any esthetic whole or of an esthetic whole to its part
or parts or of any part to the esthetic whole of which it is a
part." It does not reflect the harmony of God's universe. Seen
thus, Joyce is thinking simply of the importance of form, the
well-made work of art, and this point of Stephen's theory is

[11] *Poetic Experience: An Introduction to Thomist Aesthetic* (New York,
1934), p. 99 and p. 108.
[12] *Art and Scholasticism, with Other Essays*, trans. J. F. Scanlon (London,
1943), p. 23. The most complete statement of the neo-Thomist view of "due
proportion" is Edward I. Watkin, *A Philosophy of Form* (New York, 1935).
[13] *The Significance of Beauty in Nature and Art* (Milwaukee, 1948), p. 67.

closer to Henry James than to Saint Thomas. Joyce's "rhythm" places no emphasis on the *due* of Aquinas's "due proportion." Perhaps this is what Francis Fergusson had in mind when he wrote that Joyce makes his Thomism godless.

II. THE BEAUTIFUL, THE GOOD, AND THE TRUE

In *Stephen Hero* the aesthetic theory is presented not as an exposition of abstract principles, but in terms of dramatic conflict. Many of the points which Stephen explains to Lynch, who offers [25] only passive resistance and an occasional sarcasm, appear in the earlier version as part of the paper on "Art and Life" which Stephen read before the Literary and Historical Society of University College. The paper met with a hostile reception, mainly on the charge that it absolved art and artist from all patriotic and moral obligations. Previously, Dr. Dillon, President of the University, had said to him: "This theory you have—if pushed to its logical conclusion—would emancipate the poet from all moral laws. I notice too that in your essay you allude satirically to what you call the 'antique' theory—the theory, namely, that the drama should have special ethical aims, that it should instruct, elevate, and amuse. I suppose you mean Art for Art's sake." Stephen replied that he "only pushed to its logical conclusion the definition Aquinas has given of the beautiful." (95) After the reading of his paper, he remained silent, refusing to debate with his critics. And when, in the process of revision, the audience of many becomes the single auditor Lynch, the ethical objections disappear altogether. Thus, the only defense which Stephen makes at any time to the moralistic criticism is the testimonial of Saint Thomas—he has simply pushed to its logical conclusion Aquinas's definition of beauty.

Only by taking the part for the whole is Stephen's summary dismissal of the good from any consideration of the beautiful to be justified in terms of Thomist doctrine. The difference which Aquinas notes between the aspects of the good and the beautiful is, in the total theological view, less important than the similarity. They are "identical fundamentally," Aquinas said in the passage already quoted, and in another section of the *Summa:*

The beautiful is the same as the good, and they differ in aspect only. For since good is what all seek, the notion of good is that which calms the desire; while the notion of the beautiful is that which calms the desire, by being seen or known. Consequently those senses chiefly regard the beautiful, which are the most cognitive, viz., sight and hearing, as ministering to reason; for we speak of beautiful sights and beautiful sounds. But in reference to the other objects of the other senses, we do not use the expression *beautiful,* for we do not speak of beautiful tastes, and beautiful odours. Thus it is evident that beauty adds to goodness a relation to the cognitive faculty: so that *good* means that which simply pleases the appetite; while the *beautiful* is something pleasant to apprehend.[14]

It will be noticed that this passage makes beauty and goodness less divergent than does the passage from which Joyce drew his first [26] premise. Aquinas's phrase "beauty adds to goodness a relation to the cognitive faculty" sanctions the neo-Thomist acceptance of Cajetan's interpretation of this passage: "Beauty is a certain kind of good."[15]

Although most neo-Thomists agree with Joyce that art should not be didactic, that the artist's "only thought for the spectator should be to give him something beautiful, or *well-made*"[16] and that "the poetic experience in itself teaches nothing, making neither for edification nor appearing to lead onwards to higher truths,"[17] they do feel that art must be subject to moral censorship. This seeming paradox is to be explained by the scholastic distinction between art and artist. Art, says Maritain, is in the realm of Making, which is related solely to the good and perfection of the work produced; it "remains outside the line of human conduct, with an end, rules, and values, which are not those of the man, but of the work to be produced."[18] Art is a *habitus* of the practical understanding, and it is always good because it always strives towards perfection. Moral considera-

[14] *Summa Theologica,* Part II, question 27, article 1.
[15] *Prima Secundae,* question 27, article 1. Quoted by Maritain, *Art and Scholasticism,* p. 166.
[16] Maritain, *op. cit.,* p. 66.
[17] Gilby, *op. cit.,* p. 99.
[18] Maritain, *op. cit.,* p. 7.

tions, on the other hand, are in the realm of Doing or Action, the use made of free will. Thus the artist's decisions are ethically vulnerable. Art is infallibly right; when the art-work seems to fail, it is because the artist has failed his art. And since Prudence must rule the affairs of men, the artist must be moral. "Because art, the virtue of making, is specifically human rather than merely animal or merely mechanical," Cory explains, "it can never *persist* in its sanity unless it acts in fellowship with the moral virtues." [19] Art that is irreverent must be prohibited, for art, says Maritain, "has no right against God." [20] The neo-Thomists are not here speaking entirely for themselves; Aquinas himself says, "In the case of an art that produces things which for the most part some people put to an evil use, although such arts are not unlawful in themselves, nevertheless, according to the teaching of Plato, they should be extirpated from the State by the governing authority." [21] [27]

The Very Reverend Dr. Dillon charged that Stephen's theory would lead him to Art for Art's sake. If this expression means an art which is an escape from life, then the criticism is unjustified, for Joyce had no quarrel with the alliance of art and truth. The Stephen of *Stephen Hero* "did not attach himself to art in any spirit of youthful dilettantism but strove to pierce to the significant heart of everything" (*SH*, 33), and he told his mother, "Art is not an escape from life. It's just the very opposite. Art, on the contrary, is the very central expression of life" (*SH*, 86). In the *Portrait*, the theme of the artist's reliance upon life is expressed more symbolically, especially when Stephen, reacting bitterly from his religious crisis, seems to re-affirm the value of life as he watches the young girl wading in the river. In that moment of revulsion from the Church, it is religion—or, at any rate, the religion represented by the Jesuit priests—which seems to stand for the negation of life, and art which affirms the significance of experience. The *Portrait* concludes with the cry, "Welcome, O life! . . ." Thus, if Stephen is eager to separate beauty from goodness, he is also determined to associate beauty with truth.

[19] Cory, *op. cit.*, pp. 158-159.
[20] Maritain, *op. cit.*, p. 75.
[21] *Summa Theologica*, Part II, question 169, article 2.

Joyce's essay on James Clarence Mangan, published in 1902, contains the sentence, "Beauty, the splendour of truth, is a gracious presence when the imagination contemplates intensely the truth of its own being or the visible world and the spirit which proceeds out of truth and beauty is the holy spirit of joy." [22] By the time that Joyce wrote the *Portrait*, "the holy spirit of joy" had become less celestial, but he retained the conviction that beauty is the "splendour of truth."

Stephen continues his discourse. He has already cited Aquinas as an authority on the alliance of beauty and truth; he now brings in additional support:

> Plato, I believe, said that beauty is the splendour of truth. I don't think that it has a meaning but the true and the beautiful are akin. Truth is beheld by the intellect which is appeased by the most satisfying relations of the intelligible: beauty is beheld by the imagination which is appeased by the most satisfying relations of the sensible. The first step in the direction of truth is to understand the frame and scope of the intellect itself, to comprehend the act itself of intellection. Aristotle's entire system of philosophy rests upon his book of psychology and that, I think, rests on his statement that the same attribute cannot at the same time and in the same connexion belong to and not belong to the same subject. The first step in the direction of beauty is to understand the frame and scope of the imagination, to comprehend the act itself of esthetic [28] apprehension. (243-244)

Therefore, the qualities of beauty are akin to the stages of apprehension: "Though the same object may not seem beautiful to all people, all people who admire a beautiful object find in it certain relations which satisfy and coincide with the stages themselves of all esthetic apprehension. These relations of the sensible, visible to you through one form and to me through another, must be therefore the necessary qualities of beauty." (245)

This part of Stephen's theory clearly agrees with Thomist doctrine. Aquinas wrote that "since truth is in the intellect in proportion to its conformity with the object understood, the idea of truth must needs flow from the intellect to the object of the in-

[22] Quoted by Gorman, *op. cit.*, p. 80.

tellect, so that the thing understood is said to be true in so far as it is conformed in relation to the intellect" and that therefore "truth is defined by the conformity of intellect and thing." [23] Cory adds that "when we discern the beauty of an object our own spiritual powers and operations assume themselves a form, a harmony and equilibrium." [24] The interrelationship of subject and object is the basis of Maritain's definition of poetry: "that intercommunication between the inner being of things and the inner being of the human Self which is a kind of divination." [25]

What is the significance of this association of beauty with truth, of the stages of apprehension with the qualities of beauty? For Joyce, it provided a defense to the charge that his was a dilettante's art. Art, he insisted, is neither something found, a pretty object to be copied in a servile manner, nor entirely something invented. Pure art exists as a delicate balance between the artist-creator and that which he perceives, between the art-object and the one who perceives it. Joyce secularizes the Thomist insistence on the moral obligations of the artist by demanding instead intellectual or psychological obligations. There are definite standards for art which are rooted in human psychology. Art is a discipline and the artist a responsible creature.

III. THE THREE QUALITIES OF BEAUTY

In stating Aquinas's definition of the three qualities of beauty, Stephen again simplifies and misquotes the original Latin. He tells Lynch, "Aquinas says: *Ad pulcritudinem tria requiruntur integritas, consonantia, claritas.* I translate it so: *Three things are* [29] *needed for beauty, wholeness, harmony and radiance"* (248). Actually, Aquinas wrote: *"Nam ad pulchritudinem tria requiruntur: primo quidem integritas sive perfectio; quae enim diminuta sunt, turpia sunt; et debita proportio sive consonantia; et iterum claritas, unde, quae habent colorem nitidum, pulchra esse dicunter."* This the Dominican Fathers translate:

---

[23] *Summa Theologica*, Part I, question 16, articles 1 and 2.
[24] Cory, *op. cit.*, pp. 66-67.
[25] *Creative Intuition in Art and Poetry* (New York, 1953), p. 3.

"For beauty includes three conditions, *integrity* or *perfection,*
for those things which are impaired are by the very fact ugly;
and then due *proportion* or *harmony* is required; and lastly,
brightness or *clarity,* whence things are called beautiful which
have a bright color." [26]

We need not linger over the first two of these qualities. *Integritas* Stephen interprets as *wholeness.* In looking at a basket,
he tells Lynch, the mind first separates the basket from its surroundings and thus sees it as *one* thing. Joyce's definition is
probably even closer to the Latin text than the translation given
above, for *integritas* has also the meaning of wholeness or completeness, which fits better the *diminuta.* Father Gilby translates
this part of the definition, "a certain wholeness or perfection, for
whatever is incomplete is to that extent ugly." [27] *Wholeness*
obviously has greater application to Joyce's carefully unified art,
especially in *Ulysses* and *Finnegans Wake,* than does the more
vague *perfection.*

Stephen's interpretation of *consonantia* accords generally with
that "due proportion" Aquinas noted as a characteristic of
beauty. Having recognized the basket as *one* thing, Stephen tells
Lynch, you now notice "its formal lines . . . you feel the rhythm
of its structure . . . you feel now that it is a *thing.*" (249)
We have already noted the difference between Aquinas's concept of form and rhythm as a manifestation of Being and Joyce's
more mundane, mechanistic interpretation.

With *claritas,* Stephen sharply diverges from the orthodox interpretations of Saint Thomas. On this point we need not assume
what would be the attitude of the neo-Thomists towards Joyce's
explication. Cory, in his *The Significance of Beauty in Nature and
Art,* uses Joyce's explanations of *integritas* and *consonantia* as a
rebuttal to an attack on medieval aesthetic theory as sterile and
shallow, but he disagrees with Joyce's understanding of *claritas.*
Stephen himself points out the ambiguous nature of the
word: [30] "Aquinas uses a term which seems to be inexact. It
baffled me for a long time. It would lead you to believe that he
had in mind symbolism or idealism, the supreme quality of

[26] *Summa Theologica,* Part I, question 39, article 8.
[27] Gilby, *op. cit.,* p. 89.

beauty being a light from some other world, the idea of which the matter was but the shadow, the reality of which it was but the symbol. I thought he might mean that *claritas* was the artistic discovery and representation of the divine purpose in anything or a force of generalization which would make the esthetic image a universal one, make it outshine its proper conditions." (249-250) Cory interrupts his quoting of this passage to remark, "Precisely so; for Thomists also like the very powerful word *effulgence*. Joyce, the apostate, here loses his grip." Stephen continues: "But that is literally talk. I understand it so. When you have apprehended that basket as one thing and have then analysed it according to its form and apprehended it as a thing you make the only synthesis which is logically and esthetically permissible. You see that it is that thing which it is and no other. The radiance of which he speaks is the scholastic *quidditas*, the *whatness* of a thing." (250) To this, Cory replies:

> But St. Thomas also said elsewhere that one of the three ways in which God is present in all things is by His *quidditas*, His Essence. Just what *claritas* meant to St. Thomas we may gather from his account of what the glorified human body will be after its resurrection. The glory of the soul, already in heaven, will glow through its restored body and make it splendid. For this once too often recalcitrant flesh will now be ablaze in its every part with the effulgence of the soul which has experienced the Beatific Vision. Even so, even on earth, objects inanimate as well as animate, though their *claritas* is, of course, immeasurably below that of the saints in heaven, yet do, in so far as they are beautiful, beacon forth Divine Providence in so far as it is not impeded by imperfections which are never created by God. Even on earth, then, *claritas*, the crowning attribute of beauty is the shining through, to some greater or less degree, of the operative and essential presence of God. In his last sentences which I do not here quote Joyce falteringly reduces this *claritas* to a sort of metaphorical materialistic sentimentality.[28]

Apparently Joyce substituted *quidditas* for *claritas* in order to avoid the spiritual connotation of the latter. He left himself open to the objection of Cory by confusing *quidditas*, which in

[28] Cory, *op. cit.*, p. 227.

scholastic philosophy means specific essence (e.g. the manhood of Socrates, the correct answer to What is Socrates?), with the scholastic *haecceitas,* individual thisness.[29] In this instance, as "the scholastic *quidditas"* seems to imply, Joyce wanted to claim the sanction of [31] Aquinas without accepting the meaning of Aquinas. If the "bright color" in Aquinas's explanation of *claritas* seems to justify Joyce's mundane interpretation, the context in which it appears does not. The sentence immediately preceding is translated, "Species or Beauty has a likeness to the property of the Son." Following the list of the three conditions is Saint Thomas's explanation of how each applies to Christ. *Claritas,* he says, "agrees with the property of the Son, as the Word, which is the light and splendour of the intellect."

To say that beauty is *like* the property of the Son is not, of course, to say that all earthly beauty is but a shadow of divine form. Yet here Aquinas is more conservative than his modern interpreters. Although Maritain, the most authoritative of these commentators, is more cautious than Cory, he says of the third quality of beauty:

> A certain splendour is indeed according to all the Ancients the essential character of beauty. . . . *splendor formae,* said St. Thomas with a metaphysician's precision of language: for *form,* that is to say the principle determining the peculiar perfection of everything which is, constituting and completing things in their essence and their qualities, the ontological secret, so to speak, of their innermost being, their spiritual essence, their operative mystery, is above all the peculiar principle of intelligibility, the peculiar *clarity* of everything. Every form, moreover, is a remnant or a ray of the creative Mind impressed upon the heart of the being created. All order and proportion, on the other hand, are the work of the mind.[30]

What Joyce called "epiphany" gives us a clue by which we can trace the gradual development of his alienation from Thomist aesthetic. It is not impossible that Joyce first formulated his theory before his final break with the Church, then altered and

[29] I am indebted to Professor W. K. Wimsatt of Yale University for this information.
[30] Maritain, *Art and Scholasticism,* pp. 24-25.

modified it to suit his new attitude. We have already noticed that the phrase "the holy spirit of joy" in his essay on Mangan implies a greater reliance on the spiritual value of art than is apparent in the *Portrait*. In *Stephen Hero* Joyce described *claritas* in terms more congenial to the Thomistic interpretation:

> *Claritas* is *quidditas*. After the analysis which discovers the second quality the mind makes the only logically possible synthesis and discovers the third quality. This is the moment which I call epiphany. First we recognize that the moment is *one* integral thing, then we recognize that it is an organised composite structure, a *thing* in fact: finally, when the relation of the parts is exquisite, when the parts are adjusted to the special point, we recognise that it is *that* thing which it is. Its soul, its whatness, leaps to us from the vestment of its appearance. The soul of the commonest object, the structure of which is so adjusted, seems to us radiant. The object achieves its epiphany. (*SH*, 213) [32]

In this stage, Stephen's interpretation of *claritas* is orthodox.[31] The word *epiphany*, which he defines as "a sudden spiritual manifestation" (*SH*, 211), has, of course, the religious connotation of Christ's manifestation to the wise men. Stephen speaks of the soul. Maritain says of the third quality of beauty that "above all it is the profound splendour of the soul shining through." [32]

In the *Portrait* there is no mention of the epiphany. Here is how Stephen develops his explanation of *claritas* with what Cory calls "metaphorical materialistic sentimentality": "The radiance of which he speaks is the scholastic *quidditas*, the *whatness* of a thing. This supreme quality is felt by the artist when the esthetic image is first conceived in his imagination. The mind in that mysterious instant Shelley likened beautifully to a fading coal. The instant wherein that supreme quality of beauty, the clear

---

[31] It is perhaps for this reason that Catholic critics of Joyce use the presentation of the theory in *Stephen Hero* as a basis for their argument that the Stephen of the *Portrait* is a satirized, romanticized figure whose statements on art cannot always be taken seriously. See McLuhan (pp. 249-265), and Hugh Kenner, pp. 25-60. The assumption that Joyce is speaking for himself in *Stephen Hero*, but not in the *Portrait*, fails to account for the abundant evidence that Joyce shared Stephen's rejection of the Church. See, for example, Mary Colum, *Life and the Dream* (Garden City, 1947), pp. 388-389 and Georges Borach, "Conversations with James Joyce," trans. Joseph Prescott, *College English*, XV, 326.

[32] Maritain, *Art and Scholasticism*, p. 28.

radiance of the esthetic image, is apprehended luminously by
the mind which has been arrested by its wholeness and fascinated by its harmony is the luminous silent stasis of esthetic
pleasure." (250) The reference to Shelley is particularly significant because it refers to that passage in A *Defence of Poetry*
which describes the creative process as an unfortunate *moving
away* from divine inspiration.[33] The man-made nature of art, a
condition which Shelley, the translator of Plato's *Ion,* largely
regrets, Joyce exalts as the factor which enables the artist to
exist as a god in himself.

This explains why the epiphanies, now reduced simply to
revelations of whatness rather than of soul, which appear in the
Portrait and *Ulysses* do not imply the existence of an all-encom-
passing Unity. In *Ulysses,* for example:

> From the playfield the boys raised a shout. A whirring whistle:
> goal. . . .
> —The ways of the Creator are not our ways, Mr Deasy said.
> All history moves towards one great goal, the manifestation of
> God. [33]
> Stephen jerked his thumb towards the window, saying:
> —That is God.
> Hooray! Ay! Whrrwhee!
> —What? Mr Deasy asked.
> —A shout in the street, Stephen answered, shrugging his
> shoulders. (*UL,* 35)

Aquinas and Maritain, like Mr. Deasy, would undoubtedly agree
that God manifests Himself in the shout, but the implication of
Stephen's remark is that a shout in the street is all the God
there is.

<h3 style="text-align:center">CONCLUSION</h3>

We have seen that Joyce consistently secularizes Aquinas. He
adheres to the Thomist categories, but interprets them to suit his
own purposes. Yet, in doing so, he uses much of Aquinas and does
not so much dispute as distort the scholastic argument. At least
one important doctrine he accepts completely: the identification
of truth as the conformity of mind and object he finds useful

[33] *Works,* ed. Harry Buxton Forman (London, 1880), VII, 137.

because it provides him with a justification of absolute, psychological standards for art and a defense against the charge that his theory is that of a dilettante or an Art-for-Art's sake advocate. Each of the other principles, however, he interprets—against the spirit, if not the letter, of the *Summa*—in secular, mundane terms that permit him to discard the supernatural implications of Thomist doctrine. Aquinas's "due proportion" he accepts to the extent that it supports his objective, non-emotional art, but he denies the scholastic interpretation of "due proportion" as a semblance of Divine Order or Unity. He exalts the art-work as a world in itself, with the appropriate standards of completeness, harmony, and clarity, but he sees it as complete in itself, harmonious in itself, and clear in itself, rather than as a fragment or a symbol of a broader, more extensive Unity. Thus he makes the artist equal to God and under the guise of traditionalism advances a theory that is revolutionary—or if traditional, closer to the tradition of Gustave Flaubert, Henry James, and Walter Pater than to the tradition of the Thomists.

In the satirical poem "The Holy Office" (1904), Joyce wrote:

> I turn to view
> The shamblings of that motley crew,
> Those souls that hate the strength that mine has
> Steeled in the school of old Aquinas.
> Where they have crouched and crawled and prayed
> I stand, the self-doomed, unafraid,
> Unfellowed, friendless and alone, [34]
> Indifferent as the herring-bone,
> Firm as the mountain ridges where
> I flash my antlers on the air.[34]

Joyce was steeled in the school of Aquinas to the extent that he could use the scholastic method of logical argument against the vague generalities of the moralists or the dilettantes. But as far as his thought itself was concerned, he stood "unfellowed, friendless and alone." *A Portrait of the Artist as a Young Man* tells how Stephen discovered that his weapons were to be "silence, exile and cunning." (291) The cunning preceded the writing of the novel. [35]

[34] Quoted by Gorman, *op. cit.*, p. 140.

J. MITCHELL MORSE
Augustine's Theodicy and Joyce's Aesthetics

SAINT AUGUSTINE, whose name Joyce bore within his own, was partly responsible for the dramatistic theory of art set forth in *A Portrait of the Artist as a Young Man* and followed to a greater or less degree in all Joyce's works. He was also partly responsible for Joyce's theory of the godlike artist, and perhaps to some extent even for his conviction of the irrelevance of moral standards to artistic judgment.[1] The three ideas are all of a piece, each supporting and supported by the others, in Augustine's theodicy as in Joyce's aesthetics. This is not to say that Joyce was an Augustinian, except in the sense that, being preoccupied with the ideas we most strongly oppose, we are willy-nilly influenced by them; in the same way that Augustine turned the devices of pagan rhetoric "to a Christian use, . . . to the defense of our way,"[2] Joyce turned certain Augustinian notions to the service and defense of art.

Genius has little reverence for ideas. It uses them. Joyce used Augustine and the whole classic tradition for new purposes. The Platonic notion that the arts and sciences were properly

Reprinted by permission of the author and The Johns Hopkins Press. The essay originally appeared in *ELH, A Journal of English Literary History* in March, 1957. References to *A Portrait* are to P-2; *Stephen Hero* to SH-2.
[1] The chief source of this last theory was Thomas Aquinas. See my paper, "Art and Fortitude: Joyce and the *Summa Theologica*," *The James Joyce Review*, I (February, 1957).

[2] *De Doctrina Christiana* II.40, IV.2 (Migne, *Patrologia Latina*, XXXIV, 63 [C], 64 [A], 89 [D]–90 [A]): "*in usum convertanda Christianum . . . in usum nostrum vindicanda. . . . Cum ergo sit in medio posita facultas eloquii, quae ad persuadenda seu prava seu recta valet plurimum; cur non bonorum studio comparatur, ut militet veritati . . . ?*"

subordinate to politics became among Christian thinkers the belief that they were properly handmaids of theology; not until Joyce did any artist dare to "kill the priest and the king" within himself (*UL,* 574), to regard both politics and [30] theology as nothing more than materials for art, and to subordinate both church and state to the personality of the artist. "You die for your country, suppose," says Stephen Dedalus to the British soldiers. "Not that I wish it for you. But I say: Let my country die for me." (*UL,* 576) And to Bloom he says, "You suspect . . . that I may be important because I belong to the *faubourg Saint-Patrice* [that suburb of the Church] called Ireland for short. . . . But I suspect . . . that Ireland must be important because it belongs to me." (*UL,* 629) The same notion appears in *Stephen Hero.* (*SH,* 246) In the *Portrait,* announcing his artistic intention, he asserts that he will try to fly by means of (as well as past) the nets that have been flung at him—the nets of nationality, language and religion. (238) Joyce was aided in his flight by the net of Augustinian theodicy.

Augustine worked in the shadow of Tertullian by the light of Cicero and Quintilian. Though he had the best education the age afforded, though he was the master of an ornately beautiful Latin style and (to his sorrow) never lost his pagan delight in a well-turned sentence, he did not approve of secular learning or literary art except as means of propagating the faith. The roots of his attitude were in the classic tradition itself. Under the dictatorship of Julius Caesar, when thoughtful public discussion was penalized, when fools orated and wise men stayed at home, when rhetoric had no content and wisdom no tongue, Cicero set forth a regime of education for the man who he hoped would one day restore republican liberty—the informed and intelligent speaker, the *doctus orator,* no philosopher king but a private citizen willing to speak out for the public good and able to speak effectively.[3] Quintilian—for whom, as a Stoic, virtue was an end in itself and outward circumstances could not be helped—was less interested in promoting liberty than in persuading individuals to amend their lives. At his hands, therefore, the ideal of the informed speaker was transmogrified into that

[3] *De Oratore* II.xx.85, II.xliii.182.

of the good man skilled in speaking—Cato's *vir bonus dicendi peritus*.[4] Quintilian's *Institutio* [31] *Oratoria*, the fruit of twenty years of teaching, had a strong effect on such early Christian thinkers as were not absolutely opposed to the reading of pagan books, notably on Saint Augustine, who in any case had read it before his conversion. From the good man skilled in speaking it was an easy transition to the Christian skilled in teaching, the ideal of *De Doctrina Christiana*.[5] That was a considerable advance over the attitude of Tertullian, who (having a magnificently developed *odium theologicum*) had written, "What has Jerusalem to do with Athens? Or the Church with the Academy? Or Christians with heretics? . . . We who have Jesus Christ need no curiosity; we who have the Gospel need no investigation."[6] But Saint Augustine, who was concerned to explain the fact of evil in a world made by a good and omnipotent God, took a more liberal attitude: "Let everyone who is a good and true Christian know that truth is the truth of his Lord, wheresoever it be found"; since the liberal arts developed by the pagans are "better suited to the service of truth," and since even pagan philosophy contains truths that support the faith, Christians should take such arts and truths from their "wrongful possessors"[7] and use them "for the confuting of heretics."[8]

Augustine's specific use of them was to justify God's ways

[4] *Institutio Oratoria* X.i.1.

[5] *De Doctrina Christiana* IV.15, 16, 27, 28 (Migne, *P.L.*, XXXIV, 103 [A]–104 [D], 118 [A]–120 [C]).

[6] *Liber De Praescriptionibus Adversus Haereticos* VII (Migne, *P.L.*, II, 20 B–21 A): "*Quid ergo Athenis et Hierosolymis? quid Academiae et Ecclesiae? quid haereticis et Christianis?* . . . *Nobis curiositate opus non est, post Christum Jesum; nec inquisitione, post Evangelium.*" Cf. II Corinthians 6: 14-16.

[7] *De Doctrina Christiana* II.18, 40 (Migne, *P.L.*, XXXIV, 49 [D], 63 [A-B]): "*imo verus quisquis bonus verusque christianus est, Domini sui esse intelligat, ubicumque invenerit veritatem. . . . Philosophi autem qui vocantur, si qua forte et fidei nostrae accommodata dixerunt, maximi Platonici* [i.e., the Neo-Platonists], *non solum formidanda non sunt, sed ab eis etiam tanquam injustis possessoribus in usum nostrum vindicanda . . . etiam liberales disciplinas usui veritatis aptiores, et quaedam morum praecepta utilissima continent, deque ipso uno Deo colendo nonnulla vera inveniuntur apud eos.*"

[8] *De Musica* VI.xvii.59 (Migne, *P.L.*, XXXII, 1194 [A]): "*Quod tamen facere non auderemus, nisi multos pios Ecclesiae catholicae matris optimae filios, qui puerilibus studiis loquendi ac disserendi facultatem quantum satis est*

by portraying Him as an artist—a conception that profoundly influenced Joyce's view of himself as artist and of the creative process. Though it is wicked to study music for its own sake, [32] said Augustine, we can learn from it what great souls learn by flights of intuition: that in nature, as in a perfect poem, nothing is accidental or unintended; that just as a syllable may be replaced by an interval of silence, or a long syllable by two short ones or by a short one and a rest, and the whole poem gain in artistic interest by the variations thus achieved without breaking the rhythmic pattern, so all seeming inequalities, whether of the stars in their courses or of human beings in theirs, "join in melodious succession, as it were in a song of the universe." [9] Let us not complain if it falls to our lot to be a short syllable or even a rest. If we cannot apprehend the harmony, the order, the justice of the whole and of our position in it, neither can a statue in an outer niche of a building see the whole building, or a soldier in the front line of battle the disposition of the whole army. We are disposed in the order of things according to our merit as predetermined by God's will, "not knowing what beauty divine providence will bring forth by means of us." If, for example, God ordains us to have a wicked will and violate His law, that is not wicked of Him: He does it only in order that the punishment of our imperfection may fulfill the law and demonstrate its perfection. Thus God's good works subsist even in man's bad works. [10]

This notion is developed more fully in the *Enchiridion.* Since

---

consecuti essent, eadem refellendorum haereticorum necessitate fecisse videremus."

[9] *Ibid.,* VI.xi.29 (Migne, *P.L.,* XXXII, 1179 [D]): *"Ita coelestibus terrena subjecta, orbes temporum suorum numerosa successione quasi carmini universitatis associant."*

[10] *Ibid.,* 1179 [D]–1180 [A-B]: *"In quibus multa nobis videntur inordinata et perturbata, quia eorum ordini pro nostris meritis assuti sumus, nescientes quid de nobis divina providentia pulchrum gerat. Quoniam si quis, verbi gratia, in amplissimarum pulcherrimarumque aedium uno aliquo angulo tanquam statua collocetur, pulchritudinem illius fabricae sentire non poterit, cujus et ipse pars erit. Nec universi exercitus ordinem miles in acie valet intueri. Et in quolibet poemate si quanto spatio syllabae sonant, tanto viverent atque sentirent, nullo modo illa numerositas et contexti operis pulchritudo eis placeret, quam totam perspicere atque approbare non possent, cum de ipsis singulis praetereuntibus fabricata esset atque perfecta. Ita*

nothing happens against God's will; since even when the wicked, "as far as they themselves are concerned," act against His will, His will concerning them is thereby fulfilled; since "as far as His omnipotence is concerned" they do His will by opposing [33] it; since He thus achieves His good purposes "through the evil wills of evil men," [11] it follows that the individual is of no consequence or value as such but only as part of the grand design. In his polemic *Against the So-called Fundamental Letter of Manichaeus*, Augustine states this clearly and justifies it in terms of God's artistry: "Just as the utterance of the voice passes away and perishes in silence, and yet our speech is formed by the departure and succession of passing words, and is properly and pleasantly divided by intervals of silence, so likewise the humble beauty of temporal natures is formed and made distinct by the passing away of things and the death of those born." [12] Their beauty, that is, inheres less in themselves than in their relationships and the patterns they make. The same notion appears in *De Musica*: since the perfection of a poem requires that the individual syllables pass away, and since man is an instrument of God's will as a syllable is an instrument of the poet's will, "God, supremely good and supremely just, grudges no beauty, whether it be achieved by the soul's damnation, or retreat, or endurance." [13] Evil being

---

peccantem hominem ordinavit Deus turpem, non turpiter. Turpis enim factus est voluntate, universum amittendo quod Dei praeceptis obtemperans possidebat, et ordinatus in parte est, ut qui legem agere noluit, a lege agatur . . . quia et in malis operibus nostris Dei opera bona sunt."

[11] *Enchiridion de Fide, Spe et Charitate* C, CI (Migne, *P.L.*, XL, 297 [B], [C]): *"Quantum enim ad ipsos attinet, quod Deus noluit fecerunt; quantum vero ad omnipotentiam Dei, nullo modo id efficere valuerunt. Hoc quippe ipso quod contra voluntatem facerunt ejus, de ipsis facta est voluntas ejus. . . . Nam Deus quasdam voluntates suas, utique bonas implet per malorum hominum voluntates malas."*

[12] *Contra Epistolam Manichaei quam vocant Fundamenti* XLI.47 (Migne, *P.L.*, XLII, 205 [D]): *"Nam et species vocis emissae praeterit, et silentio perimitur; et tamen sermo noster ex praeteriuntium verborum decessione ac successione peragitur, et moderatis silentiorum intervallis decenter suaviterque distinguitur: ita sese habet etiam temporalium naturarum infima pulchritudo, ut rerum transitu peragatur, et distinguatur morte nascentium."*

[13] *De Musica* VI.xvii.56 (Migne, *P.L.*, XXXII, 1191 [B]): *"Deus autem summe bonus, et summe justus, nulli invidet pulchritudini, quae sive damnatione animae, sive regressione, sive permansione fabricatur."*

a merely negative condition, an absence or deficiency of good, the function of the evil man in God's work is analogous to that of a rest in music. Thus does God compose the poem of the universe without regard to man's limited and self-interested notions of right and wrong. God is an artist, not a humanitarian. Augustine says specifically, quoting Romans 9: 11-21, that we are not qualified to impugn His justice.[14]

It hardly needs saying that such a God is not understandable [34] in human terms; that is one of the central doctrines of Augustine's Neo-Platonic Christianity. Rare spirits at rare moments have had glimpses of the inexplicable splendor, but their efforts to communicate the experience to us who are more grossly made or less finely tuned are never quite successful; they all have reason to complain with Richard Rolle that we understand the verses of their song but not the song of their verses.[15] Joyce had more natural piety than most of us, and in the *Portrait* Stephen once experiences the mystic union, "the ecstasy of seraphic life." (255) But the experience takes place in a dream, and is never repeated in any waking hour. The child who can "encounter reality" only through imaginary participation in formal religious rites (184) becomes a youth who can encounter it only through art. (299) But the need to encounter it remains unchanged. Stephen recalls how one evening "he had dismounted from a borrowed creaking bicycle to pray to God in a wood near Malahide. He had lifted up his arms and spoken in ecstasy to the sombre nave of trees, knowing that he stood on holy ground and in a holy hour. And when two constabulary men had come into sight round a bend in the gloomy road he had broken off his prayer to whistle loudly an air from the last pantomime." (273) The disposition that led to such a moment, however, was forced to find a different mode of expression. There were too many constables in Joyce's own mind. There was Moynihan, for example, speaking of ellipsoidal balls (224, 256); and there was William of Ockham,

[14] *Enchiridion* XCIX (Migne, *P.L.*, XL, 278).
[15] C. Horstman[n] ed., *Yorkshire Writers: Richard Rolle of Hampole and his Followers* (London, 1896), II, xxx: "*Mundi amatores scire possunt verba vel carmina nostrarum cantionum, non autem cantica nostrorum carminium.*"

asking, if the whole body of Christ was physically present in the Host, how it could be in two churches at the same time. (*UL*, 41) Thus Joyce faced the dilemma every intellectual with a strong religious impulse must face, but his solution was the opposite of the mystics'. They disavow reason; he disavowed faith. It was difficult. "I am a product of Catholicism," said the hero of *Stephen Hero;* "I cannot in a moment destroy every feeling in my nature. That takes time." (*SH*, 139) It took his whole life. Joyce never destroyed his native piety to such an extent that he could ignore it. Like the reformed drunkard who, lacking a normal ability to take it or leave it, [35] regards alcohol with a horror as obsessive as his former craving, Joyce could never be indifferent to religion. He fought it all his life, as for some years he fought a tendency to drink too much, and for essentially the same reason. The slogan "Guinness is good for you" rings throughout *Finnegans Wake,* always in the same ironical tone as do certain formulas of piety, "Hail, Mary, full of grace," "Holy Mary, Mother of God," "The Father, the Son and the Holy Ghost," "Matthew, Mark, Luke and John," and Augustine's joyful cry of amazement, "O felix culpa!" The mystical consciousness, says William James, like the drunken consciousness, rises above "the cold facts and dry criticisms of the sober hour. Sobriety diminishes, discriminates, and says no; drunkenness expands, unites, and says yes." [16] Stephen's conversation was full of cold facts and dry criticisms because Joyce needed them. They were an antidote not only to his companions' muddleheadedness but to his own mystical tendencies. Every writer, in order to compose in tranquillity, must get above his material, diminish it, discriminate, and say no; for Joyce especially this was an absolute necessity, since when he worked he consciously imitated Augustine's God.

The side of his aesthetic that he got from Aquinas emphasized the irrelevance of non-artistic standards in judging works of art; the side that he got from Augustine emphasized the irrelevance of non-artistic standards in creating works of art. From Aquinas he learned to see, through the accidents of sound and shape and

16 William James, *The Varieties of Religious Experience* (New York: Modern Library, n.d.), pp. 377-378.

color (242), the formal relations (241) which are "the essence of beauty." (205) From Augustine he learned not to distort such relations by bending them to human requirements, political, moral or emotional. Just as Augustine denies that God can be understood in terms of human morality, so Stephen denies that art can be either created or understood in terms of values other than its own. "Our flesh shrinks from what it dreads and responds to the stimulus of what it desires by a purely reflex action of the nervous system. . . . Beauty expressed by the artist cannot awaken in us an emotion which is kinetic or a sensation which is purely physical. It awakens, or ought to awaken, or induces, or ought to induce, [36] an esthetic stasis, an ideal pity or an ideal terror." (241) The ideal is almost mathematical in its purity. The highest form of art, the dramatic, is not merely a reproduction of life, but "life purified and reprojected from the human imagination" (252), the function of the imagination being to work the raw material of life into "the most satisfying relations of the sensible" and "of the intelligible." (243) The most important words here are "purified" and "ideal." They are the keys to Joyce's intention. Stephen is careful to distinguish between the uses of words "in the literary tradition," which has nothing to do with current practicalities, and "in the marketplace" (219, 250); in the marketplace their purity of meaning is compromised by the immediate human context—when the word *detain* is adapted to the practical considerations of the moment it loses something of its essential or ideal meaning (219), and the word *beauty* as used in the marketplace loses its "wider sense." (250) The uses of the marketplace, that is to say, are rough and inaccurate, and therefore unsuited to the requirements of art. The dean of studies uses the vague language of the marketplace, calling a tundish a funnel, and Stephen makes bold to correct him. (219-220, 297) A tundish is a particular kind of funnel; when Stephen, to make himself understood, has to use the merely generic term, he does so reluctantly. Call this pedantry if you will. He takes unfavorable notice of Cranly's using the word "eke" for "e'en" (238, 281), is irritated when McCann calls him "a reactionary" because he will not sign a resolution for universal peace sponsored by the Czar of Russia

(231), and is disheartened by the "sour smelling" question, "What then is your point of view?" (291) In one of his early book reviews Joyce chided an author who used the word "certainty" for "certitude." [17] Stephen too, requiring precision of thought and speech, cultivates it in himself, for if he is to purify life he must have a pure medium. He must divorce his speech from the common speech of men. He must be able to report their speech accurately in all its inaccuracy, but if he is to do anything more, if he is to express beauty from such "sluggish matter" (196), such "lumps of earth" (221), "the [37] gross earth or what it brings forth" (242), "the daily bread of experience" (260), "the reality of existence" (299), he must command a fine instrument, "a lucid supple periodic prose." (194) The beauty of literature thus inheres not in the material but in the art of writing; what Stephen chiefly likes about words is "the poise and balance of the period itself," and what he most enjoys about writing is not "the reflection of the glowing sensible world through the prism of a language manycoloured and richly storied," not language's "associations of legend and colour," not even his own "inner world of individual emotions"—not any subject matter—but the contemplation of the inner world "mirrored perfectly": the contemplation of his own artistry. (193-194) The opening chapter of Genesis is punctuated with the joyful refrain, "And God saw that it was good." Augustine's whole conception of God as artist is a development of that theme, and Joyce's conception of drama as the highest form of literature follows Augustine very closely.

Literature, says Stephen, is "the highest and most spiritual form of art." Even in its simplest form, the "rhythmical cry" that constitutes a lyric expressing an instant of emotion, the artist begins to rise above himself, since he is "more conscious of the instant of emotion than of himself as feeling emotion." (251) This is a fair description of the *Portrait*, an essentially lyrical utterance, though, as Stephen admits, the forms are often blended and confused. From the lyric emerges the simplest

---

[17] Stanislaus Joyce and Ellsworth Mason, eds., *The Early Joyce: The Book Reviews, 1902-1903* (Colorado Springs, Colo., 1955), p. 15.

form of the epic, in which "the narrative is no longer purely personal," since "the personality of the artist passes into the narration itself" in which the characters and the action are bathed as in "a vital sea." This is a fair description of *Ulysses*. The narrative is no longer purely personal, since the author, though he is the central character, is no longer the only character. Being involved with others, he necessarily regards them with interest and thereby attains a greater distance from himself. In the *Portrait* the other characters serve merely as background for Stephen; they are seen only through his eyes, and they talk only that he may reply or react; there is no scene in which he is not the central figure. *Ulysses* is a different matter. Here the artist is concerned primarily with art and only incidentally with his personal emotions. He achieves the [38] dramatic form, however, only when he can develop a story independently of his own feelings and attitudes; when, regarding life like Stephen Hero with a "remorseless lack of sentiment for himself no less than for others" (*SH*, 151), he can use characters, including himself, for purely artistic purposes as if they were so many syllables; when he can therefore endow them with such independent life that they can work out their history—however preordained by him—in accordance with their own natures and, as far as they are concerned, by their own free will.[18] At this stage, says Stephen in the *Portrait*, "the personality of the artist . . . refines itself out of existence." (252) Thus life is purified and reprojected from an imagination as free as a mathematician's, and "the mystery of esthetic like that of material creation is accomplished." The author, like God, is completely detached, "invisible, refined out of existence, indifferent." (252) The final clause, however, "paring his fingernails," is a giveaway (doubtless intentional) of both Stephen and Joyce. A person who is really indifferent has no need for such a self-conscious pantomime of indifference. That is a fair description of *Finnegans Wake*.

In the *Portrait* Stephen does not quite claim to be God; he

[18] For an orthodox resolution of the conflict between God's foreknowledge and man's free will, cf. *Enchiridion* XXX, CIV, CV (Migne, *P.L.*, XL, 246 [C]–247 [B], 281 [B-D]).

calls himself rather "the priest of the eternal imagination" (260); on the beach, after having decided not to join the Jesuits, he discovers the one God he can serve, art: the art of using language to express the meaning of life—and to create meaning —in works whose beauty is a matter of their perfect efficacy. (190-201) The principle is illustrated in the Telemachus and Eumaeus episodes of *Ulysses.* When Stephen composes the phrase, "White breast of the dim sea," what interests and pleases him is not so much the sea as the phrase itself and his own activity as poet: "The twining stresses, two by two. A hand plucking the harpstrings merging their twining chords. Wavewhite wedded words shimmering on the dim tide." (*UL*, 11) This is the work of a linguistic genius who, like Augustine, thinks of poetry chiefly in terms of its musical qualities. Joyce, however, recognizes the limitations of that view. When Bloom, passing a group of Italians, is charmed by the sound of their [39] speech—"it is so melodious and full"—Stephen wearily informs him that they are "haggling over money." (*UL*, 606) Yet Bloom is not deluded until he devalues his own experience by saying, "It may be only the southern glamour that surrounds it." His naive first impression was right: animated speech has a beauty of its own, regardless of content or vocabulary, and certainly *"Putanna madona, che ci dia i quattrini!"* (*UL*, 605) for all its obscene irreverence is as musical as "White breast of the dim sea." Yet Stephen is right too, for the content is certainly offensive and if we perceive it we cannot honestly ignore it. Joyce, however, being above Stephen, Bloom and the quarreling Italians, uses the ludicrous unlovely incident to create a complex beauty, that artistic beauty which Stephen calls in the *Portrait* the radiance of truth (243, 250)—the revelation of the inner and outer relations of things and thus of their meaning. This does not shine from the Italians' speech or from anything that Bloom or Stephen says about it; there is little natural beauty in any one of these elements, but Joyce creates artistic beauty from them by showing us the truth of which they are an epiphany and by making us admire the skill with which he shows it. Bloom's pitifully dull remark about Southern glamour, for example, is so justly recorded that the contempla-

tion of the recording gives us an intellectual pleasure of the
aesthetic kind. Thus, just as God accomplishes His good work
through man's bad works, so the priest of the imagination
creates beauty from ugly materials—or rather, as Stephen
would say, expresses the beauty he can see in their relations.
There is thus an essentially romantic attitude behind all Joyce's
work, however unromantic the details may seem, and an essentially Augustinian acceptance of things as they are. Augustine
came to acceptance through religion, Joyce through art. One
is perhaps as evil as the other.

The artist's task, however, is more difficult, for he must at
all times be clearheaded about his work, and the priestly imagination is liable to a peculiarly seductive kind of doublethink.
The priest is a vicar, a vicarious God, so that even though he
denies that he is God he can hardly help acting as if he were.
However long the chain of command may be, still the Pope is
God's vicar and the village priest acts for him; the village priest,
no less than the Pope, can hardly permit himself to be gain-
said, [40] and is therefore liable to regard all who disagree with
him in anything as enemies of God. Joyce's self-confidence seems
to have been of this kind. Those who disagreed with him he
tended to consider enemies of art. He was always a man of
faith; as an adult he lived by the truth of art as intensely as
he had formerly lived by the truth of the Catholic religion. In
the *Portrait* Stephen deplores a girl's preferring the false priest
of Catholicism, who merely goes through the motions of communion with the divine, to himself, in whom divinity lives
although as yet there are no outward signs of it. What he
deplores in her is lack of faith, lack of that spiritual vision
which would have enabled her to make a better choice. He
frankly regards himself as one of the elect of his race, in betraying whom the mocker Moynihan (a forerunner of Buck Mulligan) betrays the whole race. (226) In *Ulysses* he deplores
the old milkwoman's preferring Mulligan to himself (*UL*, 16),
and Joyce implies that the barmaids at the Ormond are equally
blind in preferring the mocker Boylan, in whom there is no
truth, to the good Bloom, who in his fallen condition is yet also
a man of faith. (*UL*, 256, 262) In *Finnegans Wake* Shem

"lifts the lifewand and the dumb speak" (*FW*, 195), but the Rain-
bow Girls and the Leapyear Girls have no use for him; they
flock around Shaun, though—or because—"he points the deathbone and the quick are still." (*FW*, 193, 595) This is one of the
major themes of Joyce's work as a whole: the tendency of
"ordinary people," as Stephen Hero says, to commit "moral
suicide" (*SH*, 200-201) or to reveal the fact that they are already
dead by choosing Barrabas instead of God. "No honourable
and sincere man," says Stephen to the nationalists in the
Portrait, "has given up to you his life and his youth and his
affections . . . but you sold him to the enemy or failed him in
need or reviled him and left him for another. And you invite
me to be one of you. I'd see you damned first." (237-238)
He himself does not fear to be "spurned for another." (292) He
thus explicitly rejects not the role of savior but the role of
one who kills the savior. His attitude is close to that of God
in the *Enchiridion*, who willingly sees the majority of men
damned because it is their nature to be damned.[19] [41]

But God is the savior too—of those who by His own decree
have natures capable of being saved. Stephen likewise, as artist,
hopes to save from spiritual death those who are capable of
being quickened by his art: "How could he hit their conscience
or how cast his shadow over the imaginations of their daughters,
before their squires begat upon them, that they might breed
a race less ignoble than their own?" (280) The answer Joyce
proposed can be found in his youthful criticism and in all his
works: the art itself must create its audience—must create those
who can respond to it and be saved. Not the majority, of
course, who have no desire to rise any higher than they must,
but the elect, who by their aspiration cut themselves off from
the majority. The artist who ministers to and in part creates

[19] *Enchiridion* XCIX (Migne, *P.L.*, XL, 278 [D]): "*Videt enim, si capit,
universum genus humanum tam justo judicio divino in apostatica radice
damnatum, ut etiamsi nullus inde liberaretur, nemo recte posset Dei
vituperare justitiam; et qui liberantur, sic opportuisse liberari, ut ex pluribus
non liberatis, atque in damnatione justissima derelictis, ostenderetur quid
meruisset universa conspersio, et quo etiam istos debitum judicium Dei
duceret, nisi eis indebita misericordia subveniret: ut volentium de suis meritis
gloriari, omme os obstruatur* (Romans 3: 19); *et qui gloriatur, in Domino
glorietur.*"

aspiration is not quite God, but his activity is godlike. He makes the most difficult of all human choices. He risks cutting himself off from all human understanding, for a purpose which may very well turn out to be of no consequence after all. Joyce made that hard decision. So great was his faith in art, he was willing to risk damnation for it. In the *Portrait* Stephen tells Cranly, "I am not afraid to make a mistake, even a great mistake, a lifelong mistake and perhaps as long as eternity too." To Cranly's question if he would be willing to stand "quite alone . . . separate from all others" and "to have not even one friend," he replies, "I will take the risk." (292) Joyce suffered intensely from his isolation, but contrived to create beauty from it: the picture of Shem in *Finnegans Wake* is a nightmare of loneliness (*FW*, 169-187), but the author looks down and describes it with godlike levity and joy. He is never completely detached, because he can never quite forget that he is being detached, and because after all he is not without human passion. His own voice can be heard in Anna Livia's cry, "A hundred cares, a tithe of troubles and is there one who understands me?" (*FW*, 627); he knows that in eternity not only his own work but all [42] life, all variety, all joy and all creation will be drowned in the conformity of death and total darkness; nevertheless he will continue to lift the lifewand that the dumb may sing the song of the universe: "Till tree from tree, tree among trees, tree over tree become stone to stone, stone between stones, stone under stone for ever." (*FW*, 259)

That is perhaps as near to the purely intellectual joy of God as man can come. [43]

APPENDICES

DOROTHY VAN GHENT

Problems for Study and Discussion for

A Portrait of the Artist
as a Young Man

1. THIS NOVEL is not without narrative design; that is, events involving external action do occur in it—like the incident of the pandying in the first chapter, and of Stephen's going to the rector's office. But these events are absorbed into the larger and more constant movement of an "internal action," the action of Stephen's mind and sensibility as he seeks the meaning of things. In what sense does this displacement of emphasis from external action to internal action reflect an extreme development of that "moral isolation" of the protagonist . . .

2. Let us break the first chapter down into three divisions, the first ending with Stephen in the infirmary, the second comprising the episode of the Christmas dinner, the third the episode of the pandying. Having found these divisions in your book, what means would you say Joyce used, if any, to make his transitions between them? [1]

3. To speak now of what we have called the first division of

From *The English Novel: Form and Function,* by Dorothy Van Ghent. Copyright © 1953. By permission of Holt, Rinehart and Winston, Inc., publishers. References to *A Portrait* are to P-3.

[1] Readers of American editions of the novel work under a handicap in answering this question, for the errata lists sent by Joyce to his American publisher were ignored. Among the corrections that were not made (see pp. 318-328) was the insertion of a set of asterisks to terminate the first division of the chapter. If these are inserted it will become apparent that Joyce divided the chapter into *four* sections by asterisks.

this chapter and the motifs and associative patterns worked up in it, what structural significance do you find in the fact that the first piece of dialogue on the school grounds involves the question of Stephen's name? Why does Nasty Roche's question stir anxiety in Stephen about his father, and how is this anxiety developed in the rest of the chapter? How is the same anxiety developed in the book as a whole? One of the themes of Joyce's *Ulysses* is a son's quest for his "spiritual father": would you say that there is the same theme in the *Portrait?*

4. Referring only to this first division of the chapter, work out carefully, with close textual illustration, the patterns of association between coldness, dampness, sliminess, limpness, whiteness, water sounds in the lavatory, the color of the water in the bath, the smell of the bath, and feelings of repugnance and fear. In what sense can associative patterns of this kind be said to be, for Stephen, an approach toward [463] understanding of the world? What bearing on Stephen's quest for understanding has the bit of dialogue beginning with Wells's question as to whether Stephen kisses his mother before he goes to bed? What bearing on it has Athy's riddle? Two passages from the evening prayers are given. The first is: "O Lord, open our lips/ And our mouths shall announce Thy praise . . ." (257) Does this seem to have any connection with a major theme in the book? The second is: "Visit, we beseech Thee, O Lord, this habitation and drive away from it all the snares of the enemy . . ." (258) With what major theme is this passage implicitly connected? In what sense could you speak of the passage about the peasants at Sunday Mass, their "smell of air and rain and turf and corduroy," (260) as an epiphany of a kind? Referring again to this passage, with its vision of the peasant cottage at night, the darkness of the road between the trees, and the woman standing at the half door, with what kind of emotion is the vision associated, and in what way is it connected with one of the major themes of the book?

5. Referring now to the second division of the chapter, describing the Christmas dinner at home, how in general would you define its structural connection with the rest of the novel? What two dominant concerns of Irish life, as Joyce represents

that life, appear in the argument between Mr. Casey and Dante? (You should look up some information about Parnell in order to understand this section.) Athletics is another dominant concern of the national life that Joyce depicts: in what way, in the first and third divisions of this chapter, is this national interest symbolized? Do you find it recurrent elsewhere in the book?

6. With reference to the transgression of the boys who are going to be flogged, three different crimes are suggested: what significance has it for Stephen's quest for understanding that the crime is problematic and may be any one of three different things? The sins suggested fall into the three medieval theological categories of (*a*) sin against one's neighbor (stealing the rector's cash), (*b*) sin against God (drinking the altar wine), and (*c*) sin against oneself (the smugging in the square). Which of these later becomes Stephen's own guilt obsession? In Stephen's image of the square where the smugigng went on, what has the smell of stale water to do with his confused approach to understanding of what it was the boys had done? [464]

7. In what way does the pandying contribute massively to Stephen's understanding of his environment?

8. All through the chapter there have been references to water, to the sound made by drops of water and by water flushed out of a basin, to the smell and the color of the water in the bath, to the slimy water of the ditch where Stephen was pushed; and at the very end of the chapter it is said that the sound of the cricket bats was "like drops of water in a fountain falling softly in the brimming bowl." (285) Since the book as a whole is (as Cranly says of Stephen's mind in the last chapter) "supersaturated" with Roman Catholicism, would you trace any connection between the frequent water images here and the sacrament of baptism? If there is a connection, how would you explain the differences of emotional tone between the various water images?

9. In the first paragraphs of the second chapter, having to do with Uncle Charles, music, athletics, and religion are the thematic notes—as if to set up the span of those traditional Irish concerns into which Stephen is being initiated and with which he is experiencing disenchantment. The image of Uncle Charles

humming his favorite songs in the outhouse is a kind of epiphany; and that of Mike Flynn rolling a cigarette is another; and that of Uncle Charles kneeling on his red handkerchief is another— what emotional comment does each of these images make on music, athletics, religion? Note that there follows almost immediately Stephen's fantasy about Mercedes in the country cottage: how would you justify this sequence structurally? And how would you justify structurally the immediately following sequence—the cowyard with its "foul green puddles"? (309) With reference to the paragraph just preceding the first transition (the first set of asterisks), a paragraph concerning Stephen's desire "to meet in the real world the unsubstantial image which his soul so constantly beheld" (311): how is this a prophecy of the final event in the chapter? Note that these first few pages of the chapter have recapitulated the chief elements of Irish life and presented them in an atmosphere of vague sordidness, and have set against that sordidness the dream of Mercedes: in what way does this opposition represent the conflict followed throughout the book?

10. Let us say that the next division of material in this second chapter begins with the removal to Dublin and ends with Mr. Dedalus' account [465] of his conversation with the rector (at the point of transition to the Whitsuntide play). It is said that the change of fortune which sends the family to Dublin was "reshaping the world" for Stephen "into a vision of squalor and insincerity." (313) How would you justify, in terms of epiphany, the "beautiful Mabel Hunter" (314) episode, and that of the old woman making tea while "a skull appeared suspended in the gloom" of the doorway with something like a monkey under it? (314) Note that there follows an image of Emma (after the children's party) with "cowled head" and standing on some steps with Stephen: how is this image taken up again in the final chapter of the book? What connection is there between this inconclusive episode with the girl and the fact that Stephen begins to write?

11. The next division of material is concerned with Stephen's college experience at Belvedere (ending with the row of asterisks just before the trip to Cork). In terms of the factors of Irish life

that have thematic importance, how would you comment on the references to "the smiling face of a priest" (320) and the removal of the Blessed Sacrament to make room for the dumbbells, Indian clubs, gymnasium shoes, and so forth? In what sense is the scene of the inquisition into Stephen's literary "heresy" an extension, on a more mature level, of those passages in the first chapter where Nasty Roche asks Stephen's name, Wells asks him if he kisses his mother, and Athy asks him a riddle? And would you say that the beating administered by Heron, to force a "confiteor," was a kind of duplication, on a more mature level, of the incident of the pandying in the first chapter? Does the motif of the "confiteor" appear significantly anywhere else in the book?

12. Interpret the following (the passage occurs in the context of the Whitsuntide play): ". . . he saw a likeness between his father's mind and that of this smiling welldressed priest: and he was aware of some desecration of the priest's office or of the vestry itself whose silence was now routed by loud talk and joking and its air pungent with the smells of the gasjets and the grease." (333)

How is this a duplication, on a more mature level, of Stephen's early apprehensive image, in the first chapter, of the stealing of the altar wine? How is it a prophecy of Stephen's final rejection of home, fatherland, and church? Is there any particular point in the fact that Mr. [466] Dedalus' first name is *Simon*? Interpret whatever symbolism there may be in the last lines before the asterisks, where Stephen is looking up at a morgue and smells the stable smell in the lane and says, "It is a good odour to breathe. It will calm my heart. My heart is quite calm now. I will go back." (335)

13. The next division of material concerns the visit to Cork. Is there any significance in the fact that the father is searching the desks in the anatomy theater for his own initials when Stephen sees the word "Foetus" cut there. In what way is this detail—"It shocked him to find in the outer world a trace of what he had deemed till then a brutish and individual malady of his own mind." (339) an ironic commentary on the line in the first part of the chapter concerning the fantasy-Mercedes:

"He wanted to meet in the real world the unsubstantial image which his soul so constantly beheld"? (311) How does this epiphany (through the word "Foetus") comment on Mr. Dedalus' succeeding remarks? ". . . remember, whatever you do, to mix with gentlemen. When I was a young fellow I tell you I enjoyed myself. I mixed with fine decent fellows . . . we were all gentlemen, Stephen . . . That's the kind of fellows I want you to associate with, fellows of the right kidney." (341)

Feeling cut off from reality by his "monstrous way of life," Stephen repeats to himself, "I am Stephen Dedalus. I am walking beside my father whose name is Simon Dedalus. We are in Cork, Ireland. Cork is a city. Our room is in the Victoria Hotel . . ." (342)

In what way is this passage a duplication of the notes on the geography flyleaf in the first chapter, and how does it differ in significance? In what sense do the lines from Shelley that close this division repeat the geographical motif, and on what level of significance?

14. How does the disposition of the prize money prophesy Stephen's spiritual dryness at the beginning of Chapter 4? Note that Joyce uses the metaphor of a "breakwater" against a "tide." [467] "He had tried to build a breakwater of order and elegance against the sordid tide of life without him and to dam up, by rules of conduct and active interests and new filial relations, the powerful recurrence of the tide within him. Useless. From without as from within the water had flowed over his barriers: their tides began once more to jostle fiercely above the crumbled mole." (349)

What connection would you make between this metaphor and the water images in the first chapter and the sea in the fourth chapter? Account for the exalted lyric handling of the encounter with the whore.

15. How are the first two paragraphs of the third chapter an ironic commentary on the last paragraphs of the preceding chapter? In the paragraph about the equation with its widening tail of starry eyes, how do you account for the association with the lines from Shelley about the moon wandering companionless? The equation becomes Stephen's own soul "going forth to expe-

rience, unfolding itself sin by sin" (354): how does this sequence of associations develop the geographical motif that started with the notations on the flyleaf of the geography book? The symbols for the Virgin that Stephen recites to himself are taken from the Song of Solomon: why is this significant? Do you find any implicit connection between this passage and the Mercedes-fantasy and the encounter with the whore? You will note that Stephen is most a theologian when he is deepest in sin. He formulates questions that (as Lynch says later of his aesthetics) have "the true scholastic stink." One of these questions is: "If the wine change into vinegar and the host crumble into corruption after they have been consecrated, is Jesus Christ still present under their species as God and as man?" (358) In what sense could one say that Stephen's whole experience with the church shows the wine changed into vinegar and the host crumbled into corruption? Referring to Stephen's final talk with Cranly, in the fifth chapter, would you say that he rejects his religion because he does not believe in it or because its service has become corrupted?

16. Formulate, with clear textual reference, the divisions of the material in the section of sermons: that is, with what "last thing" has each sermon to do? What reason would you suggest for Joyce's representing these sermons in full? What development is given to what we have called the "geographical motif" in the sermon on doomsday? What is the specific effect of each sermon on Stephen? When he hears [468] the rain falling, and thinks, "The water would rise inch by inch, covering the monuments and the mountain tops . . . ," (370) what association would you make between this image and other water images? What is the sin of Lucifer said to be, and how is this motif picked up in the last chapter during Stephen's walk with Cranly? What specific portions of the description of hell and its torments would you point to as absurdly materialistic? Does the materialism of this vision of hell seem to you to have any connection with Stephen's eventual decision not to "serve"? The priest speaks of special torments for each of the senses—eyes, nose, ears, taste, touch: in what sense is this description a development of the sense impressions recorded on the first page of the book;

and how is this particular pattern (associated with the five senses) developed still further in Chapter 4, where Stephen attempts to discipline himself spiritually. Why is the portentous mountain of sand given such full and detailed description?

17. Is the vision of the field of thistles an "epiphany," and if so, in what sense? Does the scene in the chapel where Stephen makes his confession suggest any development of his childish impression, in the first chapter, of the "holy smell" of the peasants at Sunday Mass? At the end of this chapter, after taking the Mass [Eucharist, ed.], Stephen goes about "in a dream." "Another life. A life of grace and virtue and happiness! It was true. It was not a dream from which he would wake." (403) How does this reference to the "dream" reflect the conflict that we have seen in the book so far?

18. With reference to the beginning of Chapter 4, where Stephen is disciplining himself, interpret the associations between the following passage and Stephen's disposition of his prize money (in Chapter 2) and his vision of his sins in the form of an *equation* (in Chapter 3): ". . . at times his sense of such immediate repercussion was so lively that he seemed to feel his soul in devotion pressing like fingers the keyboard of a great cash register and to see the amount of his purchase start forth immediately in heaven." (405)

Why, given Stephen's sensibility, is the "august incomprehensibility" of the Trinity more easily acceptable to his mind than God's eternal [469] love? Interpret the association between the following metaphors and the water images that we have considered: it is said that "To merge his life in the common *tide* of other lives was harder for him than any fasting or prayer," (409) and his difficulty is given the name of spiritual "*dryness*"; temptation to sin comes to him like waves of a flood "slowly advancing towards his naked feet . . . Then, almost at the instant of that touch, almost at the verge of sinful consent, he found himself standing far away from the flood upon a dry shore, saved by a sudden act of the will or a sudden ejaculation. . . ." (410)

In this latter passage, do you find a complex irony that associates itself with the sea scene at the end of this chapter?

19. In the scene between Stephen and the director, his secret musing on the pride of the priestly office is described: how is this impulse toward the priesthood inflected later when Stephen has a revelation of his vocation as artist? The director tells Stephen to pray for enlightenment to his patron saint, the first martyr, Stephen, "who is very powerful with God" (418) (for background refer to Acts, Chapter 7): what significance do you find in Stephen's first name? How does this reference to his name develop and deepen the motif of the *name* which began with Nasty Roche's question, in the first chapter, about Stephen's name? Note that at the end of this chapter, the boys who call to Stephen on the beach give his name a Greek form (Stephanos): suggest a reason for this change in the form of the name.

20. After the discussion with the director, Stephen goes home and confronts "the faint sour stink of rotted cabbages" (421) and other tokens of "the misrule and confusion of *his father's house.*" What reverberations of significance does the last phrase, "his father's house," raise? Is the "father" that is suggested here only Simon Dedalus—or has Stephen known other "fathers" who misrule and confuse their house?

21. On the beach, Stephen sees the reflections of the clouds drifting in the water along with the tangle of seaweed: interpret the expressive value of this mobile image of clouds and water, clouds in water. Does it have any connection with the "geographical motif" that we have followed from the beginning, and what connection has the "geographical motif" itself with Stephen's search for God (who is also a "father")? The girl's thighs are said to be "softhued as ivory" (432): what associative [470] cluster is contained here? In the fifth chapter, Stephen defines "beauty" as being the "most satisfying relations of the sensible," (473) as against "truth," which is the "most satisfying relations of the intelligible." (473) If we should say that the synthesis at the end of the fourth chapter is a synthesis in terms of "beauty," as defined, in what sense could one say that the fifth chapter develops this synthesis as "truth"?

22. The material of the fifth chapter is derived from Stephen's experience of the university, and the word "university" has been

fairly frequently present during the preceding pages. Would you say that there might be here a pun on "universe" and "city"— and if so, what would be the significance of the pun for the whole book? In what sense is there an epiphany in the appearance of the box of pawn tickets with the louse marks on it, and in the alarm clock lying on its side? How would you interpret, in terms of the water symbolism that we have remarked, the passage where Stephen's mother washes him in the bowl?

23. Stephen walks to the university "among heaps of dead language," (439) and his language-consciousness suddenly deteriorates into the absurd rhyme about the yellow ivy whining on the wall, which leads him to the epithets "yellow ivory" and "ivory ivy" and so on; then he thinks of the name for ivory in several different languages: what associative cluster is suggested here by the word "ivory," and what reason would you suggest for the passage of the cluster into French and Spanish and Italian?

24. What is Davin's significance in the book? Why is Stephen drawn particularly to Davin although he has a serflike mind?

25. What is the expressive value of the scene with the dean of studies? There is a network here of oblique associations with the function and meaning of epiphany, in the business about lighting the fire, the reference to Epictetus' lamp, the smell of the molten tallow from the candle butts, the dean's face that is like an "unlit lamp," (450) the quibble about funnel and tundish, the reference to the fact that the dean has in him no "fire" (448) of apostleship, and Stephen's phrasing in the statement that he "can work at present *by the light* of one or two ideas of Aristotle and Aquinas." (449) Attempt to define the relationship of these references to the doctrine of epiphany. (For background, you might look up the fire epiphanies in Acts II: 1-4 and IX: 3-8.)

26. How does Cranly's language ("flaming bloody sugar" etc.) differ significantly from Davin's language, and why is the character of the language of each emphasized? Why is the scene with Davin located on [471] the playing field and why is Davin's uncle said to be a famous athlete? Interpret this statement,

which Stephen makes to Davin: "You talk to me of nationality, language, religion. I shall try to fly by those nets." (468) Later Stephen says to Cranly that his only tools will be silence, exile, and cunning: in what sense is this triad an inversion of the triad through which Davin tries to appeal to him?

27. Analyze term by term Stephen's aesthetics. According to his definitions of the lyrical, epical, and dramatic modes, in what category would you place the *Portrait* itself? In what sense is Stephen's aesthetics also a description of the life experience that the *Portrait* records?

28. What structural justification would you suggest for the fact that, after the discussion of aesthetics, there is the episode of the writing of the villanelle?

29. Stephen is thinking of a lyric of Nash's, and thinking with desire of Emma, when a louse crawls over the nape of his neck: is this an epiphany of a kind? Interpret, with as much depth and complexity of reference as possible to associative patterns throughout the book, the following:

> How could he hit their conscience or how cast his shadow over the imaginations of their daughters, before their squires begat upon them, that they might breed a race less ignoble than their own? And under the deepened dusk he felt the thoughts and desires of the race to which he belonged flitting like bats, across the dark country lanes, under trees by the edges of streams and near the pool mottled bogs. A woman had waited in the doorway as Davin had passed by at night and, offering him a cup of milk, had all but wooed him to her bed: for Davin had the eyes of one who could be secret. But him no woman's eyes had wooed. (508)

30. In his conversation with Cranly, is Stephen's "*non serviam*" actually a "*non credo*"? Make an evaluative judgment of Stephen's attitude toward his mother, which he illustrates by speaking of Pascal, who "if I remember rightly, would not suffer his mother to kiss him as he feared the contact of her sex," (512) and which he illustrates also by Christ's attitude toward Mary: would you say that Joyce's portrait of Stephen here is wholly sympathetic or is ironical and objective and has "aesthetic dis-

tance"? While we have called this book an "autobiographical novel," [472] would you say that Joyce wholly identified himself with Stephen, in sympathy, or not?

31. Make a brief formulation of the total conflict represented in the book, and of each of the five modes under which it appears. Does Joyce's Stephen make any approach to solution of the problems of "moral isolation" and "how to be," and if so, how? [473]

PETER SPIELBERG
James Joyce's Errata
for American Editions of
A Portrait of the Artist

IN RECENT YEARS James Joyce's popularity with the critics has undoubtedly been on the rise; the *PMLA* bibliography for 1960 lists forty-eight items dealing with Joyce—a quick check shows that Joyce is behind only T. S. Eliot and William Faulkner among twentieth-century English-speaking authors in scholar appeal. To illustrate this point of popularity further, the copyright page of the Compass Books edition of *A Portrait of the Artist as a Young Man* shows that between August 1956 and December 1960 fourteen printings were called for. Surprising as may be this upturn in the appeal of *A Portrait,* it is even more surprising that, although forty-five years have elapsed since the first

Reprinted by permission of the author, The Society of Authors (London), and the Lockwood Memorial Library of The University of Buffalo. This essay is here published for the first time.

American edition, most of the errors that had crept into the 1916 edition are still to be found in the 1961 printing of the 1956 edition.[1]

Although Joyce carefully prepared a list of errata in April, 1917, these misprints have not been corrected and the errors have been compounded in the Viking Press, the Modern Library, Signet Books, the Viking Portable, and Compass Books editions. "On April 10 [Joyce] sent Pinker the corrections and asked that they be typed and forwarded to Huebsch [Joyce's American publisher]."[2] J. B. Pinker, Joyce's literary agent, carried out the request. Mr. Huebsch received a typed copy of Joyce's corrections plus an additional sheet of corrections in the hand of Miss Harriet Shaw Weaver in May 1917.[3] However, the requested corrections were never made in the subsequent American editions, although a number of errors were independently cor-

[1] See John J. Slocum and Herbert Cahoon, *A Bibliography of James Joyce* (New Haven, 1953), pp. 18-19, "*A Portrait of the Artist as a Young Man* was reprinted by Huebsch as follows: second, April, 1917; third, January or June, 1918; fourth, September, 1921; fifth, September, 1922; sixth, by the Viking Press and B. W. Huebsch, September, 1925; seventh, . . . August, 1927. In March, 1928 it was issued in the Modern Library, New York, . . . and has been reprinted thirty-seven times in this series, most recently in May, 1950, all from the original Huebsch plates. The total number printed to date [1953] is 99,000 copies. *A Portrait of the Artist as a Young Man* was reset and published by Signet Books, New York, in March, 1948 and reprinted in March, 1949, November, 1950, and March, 1952. . . . [It] is included in *The Portable James Joyce* [Viking Press, 1947]." The novel was also included in *The Indispensable James Joyce,* a reissue of *The Portable James Joyce* by the Book Society, New York, 1949. (See *Ibid.,* p. 67.) *A Portrait of the Artist as a Young Man* was then published in August, 1956 by the Viking Press in its Compass Books edition and reprinted at least fourteen times since.
[2] *Ibid.,* p. 136.
[3] In December, 1959 B. W. Huebsch donated these two manuscripts of Joyce's errata for *A Portrait* to the University of Buffalo's Lockwood Library Joyce Collection. The MS in Miss Weaver's hand is headed by a pencil note, probably in the hand of Mr. Huebsch, "sent by Miss Weaver May 2/17." The typescript MS of errata, consisting of sixteen sheets and containing three hundred and sixty-four corrections (See *Ibid.,* p. 136, item E.3.d. for a description of the autograph MS of the corrections now in the Yale University Library. I have examined the Yale MS and have followed its corrections wherever a discrepancy between the Yale and University of Buffalo MSS occurred.), has the date "May 7–1917" stamped on the verso of the last sheet, indicating the date Huebsch received the corrections.

rected "at the instance of the proofreaders." [4] The English and continental editions incorporated Joyce's corrections beginning with the "new edition, type re-set" of Jonathan Cape, London, 1924. [5]

Therefore, the Joyce scholar in America must either use a European edition of *A Portrait* for his references or incur the danger of basing his interpretations on a faulty text. For the common reader the disadvantage of a faulty text may at first not seem to be serious, but in the work of an author who is often accused of being deliberately obscure these errors can add unnecessary confusion and ambiguity.

Of the three hundred and eighty errors that Joyce located and asked to be rectified, one hundred and forty-seven were spotted by the American proofreaders and corrected in subsequent editions; two hundred and thirty-three errors remain to be corrected.

Though most of Joyce's errata for *A Portrait* are concerned with matters of punctuation—the change of hyphenated compounds to solid compounds, the deletion of unnecessary commas, and the deletion of unnecessary capitals—it should be remembered that Joyce attached more importance to having his works printed exactly as he wrote them than do most prose writers. [6]

---

[4] *Ibid.*, p. 136. It is possible though that some of the "independent" corrections were based not on the proofreaders' judgment but on Joyce's list of errata. One correction on 157.6 of the novel (Compass Books edition) would seem to indicate this, since here "chocolate" has been changed to "slim jim" as Joyce requested. (Some of the corrections in the Compass Books edition, such as the one here cited, are not to be found in the Modern Library edition.) I doubt that such a change could have been made "at the instance of the proofreaders." It is, of course, possible that this change was also called for in a separate letter or in yet another list of errata submitted by Joyce.

[5] A few of Joyce's corrections were not made in the new English and continental editions. A brief check shows that the Jonathan Cape *"Flexibles"* edition, London, 1934, misses at least seventeen of the corrections, while the Tauchnitz Edition, Leipzig, 1930, overlooks at least twelve corrections.

[6] Joyce's dislike for inverted commas, unnecessary commas, superfluous capitals, and all hyphens is well known. See *Letters of James Joyce,* Stuart Gilbert, ed. (New York, 1957), p. 93 for a letter from Harriet Shaw Weaver to B. W. Huebsch, dated 24 July 1916, ". . . I have written to ask Mr. Marshall to send on to you his copy of the text [of *A Portrait* as it appeared in the *Egoist,* London Vol. I, No. 3 (Feb. 2, 1914)—Vol. II, No. 9

A number of other corrections may be of greater significance since they clarify the meaning of hitherto confusing passages. A random selection of such corrections follows: On p. 12, of the Compass Books edition, where a sentence as it stands makes little sense, "And the cards for first place and third place were beautiful colours too: pink and cream and lavender," Joyce's correction adds the necessary missing words and the necessary sense, "And the cards for first place and second place and third place were beautiful colours too: pink and cream and lavender." On p. 89, a missing dash (Joyce uses the dash to indicate the beginning of a quotation) may cause some confusion. On p. 36, Mr. Casey's story of his trip to Arklow should begin, "—It was down in Arklow one day," not, "—He was down in Arklow one day." On p. 152, Stephen, thinking of the temptation of the flesh and comparing this temptation to a flood, does not see "the silver line of the floor far away and beginning again its slow advance towards his feet" but rather sees "the silver line of the flood." On p. 102, Stephen's eyes are "wounded or shamed" not by two items, "a ring of porter froth on a clothless table or a photograph of two soldiers standing to attention on a gaudy playbill," but by three items, "a ring of porter froth on a clothless table or a photograph of two soldiers standing to attention or a gaudy playbill." On p. 227, the title of Cranly's book obviously should be "printed" not "written." On p. 242, there is a vast difference in connotation between a "white sepulchre" and Joyce's correction to a "whited sepulchre." Even more misleading is the omission of requested asterisks in two places in the novel. Joyce's use of asterisks in *A Portrait* is of great interest since this device was used by the author to indicate a division within a chapter, usually a change in both time and scene. Joyce's errata sheets indicate that such a division should appear on p. 28 after the second line, thus dividing the first chapter into four major parts (instead of three): *(1)* pp. 7-8, Stephen's

---

(Sept. 1, 1915)] which contains Mr. Joyce's corrections (chiefly the deletion of unnecessary commas and capitals put in by the printer). Mr. Joyce would like the book printed exactly according to this corrected text . . . without any further alteration in the punctuation. On the enclosed slip are two corrections he has since sent to me."

early childhood (2) pp. 8-28, Stephen sick at Clongowes Wood College (3) pp. 28-40, the Christmas dinner (4) pp. 40-59, Stephen back in school and his trouble with Father Dolan and the rector. Joyce also indicates that a division is to be shown by asterisks on p. 73 after the third line, thus dividing the second chapter into five major parts (instead of four): (1) pp. 60-65, summer and autumn in Blackrock (2) pp. 65-73, the move to cheaper quarters in Dublin (3) pp. 73-86, Stephen at Belvedere College (4) pp. 86-96, Stephen and Simon Dedalus at Cork (5) pp. 96-101, Stephen with the prize money and Stephen with the prostitute.

In the following corrections Joyce has also weeded out a number of grammatical errors, spelling mistakes, and awkwardnesses of style. Individually most of these errors are slight, but the cumulative effect of such errors equals more than the sum of the parts.

I have listed below only those corrections found in the two errata MSS. which have *not* been made in the American editions of *A Portrait* (page and line references are to the Compass Books edition, Viking Press, 1956):

Page & Line	For	Read
7.3	down	coming down
7.13	bed,	bed
7.23	Uncle	uncle
9.37; 10.1	Good-bye	Goodbye
11.11	Uncle	uncle
12.26	Elements	elements
12.34	first place and	first place and second place and
13.23	bread basket	breadbasket
17.9	Uncle	uncle
17.15	Poetry and Rhetoric	poetry and rhetoric
19.12	Uncle	uncle
20.1; 11	death wound	deathwound
23.13	turf-coloured	turfcoloured
26.8	Kildare,	Kildare
26.34	Liberator	liberator
28.2	after "edge." insert asterisks *** in empty space	

Page & Line	For	Read
28.10	Uncle	uncle
30.1	"	"
31.1; 13	"	"
32.11	"	"
33.9; 15	"	"
36.34	He	It
37.25	Phth!	*Phth!*
37.33	Uncle	uncle
54.1	Lent	lent
61.26	stubble-covered	stubblecovered
63.8-9	love, and	love and,
66.21	Custom House	customhouse
68.8	there [second *there* in line]	thither
71.8	dressing table	dressingtable
72.4	thick-headed	thickheaded
72.11	both of	both
73.3	under "Ha! Ha! Ha!" insert asterisks *** in space to be made so as to separate paragraph following [7]	
73.5	dressing room	dressingroom
73.25	programme,	programme
74.13	pink dressed	pinkdressed
74.14	old fashioned	oldfashioned
77.18	him,	him
78.21	there should not be a space here after "—Admit."	
78.27	reverie	revery
80.28	explanation;	explanation,
82.25	description	descriptions
82.29	sudden woven	suddenwoven
84.6	school-comrades	schoolcomrades [8]
84.22	side pockets	sidepockets [9]
87.8	youth—	youth,
87.10	it,	it
87.12	heard,	heard
87.13	Uncle	uncle
88.4	water jug	waterjug
89.10	Well,	—Well,
89.38-90.1	broad shouldered	broadshouldered
90.2	jack knife	jackknife
90.17	them,	them
93.11	chapel,	chapel

Page & Line	For	Read
93.15	death,	death
93.19	side pockets	sidepockets
94.6	Dilectus,	Dilectus
94.8	*illis,*	*illis*
94.37	great grandfather	greatgrandfather
95.9	there,	there
95.18	fire-barred	fivebarred [10]
96.13	him,	him
98.13	ill plastered	illplastered
98.22	tide	tides
98.34	foster child and foster brother	fosterchild and fosterbrother
100.21	Jews	jews
102.23	on	or
103.22	maimed,	maimed
104.10	church door	churchdoor
105.2	*plantanus*	*platanus*
105.10	repent,	repent
105.11	re-entering	reentering
106.24	heart,	heart
106.33	consecrated,	consecrated
107.7; 22; 25	Saint	saint
107.29	founder,	founder
107.30	Saint	saint
108.1; 12	Saint, Saint	saint, saint
109.4	Saint	saint
109.26	Christian	christian
110.17	Holy Angels	holy angels
110.17	fellow-students	fellowstudents
110.22	may be	maybe
110.27	Christian	christian
111.3	thoughts,	thoughts
112.20; 35	judgment seat	judgmentseat
113.6	The doomsday	Doomsday
113.33	Kingdom	kingdom
114.16	die,	die
117.16	parents,	parents
119.1	Jewish	jewish
119.8	Holy	holy
119.8-9	Catholic Church	catholic church

Page & Line	For	Read
119.13	Church	church
119.13	life,	life
125.27	well;	well,
127.5	twenty-third	twentythird
127.29	Church	church
129.6	hell-fire	hellfire
130.16	another,	another
130.31	co-existent	coexistent
131.8	habit,	habit.
134.9	Jews	jews
136.9	although	though
137.6	time after time	time after time,
137.17	nor	or
137.30	horny browed	hornybrowed
138.18	and	and,
140.28	souls,	souls
147.27	moisture	moisture,
148.18	him, [second *him* in line]	him
149.1	eternal,	eternal
149.20	him,	him
149.37	giver	Giver
151.32	prayer,	prayer
152.29	floor	flood
153.32	blind,	blind.
153.36	shadow,	shadow
154.20	Dominican	dominican
154.21	Franciscan	franciscan
154.21; 22	Saint	saint
154.22	Capuchin	capuchin
154.28	Capuchins	capuchins
154.29	Franciscans	franciscans
154.33	right,	right
155.11	and	and of
156.23	heard	had heard
159.36	martyr	martyr,
160.10	hall door	halldoor
160.14	quartette	quartet
161.1	air,	air
161.5	piety	piety,
161.29	Gardimer Street,	Gardiner Street

Page & Line	For	Read
162.16	Tolka,	Tolka
162.29; 31	The Man with the Hat	the man with the hat
163.16	, in Belvedere,	in Belvedere
163.25-26	"Oft in the Stilly Night"	*Oft in the Stilly Night*
164.11	, and	and
165.7	triple-branching	triplebranching
165.30	Christian Brothers	christian brothers
165.34	and	and,
166.2	hats,	hats
167.30	long-drawn	longdrawn
168.11	rough-hewn	roughhewn
168.12	horseplay,	horseplay
168.19	clasp,	clasp
168.21	sword-like	swordlike
169.31	the cerements	cerements
170.21	pockets,	pockets
171.1	happy,	happy
172.27	glimmer,	glimmer
174.4	boghole,	boghole
175.1	it,	it
175.15-16	—Sure?	—Sure?
	—Hm!	—Yes, father.
		—Hm!
175.28	nun's	nuns'
176.4	rain laden	rainladen
176.14	stone cutting	stonecutting
176.35	Poetics and Psychology	poetics and psychology
177.2	fire consumed	fireconsumed
177.5	reverie	revery
177.31	Physics	physics
178.3	Green	green
180.20	them,	them
182.26	Hills,	hills;
183.14	*no one in*	*no one in it*
185.11	task—	task,
185.20	bellybordered	bellbordered
188.8	Newman's,	Newman's
189.11	principal	principle
189.18	zinc roofed	zincroofed

Page & Line	For	Read
190.38	began,	began
191.28	Oh,	O
192.9	fellow student's	fellowstudent's
193.33	whey pale	whey-pale
196.3	silver wrapped	silverwrapped
196.5	breast-pocket	breastpocket
197.2	dark, oval	dark oval
198.6	you	we
198.6	Jesus,	Jesus
199.26	brow,	brow
202.10	are	Are
203.28	or	or a
207.15	forgot	forget
207.34	evil,	evil
209.32	reproduction,	reproduction
210.26	fat encircled	fatencircled
210.29	lurking places	lurkingplaces
210.35	breast,	breast
211.15	ultra profound	ultraprofound
212.16	But	But,
213.1; 2; 3	was	is
213.25-26	thought enchanted	thoughtenchanted
214.10	of the esthetic	of esthetic
215.18	lawn,	lawn
219.14	listen	listen,
220.30	mouth	mouth,
222.26	armchair	armchair,
223.11	radiant,	radiant
224.10	limp hung	limphung
225.30	*Aleel,*	*Aleel.*
226.27	atheist	atheists
227.13	written	printed
227.18	well shod	wellshod
227.31	stubble grown	stubblegrown
227.35	monkey puckered	monkeypuckered
229.35	fig seed	figseed
230.3	Forster,	Forster
236.3	and, pushing past Cranley	and, pushing past Cranley,
237.25	fleet footed	fleetfooted

Page & Line	For	Read
238.25	bats,	bats
239.1	so far	so
242.28	Suarez	Suarez,
242.36	white	whited
244.27	white robed	whiterobed
244.28	boy,	boy
246.36	do	do so
247.18	lead	lead him
247.19	Lesson	Leeson
248.17	sixty-one	sixtyone
251.4	Father,	Father
252.28	me,	me [11]

[7] In the Compass Books edition the requested space has been provided, but the asterisks are still missing.

[8] Changed to "school comrades" in the Compass Books edition.

[9] Changed to "side-pockets" in the Compass Books edition.

[10] Correction in Compass Books edition made from "fire-barred" to "five-barred."

[11] I have not attempted to reproduce Joyce's errata MSS here (although I have adhered to his wording and set-up as much as possible). Therefore, I have not reproduced typing errors or other peculiarities, nor have I indicated where the errors or peculiarities occur; I have, rather, taken the liberty of presenting Joyce's errata as clearly as possible, with a minimum of footnotes or what I believe would have been unnecessary explanations. For example, the correction for 94.37, "for 'great grandfather' read 'greatgrandfather'" appears in the errata MS as, "for 'great grand-' read 'greatgrand-'"; I have added the final syllables since in the Compass Books edition the words "great grandfather" are printed on the same line, unlike the first edition (New York: B. W. Huebsch, 1916) where grandfather was hyphenated because it was printed on two lines. (See first edition 106.26.) Another example of my emendations is my correction without comment of the few obvious typing errors in the MSS; *e.g.*, because of such a slip on the typist's part a correction calls for the deletion of the comma after "then," rather than after "them." (90.17) Again, on 154.20 the MS calls for a change from "dominican" to "dominican" rather than from "Dominican" to "dominican".

SELECTIVE BIBLIOGRAPHY

A. *Bibliographical Studies*

BEEBE, Maurice, and LITZ, Walton. "Criticism of James Joyce: A Selected Checklist with an Index to Studies of Separate Works." *Modern Fiction Studies*, IV (1958), 71-99.

COHN, Alan M. "Further Supplement to James Joyce Bibliography 1950-1957," *James Joyce Review*, II, 1-2 (1958), 40-54.

CONNOLLY, Thomas E. *The Personal Library of James Joyce: A Descriptive Bibliography*. University of Buffalo Monographs in English No. 6. Buffalo, 1955; 2nd ed. (Buffalo, 1957).

KAIN, Richard M. "Supplement to James Joyce Bibliography, 1954-1957," *James Joyce Review*, I, 4 (1957), 38-40.

McLUHAN, Herbert M. "A Survey of Joyce Criticism," *Renascence*, IV (Autumn, 1951), 12-18.

PARKER, Alan. *James Joyce: A Bibliography of His Writings, Critical Material, and Miscellanea*. Boston: F. W. Faxon & Co., 1948.

SLOCUM, John F., and CAHOON, Herbert. *A Bibliography of James Joyce (1882-1941)* (New Haven: Yale University Press, 1953).

WHITE, William. "James Joyce: Addenda to Alan Parker's Bibliography," *Papers of the Bibliographical Society of America*, XLIII (1949), 401-411.

————. "Addenda to James Joyce Bibliography 1950-1953," *James Joyce Review*, I, 2 (June, 1957), 9-25.

————. "Addenda to James Joyce Bibliography 1954-1957," *James Joyce Review*, I, 3 (September, 1957), 3-24.

B. *About Joyce*

BEACH, Sylvia. *Shakespeare and Company* (New York: Harcourt, Brace & World, 1959).

BUDGEN, Frank. *James Joyce and the Making of Ulysses* (London: Grayson, 1934).

BYRNE, J. F. *Silent Years: An Autobiography, with Memoirs of James Joyce and Our Ireland* (New York: Farrar, Straus & Cudahy, 1953).

COLUM, Mary and COLUM, Padraic. *Our Friend James Joyce* (Garden City, N.Y.: Doubleday, 1958).

ELLMANN, Richard. *James Joyce* (New York: Oxford University Press, 1959).

————. *Joyce in Love* (Ithaca, New York: Cornell University Library, 1959).

GILBERT, Stuart, ed. *Letters of James Joyce* (New York: Viking Press, 1957).

GORMAN, Herbert. *James Joyce* (New York: Holt, Rinehart and Winston, 1940; 1948 revised).

HUTCHINS, Patricia. *James Joyce's Dublin* (London: Grey Walls Press, 1950).

————. *James Joyce's World* (London: Methuen, 1957).

JOYCE, Stanislaus. *Recollections of James Joyce* [first published 1941]. Translated by Ellsworth Mason (New York: James Joyce Society, 1950).

————. *My Brother's Keeper,* ed. ELLMAN, Richard (New York: Viking Press, 1958).

MASON, Ellsworth, and ELLMAN, Richard, eds. *The Critical Writings of James Joyce* (New York: Viking Press, 1959).

MORSE, J. Mitchell. *The Sympathetic Alien: James Joyce and Catholicism* (New York: New York University Press, 1959).

SILVERMAN, Oscar A., ed. *Epiphanies by James Joyce* (Buffalo: Lockwood Memorial Library, 1956).

STEWART, J. I. M. *James Joyce* (London: Longmans, Green, 1957).

SULLIVAN, Kevin. *Joyce Among the Jesuits* (New York: Columbia University Press, 1958).

TINDALL, William Y. *The Joyce Country* (University Park, Pa.: Pennsylvania State University Press, 1960).

C. *General Studies*

GIVENS, Seon, ed. *James Joyce: Two Decades of Criticism* (New York: Vanguard Press, 1948).

GOLDING, Louis. *James Joyce* (London: Thornton Butterworth Ltd., 1933).

HODGART, Matthew J. C., and WORTHINGTON, Mabel P. *Song in the*

Works of James Joyce (New York: Columbia University Press, 1959).

KENNER, Hugh. *Dublin's Joyce* (Bloomington, Ind.: Indiana University Press, 1956).

LEVIN, Harry. *James Joyce: A Critical Introduction* (Norfolk, Conn.: New Directions, 1941; revised edition, augmented, 1960).

————. ed. *The Portable James Joyce* (New York: Viking Press, 1947).

MAGALANER, Marvin. ed. *A James Joyce Miscellany* (New York: James Joyce Society, 1957).

————. ed. *A James Joyce Miscellany: Second Series* (Carbondale, Ill.: Southern Illinois University Press, 1959).

————, and KAIN, Richard M. *Joyce: The Man, the Work, the Reputation* (New York: New York University Press, 1956).

NOON, William. *Joyce and Aquinas* (New Haven: Yale University Press, 1957).

SMIDT, Kristian. *James Joyce and the Cultic Use of Fiction.* Oslo Studies in English, No. 4 (Oxford: Basil Blackwell, 1955).

TINDALL, William Y. *James Joyce: His Way of Interpreting the Modern World* (New York: Scribners, 1950).

————. *A Reader's Guide to James Joyce* (New York: Noonday Press, 1959).

D. *Stephen Hero* and *A Portrait of the Artist*

ANDERSON, C. G. "The Sacrificial Butter," *Accent*, XII (Winter, 1952), 3-13.

————. *A Word-Index to James Joyce's Stephen Hero* (Ridgefield, Conn.: Ridgebury Press, 1958).

BAKER, James R. "Esthetic Freedom and Dramatic Art," *Western Humanities Review*, V (Winter, 1950-1951), 29-40.

BEEBE, Maurice. "James Joyce: Barnacle Goose and Lapwing," *PMLA*, LXXI (June, 1956), 302-320.

————. "Joyce and Aquinas: The Theory of Aesthetics," *Philological Quarterly*, XXXVI (January, 1957), 20-35.

————. "James Joyce and Giordano Bruno: A Possible Source for 'Dedalus,'" *James Joyce Review*, I, 4 (1957), 41-45.

BLOCK, Haskell M. "The Critical Theory of James Joyce," *Journal of Aesthetics and Art Criticism*, VIII (March, 1950), 172-184.

CONNOLLY, Thomas E. "Joyce's Aesthetic Theory," *UKCR*, XXIII (October, 1956), 47-50.

————. "Stephen Hero Revisited," *James Joyce Review*, III, 1-2 (1959), 40-46.

DAICHES, David. *The Novel and the Modern World* (Chicago: University of Chicago Press, 1939), pp. 101-110.

————. "James Joyce: The Artist as Exile," in *Forms of Modern Fiction*, ed., William Van O'Connor (Minneapolis: University of Minnesota Press, 1948), pp. 62-65.

ELLMANN, Richard. "A Portrait of the Artist as Friend." *Kenyon Review*, XVIII (Winter, 1956), 53-67.

FARRELL, James T. "Joyce's *A Portrait of the Artist as a Young Man*," in Givens, *James Joyce: Two Decades of Criticism*, pp. 175-190.

————. "Postscript on *Stephen Hero*," in Givens, *ibid*., pp. 190-197.

FEEHAN, Joseph, ed. *Dedalus on Crete: Essays on the Implications of Joyce's Portrait* (Los Angeles: Saint Thomas More Guild, Immaculate Heart College, 1957).

FLEMING, Rudd. "*Quidditas* in the Tragi-Comedy of Joyce," *UKCR*, XV (Summer, 1949), 288-296.

FRIEDMAN, M. J. *Stream of Consciousness: A Study in Literary Method* (New Haven: Yale University Press, 1956), pp. 214-220.

FRIERSON, William C. *The English Novel in Transition*. Norman: University of Oklahoma Press, 1942, pp. 200-203.

GILBERT, Stuart. "James Joyce," in Givens, *James Joyce: Two Decades of Criticism*, pp. 458-461.

————. "The Latin Background of James Joyce's Art," *Horizon*, X (September, 1944), 178-188.

GORDON, Caroline. "Some Readings and Misreadings," *Sewanee Review*, LXI (Summer, 1953), 388-407.

————. *How to Read a Novel*. (New York: Viking Press, 1957), pp. 210-214.

HENDRY [Chayes], Irene. "Joyce's Epiphanies," *Sewanee Review*, LIV (Summer, 1946), 1-19.

HONIG, Edwin. "Hobgoblin or Apollo," *Kenyon Review*, X (Autumn, 1948), 664-681.

HOPE, A. D. "The Esthetic Theory of James Joyce," *Australasian Journal of Psychology and Philosophy*, XXI (December, 1943), 93-114.

JACK, Jane H. "Art and the *Portrait of the Artist*," *Essays in Criticism*, V (October, 1955), 354-364.

KAIN, Richard M. and SCHOLES, Robert E., eds. "The First Version of Joyce's *Portrait*," *Yale Review*, XLIX, 355-369.

KAYE, Julian B. "Who is Betty Byrne?" *Modern Language Notes,* LXXI (February, 1956), 93-95.

————. "Simony, the Three Simons, and Joycean Myth," in *A James Joyce Miscellany,* pp. 20-36.

KENNER, Hugh. "The Portrait in Perspective," in Givens, *Two Decades of Criticism,* pp. 132-174. See also, *Dublin's Joyce* for a variant version of this essay.

KUMAR, Shiv K. "Bergson and Stephen Dedalus' Aesthetic Theory," *Journal of Aesthetics and Art Criticism,* XVI (September, 1957), 124-127.

KUNKEL, Frank L. "Beauty in Aquinas and Joyce," *Thought Patterns,* II (1951), 61-68.

LIND, Ilse Dusoir. *"The Way of All Flesh* and *A Portrait of the Artist as a Young Man:* A Comparison," *Victorian Newsletter,* No. 9 (Spring, 1956), 7-10.

MACGREGOR, Geddes. "Artistic Theory in James Joyce," *Life and Letters,* LIV (July, 1947), 18-27.

McLUHAN, Herbert M. "Joyce, Aquinas, and the Poetic Process," *Renascence,* IV (Autumn, 1951), 3-11.

MAGALANER, Marvin. "James Mangan and Joyce's Dedalus Family," *Philological Quarterly,* XXXI (October, 1952), 363-371.

————, and KAIN, Richard M. *Joyce: The Man, the Work, the Reputation* (New York: New York University Press, 1956), pp. 102-129.

MASON, Ellsworth. "Joyce's Categories," *Sewanee Review,* LXI (Summer, 1953), 427-432.

MORIN, Edward. "Joyce as Thomist," *Renascence,* IX (Spring, 1957), 127-131.

MORSE, J. Mitchell. "Art and Fortitude: Joyce and the Summa Theologica," *James Joyce Review,* I (February, 1957), 19-30.

————. "Augustine's Theodicy and Joyce's Aesthetics," *ELH,* XXIV (March, 1957), 30-43.

NOON, William. *Joyce and Aquinas* (New Haven: Yale University Press, 1957), pp. 18-59.

PEARCE, Donald R. "My Dead King!: The Dinner Quarrel in Joyce's Portrait of the Artist," *Modern Language Notes,* LXVI (April, 1951), 249-251.

PRESCOTT, Joseph. "James Joyce: A Study in Words," *PMLA,* LIV (March, 1939), 304-315.

————. "James Joyce's Epiphanies," *Modern Language Notes,* LXIV (May, 1949), 346.

————. "James Joyce's Stephen Hero," *Journal of English and Germanic Philology*, LIII (April, 1954), 214-223. Reprinted many times, most recently in *The Diliman Review*, 1961.

REDFORD, Grant H. "The Role of Structure in Joyce's 'Portrait'," *Modern Fiction Studies*, IV (Spring, 1958), 21-30.

ROBERTS, John H. "James Joyce: From Religion to Art," *New Humanist*, VII (May-June, 1934), 7-13.

SAVAGE, D. S. *The Withered Branch: Six Studies in the Modern Novel* (London: Eure & Spottiswoode, 1950), pp. 160-168.

SCHORER, Mark. "Technique as Discovery," *Hudson Review*, 1948, in John Aldridge, ed. *Critiques and Essays on Modern Fiction* (New York: Ronald Press, 1952), pp. 75-77.

SCHWARTZ, Edward. "Joyce's Portrait," *Explicator*, XI (February, 1953), item 27.

SEWARD, Barbara. "The Artist and the Rose," *University of Toronto Quarterly*, XXVI (January, 1957), 180-190.

SLOCUM, John J., and CAHOON, Herbert, eds. *Stephen Hero by James Joyce: A New Edition Incorporating the Additional Manuscript Pages in the Yale University Library* (Norfolk, Conn.: New Directions, 1955).

SMIDT, Kristian. *James Joyce and the Cultic Use of Fiction.* Oslo: Studies in English, No. 4 (Oxford: Basil Blackwell, 1955), pp. 35-42, 53-61, and *passim.*

SPENCER, Theodore, ed. *Stephen Hero: A Part of the First Draft of A Portrait of the Artist as a Young Man* (Norfolk, Conn.: New Directions, 1944).

STERN, Richard G. "Proust and Joyce Underway: Jean Santeuil and Stephen Hero," *Kenyon Review*, XVIII (Summer, 1956), 486-496.

STEWART, J. I. M. *James Joyce* (London: Longmans, 1957), pp. 15-22.

STRONG, L. A. G. *The Sacred River: An Approach to James Joyce.* London: 1949 (New York: Pellegrini and Cudahy, 1951), pp. 23-27.

SYPHER, Wylie. "Portrait of the Artist as John Keats," *Virginia Quarterly Review*, XXV (Summer, 1949), 420-428.

TINDALL, William York. *James Joyce: His Way of Interpreting the Modern World* (New York: Scribners, 1950), pp. 16-22.

————. "The Symbolic Novel," *A. D.*, III (Winter, 1952), 56-68.

————. *The Literary Symbol* (New York: Columbia University Press, 1955), pp. 76-86, 239-246.

——. *A Reader's Guide to James Joyce* (New York: Noonday Press), pp. 50-103.

VAN GHENT, Dorothy. *The English Novel: Form and Content* (New York: Holt, Rinehart and Winston, 1953), pp. 263-276, 463-473.

WAITH, Eugene M. "The Calling of Stephen Dedalus," *College English*, XVIII (February, 1957), 256-261.

WELLS, H. G. "James Joyce," [written 1917] in Groff Conklin, ed. *New Republic Anthology* (New York: Dodge Press, 1936), pp. 45-48.

WHALLEY, George. *Poetic Process* (London: Routledge and Kegan Paul, 1953), pp. 16-24.